# SOMETHING ABOUT THE AUTHOR®

Something about the Author *was named an* ***"Outstanding Reference Source,"*** *the highest honor given by the American Library Association Reference and Adult Services Division.*

ISSN 0276-816X

# SOMETHING ABOUT THE AUTHOR®

Facts and Pictures about Authors and Illustrators of Books for Young People

volume 182

THOMSON
GALE

Detroit • New York • San Francisco • New Haven, Conn. • Waterville, Maine • London

THOMSON
GALE

**Something about the Author, Volume 182**

**Project Editor**
Lisa Kumar

**Editorial**
Dana Ferguson, Amy Elisabeth Fuller, Michelle Kazensky, Kathy Meek, Jennifer Mossman, Joseph Palmisano, Mary Ruby, Robert James Russell, Amanda D. Sams, Marie Toft

**Permissions**
Scott Bragg, Jackie Jones, Sue Rudolph

**Imaging and Multimedia**
Leitha Etheridge-Sims, Lezlie Light

**Composition and Electronic Capture**
Tracey L. Matthews

**Manufacturing**
Drew Kalasky

**Product Manager**
Peg Knight



*For more information, contact*
The Gale Group, Inc.
27500 Drake Rd.
Farmington Hills, MI 48331-3535
Or you can visit our internet site at
http://www.gale.com



**LIBRARY OF CONGRESS CATALOG CARD NUMBER 62-52046**

ISBN-13: 978-0-7876-8806-6
ISBN-10: 0-7876-8806-1
ISSN 0276-816X

This title is also available as an e-book.
ISBN-13: 978-1-4144-3285-4, ISBN-10: 1-4144-3285-2
Contact your Gale Group sales representative for ordering information.

Printed in the United States of America
10 9 8 7 6 5 4 3 2 1

# Contents

# Authors in Forthcoming Volumes

Below are some of the authors and illustrators that will be featured in upcoming volumes of *SATA*. These include new entries on the swiftly rising stars of the field, as well as completely revised and updated entries (indicated with *) on some of the most notable and best-loved creators of books for children.

**Aileen Arrington ▌** An elementary-school teacher, Arrington began her career as an illustrator while collaborating with her twin sister and writer Frances Arrington. Almost a decade later, in 2003, Arrington's debut chapter book, *Camp of the Angel* was released to critical acclaim, followed by her middle-grade novel *Paper Heart.* Both set in South Carolina, the novels find preteens making the transition from childhood to adulthood despite a lack of positive parental guidance.

***Lauren Child ▌** Fans of the "Clarice Bean" book series and the popular "Charlie and Lola" television series will likely count British author and collage artist Child among their favorite children's book authors. Her award-winning self-illustrated picture books include the standalone titles *The Pesky Rat* and *Who's Afraid of the Big Bad Book?,* each of which captures Child's whimsical, lighthearted view of life. Brought to life via her intricate, theatrically inspired cut-paper art, Child has also created a version of Hans Christian Andersen's classic fairy tale *The Princess and the Pea* that is set in a magical dollhouse world.

**Ron Fontes ▌** Working with prolific writer and partner Justine Korman Fontes, Ron Fontes has published over four hundred books. Ranging from historical fiction such as the "Wooden Sword" trilogy to middle-grade novels that include *Wild America* and *Tower of Terror,* the Fontes' capture readers with fast-moving plots and compelling characters. The couple also woo younger fans, who enjoyed their many interactive picture books. If that is not enough, a former job at Marvel Comics has also inspired Fontes to create and edit the Sonic Comics line, which features illustrated stories by a variety of comic-book writers.

***Iain Lawrence ▌** The novels of Canadian writer Lawrence transport readers to the past, and have been praised for their realistic and memorable characters and their evocative settings. The high-seas adventures of young John Spencer are the focus of his high-action trilogy *The Wreckers, The Smugglers,* and *The Buccaneers,* while *Ghost Boy* finds an albino youth working for a circus in the American West shortly after World War II. Moving closer to the present, *Gemini Summer* maps the fallout of a tragedy that hits a rural family in the 1960s while *The Lightkeeper's Daughter* focuses on a young woman coming to terms with her family's troubled past in her a remote island community.

**Christopher Myers ▌** A graduate of Brown University and the Whitney Museum of American Art Independent Studio Program, Myers turned to children's book illustration while working with his father, noted writer Walter Dean Myers. After collaborating on *Shadow of the Red Moon* and the award-winning *Harlem,* the younger Myers decided to tackle both text and pictures, producing an auspicious debut with the Coretta Scott King Honor Book *Black Cat.*

**Rhea Perlman ▌** Many adults know Perlman as the Emmy Award-winning actress who starred as Carla Tortelli on the popular television series "Cheers". To young readers, however, her name recognition comes as the popular author of the "Otto Undercover" series, which features the titles *Born to Drive, Water Balloon Doom, Brink of the Ex-stink-tion,* and *Brain Freeze,* among others.

**Henry Selick ▌** An innovator in his field, Selick is the stop-motion animation director of such films as *The Nightmare before Christmas* and *James and the Giant Peach.* He moved onto the radar of young bookworms when his animated short film *Moongirl* was adapted in picture-book form. Selick's award-winning story finds a young boy transported into the magical nighttime world of the luminous Moongirl while fishing in the bayou.

***David Small ▌** Small made the transition from college art teacher to author/illustrator with his first book, *Eulalie and the Hopping Head.* Acclaimed for his clever texts and detailed, engaging art, Small has also earned praise for the illustrations he creates for stories by Beverly Cleary, Eve Merriam, and his most frequent collaborator, his wife, Sarah Stewart. Best known for his work for Judith St. George's *So You Want to Be President?,* which earned him the 2001 Caldecott Medal, Small's most engaging books may be his original self-illustrated picture books, such as *Imogen's Antlers* and *George Washington's Cows.*

**Zai Whitaker ▌** A native of Mumbai, India, Whitaker is principal of the Outreach School in Bangalore, where she dedicates her efforts to providing an education to children growing up in rural areas. In her books for children, which include *Cobra in My Kitchen* and *Kali and the Rat Snake,* Whitaker draws on her lifelong interest in nature as well as her work with the women of the Irula tribe of hunter-gatherers and snake catchers.

# Introduction

*Something about the Author* (*SATA*) is an ongoing reference series that examines the lives and works of authors and illustrators of books for children. *SATA* includes not only well-known writers and artists but also less prominent individuals whose works are just coming to be recognized. This series is often the only readily available information source on emerging authors and illustrators. You'll find *SATA* informative and entertaining, whether you are a student, a librarian, an English teacher, a parent, or simply an adult who enjoys children's literature.

## What's Inside *SATA*

*SATA* provides detailed information about authors and illustrators who span the full time range of children's literature, from early figures like John Newbery and L. Frank Baum to contemporary figures like Judy Blume and Richard Peck. Authors in the series represent primarily English-speaking countries, particularly the United States, Canada, and the United Kingdom. Also included, however, are authors from around the world whose works are available in English translation. The writings represented in *SATA* include those created intentionally for children and young adults as well as those written for a general audience and known to interest younger readers. These writings cover the entire spectrum of children's literature, including picture books, humor, folk and fairy tales, animal stories, mystery and adventure, science fiction and fantasy, historical fiction, poetry and nonsense verse, drama, biography, and nonfiction. Obituaries are also included in *SATA* and are intended not only as death notices but also as concise overviews of people's lives and work. Additionally, each edition features newly revised and updated entries for a selection of *SATA* listees who remain of interest to today's readers and who have been active enough to require extensive revisions of their earlier biographies.

## Autobiography Feature

Beginning with Volume 103, many volumes of *SATA* feature one or more specially commissioned autobiographical essays. These unique essays, averaging about ten thousand words in length and illustrated with an abundance of personal photos, present an entertaining and informative first-person perspective on the lives and careers of prominent authors and illustrators profiled in *SATA*.

## Two Convenient Indexes

In response to suggestions from librarians, *SATA* indexes no longer appear in every volume but are included in alternate (odd-numbered) volumes of the series, beginning with Volume 57.

*SATA* continues to include two indexes that cumulate with each alternate volume: the Illustrations Index, arranged by the name of the illustrator, gives the number of the volume and page where the illustrator's work appears in the current volume as well as all preceding volumes in the series; the Author Index gives the number of the volume in which a person's biographical sketch, autobiographical essay, or obituary appears in the current volume as well as all preceding volumes in the series.

These indexes also include references to authors and illustrators who appear in *Gale's Yesterday's Authors of Books for Children, Children's Literature Review,* and *Something about the Author Autobiography Series.*

## Easy-to-Use Entry Format

Whether you're already familiar with the *SATA* series or just getting acquainted, you will want to be aware of the kind of information that an entry provides. In every *SATA* entry the editors attempt to give as complete a picture of the person's life and work as possible. A typical entry in *SATA* includes the following clearly labeled information sections:

***PERSONAL:*** date and place of birth and death, parents' names and occupations, name of spouse, date of marriage, names of children, educational institutions attended, degrees received, religious and political affiliations, hobbies and other interests.

***ADDRESSES:*** complete home, office, electronic mail, and agent addresses, whenever available.

***CAREER:*** name of employer, position, and dates for each career post; art exhibitions; military service; memberships and offices held in professional and civic organizations.

***MEMBER:*** professional, civic, and other association memberships and any official posts held.

***AWARDS, HONORS:*** literary and professional awards received.

***WRITINGS:*** title-by-title chronological bibliography of books written and/or illustrated, listed by genre when known; lists of other notable publications, such as plays, screenplays, and periodical contributions.

***ADAPTATIONS:*** a list of films, television programs, plays, CD-ROMs, recordings, and other media presentations that have been adapted from the author's work.

***WORK IN PROGRESS:*** description of projects in progress.

***SIDELIGHTS:*** a biographical portrait of the author or illustrator's development, either directly from the biographee—and often written specifically for the *SATA* entry—or gathered from diaries, letters, interviews, or other published sources.

***BIOGRAPHICAL AND CRITICAL SOURCES:*** cites sources quoted in "Sidelights" along with references for further reading.

***EXTENSIVE ILLUSTRATIONS:*** photographs, movie stills, book illustrations, and other interesting visual materials supplement the text.

## How a *SATA* Entry Is Compiled

*SATA* editors examine a wide variety of published sources to gather information for an entry. Biographical and bibliographic sources are consulted, as are book reviews, feature articles, published interviews, and material sometimes obtained from the biographee's family, publishers, agent, or other associates. Whenever possible, the author or illustrator is sent a copy of the entry to check for accuracy and completeness.

Entries that have not been verified by the biographees or their representatives are marked with an asterisk (*).

## Contact the Editor

We encourage our readers to examine the entire *SATA* series. Please write and tell us if we can make *SATA* even more helpful to you. Give your comments and suggestions to the editor:

Editor
Something about the Author
The Gale Group
27500 Drake Rd.
Farmington Hills MI 48331-3535

Toll-free: 800-877-GALE
Fax: 248-699-8070

# *Something about the Author* Product Advisory Board

The editors of *Something about the Author* are dedicated to maintaining a high standard of excellence by publishing comprehensive, accurate, and highly readable entries on a wide array of writers for children and young adults. In addition to the quality of the content, the editors take pride in the graphic design of the series, which is intended to be orderly yet inviting, allowing readers to utilize the pages of *SATA* easily and with efficiency. Despite the longevity of the *SATA* print series, and the success of its format, we are mindful that the vitality of a literary reference product is dependent on its ability to serve its users over time. As literature, and attitudes about literature, constantly evolve, so do the reference needs of students, teachers, scholars, journalists, researchers, and book club members. To be certain that we continue to keep pace with the expectations of our customers, the editors of *SATA* listen carefully to their comments regarding the value, utility, and quality of the series. Librarians, who have firsthand knowledge of the needs of library users, are a valuable resource for us. The *Something about the Author* Product Advisory Board, made up of school, public, and academic librarians, is a forum to promote focused feedback about *SATA* on a regular basis. The nine-member advisory board includes the following individuals, whom the editors wish to thank for sharing their expertise:

**Eva M. Davis**
*Youth Department Manager,*
*Ann Arbor District Library,*
*Ann Arbor, Michigan*

**Joan B. Eisenberg**
*Lower School Librarian,*
*Milton Academy,*
*Milton, Massachusetts*

**Francisca Goldsmith**
*Teen Services Librarian,*
*Berkeley Public Library,*
*Berkeley, California*

**Susan Dove Lempke**
*Children's Services Supervisor,*
*Niles Public Library District,*
*Niles, Illinois*

**Robyn Lupa**
*Head of Children's Services,*
*Jefferson County Public Library,*
*Lakewood, Colorado*

**Victor L. Schill**
*Assistant Branch Librarian/Children's Librarian,*
*Harris County Public Library/Fairbanks Branch,*
*Houston, Texas*

**Caryn Sipos**
*Community Librarian,*
*Three Creeks Community Library,*
*Vancouver, Washington*

**Steven Weiner**
*Director,*
*Maynard Public Library,*
*Maynard, Massachusetts*

# SOMETHING ABOUT THE AUTHOR

## ABERCROMBIE, Barbara 1939-
## (Barbara Mattes Abercrombie)

### Personal

Born April 6, 1939, in Evanston, IL; daughter of William F. (a businessman and writer) and Grace (a pianist) Mattes; married second husband, Robert V. Adams, 1997; children: Brooke, Gillian, three stepchildren. *Education:* Attended Briarcliff College and Los Angeles Harbor College.

### Addresses

*Home and office*—Santa Monica, CA; Twin Bridges, MT. *E-mail*—Barbara@BarbaraAbercrombie.com.

### Career

Actor, educator, and author. Actor in stage and television productions, including television series *Ironside* and *Route 66;* freelance writer. University of California, Los Angeles, Extension, teacher in The Writers' Program; teacher of creative writing to children. Conductor of workshops for Wellness Community.

### Awards, Honors

University of California, Los Angeles, Extension Outstanding Teacher Award, 1994,

### Writings

*FOR YOUNG PEOPLE*

(Editor) *The Other Side of a Poem,* Harper (New York, NY), 1977.
*Amanda and Heather, and Company,* illustrated by Mimi St. John, Dandelion (New York, NY), 1979.
*Cat-Man's Daughter,* Harper (New York, NY), 1981.
*Charlie Anderson,* illustrated by Mark Graham, Margaret K. McElderry Books (New York, NY), 1990.
*Michael and the Cats,* illustrated by Mark Graham, Macmillan (New York, NY), 1993.
*Bad Dog, Dodger!,* illustrated by Adam Gustavson, Margaret K. McElderry Books (New York, NY), 2002.
*The Show-and-Tell Lion,* illustrated by Lynne Avril Cravath, Margaret K. McElderry Books (New York, NY), 2006.

*OTHER*

(With Norma Almquist and Jeanne Nichols) *Traveling without a Camera* (poems), Peck Street Press, 1978.
*Good Riddance* (adult novel), Harper (New York, NY), 1979.
*Run for Your Life* (adult novel), Morrow (New York, NY), 1984.
*Writing out the Storm: Reading and Writing Your Way through Serious Illness or Injury,* St. Martin's Press (New York, NY), 2002.
*Courage and Craft: Writing Your Life into Story,* New World Library, 2007.

***Barbara Abercrombie*** (Courtesy of Barbara Abercrombie.)

Contributor of articles, essays, and poems to newspapers and magazines, including *Los Angeles Times, Christian Science Monitor,* and *United Airlines Hemisphere* magazine.

## Sidelights

Barbara Abercrombie is the author of two adult novels and several books for children, as well as of *Writing out the Storm: Reading and Writing Your Way through Serious Illness or Injury,* which is based on her personal struggle with breast cancer. "I write to make things clear to myself," she once explained in discussing her books for children, such as the picture books *Charlie Anderson* and *The Show-and-Tell Lion.* "I write about the things that happen in my own family from my own viewpoint," she added, noting that, as an adult, that viewpoint is "not very different from the way I was in terms of thoughts and feelings at age ten."

In Abercrombie's picture book *Michael and the Cats,* a young boy visiting his aunt tries to befriend the woman's two cats by attempting "things that would make him happy if he were a cat," as Ellen Fader explained in *Horn Book.* Nothing the boy tries seems to work, until he learns what it is that cats actually like. Emily Melton, reviewing the work for *Booklist,* noted that in *Michael and the Cats* "children will learn . . . that imposing their own ideas of friendship may not work, but putting themselves in another's place usually produces the desired response." "Abercrombie perfectly captures the tenuous nature of friendship between pets and small children," Fader concluded: "she never preaches, yet manages to convey the necessity of accepting animals on their own terms."

Another child befriends an animal in *Bad Dog, Dodger!,* which features oil paintings by illustrator Adam Gustavson. Abercrombie's story introduces readers to Sam, a nine year old who wants to have a dog. Sam's parents insist that he prove he is responsible enough, but when he does so, and the dog is acquired, a new problem surfaces. The rambunctious new pup, aptly named Dodger, is full of energy. It knocks over the garbage, chews things, and even follows Sam to school, until the boy decides to get up early each morning and put the puppy through a training program. A critic for *Kirkus Reviews* called *Bad Dog, Dodger!* "a perfect cautionary tale for a youngster about to get a first dog." According to Dorian Chong, reviewing the book for *School Library Journal,* Abercrombie presents readers with "a well-written, charmingly illustrated story with a satisfying, happy ending."

Critters of a different sort are the focus of both *Charlie Anderson* and *The Show-and-Tell Lion.* In *Charlie Anderson* two sisters think that they are adopting a stray cat, until they learn that the cat has, in fact, adopted their family as its second home. Reviewing *Charlie Anderson* for *School Library Journal,* Shirley Wilton noted the story's gentle message and praised the "soft-toned, realistic paintings" by illustrator Mark Graham.

Accompanied by what *Booklist* contributor Ilene Cooper described as "imaginative, wonderfully child-friendly artwork" by Lynne Avril Cravath, *The Show-and-Tell Lion* finds Matthew at a loss when his turn for show-and-tell arrives, until his vivid imagination solves the problem. Everyone in class is impressed to learn that Matthew shares his house with a baby lion named Larry. When the boy embellishes his tall tale with daily updates about his "house-lion", his classmates ask to see the creature, creating something of a quandary for the imaginative boy. In *School Library Journal,* Grace Oliff noted that *The Show-and-Tell Lion* "could spark discussions about the value of honesty and facing up to bad decisions," and a *Kirkus Reviews* writer praised the fact that Abercrombie's tale "perfectly embodies the importance of creativity, honesty and acceptance."

In *Writing out the Storm* Abercrombie draws on her experiences battling breast cancer to demonstrate how writing can be a faith-building activity for those going through a serious illness. A critic for *Publishers Weekly* praised the work as "a moving, unsentimental portrait of the author with breast cancer," noting that the book

***The spirit of Abercrombie's* Charlie Anderson, *a gentle story about a beloved family pet, is captured in Mark Graham's soft-edged paintings.*** (Illustration © 1990 by Mark Graham. Reprinted by permission of Aladdin Paperbacks, an imprint of Simon & Schuster Macmillan. )

includes excerpts from such writers as Raymond Carver, Gilda Radner, Andre Dubus, and other who have weathered adversity. Discussing her bout with cancer in the *Baltimore Sun,* Abercrombie refuses to refer to herself as a "survivor." For her, that term is "overly dramatic, implying courage that hadn't been earned." "The majority of women I know who are diagnosed with breast cancer get treatment and go on with their lives," Abercrombie added, "and many of these women don't want to be identified for all time as a breast cancer survivor."

## Biographical and Critical Sources

*PERIODICALS*

*Baltimore Sun,* October 30, 2002, Barbara Abercrombie, "A Brighter Outlook on Breast Cancer," p. A11.

*Booklist,* December 15, 1993, Emily Melton, review of *Michael and the Cats,* p. 762; September 15, 2006, Ilene Cooper, review of *The Show-and-Tell Lion,* p. 193.

*Bulletin of the Center for Children's Books,* December, 1981, review of *Cat-Man's Daughter,* p. 61.

*Horn Book,* January-February, 1994, Ellen Fader, review of *Michael and the Cats,* p. 58; February, 1982, Karen M. Klockner, review of *Cat-Man's Daughter,* p. 49.

*Kirkus Reviews,* April 15, 2002, review of *Bad Dog, Dodger!,* p. 560; June 1, 2006, review of *The Show-and-Tell Lion,* p. 567.

*New York Times Book Review,* March 18, 1984, Newgate Callendar, review of *Run for Your Life,* p. 27.

*Publishers Weekly,* August 29, 1980, review of *Good Riddance,* p. 364; December 2, 1983, review of *Run for Your Life,* p. 81; June 24, 2002, review of *Writing out the Storm: Reading and Writing Your Way through Serious Illness or Injury,* p. 52.

*School Library Journal,* October, 1981, Karen Stang Hanley, review of *Cat-Man's Daughter,* p. 148; October, 1990, Shirley Wilton, review of *Charlie Anderson;* October, 1993, Nancy Seiner, review of *Michael and the Cats,* p. 90; November, 2002, Dorian Chong, review of *Bad Dog, Dodger!,* p. 110; July, 2006, Grace Oliff, review of *The Show-and-Tell Lion,* p. 68.

*Tribune Books* (Chicago, IL), June 23, 2002, review of *Bad Dog, Dodger!,* p. 5.

*ONLINE*

*Barbara Abercrombie Home Page,* http://www.barbaraabercrombie.com (August 8, 2007).

*Writing Time Web site,* http://www.writingtime.net/ (August 27, 2007).

* * *

## ABERCROMBIE, Barbara Mattes
## See ABERCROMBIE, Barbara

* * *

## ALEXANDER, Lloyd 1924-2007
## (Lloyd Chudley Alexander)

*OBITUARY NOTICE—* See index for *SATA* sketch: Born January 30, 1924, in Philadelphia, PA; died of cancer, May 17, 2007, in Drexel Hill, PA. Author. Alexander was a Newbery and National Book Award winner best known for his "Prydain Chronicles" fantasy novel series. Although he was a bookish boy who desired to be a writer at a young age, his stockbroker father insisted he pursue a more stable career. He therefore got a job as a bank messenger. His life was changed during World War II, however, when he enlisted in the British Army in 1943 and was sent to Wales. Here he was deeply inspired by that ancient land, which reminded him of fairy tales and legends of enchantment. After the war, the army sent him to France and he studied at the Sorbonne in Paris. Moviing to the United Statesin 1947, Alexander found various jobs, including as a cartoonist, layout artist, advertising writer, and magazine editor. In his spare time, he wrote. His first book was *And Let the Credit Go* (1955), a novel for adults that drew heavily on his early experience in the banking world. Other works for adults followed, including *My Five Tigers*

(1956) and *Janine Is French* (1959). By the late 1950s, he began writing for younger audiences, initially penning biographies but then publishing a fantasy for children called *Time Cat: The Remarkable Journeys of Jason and Gareth* (1963). The next year he released the first of his "Prydain Chronicles" books, *The Book of Three.* Inspired by Welsh mythology, the fantasy novels addresses modern themes in a medieval setting. The other works in the series include *The Black Cauldron* (1965), which was a Newbery honor book, *The Castle of Llyr* (1966), *Taran Wanderer* (1967), and *The High King* (1968), which won a Newbery Medal and was a National Book Award nominee. Alexander also earned a National Book Award for the stand-alone novel *The Marvelous Misadventures of Sebastian* (1970) as well as for *Westmark* (1981), the first of a trilogy about a printer's apprentice. Another popular series by Alexander features Vesper Holly, a girl growing up in 1870s Philadelphia. Among the author's many other works are *Coll and His White Pig* (1965) and *The Truthful Harp* (1967), which are both set in the Prydain world; *The Town Cats and Other Tales* (1977); *The Remarkable Journey of Prince Jen* (1991); *Gypsy Rizka* (1997); *The Rope Trick* (2002); *The Xanadu Adventure* (2005); and *The Golden Dream of Carlo Chuchio,* the last scheduled for posthumous publication.

*OBITUARIES AND OTHER SOURCES:*

*BOOKS*

Alexander, Lloyd, *My Love Affair with Music,* Crowell (New York, NY), 1960.

*PERIODICALS*

*Los Angeles Times,* May 19, 2007, p. B12.
*New York Times,* May 19, 2007, p. A26.
*Washington Post,* May 18, 2007, p. B8.

* * *

## ALEXANDER, Lloyd Chudley
## See ALEXANDER, Lloyd

* * *

## ANDERSON, Jodi Lynn

### Personal

Female. *Education:* University Maryland-College Park, B.A. (American and British literature).

### Addresses

*Home and office*—Atlanta, GA.

### Career

Author. HarperCollins Publishers, New York, NY, editorial assistant, 1998-2000; 17th Street Productions, New York, NY, editor, 2000-02.

### Writings

*Peaches,* HarperCollins Publishers (New York, NY), 2005.

*May Bird and the Ever After* (first part of trilogy), illustrated by Leonid Gore, Atheneum Books for Young Readers (New York, NY), 2005.

*May Bird among the Stars* (second part of trilogy), illustrated by Eric Fortune, Atheneum Books for Young Readers (New York, NY), 2006.

*May Bird: Warrior Princess* (third part of trilogy), Atheneum Books for Young Readers (New York, NY), 2007.

*The Secret of Peaches* (sequel to *Peaches*), HarperTempest (New York, NY), 2007.

### Adaptations

*May Bird and the Ever After* was adapted as an audiobook, read by Bernadette Dunne, Listening Library, 2005.

### Sidelights

Jodi Lynn Anderson's first book, the young-adult novel *Peaches,* focuses on three teens who spend the last summer of high school working as peach pickers in an orchard in rural Georgia. Birdie is no stranger to the job; shy and socially awkward, she is the daughter of the orchard's owners, while Leeda is Birdie's far-more-sophisticated cousin and Murphy is an impressionable teen fulfilling a community-service requirement. Summer romances, problems with a land developer, and the everyday challenges and struggles of farming all feature in Anderson's "charming, breezy" novel, according to *Booklist* contributor Gillian Engberg. In *Kliatt* Stephanie Squicciarini wrote that *Peaches* is "beautifully and richly descriptive and surprisingly strong in its sparse dialogue," while *School Library Journal* reviewer Angela M. Boccuzzi-Reichert cited Anderson's ability to create "realistic" teen protagonists and "fresh" dialogue. A sequel, *The Secret of Peaches,* finds the summer coming to an end and each girl returning to her separate life with new confidence and a changed perspective. *The Secret of Peaches* "is well paced and resolves the interwoven story lines tidily but authentically," according to *School Library Journal* contributor Daisy Porter, and Squicciarini wrote that the novel's characters "are strong but also vulnerable as they learn to battle the demons within themselves and to accept the flawed natures of those around them."

Geared for middle-grade readers, *May Bird and the Ever After* is a fantasy that allows readers to travel between the worlds of the living and the dead. Anderson's protagonist, May Bird, is a lonely and awkward ten year old whose life changes after she finds a letter in the ruins of an abandoned post office. The letter, eerily addressed to May, directs her to a lake which, the girl discovers, is a gateway to the afterlife, also known as Ever After. In her story, Anderson details the adventures of May and May's pet cat, Somber Kitty, as they try to find their way out of Ever After and back to the living world. *May Bird and the Ever After* is the first volume of a three-book series and is followed by *May Bird among the Stars* and *May Bird: Warrior Princess.* A *Kirkus Reviews* critic noted that Anderson's fantasy debut is "vividly envisioned" and composed of "equal parts terror and tongue-in-cheek." In her *Booklist* review, Karen Cruze called *May Bird and the Ever After* a "superior entry in the fantasy genre" and cited Anderson's ability to entertain readers with stories featuring "unique characters."

## Biographical and Critical Sources

*PERIODICALS*

*Booklist,* October 1, 2005, Gillian Engberg, review of *Peaches,* p. 47; October 15, 2005, Chris Sherman, review of *May Bird and the Ever After,* p. 48; December 1, 2006, Krista Hutley, review of *May Bird among the Stars,* p. 44.

*Bulletin of the Center for Children's Books,* November, 2005, Karen Coats, review of *Peaches,* p. 128.

*Kirkus Reviews,* September 15, 2005, review of *May Bird and the Ever After,* p. 1019; September 15, 2006, review of *May Bird among the Stars,* p. 945.

*Kliatt,* November, 2006, Stephanie Squicciarini, review of *Peaches,* p. 17; January, 2007, Stephanie Squicciarini, review of *The Secrets of Peaches,* p. 6.

*Publishers Weekly,* August 8, 2005, review of *Peaches,* p. 236.

*School Library Journal,* August, 2005, Angela M. Boccuzzi-Reichert, review of *Peaches,* p. 121; December, 2005, Tasha Saecker, review of *May Bird and the Ever After,* p. 136; February, 2006, Charli Osborne, review of *May Bird and the Ever After,* p. 75; November, 2006, Tim Wadham, review of *May Bird among the Stars,* p. 129; January, 2007, Daisy Porter, review of *The Secrets of Peaches,* p. 123.

*Voice of Youth Advocates,* February, 2006, Lisa A. Hazlett, review of *Peaches,* p. 480; August, 2007, Lisa A. Hazlett, review of *The Secret of Peaches,* p. 234.

*ONLINE*

*HarperCollins Web site,* http://www.harpercollins.com/ (August 5, 2007), "Jodi Lynn Anderson."

*Simon & Schuster Web site,* http://www.simonsays.com/ (August 6, 2007), "Jodi Lynn Anderson."*

* * *

## ANDERSON, K.J.
See MOESTA, Rebecca

## ANDERSON, Matthew Tobin
See ANDERSON, M.T.

* * *

## ANDERSON, M.T. 1968-
## (Matthew Tobin Anderson)

### Personal

Born November 4, 1968, in Cambridge, MA; son of Will (an engineer) and Juliana (an Episcopal priest) Anderson. *Education:* Attended Harvard University, 1987; Cambridge University, B.A. (English literature), 1991; Syracuse University, M.F.A. (creative writing), 1998.

### Addresses

*E-mail*—Matthew.Anderson@tui.edu.

### Career

Writer. Candlewick Press, Cambridge, MA, editorial assistant, 1993-96; *Boston Review,* intern; WCUW-Radio, disk jockey; Union Institute & University, Vermont College, Montpelier, visiting instructor in M.F.A. program in writing for children, 2000-06. *3rd bed* (literary journal), fiction editor, 1999-2006.

### Awards, Honors

*Boston Globe/Horn Book* Nonfiction Honor, 2002, for *Handel, Who Knew What He Liked;* National Book Award finalist, National Book Foundation, 2002, Best Book for Young Adults selection, American Library Association, *Boston Globe/Horn Book* Honor Book designation for Fiction, and *Los Angeles Times* Book Award, all 2003, all for *Feed;* National Book Award for Young People's Literature, 2006, Michael L. Prinz Award Honor Book designation, and *Boston Globe/Horn Book* Award in fiction and poetry, all 2007, all for *The Astonishing Life of Octavian Nothing, Traitor to the Nation.*

## Writings

*YOUNG-ADULT NOVELS*

*Thirsty,* Candlewick Press (Cambridge, MA), 1998.

*Burger Wuss,* Candlewick Press (Cambridge, MA), 1999.

*Feed,* Candlewick Press (Cambridge, MA), 2002.

*The Astonishing Life of Octavian Nothing, Traitor to the Nation, Volume One: The Pox Party,* Candlewick Press, 2006.

*FOR CHILDREN*

*Handel, Who Knew What He Liked* (picture book), illustrated by Kevin Hawkes, Candlewick Press (Cambridge, MA), 2001.

*M.T. Anderson*

*Strange Mr. Satie* (picture book), illustrated by Petra Mathers, Viking Penguin (New York, NY), 2003.

*The Game of Sunken Places* (middle-grade novel), Scholastic (New York, NY), 2004.

*The Serpent Came to Gloucester* (picture book), illustrated by Bagram Ibatouline, Candlewick Press (Cambridge, MA), 2005.

*Whales on Stilts!* (chapter book; "M.T. Anderson's Thrilling Tales" series), illustrated by Kurt Cyrus, Harcourt (New York, NY), 2005.

*The Clue of the Linoleum Lederhosen* (chapter book; "M.T. Anderson's Thrilling Tales" series), illustrated by Kurt Cyrus, Harcourt (New York, NY), 2005.

*Me, All Alone, at the End of the World* (picture book), illustrated by Kevin Hawkes, Candlewick Press (Cambridge, MA), 2005.

*OTHER*

Contributor of articles and reviews to periodicals, including *Improper Bostonian, BBC Music, Pulse!,* and *Cobblestones.* Contributor of short story to *Open Your Eyes: Extraordinary Experiences in Far Away Places,* edited by Jill Davis, Viking (New York, NY), 2003. Adult fiction published in *Northwest Review, Colorado Review,* and *Conjunctions.*

## Adaptations

Several books by Anderson have been adapted for audiobook, including *Whales on Stilts!, Feed,* and *The Astonishing Life of Octavian Nothing, Traitor to the Nation, Volume One: The Pox Party,* all released by Listening Library.

## Sidelights

Winner of the 2006 National Book Award for Young People's Literature for his quirkily titled novel *The Astonishing Life of Octavian Nothing, Traitor to the Nation, Volume One: The Pox Party,* M.T. Anderson is noted for penning young-adult novels that challenge readers to look at the world in new ways. "Writing is a kind of weakness, I think," Anderson once told *SATA.* "We write because we can't decipher things the first time around. As a reader, I like best those books in which the author, mulling things over for him or herself, enables readers to see a world anew." While Anderson's middle-grade novels, such as *Whales on Stilts!, The Clue of the Linoleum Lederhosen,* and *The Game of Sunken Places,* feature an entertaining mix of fantasy, mystery, and spine-tingling supernatural elements, novels such as *Thirsty,* about a teenage vampire, *Feed,* about rebellion against futuristic media control of the world, and *The Astonishing Life of Octavian Nothing, Traitor to the Nation,* about the hypocrisy of Enlightenment-era morality, aim their wit and satire at society. "We are so used to the bizarre images, cabals, rituals, and rites that constitute our lives that they seem natural, even invisible, to us," Anderson explained. "I admire books that facilitate renewed awareness of the way we live, and this is what I'm attempting in my own work: renewed awareness both for myself and, I hope, for my readers. That's my goal, in any case."

*Thirsty,* set in a small town in Massachusetts, features a high school freshman named Chris who realizes that he is on the verge of growing into a vampire—despite his town's elaborate and ritualistic attempts to fight the dreaded monsters. "Chris's turbulent transformation . . . is paralleled by and inextricable from the changes of adolescence: insatiable appetite, sleepless nights, and a deep sense of insecurity and isolation," noted *Horn Book* reviewer Lauren Adams. "The unusual blend of camp horror and realistic adolescent turmoil and the suspenseful plot affirm a new talent worth watching," Adams added of Anderson's fiction debut. A *Kirkus Reviews* critic also praised *Thirsty,* calling the book a "startling, savagely funny debut," and *School Librarian* contributor Julie Blaisdale deemed the work "at once creepy and yet extremely funny." While noting some flaws in the plot, a *Publishers Weekly* reviewer described *Thirsty* as a "vampire novel a bloody cut above the usual fare."

Anderson's young-adult novels *Burger Wuss* and *Feed* take place in settings that are both disturbing and familiar. In *Burger Wuss* teen narrator Anthony is determined to get revenge on another teen who has "stolen" his girlfriend. The romantic rival, Turner, is a hot-shot employee at the local burger joint, and by getting a job at the same restaurant Anthony begins enacting his revenge. According to a *Publishers Weekly* critic,

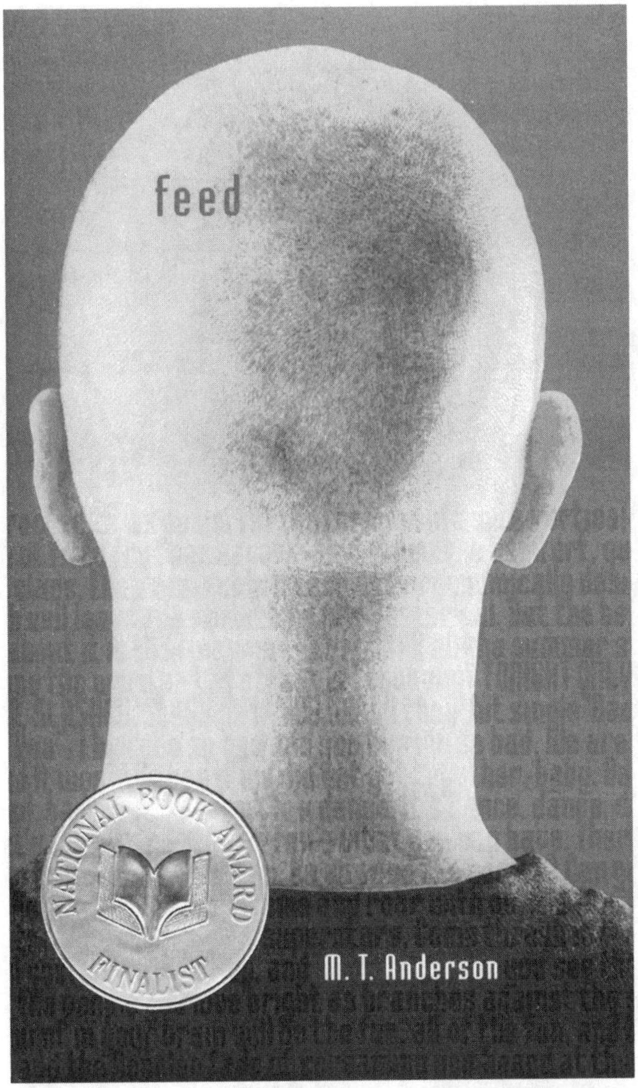


***Cover of Anderson's award-winning young-adult novel* Feed, *which takes readers into a chilling possible future.*** (Illustration © 2002. Reproduced by permission of the publisher, Candlewick Press, Inc., Cambridge, MA.)

"Anderson's witty tale of a lovelorn boy and his corporate antagonists is both a tasty read and a stinging satire." Focusing on the novel's abundant "black humor and satire," *Booklist* critic Jean Franklin cited "a marvelous parody of a television commercial" for particular praise. In *Horn Book* Peter D. Sieruta likewise commented on Anderson's "eye for the dark and demented aspects of everyday life," adding that Anthony's narration "serves up a lot of laughs."

*Feed* takes readers into a distant and frightening future in which the media controls the world and individuals are linked into the propagandizing system via an electronic feed inserted into the brain. Titus, a typical teen, is connected to the educational system as well as to entertainment, merchandise, and friends through this feed. The constant information stream means that there is little need to speak, read, or write. While vacationing on the moon with a group of friends, Titus meets Violet, who, having been home schooled, is somewhat of a Luddite in that she eschews the feed technology. When hackers temporarily disconnect the vacationers' brain feeds and Titus wakes up in the hospital, he experiences silence for the first time. Although Violet tries to recruit Titus to resist the feed and all it implies, the teen is unable to reject his previous lifestyle.

Reviewers saw much to like in *Feed,* particularly Anderson's wit and imagination. A *Kirkus Reviews* contributor called the novel's plot "satire at its finest," and a *Publishers Weekly* critic described Titus as a "believably flawed hero" and the work a "thought-provoking and scathing indictment." According to Elizabeth Devereaux, writing in the *New York Times Book Review,* Anderson's novel is "subversive, vigorously conceived, [and] painfully situated at the juncture where funny crosses into tragic." Although Sharon Rawlins remarked in *School Library Journal* that "Violet and her father are the only truly sympathetic characters" in the book, the critic also asserted that *Feed* is a "gripping, intriguing, and unique cautionary novel." Several reviewers noted Anderson's use of language, particularly his tone and his creation of a unique dialect. "Anderson's hand is light throughout; his evocation of the death of language is as hilarious as it is frightening," wrote *Horn Book* critic Lauren Adams. "Inventive details help evoke a world that is chillingly plausible," Adams continued. "Like those in a funhouse mirror, the reflections the novel shows us may be ugly and distorted, but they are undeniably ourselves." Winner of the *Los Angeles Times* Book Award, *Feed* was also a finalist for the National Book Award, as well as a *Boston Globe/Horn Book* Honor Book and an American Library Association Best Book for Young Adults selection.

Described by *Horn Book* critic Vicky Smith as "an alternative narrative of [America's] . . . national mythology, one that fascinates, appalls, condemns," *The Astonishing Life of Octavian Nothing, Traitor to the Nation* takes readers back to the birth of the United States and an age when the influences of European Enlightenment thinkers such as Voltaire and Rousseau were meshing with the economic realities of industrialization. As recounted by Anderson in baroque prose, the circumstances of black, sixteen-year-old Octavian Nothing rapidly decline as revolutionary activities in his native Boston accelerate. Brought to the American colonies with his mother, an African princess, Octavian was raised in unique circumstances, amid an intellectual elite at the city's Novanglian College of Lucidity, where he was taught music and the classics. He also unknowingly served as the test subject of the college fellows, who were attempting to gauge the intelligence potential of blacks. Octavio gains an awareness of the outside world through his friendship with a slave named Pro Bono, but when the boy flees his insulated life after a college-mandated smallpox inoculation results in his mother's death, the outside world proves harsher than he ever imagined.

Praising the novel—both Octavian's narrative and the sequence of letters that comprise the second half of the

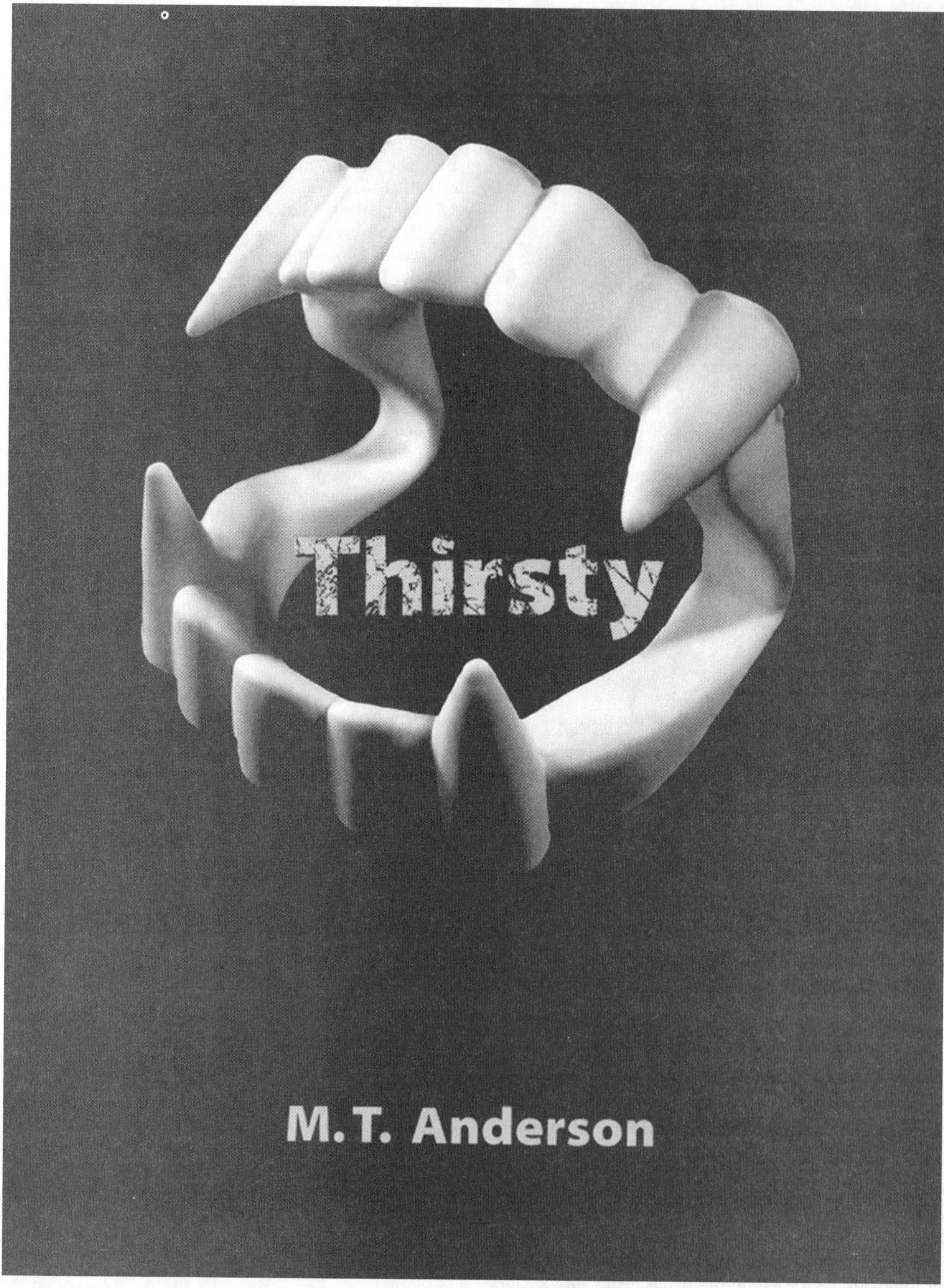


***Anderson's 1997 novel* Thirsty *served as the author's teen fiction debut.*** (Illustration © 1997. Reproduced by permission of the publisher, Candlewick Press, Inc., Cambridge, MA.)

book—as "stunningly well-researched," a *Publishers Weekly* contributor wrote that Anderson's "accessible" prose and "straight-forward" message . . . clearly delineates the hypocrisy of the Patriots," who both proclaim their right to freedom and quietly accept "the enslavement of people like Octavian." "Readers are seduced" by Anderson's "gothic introduction to the child Octavian," a *Kirkus Reviews* writer noted, calling the boy's "bizarre situation" in the Novanglian College of Lucidity "both lavish and eerie." "Teens need not understand all the historical and literary allusions to connect with Octavian's torment or to debate the novel's questions," Gillian Engberg maintained in her *Booklist* review while going on to note that *The Astonishing Life of Octavian Nothing, Traitor to the Nation* is a "chaotic and highly accomplished" novel that "demands rereading."

In addition to his genre-defying books for teen readers, Anderson also writes for a younger audience, and has created picture-book texts as well as middle-grade chapter books. He shares his interest in music in picture-book biographies of eighteenth-century German-English composer George Frideric Handel and twentieth-century French composer Erik Satie. In *Handel, Who Knew What He Liked* Anderson illustrates the life of Handel

*Cover of Anderson's highly lauded historical novel* **The Astonishing Life of Octavian Nothing, Traitor to the Nation,** *featuring artwork by Gerard Dubois.* (Illustration © 2006 by Gerard Dubois. Reproduced by permission of the publisher, Candlewick Press, Inc., Cambridge, MA.)

through anecdotes related in what *School Library Journal* critic Wendy Lukehart described as a "saucy style [featuring] impeccable pacing, and a richness of content." One such anecdote focuses on how the young Handel—whose parents did not want him to become a musician—smuggled a clavichord into the attic of his parents' house. Others provide background to the composition of such works as the *Music for the Royal Fireworks,* which bombed upon its first performance; Handel's failure as an opera composer; and the creation of the *Messiah* oratorio, which would earn the composer lasting fame. Several reviewers commented on the appropriateness of Anderson's language and tone, among them a *Publishers Weekly* contributor, who dubbed the work "wittily irreverent." Using "plain words and short sentences," Anderson describes Handel's life "with warmth and color, humor and humanity," applauded *Booklist* reviewer Carolyn Phelan, and in *Horn Book,* Mary M. Burns deemed *Handel, Who Knew What He Liked* "worthy of a standing ovation." Burns also praised Anderson's balanced tone and his ability to create a "lively text, sufficiently detailed but not overburdened with minutiae."

In *Strange Mr. Satie* Anderson once again draws on his "offbeat" but compelling storytelling skills, in the opinion of *Booklist* contributor GraceAnne A. DeCandido. An unusual man, Satie is not as universally known as Handel, but he had a lasting influence on modern music. In his day he was also known for his interesting lifestyle, throwing one girlfriend out of a window, never bathing with soap, and displaying a general disdain for rules, be they of music or society. Discussing Anderson's narrative style in *Horn Book,* Lolly Robinson claimed that the story's "words flow naturally and hypnotize the reader with oceanic rhythms." Similarly, DeCandido remarked that the author's "text has a fine rhythm, and it doesn't shirk at the strangeness" of the composer's life. Pointing out that Anderson's text mirrors Satie's own circular musical style, *School Library Journal* contributor Jody McCoy found in *Strange Mr. Satie* "a splendid alliance of topic, text, and illustration, produc[ing] a hauntingly compelling biography."

Other picture books featuring Anderson's text include *Me, All Alone, at the End of the World,* about a boy whose quiet home at the end of the world is transformed by magician-promoter Constantine Shimmer into an amusement park overrun by tourists, and *The Serpent Came to Gloucester,* a rhyming tale based on a sea-serpent sighting in coastal Massachusetts in 1817. Noting that *Me, All Alone, at the End of the World* "addresses some thought-provoking, philosophical issues," *School Library Journal* contributor Linda L. Walkins added that Kevin Hawkes' full-color illustrations for the book "resonate with old-fashioned charm." "Many will assume" that the text of *The Serpent Came to Gloucester* "came straight from some leather-bound volume of romantic poetry," maintained Jennifer Mattson in her *Booklist* review of Anderson's 2005 collaboration with illustrator Bagram Ibatouline, and Margaret

Bush described the same work in *School Library Journal* as "an evocative introduction to poetic narrative, local legends, or an exploration of a tantalizing subject."

Anderson turns to preteen readers with *The Game of Sunken Places,* an intriguing chapter book that finds Gregory and brainy best friend Brian pulled into an alternative reality while spending a holiday at Grendle Manor, the rural Vermont mansion of Gregory's eccentric uncle Max. A discarded game board discovered in the woods near the manor is the key to this sinister alternative Vermont, and the boys must unravel the many rules and dimensions of the game—as well as deal with assorted trolls, monsters, and other beasties—in order to return to their own world. With "colorful prose" and an ability to "dexterously juggl[e] . . . a seemingly impossible profusion of elements," *The Game of Sunken Places* "builds to a climactic series of surprises that . . . will almost certainly dazzle readers," wrote a *Publishers Weekly* critic. In *Kirkus Reviews* a contributor concluded that middle graders "willing to suspend every ounce of disbelief will be rewarded by this smart, consciously complex offering," and Mattson wrote in *Booklist* that the novel is "deliciously scary, often funny, and crowned by a pair of deeply satisfying surprises."

Comprising the "M.T. Anderson's Thrilling Tales" series, *Whales on Stilts!* and *The Clue of the Linoleum Lederhosen* introduce Lily Gefelty, Jasper Dash, and Katie Mulligan. Following the time-honored traditions established by the series fiction of generations past, these three friends discover a plot by a mad scientist to marshal an army of sea mammals and take over the world in *Whales on Stilts!* This revelation prompts them to shoulder the task of saving mankind when parents—including Lily's absentminded professor father—prove unmoved by their worries. *The Clue of the Linoleum Lederhosen* finds the trio looking forward to a vacation at the Moose Tongue Lodge. However, after arriving at the mountain retreat they realize that they are not the only junior sleuths there; in fact, all sorts of fictional sleuthing teams are sharing the vacation spot. When a princess's priceless necklace disappears, followed by several examples of the taxidermist's art, Lily and company prove their sleuthing superiority. Featuring "an array of adjectives, non-sequiturs, bizarre asides, irrelevant footnotes and running gags," *Whales on Stilts!* is a humorous send-up of "decades of children's book series," observed a *Publishers Weekly* contributor, while Smith wrote in *Horn Book* that the "narrative gleefully revels in each cliché it exploits." "Anderson's mind is a very strange place," quipped a *Kirkus Reviews* contributor, noting that the "almost indescribable wackiness" of *Whales on Stilts!* "is further proof." Sharing this assessment, Smith wrote of *The Clue of the Linoleum Lederhosen* that the author's "second send-up of kids' series books is, if possible, even more self-consciously metaliterary than his first."

In addition to remaining unpredictable and unclassifiable, Anderson's books continue to be acknowledged for their sophisticated wit and storylines. Asked by a *Kirkus Reviews* interviewer whether he worries that his tales might be too complex for younger readers, Anderson responded: "I think many adults underestimate kids' intelligence and capacity, and I think that's a big problem. I prefer to delude myself that we're a nation of geniuses, all just waiting to unfold."

## Biographical and Critical Sources

*PERIODICALS*

*Booklist,* November 15, 1999, Jean Franklin, review of *Burger Wuss,* p. 613; December 15, 2001, Carolyn Phelan, review of *Handel, Who Knew What He Liked,* p. 727; October 15, 2002, Frances Bradburn, review of *Feed,* pp. 400-401; January 1, 2003, review of *Feed,* p. 795; November 1, 2003, GraceAnne A. DeCandido, review of *Strange Mr. Satie,* p. 512; April 15, 2004, Jennifer Mattson, review of *The Game of Sunken Places,* p. 512; June 1, 2005, Jennifer Mattson, review of *The Serpent Came to Gloucester,* p. 1805; November 15, 2005, Jennifer Mattson, review of *Me, All Alone, at the End of the World,* p. 44; May 1, 2006, John Peters, review of *The Clue of the Linoleum Lederhosen,* p. 48; September 1, 2006, Gillian Engberg, review of *The Astonishing Life of Octavian Nothing, Traitor to the Nation, Volume One: The Pox Party,* p. 110.

*Book Report,* September-October, 1997, Charlotte Decker, review of *Thirsty,* p. 30.

*Bulletin of the Center for Children's Books,* April, 1997, review of *Thirsty,* p. 269; November, 2002, review of *Feed,* p. 95; September, 2003, Deborah Stevenson, review of *Strange Mr. Satie,* p. 5; September, 2004, Deborah Stevenson, review of *The Game of Sunken Places,* p. 5; April, 2005, Krista Hutley, review of *Whales on Stilts!,* p. 325; July-August, 2005, review of *The Serpent Came to Gloucester,* p. 476; July-August, 2006, Loretta Gaffney, review of *The Clue of the Linoleum Lederhosen,* p. 487; November, 2006, Elizabeth Bush, review of *The Astonishing Life of Octavian Nothing, Traitor to the Nation,* p. 112.

*General Music Today,* winter, 2002, Richard Ammon, review of *Handel, Who Knew What He Liked,* p. 31.

*Horn Book,* May-June, 1997, Lauren Adams, review of *Thirsty,* p. 313; November, 1999, Peter D. Sieruta, review of *Burger Wuss,* p. 732; November-December, 2001, Mary M. Burns, review of *Handel, Who Knew What He Liked,* pp. 767-768; September-October, 2002, Lauren Adams, review of *Feed,* pp. 564-566; September-October, 2003, Lolly Robinson, review of *Strange Mr. Satie,* p. 624; March-April, 2005, Vicky Smith, review of *Whales on Stilts!,* p. 197; May-June, 2006, Vicky Smith, review of *The Clue of the Linoleum Lederhosen,* p. 309; September-October, 2006, Vicky Smith, review of *The Astonishing Life of Octavian Nothing, Traitor to the Nation,* p. 573.

*Kirkus Reviews,* January 1, 1997, review of *Thirsty,* p. 56; September 15, 2001, review of *Handel, Who Knew What He Liked,* p. 1352; September 1, 2002, review of *Feed,* p. 1301; August 1, 2003, review of *Strange Mr. Satie,* p. 1011; June 15, 2004, review of *The Game of Sunken Places,* p. 575; April 1, 2005, review of *Whales on Stilts!,* p. 411; June 1, 2005, review of *The Serpent Came to Gloucester,* p. 632; September 1, 2005, review of *All Alone, at the End of the World,* p. 968; June 1, 2006, review of *The Clue of the Linoleum Lederhosen,* p. 568; September 15, 2006, review of *The Astonishing Life of Octavian Nothing, Traitor to the Nation,* p. 945; December 1, 2006, interview with Anderson.

*Kliatt,* November, 2002, Paula Rohrlick, review of *Feed,* p. 5; September, 2003, Erin Lukens Darr, review of *Thirsty,* p. 23; September, 2006, Paula Rohrlick, review of *The Astonishing Life of Octavian Nothing, Traitor to the Nation,* p. 6.

*New York Times Book Review,* November 17, 2002, Elizabeth Devereaux, review of *Feed,* p. 47; December 8, 2002, review of *Feed,* p. 74.

*Publishers Weekly,* January 27, 1997, review of *Thirsty,* p. 108; August 2, 1999, review of *Burger Wuss,* p. 86; October 15, 2001, review of *Handel, Who Knew What He Liked,* p. 72; July 22, 2002, review of *Feed,* p. 181; September 1, 2003, review of *Strange Mr. Satie,* p. 89; July 12, 2004, review of *The Game of Sunken Places,* p. 64; May 16, 2005, reviews of *The Serpent Came to Gloucester,* p. 62, and *Whales on Stilts!,* p. 63; September 18, 2006, review of *The Astonishing Life of Octavian Nothing, Traitor to the Nation,* p. 56.

*School Librarian,* fall, 1998, Julie Blaisdale, review of *Thirsty,* p. 155.

*School Library Journal,* March, 1997, Joel Shoemaker, review of *Thirsty,* p. 184; December, 2001, Wendy Lukehart, review of *Handel, Who Knew What He Liked,* p. 117; September, 2002, Sharon Rawlins, review of *Feed,* p. 219; October, 2003, Jody McCoy, review of *Strange Mr. Satie,* p. 143; May, 2005, Walter Minkel, review of *Whales on Stilts!,* p. 120; December, 2005, Linda L. Walkins, review of *Me, All Alone, at the End of the World,* p. 100; April, 2006, Ann Crewdson, review of *The Game of Sunken Places,* p. 80; October, 2006, Sharon Rawlins, review of *The Astonishing Life of Octavian Nothing, Traitor to the Nation,* p. 147; November, 2006, interview with Anderson.

*Voice of Youth Advocates,* April, 1998, review of *Thirsty,* p. 40; December, 2002, review of *Feed,* p. 394; June, 2004, Michael Levy, review of *The Game of Sunken Places,* p. 139; June, 2004, Joel Shoemaker, interview with Anderson, p. 98.

*ONLINE*

*Cynsations,* http://www.cyndialeitichsmith.blogspot.com/ (September 12, 2005), Cynthia Leitich-Smith, interview with Anderson.

*   *   *

## AVRIL, Lynne

See CRAVATH, Lynne W.

# B

## BAILEY, Linda 1948-

### Personal

Born 1948, in Winnipeg, Manitoba, Canada; married; children: two daughters. *Education:* University of British Columbia, B.A. (English), M.A. (education).

### Addresses

*Home*—Vancouver, British Columbia, Canada. *E-mail*—bestclues@shaw.ca.

### Career

Writer. Presenter to schools and other organizations.

### Member

Canadian Society of Children's Authors, Illustrators, and Performers, Children's Book Centre of Canada, Society of Children's Book Writers and Illustrators, Writers' Union of Canada, Vancouver Children's Literature Roundtable.

### Awards, Honors

4-Surrey Book of the Year award, 1993, and Langley Book of the Year Award, 1994, both for *How Come the Best Clues Are Always in the Garbage?;* Ruth Schwartz Award, Arthur E. Ellis Award for best juvenile, Crime Writers of Canada, Silver Birch Award shortlist, and Canadian Library Association Notable Canadian Fiction designation, all 1994, all for *How Can I Be a Detective If I Have to Baby-sit?;* Arthur Ellis Award, 1996, for *How Can a Frozen Detective Stay Hot on the Trail?;* Arthur Ellis Award, CLB Book-of-the-Year honor, and Manitoba Young Readers' Choice honor, all 1996, all for *Who's Got Gertie?;* Arthur Ellis Award, 1997, and Red Cedar Award shortlist, 1999, both for *What's a Daring Detective like Me Doing in the Doghouse?;* Silver Birch Award shortlist, and Our Choice selection, both 2000, and Red Cedar Award shortlist, 2002, all for *How Can a Brilliant Detective Shine in the Dark?;* Silver Birch Award for nonfiction, 2001, for *Adventures in the Middle Ages;* Great Books Award, Canadian Toy Testing Council, 2002, for *The Best Figure Skater in the Whole Wide World;* Atlantic Hackmatack Award for English Nonfiction, Blue Spruce Award shortlist, and Red Cedar Award shortlist, all 2003, all for *Adventures with the Vikings; Child* magazine Best Children's Book Award, 2003, Ontario Blue Spruce Award, CNIB Tiny Torgi Award, and University of Chicago Zena Sutherland Award, all 2004, and Saskatchewan Shining Willow Award and Georgia Picture Storybook Award, both 2005, all for *Stanley's Party;* Atlantic Hackmatack Award for English Nonfiction shortlist, and Red Cedar Award shortlist, both 2004, both for *Adventures in Ancient Greece;* Silver Birch Award shortlist, 2004, and Atlantic Hackmatack Award for English Nonfiction shortlist, 2006, both for *Adventures in Ancient China;* Atlantic Hackmatack Award for English Nonfiction, 2006, for *Adventures in the Ice Age.*

### Writings

*FOR CHILDREN*

*Petula, Who Wouldn't Take a Bath,* illustrated by Jackie Snider, HarperCollins (Toronto, Ontario, Canada), 1996.

*Gordon Loggins and the Three Bears,* illustrated by Tracy Walker, Kids Can Press (Toronto, Ontario, Canada), 1997.

*When Addie Was Scared,* illustrated by sister, Wendy Bailey, Kids Can Press (Tonawanda, NY), 1999.

*The Best Figure Skater in the Whole Wide World,* illustrated by Alan Daniel and Lea Daniel, Kids Can Press (Toronto, Ontario, Canada), 2001.

*Stanley's Party,* illustrated by Bill Slavin, Kids Can Press (Toronto, Ontario, Canada), 2003.

*Stanley's Wild Ride,* illustrated by Bill Slavin, Kids Can Press (Toronto, Ontario, Canada), 2006.

*The Farm Team,* illustrated by Bill Slavin, Kids Can Press (Toronto, Ontario, Canada), 2006.

*Goodnight, Sweet Pig,* illustrated by Josee Masse, Kids Can Press (Toronto, Ontario, Canada), 2007.

*FOR CHILDREN; "STEVIE DIAMOND" MYSTERY SERIES*

*How Come the Best Clues Are Always in the Garbage?,* illustrated by Pat Cupples, Kids Can Press (Toronto, Ontario, Canada), 1992.
*How Can I Be a Detective If I Have to Baby-sit?,* illustrated by Pat Cupples, Kids Can Press (Toronto, Ontario, Canada), 1993.
*Who's Got Gertie? And How Can We Get Her Back?,* illustrated by Pat Cupples, Kids Can Press (Toronto, Ontario, Canada), 1994.
*How Can a Frozen Detective Stay Hot on the Trail?,* illustrated by Pat Cupples, Albert Whitman (Morton Grove, IL), 1996.
*What's a Daring Detective like Me Doing in the Doghouse?,* illustrated by Pat Cupples, Albert Whitman (Morton Grove, IL), 1997.
*How Can a Brilliant Detective Shine in the Dark?,* Kids Can Press (Tonawanda, NY), 1999.
*What Is a Serious Detective like Me Doing in Such a Silly Movie?,* Kids Can Press (Tonawanda, NY), 2002.

Author's books have been translated into several languages, including French, Chinese, Polish, and Danish.

*FOR CHILDREN; "GOOD TIMES TRAVEL AGENCY" SERIES*

*Adventures in Ancient Egypt,* illustrated by Bill Slavin, Kids Can Press (Toronto, Ontario, Canada), 2000.
*Adventures in the Middle Ages,* illustrated by Bill Slavin, Kids Can Press (Toronto, Ontario, Canada), 2000.
*Adventures with the Vikings,* illustrated by Bill Slavin, Kids Can Press (Toronto, Ontario, Canada), 2001.
*Adventures in Ancient Greece,* illustrated by Bill Slavin, Kids Can Press (Toronto, Ontario, Canada), 2002.
*Adventures in Ancient China,* illustrated by Bill Slavin, Kids Can Press (Toronto, Ontario, Canada), 2003.
*Adventures in the Ice Age,* illustrated by Bill Slavin, Kids Can Press (Toronto, Ontario, Canada), 2004.

## Adaptations

*Stanley's Party* and *Stanley's Wild Ride* were adapted for videocassette, Nutmeg Media, 2006.

## Sidelights

Canadian author Linda Bailey is the creator of the "Stevie Diamond Mystery" and "Good Times Travel Agency" series for middle-grade readers. Other children's books by Bailey include *Gordon Loggins and the Three Bears, The Farm Team, Goodnight, Sweet Pig,* and a pair of books that focus on a rambunctious dog named Stanley. *Gordon Loggins and the Three Bears,* a send-up of the classic Goldilocks story that finds a boy slipping through a door in the school library bookshelf and ending up starring in the librarian's story-hour tale, was described by *Quill & Quire* contributor Anne Louise Mahoney as a "hilarious story [that] will be a big hit with kids who know the classic tale." Praising Josee Masse's illustrations for *Goodnight, Sweet Pig, School Library Journal* contributor Donna Atmur added that Bailey's tale about Hamlette, a piglet who cannot fall asleep, "would also make an excellent bedtime story for restless children." In *Booklist,* Ilene Cooper dubbed *Stanley's Party* "a well-plotted delight," and Shawn Brommer predicted in *School Library Journal* that Bailey's energetic pooch will make "dog lovers and party animals alike . . . howl with delight."

In *How Come the Best Clues Are Always in the Garbage?,* the first novel in the "Stevie Diamond Mystery" series, eleven-year-old Stevie and friend Jesse Kulniki set out to find out who stole the funds of Garbage Busters, an environmental group that is protesting a fast-food restaurant's excessive use of packaging. *How Can I Be a Detective If I Have to Baby-sit?* finds Stevie and Jesse spending a week at a British Columbian reforestation camp, where Stevie's father is working. Although the girls look forward to enjoying the great outdoors, they quickly realize that they were invited along so that

***Cover of Linda Bailey's middle-grade novel* How Come the Best Clues Are Always in the Garbage?, *featuring artwork by Pat Cupples.*** (Illustration © 1994 by Pat Cupples. Reproduced by permission of Kids Can Press Ltd., Toronto, Ontario, Canada.)

***Bailey pairs up with frequent collaborator Bill Slavin on a humorous story about an adventurous pup in* Stanley's Wild Ride.** (Illustration © 2006 by Bill Slavin. Reproduced by permission of Kids Can Press Ltd., Toronto, Ontario, Canada.)

they could baby-sit five-year-old Alexander, the camp cook's son. When Stevie and Jesse discover that Alexander's family is in some kind of trouble, their vacation becomes a sleuthing job.

Joseph J. Rodio, writing in *Catholic Library World,* noted the "humorous insights" into the adult world in Bailey's series opener, as well as her portrayal of the well-developed friendship between the two girls. Gisela Sherman, writing in *Canadian Children's Literature,* praised the quick-paced plot, "great dialogue, comic timing, odd clues and hilarious situations" in *How Come the Best Clues Are Always in the Garbage?,* adding that the novel's environmental message "fits in naturally." Calling *How Can I Be a Detective If I Have to Baby-sit?* "a cut above most detective series for the age group," *School Library Journal* contributor Linda Wicher described the plot as "nimble," and *Booklist* reviewer Chris Sherman called Bailey's story "entertaining" and its heroine "engaging," going on to predict that the novel's fast pace will appeal to young readers.

The "Stevie Diamond Mystery" series continues with *Who's Got Gertie? And How Can We Get Her Back?, How Can a Frozen Detective Stay Hot on the Trail?,* and *What's a Daring Detective like Me Doing in the Doghouse?* In *Who's Got Gertie?* thirteen-year-old Stevie and Jesse try to locate a missing neighbor, a retired actress, while *How Can a Frozen Detective Stay Hot on the Trail?* finds the sleuthing duo tracking down missing carnivorous plants in chilly Winnipeg, where one of the suspects is Stevie's uncle. *Who's Got Gertie?* was praised by *Quill & Quire* contributor Sarah Ellis, who cited Bailey's successful depiction of "middle-grade-mayhem" and described the novel as "colourful, lively, ephemeral, attention-getting, extravagant, and a crowd pleaser." Janet McNaughton, reviewing *How Can a Frozen Detective Stay Hot on the Trail?* for *Quill & Quire,* praised the author's characterization, plotting, and use of local color, and added that "the mystery works well, too."

*What's a Daring Detective like Me Doing in the Doghouse?* finds Stevie working at a day-care center for dogs while someone known only as the "Vancouver Prankster" causes all manner of mischief, eventually stealing the Canadian prime minister's underwear. When a stray dog appears to have a connection to the prankster, the girls investigate. Other novels include *How Can a Brilliant Detective Shine in the Dark?,* in which a family reunion leads to a lost treasure, a hidden cave, and maybe murder, while *What Is a Serious Detective like Me Doing in Such a Silly Movie?* follows the girls' experiences as part of the cast of a horror film called *Night of the Neems.* Reviewing the last-named title, Phelan cited Bailey's "flair for crisp dialogue," while *School Library Journal* contributor Tina Zubak wrote of *How Can a Brilliant Detective Shine in the Dark?* that "the book's humor and fast pace make it an enjoyable, old-fashioned whodunit."

Bailey begins her "Good Times Travel Agency" series with *Adventures in Ancient Egypt,* which introduces twins Josh and Emma Binkerton. Together with tag-along little sister Lizzy, the twins find themselves transported into the past via the pages of a magical travel guide they discover in a strange travel agency. Trapped in the year 2500 B.C., the children discover that the only way to return to their own time is to read the entire travel guide, cover to cover, and a number of interesting adventures occur while they do so. "Bailey delivers not only a fast-paced story but also a fun way to convey information" regarding her ancient setting, noted Shelley Townsend-Hudson in a *Booklist* review of *Adventures in Ancient Egypt.*

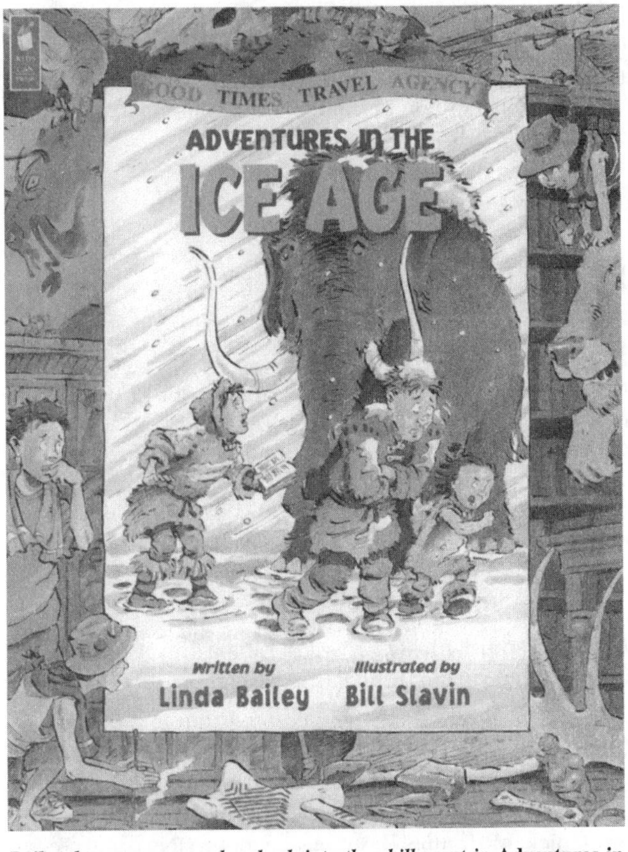


***Bailey draws young readers back into the chilly past in* Adventures in the Ice Age, *featuring artwork by Bill Slavin.*** (Illustration © 2004 by Bill Slavin. Reproduced by permission of Kids Can Press Ltd., Toronto, Ontario, Canada.)

**Adventures in the Middle Ages, *Bailey's detailed account of life in historic Europe, is enhanced by Slavin's detailed art.*** (Illustration © 2000 by Bill Slavin. Reproduced by permission of Kids Can Press, Ltd., Toronto, Ontario, Canada.)

Readers are carried along on the Binkerton children's further time-travel adventures in *Adventures in the Middle Ages, Adventures in Ancient Greece, Adventures in Ancient China, Adventures in the Ice Age,* and *Adventures with the Vikings,* the last which finds the children stowed away on a Viking ship in 800 A.D. Calling the Binkertons' escapades in *Adventures in Ancient Greece* "as hilarious as they are exciting," *Resource Links* contributor Veronica Allan added that Bailey's novel blends "historical information with fictional adventure in a way that cleverly presents facts" while also "entertaining . . . readers." Praising "the creative pen and ink, watercolour drawings and cartoon captions of Bill Slavin" that bring each series installment "to life," *Resource Links* writer Gail Lennon described *Adventures with the Vikings* as "interesting and innovative" in its approach to teaching about ancient cultures. In *Booklist,* Carolyn Phelan praised the same book as a "brief, accessible introduction to the subject," while Lynda Ritterman wrote in *School Library Journal* that

*Adventures in Ancient China* is "both fun and educational" due to Bailey's unique "combination of adventure story and factual material."

## Biographical and Critical Sources

*PERIODICALS*

*Booklist,* March 15, 1996, Chris Sherman, review of *How Can I Be a Detective If I Have to Baby-sit?,* p. 1264; November 15, 1999, John Peters, review of *When Addie Was Scared,* p. 632; January 1, 2001, Shelley Townsend-Hudson, review of *Adventures in Ancient Egypt,* p. 941; October 15, 2001, Carolyn Phelan, review of *Adventures with the Vikings,* p. 391; November 1, 2004, Kay Weisman, review of *Adventures in the Ice Age,* p. 477; May 1, 2003, Carolyn Phelan, review of *How Can a Brilliant Detective Shine in the Dark?,* p. 1528; July, 2003, Ilene Cooper, review of *Stanley's Party,* p. 1895; March 1, 2006, Gillian Engberg, review of *Stanley's Wild Ride,* p. 98; October 1, 2006, Carolyn Phelan, review of *The Farm Team,* p. 56.

*Books for Keeps,* September, 1996, David Bennett, review of *How Come the Best Clues Are Always in the Garbage,* p. 13.

*Bulletin of the Center for Children's Books,* December, 1997, Deborah Stevenson, review of *Gordon Loggins and the Three Bears,* p. 117; October 4, 2002, review of *What's a Serious Detective like Me Doing in Such a Silly Movie?;* May, 2003, review of *Stanley's Party,* p. 350.

*Canadian Book Review Annual,* 1994, p. 545; 2004, Christine Linge Macdonald, review of *Adventures in the Ice Age,* p. 544.

*Canadian Children's Literature,* winter, 1994, Gisela Sherman, review of *How Come the Best Clues Are Always in the Garbage?,* p. 66.

*Canadian Review of Materials,* March, 1994, p. 44; February 15, 2003, review of *Adventures in Ancient Egypt;* March 28, 2003, review of *Stanley's Party.*

*Catholic Library World,* December, 1996, Joseph J. Rodio, review of *How Come the Best Clues Are Always in the Garbage?,* p. 55.

*Children's Book Review Service,* spring, 1996, p. 141.

*Emergency Librarian,* September, 1994, p. 56.

*Kirkus Reviews,* September 15, 2006, review of *The Farm Team,* p. 946.

*Publishers Weekly,* February 3, 2003, review of *Stanley's Party,* p. 74; March 5, 2007, review of *Goodnight, Sweet Pig,* p. 59.

*Quill & Quire,* August, 1992, p. 26; December, 1994, Sarah Ellis, review of *Who's Got Gertie?,* p. 31; September, 1996, Janet McNaughton, review of *How Can a Frozen Detective Stay Hot on the Trail?,* and Joan Findon, review of *How Come the Best Clues Are Always in the Garbage?,* both p. 74; July, 1997, Anne Louise Mahoney, review of *Gordon Loggins and the Three Bears,* p. 51; September, 2001, review of *The Best Figure Skater in the Whole Wide World,* p. 52.

*Resource Links,* December, 1999, review of *When Addie Was Scared,* p. 2; February, 2000, review of *How Can a Brilliant Detective Shine in the Dark?,* p. 7; December, 2000, review of *Adventures in Ancient Egypt,* pp. 10-11; October, 2001, Gail Lennon, review of *Adventures with the Vikings,* p. 22; December, 2001, Valerie Pollock, review of *The Best Figure Skater in the Whole Wide World,* p. 2; December, 2002, Veronica Allan, review of *Adventures in Ancient Greece,* p. 36; June, 2003, Isobel Lang, review of *Stanley's Party,* p. 1; October, 2003, Greg Bak, review of *Adventures in Ancient China,* p. 12; June, 2006, Denise Parrott, review of *Stanley's Wild Ride,* p. 2; February, 2007, Evette Berry, review of *The Farm Team,* p. 1; June, 2007, Tanya Boudreau, review of *Goodnight, Sweet Pig,* p. 1.

*School Library Journal,* May, 1996, p. 110; July, 1996, Linda Wicher, review of *How Can I Be a Detective If I Have to Baby-sit?,* p. 82; December, 2001, Rita Soltan, review of *The Best Figure Skater in the Whole Wide World,* p. 88; June, 2003, Tina Zubak, review of *How Can a Brilliant Detective Shine in the Dark?,* p. 136; July, 2003, Shawn Brommer, review of *Stanley's Party,* p. 87, and Tina Zubak, review of *What's a Serious Detective like Me Doing in Such a Silly Movie?,* p. 123; January, 2004, Lynda Ritterman, review of *Adventures in Ancient China,* p. 110; June, 2006, Suzanne Myers Harold, review of *Stanley's Wild Ride,* p. 98; November, 2006, Blair Christolon, review of *The Farm Team,* p. 84; June, 2007, Donna Atmur, review of *Goodnight, Sweet Pig,* p. 92.

*Times Educational Supplement,* July 5, 1996, review of *How Come the Best Clues Are Always in the Garbage?,* p. R8.

*ONLINE*

*Canadian Society of Children's Authors, Illustrators, and Performers Web site,* http://www.canscaip.org/ (April 1, 2006), "Linda Bailey."*

* * *

## BARBER, Ronde 1975-

### Personal

Name pronounced RON-day; born Jamael Oronde Barber, April 7, 1975, in Roanoke, VA; son of James "J.B." and Geraldine (a financial director) Barber; married; wife's name Claudia; children: Yammile Rose, Justyce Rosina. *Education:* University of Virginia, B.A. (marketing), 1997.

### Addresses

*Home*—Tampa, FL. *Office*—c/o Tampa Bay Buccaneers, One Buccaneer Pl., Tampa, FL 33607.

### Career

Professional football player and broadcaster. Played college football at University of Virginia; third-round draft pick of Tampa Bay Buccaneers in National Football League (NFL) entry draft, 1997; cornerback for Tampa Bay Buccaneers, 1997—. Cohost of *Sunday*

***Ronde Barber*** (Photograph by Bill Kostroun. AP Images.)

*Sports Extra,* WFLA, 2000, 2002-03; host of *The Ronde Barber Show* (radio program), Tampa, FL; cohost of *The Barber Shop,* Sirius Satellite Radio, 2005-06.

## Member

Fellowship of Christian Athletes.

## Awards, Honors

Society of Professional Journalists Award, for *Sunday Sports Extra;* named National Football League (NFL) Alumni Defensive Back of the Year, 2001; named to NFL All-Pro team, Associated Press, 2001, 2002, 2004, 2005, 2006; selected to NFL Pro Bowl, 2002, 2005, 2006, 2007; inducted into Virginia High School Hall of Fame, 2006; Christopher Award, 2006, for *Game Day.*

## Writings

(With brother, Tiki Barber, and Robert Burleigh) *By My Brother's Side,* illustrated by Barry Root, Simon & Schuster Books for Young Readers (New York, NY), 2004.

(With Tiki Barber and Robert Burleigh) *Game Day,* illustrated by Barry Root, Simon & Schuster Books for Young Readers (New York, NY), 2005.

(With Tiki Barber and Robert Burleigh) *Teammates,* illustrated by Barry Root, Simon & Schuster Books for Young Readers (New York, NY), 2006.

## Sidelights

For *Sidelights,* please see entry on Tiki Barber.

## Biographical and Critical Sources

*BOOKS*

*Contemporary Black Biography,* Volume 41, Thomson Gale (Detroit, MI), 2004.

*PERIODICALS*

*Black Issues Book Review,* September-October, 2004, Suzanne Rust, "He Ain't Heavy," p. 60.

*Booklist,* September 1, 2004, Todd Morning, review of *By My Brother's Side,* p. 114; September 1, 2005, Ilene Cooper, review of *Game Day,* p. 119; September 1, 2006, Carolyn Phelan, review of *Teammates,* p. 116.

*Bulletin of the Center for Children's Books,* January, 2006, Elizabeth Bush, review of *Game Day,* p. 218.

*Ebony,* December, 2005, review of *Game Day,* p. 30.

*Kirkus Reviews,* September 15, 2004, review of *By My Brother's Side,* p. 909; September 15, 2005, review of *Game Day,* p. 1020.

*New York Times,* August 12, 1997, Bill Pennington, "The Barber Brothers Stay in Touch as Rookie Rivals with the Giants and Bucs"; November 29, 1997, Bill Pennington, "It's Barber vs. Barber When Giants Play Bucs."

*Publishers Weekly,* August 30, 2004, Shannon Maughan, "Double Duty," p. 54, and review of *By My Brother's Side,* p. 55; October 3, 2005, review of *Game Day,* p. 70.

*Sarasota Herald Tribune,* October 29, 2006, Tom Balog, "Barbers' Final Meeting?," p. C3.

*School Library Journal,* November, 2004, Ann M. Holcomb, review of *By My Brother's Side,* p. 122; January, 2006, Mary Hazelton, review of *Game Day,* p. 116; November, 2006, Rachel G. Payne, review of *Teammates,* p. 117.

*Sports Illustrated,* July 23, 2001, John Ed Bradley, "Play Mates," p. 52.

*ONLINE*

*Tampa Bay Buccaneers Web site,* http://www.buccaneers.com (July 20, 2007), "Ronde Barber."

*University of Virginia Magazine Online,* http://www.uvamagazine.org/ (spring, 2006), Ben Cramer, "The Power of Two."*

* * *

# BARBER, Tiki 1975-

## Personal

Born Atiim Kiambu Barber, April 7, 1975, in Roanoke, VA; son of James "J.B." and Geraldine (a financial director) Barber; married Ginny Cha (a fashion publicist), 1999; children: A.J., Chason. *Education:* University of Virginia, B.A. (management information systems), 1997.

## Addresses

*Home*—New York, NY.

## Career

Professional football player and broadcaster. Played college football at University of Virginia; second-round draft pick of New York Giants in National Football League (NFL) entry draft, 1997; running back for New York Giants, 1997-2006. WCBS-TV, sports commentator, 2000; WFAN-AM-FM, fill-in host, c. 2000; Fox News, commentator for *Fox & Friends* (morning show), 2004-06; YES Network, host of *This Week in Football*; Sirius Satellite Radio, cohost of *The Barber Shop,* 2005-06; National Broadcasting Company, correspondent for *Today Show* and analyst on Sunday night football coverage, 2007—.

## Awards, Honors

Named National Football League (NFL) Player of the Year, *Sports Illustrated,* 2005; named to NFL All-Pro team, Associated Press, 2005; selected to NFL Pro Bowl, 2005, 2006, 2007; inducted into Virginia High School Hall of Fame, 2006; Christopher Award, 2006, for *Game Day.*

## Writings

(With brother, Ronde Barber, and Robert Burleigh) *By My Brother's Side,* illustrated by Barry Root, Simon & Schuster Books for Young Readers (New York, NY), 2004.

(With Ronde Barber and Robert Burleigh) *Game Day,* illustrated by Barry Root, Simon & Schuster Books for Young Readers (New York, NY), 2005.

(With Ronde Barber and Robert Burleigh) *Teammates,* illustrated by Barry Root, Simon & Schuster Books for Young Readers (New York, NY), 2006.

## Adaptations

Film rights to create a cartoon based on their picture books were optioned by the Barbers.

## Sidelights

Tiki Barber, a former National Football League (NFL) star with the New York Giants, and his identical twin brother Ronde Barber, an All-Pro cornerback with the Tampa Bay Buccaneers, are the coauthors of *By My Brother's Side* and several other well-received picture books. The multi-talented brothers, whose off-field activities include radio and television broadcasting, have made literacy a cornerstone of their volunteer efforts. "We work essentially as spokesmen and conduits to get the message of literacy to the public," Ronde Barber told Suzanne Rust in the *Black Issues Book Review.* "Most people in the public eye are role models by default," Tiki Barber remarked to *Publishers Weekly* interviewer Shannon Maughan. "It's something I take very seriously, because I know someone is always watching what I'm doing. One of my biggest powers is influence, even over adults sometimes, and I try to [use] it in the right way."

***Tiki and Ronde Barber's picture-book memoir* Teammates *is brought to life in Barry Root's energetic paintings.*** (Illustration © 2006 by Barry Root. Reprinted by permission of Simon & Schuster Books for Young Readers, an imprint of Simon & Schuster Macmillan.)

Born April 7, 1975 (Ronde is older by seven minutes), the Barbers excelled at both sports and academics at Cave Spring High School in Roanoke, Virginia. They decided to play football and room together at the University of Virginia, where they earned All-Atlantic Coast Conference honors their senior year and graduated from the McIntire School of Commerce. A second-round selection of the Giants in the 1997 NFL draft, Tiki enjoyed a brilliant career, becoming the first player to rush for 1,800 yards and have 500 yards receiving in a single season; he retired after the 2006 season. Ronde, who was drafted in the third round by the Buccaneers, earned a Super Bowl ring in 2003 and became the first NFL cornerback to register twenty interceptions and twenty quarterback sacks in a career. The Barbers were encouraged to enter the publishing field by editor Paula Wiseman, whose son avidly followed their careers. "It just so happens that the idea fell right into line with the initiatives and ideals that are important to my brother and me," Ronde recalled to Maughan.

In their debut work, *By My Brother's Side,* the Barbers recount a defining moment from their childhood that taught them about love and perseverance. The virtually inseparable twins must spend their first summer apart after Tiki suffers a severe leg injury in a bicycle accident. With Ronde's support and encouragement, Tiki makes a full recovery, joining his brother in time for their team's Pee Wee football league opener in the fall. According to a *Publishers Weekly* reviewer, the Barbers "give a warm focus to the family foundation they believe is instrumental to their successes and their lives." *By My Brother's Side* "will inspire those peewee football players out there who are recuperating from their own breaks," observed a critic in *Kirkus Reviews.*

*Game Day* focuses on the Barbers' exploits with the Cave Spring Vikings, their Pee Wee league team. Tiki, the squad's star halfback, gets most of the credit for his team's success. This leaves Ronde feeling a bit underappreciated, because his devastating blocks clear the way for his brother's touchdown runs. The boys' coach has noticed Ronde's contributions, however, and devises a trick play that gives Ronde a chance to demonstrate his talents. "What works best here is the feel-good mood," remarked *Booklist* contributor Ilene Cooper, and a *Publishers Weekly* reviewer similarly noted that the narrative "is equal parts sunny reminiscence and inspirational game-day pep talk; the text sails along like a skillfully thrown spiral." Mary Hazelton, writing in *School Library Journal,* described *Game Day* as "an engaging memoir that touches on themes of cooperation and individual differences."

In *Teammates,* the brothers develop a novel solution to a vexing problem. After Tiki fumbles the ball during a critical possession, his coach notes the importance of developing good habits during practice. In response, the Barbers start a secret early-morning practice club, "leading to an ending that is believable as well as happy," wrote *Booklist* contributor Carolyn Phelan. "Tiki and Ronde have a warm, supportive relationship, rare in tales featuring siblings," remarked Rachel G. Payne in *School Library Journal.*

## Biographical and Critical Sources

*BOOKS*

*Contemporary Black Biography,* Volume 57, Thomson Gale (Detroit, MI), 2007.

*Newsmakers,* Issue 1, Thomson Gale (Detroit, MI), 2007.

*PERIODICALS*

*Black Issues Book Review,* September-October, 2004, Suzanne Rust, "He Ain't Heavy," p. 60.

*Booklist,* September 1, 2004, Todd Morning, review of *By My Brother's Side,* p. 114; September 1, 2005, Ilene Cooper, review of *Game Day,* p. 119; September 1, 2006, Carolyn Phelan, review of *Teammates,* p. 116.

*Bulletin of the Center for Children's Books,* January, 2006, Elizabeth Bush, review of *Game Day,* p. 218.

*Ebony,* December, 2005, review of *Game Day,* p. 30.

*Kirkus Reviews,* September 15, 2004, review of *By My Brother's Side,* p. 909; September 15, 2005, review of *Game Day,* p. 1020.

*New York Times,* August 12, 1997, Bill Pennington, "The Barber Brothers Stay in Touch as Rookie Rivals with the Giants and Bucs"; November 29, 1997, Bill Pennington, "It's Barber vs. Barber When Giants Play Bucs"; January 8, 2007, David Picker, "Barber Leaves His Mark on Giants and Moves on to a New Career."

*Publishers Weekly,* August 30, 2004, Shannon Maughan, "Double Duty," p. 54, and review of *By My Brother's Side,* p. 55; October 3, 2005, review of *Game Day,* p. 70.

*Sarasota Herald Tribune,* October 29, 2006, Tom Balog, "Barbers' Final Meeting?," p. C3.

*School Library Journal,* November, 2004, Ann M. Holcomb, review of *By My Brother's Side,* p. 122; January, 2006, Mary Hazelton, review of *Game Day,* p. 116; November, 2006, Rachel G. Payne, review of *Teammates,* p. 117.

*Sports Illustrated,* July 23, 2001, John Ed Bradley, "Play Mates," p. 52; December 18, 2006, Karl Taro Greenfield, "Media Giant?"

*ONLINE*

*ESPN Web site,* http://espn.go.com/ (July 20, 2007), "Tiki Barber."

*University of Virginia Magazine Online,* http://www.uvamagazine.org/ (spring, 2006), Ben Cramer, "The Power of Two."*

* * *

# BAUM, Louis 1948-

## Personal

Born March 15, 1948, in South Africa; son of Rudolf Josef (an accountant) and Heather (a florist) Baum; married Stephanie Goodman (a teacher), March 26, 1971 (divorced); married Liz Calder (a publishing director); children: (first marriage) Simon. *Education:* University of Cape Town, B.A.

## Addresses

*Home and office*—London, England; Brazil.

## Career

*Bookseller,* London, England, former editor, beginning 1980. Director of J. Whitaker & Sons and Standard Book Numbering Agency.

## Member

Groucho Club (founder and director).

## Writings

*FOR CHILDREN*

*Juju and the Pirate*, illustrated by Philippe Matter, Andersen Press (London, England), 1983.

*I Want to See the Moon*, illustrated by Niki Daly, Bodley Head (London, England), 1984, Overlook Press (New York, NY), 1989.

*After Dark*, illustrated by Susan Varley, Andersen Press (London, England), 1984.

*Are We Nearly There?*, illustrated by Paddy Bouma, Bodley Head (London, England), 1986.

*One More Time*, illustrated by Paddy Bouma, Morrow (New York, NY), 1986.

*Joey's Coming Home Today*, illustrated by Susan Varley, Andersen Press (London, England), 1989.

*Milo Mouse and the Scary Monster*, illustrated by Sue Hellard, Bloomsbury (New York, NY), 2006.

*The Mouse Who Braved Bedtime*, illustrated by Sue Hellard, Bloomsbury (New York, NY), 2006.

*Tea with Bea*, illustrated by Georgie Birkett, Bloomsbury (London, England), 2006.

## Biographical and Critical Sources

*PERIODICALS*

*Bulletin of the Center for Children's Books,* February, 1987, review of *One More Time,* p. 101.

*Kirkus Reviews,* September 15, 2006, review of *The Mouse Who Braved Bedtime,* p. 946.

*Publishers Weekly,* December 12, 1986, review of *One More Time,* p. 51.

*School Library Journal,* August, 1984, Rita Soltan, review of *JuJu and the Pirate,* p. 56; June-July, 1987, Cathy Woodward, review of *One More Time,* p. 76; Jane Dyer Cook, review of *I Want to See the Moon,* p. 84; October, 2006, Tamara E. Richman, review of *The Mouse Who Braved Bedtime,* p. 102.*

* * *

# BLACKALL, Sophie

## Personal

Born in Australia; immigrated to United States, 2000; married; children: two.

## Addresses

*Home and office*—Brooklyn, NY. *E-mail*—sophie@sophieblackall.com.

## Career

Illustrator.

## Awards, Honors

Ezra Jack Keats New Illustrator Award, 2003, for *Ruby's Wish,* by Shirin Yim Bridges; Society of Illustrators Founders Award, 2005.

## Writings

*SELF-ILLUSTRATED*

*Twenty Party Tricks to Amuse and Amaze Your Friends,* Chronicle Books (New York, NY), 1997.

*ILLUSTRATOR*

Leith Hillard, *A Giraffe for France,* Watermark Press (Sydney, New South Wales, Australia), 1998.

Shirin Yim Bridges, *Ruby's Wish,* Chronicle Books (San Francisco, CA), 2002.

Meg Rosoff and Sophie Blackall, *Meet Wild Boars,* Henry Holt (New York, NY), 2005.

Annie Barrows, *Ivy and Bean,* Chronicle Books (New York, NY), 2006.

Annie Barrows, *Ivy and Bean and the Ghost That Had to Go,* Chronicle Books (New York, NY), 2006.

Phillis and David Gershator, *Summer Is Summer,* Henry Holt (New York, NY), 2006.

Annie Barrows, *Ivy and Bean Break the Fossil Record,* Chronicle Books (New York, NY), 2007.

Cari Best, *What's So Bad about Being an Only Child?,* Farrar, Straus & Giroux (New York, NY), 2007.

Deborah Noyes, *Red Butterfly: How a Princess Smuggled the Secrets of Silk out of China,* Candlewick Press (Cambridge, MA), 2007.

## Sidelights

After growing up in Australia, illustrator Sophie Blackall moved to the United States in 2000, where her unique art is enjoyed by many young fans. She was honored with the Ezra Jack Keats Award for New Illustrator in 2002 for the artwork she created for her debut picture-book project, Shirin Yim Bridges' *Ruby's Wish.* Since then, Blackall has brought to life the texts of several other authors, among them Cari Best, Meg Rosoff, and Phillis and David Gershator. In addition to her book illustration, she also contributes artwork to periodicals such as the *New York Times* and creating animation for British television commercials.

Before tackling her first picture-book project, Blackall both wrote and illustrated *Twenty Party Tricks to Amuse and Amaze Your Friends.* Here art and text combine to instruct readers in tricks such as floating a needle, seemingly transforming water into wine, and fitting a hard-boiled egg into a narrow-necked glass bottle. She turned to a younger audience to illustrate *A Giraffe for France,* which was published while Blackall was still living in Australia. The move to the United States, which Blackall made accompanied by her husband and young children, coincided with her decision to expand her work in picture books. After making the rounds of New York City publishers, she was approached by Chronicle Books as one of three illustrators they were considering for *Ruby's Wish.* As Blackall recalled to *Communication Arts* contributor Maria Piscopo, the publisher "had each of us illustrate the same passage. . . . It was a Chinese story and there were so many possible ways to approach it visually. In the end I decided to make the picture I would want to see."

In *Ruby's Wish* readers meet a young girl growing up in China during the first part of the twentieth century. Curious and intelligent, Ruby loves the color red. She also loves learning and dreams of attending college, even though this is a path traditionally followed by men. Fortunately, in Bridges' semi-autobiographical tale, Ruby's wise grandfather recognizes her talent and supports her enrollment at a Chinese university. In a review of the book, Jody McCoy wrote in *School Library Journal* that in Blackall's "exquisite" opaque watercolor art "the beauty of Asian art and motifs is captured page after page." Noting that the strong bond between grandfather and granddaughter is at the core of *Ruby's Wish,* a *Publishers Weekly* contributor wrote that "Blackall conveys th[is] . . . special relationship in subtle ways" in her art.

Paired with the upbeat rhyming text of the Gershators' *Summer Is Summer,* Blackall's "whimsical watercolor illustrations feature a dreamy world of fantasy and reality," noted *School Library Journal* contributor Marge Loch-Wouters. Rosoff's humorous picture book *Meet Wild Boars* also benefits from the illustrator's work; this time her "hulking, hairy boars . . . make a wonderful visual articulation of and counterpoint to Rosoff's arch, mock-cautionary prose," according to a *Publishers Weekly* contributor. "Blackall's roll-on-the-ground-in-laughter illustrations" bring to life Rosoff's ill-mannered but "disgustingly delightful group," concluded Ilene Cooper in *Booklist,* while *School Library Journal* contributor Mary Elam accorded special praise to "the artist's attention to detail" in *Meet Wild Boars.*

Through her art, Blackall also brings to life Annie Barrows' easy-reading chapter book *Ivy and Bean* as well as several sequels. Writing that the art in *Ivy and Bean* "captures the girls' spirit," Cooper added that the illustrations "take . . . the book to a higher level." Appraising *Ivy and Bean and the Ghost That Had to Go* in *School Library Journal,* Adrienne Furness cited Blackall's "expressive illustrations," and Sharon R. Pearce wrote in the same publication that artist's "humorous drawings add to the fun" that plays out in *Ivy and Bean Break the Fossil Record.*

## Biographical and Critical Sources

*PERIODICALS*

*Booklist,* November 15, 2002, Linda Perkins, review of *Ruby's Wish,* p. 608; March 15, 2005, Ilene Cooper, review of *Meet Wild Boars,* p. 1287; April 1, 2006, Ilene Cooper, review of *Ivy and Bean,* p. 42; April 15, 2006, Hazel Rochman, review of *Summer Is Summer,* p. 51; October 15, 2006, Ilene Cooper, review of *Ivy and Bean and the Ghost That Had to Go,* p. 44; July 1, 2007, Kay Weisman, review of *Ivy and Bean Break the Fossil Record,* p. 58.

*Bulletin of the Center for Children's Books,* October, 2002, review of *Ruby's Wish,* p. 49; June, 2006, Deborah Stevenson, review of *Ivy and Bean,* p. 440.

*Communication Arts,* July, 2007 (illustration annual), Maria Piscopo, "Getting Published—Myth or Reality?"

*Kirkus Reviews,* August 15, 2002, review of *Ruby's Wish,* p. 1217; April 15, 2005, review of *Meet Wild Boars,* p. 481; May 1, 2006, review of *Ivy and Bean,* p. 454; May 15, 2006, review of *Summer Is Summer,* p. 518; September 15, 2006, review of *Ivy and Bean and the Ghost That Had to Go,* p. 946.

*Publishers Weekly,* August 19, 2002, review of *Ruby's Wish,* p. 88; March 28, 2005, review of *Meet Wild Boars,* p. 78; May 15, 2006, review of *Ivy and Bean,* p. 72.

*School Library Journal,* February, 2003, Jody McCoy, review of *Ruby's Wish,* p. 102; July, 2005, Mary Elam, review of *Meet Wild Boars,* p. 82; June, 2006, Marge Loch-Wouters, review of *Summer Is Summer,* p. 122; July, 2006, Eve Ottenberg Stone, review of *Ivy and Bean,* p. 68; February, 2007, Adrienne Furness, review of *Ivy and Bean and the Ghost That Had to Go,* p. 84; July, 2007, Sharon R. Pearce, review of *Ivy and Bean Break the Fossil Record,* p. 67.

*ONLINE*

*Sophie Blackall Home Page,* http://www.sophieblackall.com (August 8, 2007).

* * *

# BONIFACE, William 1963-

## Personal

Born October 17, 1963, in Yankton, SD. *Education:* University of Minnesota, B.S. (marketing).

## Addresses

*Agent*—Jon Anderson, 313 W. 22nd St., No.2B, New York, NY 10011.

## Career

Publisher and children's author.

## Writings

*FOR CHILDREN*

*Welcome to Dinsmore, the World's Greatest Store,* illustrated by Tom Kerr, Andrews McMeel (Kansas City, MO), 1995.

*Mystery in Bugtown,* illustrated by Jim Harris, Accord (Denver, CO), 1997.

*The Adventures of Max the Minnow,* illustrated by Don Sullivan, Accord (Denver, CO), 1997.

*The Treasure Hunter,* illustrated by Jim Harris, Accord (Denver, CO), 1998, board-book edition, 2006.

*Trim the Tree for Christmas,* illustrated by Debbie Palen, Price, Stern, Sloan (New York, NY), 2000.

*Christmastime Is Cookie Time,* illustrated by Ronnie Rooney, Price, Stern, Sloan (New York, NY), 2001.

*What Do You Want on Your Sundae?,* illustrated by Debbie Palen, Price, Stern, Sloan (New York, NY), 2001.

*What Do You Want in Your Cereal Bowl,* illustrated by Ronnie Rooney, Price, Stern, Sloan (New York, NY), 2002.

*Santa's Sleigh Is Full!: A Top This! Book,* illustrated by Ronnie Rooney, Price, Stern, Sloan (New York, NY), 2002.

*The Stars Came out on Christmas,* illustrated by Stephen Waterhouse, Price, Stern, Sloan (New York, NY), 2002.

*Five Little Pumpkins,* illustrated by Jerry Smath, Price, Stern, Sloan (New York, NY), 2002.

*Five Little Ghosts,* illustrated by Jerry Smath, Price, Stern, Sloan (New York, NY), 2002.

*Easter Bunnies Everywhere: A Top This! Book,* illustrated by Ronnie Rooney, Price, Stern, Sloan (New York, NY), 2003.

*Five Little Bunny Rabbits,* illustrated by Lynn Adams, Price, Stern, Sloan (New York, NY), 2003.

*Five Little Candy Hearts,* illustrated by Lynn Adams, Price, Stern, Sloan (New York, NY), 2003.

*Five Little Christmas Angels,* illustrated by Lynn Adams, Price, Stern, Sloan (New York, NY), 2003.

*Five Little Easter Eggs,* illustrated by Lynn Adams, Price, Stern, Sloan (New York, NY), 2003.

*Five Little Christmas Trees,* illustrated by Lynn Adams, Price, Stern, Sloan (New York, NY), 2003.

*Five Little Christmas Turkeys,* illustrated by Lynn Adams, Price, Stern, Sloan (New York, NY), 2003.

*Max Makes Millions* (sequel to *The Adventures of Max the Minnow* ), illustrated by Dan Vasconsellos, Accord (Riverside, NJ), 2005.

*"EXTRAORDINARY ADVENTURES OF ORDINARY BOY" SERIES: FOR CHILDREN*

*The Hero Revealed,* illustrated by Stephen Gilpin, HarperCollins (New York, NY), 2006.

*The Return of Meteor Boy?,* illustrated by Stephen Gilpin, HarperCollins (New York, NY), 2007.

## Sidelights

William Boniface is the author of several amusing stories for young children, among them novelty books such as *Trim the Tree for Christmas,* a series of holiday-themed books that include *Five Little Ghosts* and *Five Little Christmas Trees,* the elementary-grade novels *The Adventures of Max the Minnow,* and several books in the "Extraordinary Adventures of Ordinary Boy" series. Boniface's first book, *Welcome to Dinsmore, the World's Greatest Store,* combines the author's background in marketing with a rhyming story. In this picture book, a doorman takes the reader—along with the story's young hero—on a tour of all nine floors of an imaginary department store. Applauding Boniface's "rhyming text" in a *Booklist* review, Lauren Peterson added that, "as a read-aloud . . . the book can't be beat."

In *The Adventures of Max the Minnow* and *Max Makes Millions* Boniface focus on a tiny fish. Readers meet Max in *The Adventures of Max the Minnow* as the little fish tries to find a way to gain in stature before realizing that he is just fine the size he is. The minnow's passion for weight lifting results in a far more husky hero in *Max Makes Millions.* Known as the "King of Fitness Fun," Max's enthusiasm for fitness is contagious among his deep-sea friends . . . that is, until Sharky enters the picture.

In his "Extraordinary Adventures of Ordinary Boy" novels, Boniface transports upper-elementary-grade readers to Superopolis, a town where everyone is a superhero of one sort or another . . . everyone, that is, except for Ordinary Boy. The series begins in the pages of *The Hero Revealed,* which finds Ordinary Boy aided by his junior-superhero friends in foiling a nefarious scheme hatched by Professor Brain-Drain. Ordinary Boy returns in *The Return of Meteor Boy,* as our hero investigates the mysterious disappearance of Meteor Boy while the young superhero was in the middle of a dangerous mission. In *Booklist,* Ed Sullivan called *The Hero Revealed* "fast-paced and silly," while Walter Minkel concluded in *School Library Journal* that, in the amusing novel, "Boniface wields a cynical, but definitely kid-friendly, sense of humor." Popular with reluctant readers, the novels in the "Extraordinary Adventures of Ordinary Boy" are heavily illustrated by Steven Gilpin and were described by Minkel as "a send-up and a celebration of the comics genre."

## Biographical and Critical Sources

*PERIODICALS*

*Booklist,* February 1, 1996, Lauren Peterson, review of *Welcome to Dinsmore, the World's Greatest Store,* p. 936; June 1, 2006, Ed Sullivan, review of *The Hero Revealed,* p. 67.

*Kirkus Reviews,* June 1, 2006, review of *The Hero Revealed,* p. 568.

*Publishers Weekly,* September 25, 2000, review of *Trim the Tree for Christmas!,* p. 74; September 24, 2001, review of *Christmastime Is Cookie Time,* p. 55; September 23, 2002, review of *Five Little Ghosts,* p. 24; December 23, 2002, review of *Five Little Easter Eggs,* p. 72; December 15, 2003, review of *Five Little Candy Hearts,* p. 75.

*School Library Journal,* June, 2006, Walter Minkel, review of *The Hero Revealed,* p. 146.

*ONLINE*

*HarperCollins Web site,* http://www.harpercollinschildrens.com/ (August 16, 2007), "William Boniface."

* * *

## BOURBONNIERE, Sylvie 1966-

### Personal

Born July, 1966, in Montréal, Québec, Canada. *Education:* University of Québec, graduate; studied at Atelier Graff. *Hobbies and other interests:* Film festivals, discovering other cultures and ways of living, hiking, bird watching, traveling.

### Addresses

*Home and office*—227 rue des Intendents, Varennes, Québec J3X 2C3, Canada. *E-mail*—sbourbon@videotron.ca.

### Career

Illustrator, 1988—. Graphic designer for kitchenware and children's clothing.

### Member

Quebec Association of Illustrators.

### Awards, Honors

First prize, *Graphika,* 1997; first prize for interactive Web corporate design, *Applied Arts,* 1997; *LUX Quebec* special selection designation, 2000, and double finalist, 2001, 2003; Parents' Choice Gold Award, 2003, for *Dream Songs Night Songs;* Golden Oak Award, 2005, for *Tales from the Isle of Spice.*

### Illustrator

Francine Cloutier, *Le kangourou,* Ovale (Montréal, Québec, Canada), 1988.

Francine Cloutier, *L'éléphant,* Ovale (Montréal, Québec, Canada), 1988.

Francine Cloutier, *La girafe,* Ovale (Montréal, Québec, Canada), 1988.

Francine Cloutier, *Le chameau,* Ovale (Montréal, Québec, Canada), 1988.

Carme Marois, *L'étrange portrait de familie,* Chouette, (Pierrefonds, Québec, Canada), 1991.

Irina Drozd, *La moette,* Hurtubise (LaSalle, Québec, Canada), 1994.

Jean-Pierre, Guillet, *Tadam!,* Héritage (Saint-Lambert, Québec, Canada), 1995.

Patrick Lacoursiere, *Dream Songs Night Songs: From Mali to Louisiana* (song lyrics), published with CD, The Secret Mountain, 2003, published in book form, 2006.

Ricardo Keens-Douglas, *Tales from the Isle of Spice: A Collection of New Caribbean Folk Tales,* Annick Press (Toronto, Ontario, Canada), 2004.

### Biographical and Critical Sources

*PERIODICALS*

*Canadian Book Review Annual,* 2004, Deborah Dowson, review of *Tales from the Isle of Spice: A Collection of New Caribbean Folk Tales,* p. 542.

*Kirkus Reviews,* May 15, 2006, review of *Dream Songs Night Songs: From Mali to Louisiana,* p. 519.

*School Library Journal,* July, 2006, Beverly Bixler, review of *Dream Songs Night Songs,* p. 57.

*ONLINE*

*Annick Press Web site,* http://www.annickpress.com/ (August 15, 2007), "Sylvie Bourbonniere."

*La Montagne Secreète Web site,* http://www.lamontagnesecrete.com/ (August 15, 2007), "Sylvie Bourbonniere."

*Margarethe Hubauer Web site,* http://www.margarethe-hubauer.de/ (August 15, 2007), "Sylvie Bourbonniere."

*Sylvie Bourbonniere Home Page,* http://www.sylvie-bourbonniere.com (August 15, 2007).

* * *

## BOWMAN, Leslie
## See BOWMAN, Leslie W.

* * *

## BOWMAN, Leslie W.
## (Leslie Bowman)

### Personal

Born in CT. *Education:* Attended Rhode Island School of Design.

### Addresses

*Home*—Minneapolis, MN. *Agent*—Libby Ford, Kirchoff/Wohlberg, 866 United Nations Plaza, No. 525, New York, NY 10017. *E-mail*—l.w.bowman@comcast.net; lwbowman@mn.rr.com.

### Career

Portrait artist and children's book illustrator. Has also worked as a courier for Federal Express.

## Writings

*ILLUSTRATOR*

M.J. Engh, *The House in the Snow,* Orchard Books (New York, NY), 1987.
Elizabeth Borton de Treviño, *El Güero: A True Adventure Story,* Farrar, Straus & Giroux (New York, NY), 1989.
Natalie Kinsey-Warnock, *The Canada Geese Quilt,* Cobblehill Books (New York, NY), 1989.
Marc Harshman, *Snow Company,* Cobblehill Books (New York, NY), 1990.
Natalie Kinsey-Warnock, *The Night the Bells Rang,* Cobblehill Books (New York, NY), 1991.
Natalie Kinsey-Warnock, *The Fiddler of the Northern Lights,* Cobblehill Books (New York, NY), 1996.
Debra Page, *Orcas around Me: My Alaskan Summer,* Albert Whitman (Morton Grove, IL), 1997.
Marc Harshman, *When the End of Summer Is Near,* Cobblehill (New York, NY), 1999.
Marc Harshman, *Snow Company,* Quarrier Press (Charleston, WV), 2002.

*ILLUSTRATOR; AS LESLIE BOWMAN*

Nancy Ruth Patterson, *The Christmas Cup,* Orchard Books (New York, NY), 1989.
Marilyn Levinson, *The Fourth-grade Four,* Holt (New York, NY), 1989.
Deborah Chandra, *Balloons and Other Poems,* Farrar, Straus & Giroux (New York, NY), 1990.
Gloria Whelan, *Hannah,* Knopf (New York, NY), 1991.
Dennis Haseley, *Shadows,* Farrar, Straus & Giroux (New York, NY), 1991.
Gary Paulsen, *A Christmas Sonata,* Delacorte Press (New York, NY), 1992.
Jeff Daniel Marion, *Hello, Crow,* Orchard Books (New York, NY), 1992.
Gloria Whelan, *Night of the Full Moon,* Knopf (New York, NY), 1993.
Dick King-Smith, *The Cuckoo Child,* Hyperion (New York, NY), 1993.
Deborah Chandra, *Rich Lizard, and Other Poems,* Farrar, Straus & Giroux (New York, NY), 1993.
Alice Ross and Kent Ross, *The Copper Lady,* Carolrhoda Books (Minneapolis, MN), 1997.
Jane Buchanan, *The Berry-picking Man,* Farrar, Straus & Giroux (New York, NY), 2003.
Kathleen McAlpin Blasi, *A Name of Honor,* Mondo (New York, NY), 2006.
William Loizeaux, *Wings,* Farrar, Straus & Giroux (New York, NY), 2006.

## Sidelights

Leslie W. Bowman is an accomplished portrait painter who has illustrated books for such esteemed authors as Gary Paulsen, Gloria Whelan, Natalie Kinsey-Warnock, and Dick King-Smith. "I have been drawing as long as I can remember," Bowman remarked on her home page, adding that her childhood experiences growing up in

*Leslie W. Bowman shows her versatility as an illustrator in books such as* **Night of the Full Moon,** *by Gloria Whelan.* (Illustration © 1993 by Leslie Bowman. Reproduced by permission of Random House Children's Books, a division of Random House, Inc.)

Connecticut allowed her to develop "a love of light and form and texture." As a teenager, Bowman discovered her talent for portraiture and later studied illustration and photography at the Rhode Island School of Design. After a move to Minnesota in 1971, she established a home studio and, with the help of Caldecott Award-winning illustrator Stephen Gammell, began providing artwork for children's titles. Bowman's first effort, creating artwork for *The House in the Snow* by M.J. Engh, was published in 1987.

*Shadows,* a story by Dennis Haseley, concerns Jamie, a young boy who is sent to live with his overprotective aunt after his father dies tragically in a fire and his mother must look for work. When Jamie's paternal grandfather arrives, he teaches the youngster how to cast hand shadows on the wall while helping the boy gain a greater understanding of his father. As a *Publishers Weekly* reviewer stated, Bowman's "minimally drawn characters work well to illuminate" the novel's "most intriguing element—the relationship between Jamie and his grandpa.

Bowman also served as the illustrator for Deborah Chandra's *Rich Lizard, and Other Poems,* a collection of twenty-four verses about life's ordinary pleasures, including cotton candy, soap bubbles, and a pair of comfortable shoes. Complimenting Bowman's black-and-white illustrations, *Horn Book* reviewer Nancy Vasilakis stated that "the well-designed pages reflect the mood of the poems with empathic intelligence."

*The Fiddler of the Northern Lights,* one of several picture books Bowman has illustrated for Natalie Kinsey-Warnock, follows a young boy and his grandfather as they skate upriver one winter to catch a glimpse of a magical musician who commands the shimmering lights of the Aurora Borealis. "Bowman's soft, dreamy illustrations complement the magical elements of the text," noted *Booklist* contributor Kay Weisman, and a critic in *Publishers Weekly* observed that the artist's "understated, realistic watercolors transform the somber woodlands with curtains of light." *The Copper Lady,* a work of historical fiction by Alice and Kent Ross, centers on a Parisian orphan who stows away on a ship and helps save the Statue of Liberty during a terrible storm. "Watercolors rendered in soft shades of browns and grays complement" the work, according to *Booklist* reviewer April Judge.

Bowman's art also appears in Debra Page's nonfiction picture book *Orcas around Me: My Alaskan Summer,* which focuses on the author's family members and their trade as commercial salmon fishermen in the North Pacific. "Bowman's handsome sun-bleached watercolors vibrantly capture" a fisherman's life on the water, observed Linda Perkins in her review for *Booklist. Horn Book* contributor Roger Sutton remarked that Bowman's illustrations, "designed to blend gracefully with the textblocks, are appropriately washed and dappled," and a *Publishers Weekly* critic noted that the artist "contributes spare, somewhat pale watercolor illustrations that evoke both the ocean's wild openness and the family's warmth."

In Jane Buchanan's *The Berry-picking Man,* nine-year-old Meggie grows increasingly annoyed by her mother's attempts to help Old Sam, a former mental patient who enjoys picking wild strawberries. Referencing the book's sensitive theme, a critic in *Kirkus Reviews* noted that Bowman's illustrations "mimic the theme of seeing beyond the black and white to understand the whole picture."

Set during the summer of 1960, *Wings,* a middle-grade novel by William Loizeaux, centers on a young boy's efforts to rescue and nurture a baby mockingbird. "The flowing narration, alight with visual detail, is reflected in Bowman's soft pencil illustrations," wrote a *Kirkus Reviews* contributor, and *Booklist* critic Carolyn Phelan concluded that the artist's "drawings illustrate this graceful story with sensitivity and subtlety."

***Bowman has contributed her art to several books by Natalie Kinsey-Warnock, among them the Vermont author's 1992 coming-of-age novel* The Canada Geese Quilt.** (Illustration © 1989 by Leslie W. Bowman. Reproduced by permission of Dell Publishing, a division of Random House, Inc.)

## Biographical and Critical Sources

*PERIODICALS*

*Booklist,* November 15, 1996, Kay Weisman, review of *The Fiddler of the Northern Lights,* p. 594; August, 1997, Linda Perkins, review of *Orcas around Me: My Alaskan Summer,* p. 1903, and April Judge, review of *The Copper Lady,* p. 1910; August, 2003, Hazel Rochman, review of *The Berry-picking Man,* p. 1980; September 1, 2006, Carolyn Phelan, review of *Wings,* p. 129.

*Horn Book,* September-October, 1993, Nancy Vasilakis, review of *Rich Lizard and Other Poems,* p. 613; January-February, 1998, Roger Sutton, review of *Orcas around Me,* p. 94; September-October, 2006, Joanna Rudge Long, review of *Wings,* p. 591.

*Kirkus Reviews,* May 15, 2003, review of *The Berry-picking Man,* p. 747; August 15, 2006, review of *Wings,* p. 847.

*New York Times Book Review,* July 14, 1991, Lawrie Mifflin, review of *Hannah,* p. 25; October 20, 1991, Liz Rosenberg, review of *Shadows,* p. 53; December 13, 1992, review of *A Christmas Sonata,* p. 35.

*Pastel Journal,* April, 2005, Loraine Crouch, "How Leslie Bowman, of Minneapolis, Got in Touch with Her Talent and Her Art."

*Publishers Weekly,* May 17, 1991, review of *Shadows,* p. 63; September 7, 1992, Elizabeth Devereaux, review of *Christmas Sonata,* p. 69; March 8, 1993, review of *The Cuckoo Child,* p. 79; November 8, 1993, review of *Night of the Full Moon,* p. 77; November 11, 1996, review of *The Fiddler of the Northern Lights,* p. 74; June 23, 1997, review of *Orcas around Me,* p. 92.

*School Library Journal,* June, 1991, Katharine Bruner, review of *Shadows,* p. 106; November, 1996, Martha Rosen, review of *The Fiddler of the Northern Lights,* p. 87; September, 2006, Susan Scheps, review of *Wings,* p. 211.

*ONLINE*

*Leslie W. Bowman Home Page,* http://www.lwbowman.com (July 20, 2007).*

* * *

# BOYCE, Frank Cottrell

## Personal

Married; wife's name Denise; children: seven. *Education:* Keble College Oxford, degree (English). *Religion:* Roman Catholic.

## Addresses

*Home*—Liverpool, England.

## Career

Screenwriter and novelist. Former television critic for *Living Marxism* magazine; creator and writer of *Captain Star* (animated television series). Participates in writing workshops.

## Awards, Honors

Writers' Guild of Great Britain Award (with others), 1993, for *Coronation Street*; British Academy of Film and Television Artist Award nomination for best screenplay, 1999, for *Hillary and Jackie;* London *Guardian* Children's Fiction Prize shortlist, and Carnegie Medal, both 2004, both for *Millions* (novel); Humanitas Prize; British Independent Film Award for best screenplay, 2005, for *Millions* (film); Digital Departures Award shortlist, 2007, for *Grow Your Own.*

## Writings

*YOUNG-ADULT NOVELS*

(Adaptor) *Millions* (novel; based on Boyce's screenplay; also see below), HarperCollins (New York, NY), 2004.

*Framed,* HarperCollins (New York, NY), 2005.

*SCREENPLAYS*

*The Real English Eddy* (television mini-series), Channel 4, 1989.

*Forget about Me,* Thames Television, 1990.

*Coronation Street* (television series), ITV, 1991.

*A Woman's Guide to Adultery,* Hartwood Films, 1993.

*Butterfly Kiss,* British Screen Productions, 1995.

*Saint-Ex,* British Broadcasting Company, 1996.

*New York Crossing,* Videa, 1996.

*Welcome to Sarajevo* (produced by Miramax, 1997), Faber & Faber (London, England), 1997.

*Hilary and Jackie,* October Films, 1998.

*Pandaemonium,* Moonstone Entertainment, 2000.

*The Claim* (produced by United Artists, 2000), Screenpress Books, 2002.

*24 Hour Party People,* United Artists, 2002.

*Revengers Tragedy,* Fantoma, 2002.

*Code 46,* Metro-Goldwyn-Mayer, 2003.

*Millions,* Fox Searchlight, 2004.

(Under pseudonym Martin Hardy) *A Cock and Bull Story,* Newmarket Films, 2005.

(With Carl Hunter) *Grow Your Own,* Pathé Distribution, 2007.

## Adaptations

*Millions* and *Framed* were both adapted as audiobooks by Harper Audio, 2004 and 2007 respectively.

## Sidelights

As a screenwriter, British author Frank Cottrell Boyce is best known for his work on the critically acclaimed films *Welcome to Sarajevo, 24 Hour Party People,* and *Hilary and Jackie.* During his career he has collaborated with such highly regarded directors as Michael Winterbottom, Alex Cox, Julien Temple, and Danny Boyle, "becoming arguably the most versatile screenwriter in the land," according to *Chicago Sun-Times* online critic Roger Ebert. In 2004, Boyce gained a new audience—a reading audience—with the publication of his highly praised young-adult novels *Millions* and *Framed.* Based on a film also by Boyce, *Millions* earned its author the prestigious Carnegie Medal in 2005.

Boyce began his career on the small screen, penning the script for the television mini-series *The Real English Eddy,* and he then spent a year working on the long-running British soap opera *Coronation Street.* In 1990 he paired with Winterbottom on the television film *Forget about Me*; the duo went on to collaborate on several other films, including *Welcome to Sarajevo, A Cock and Bull Story,* and *24 Hour Party People.*

Set in 1992, *Welcome to Sarajevo* looks at the civil war in the former Yugoslavia through the eyes of an English reporter. According to *New York Times* critic Janet Maslin, "the film's best moments are its smallest ones, the casual contrasts between the lives of interloping journalists and those of people watching their homeland torn apart." Boyce told Ebert that the film "was made with great spirit. [Director] Michael [Winterbottom] insisted on shooting it in Sarajevo in the face of incredible difficulties. It was a Herzogian thing to do." *24 Hour Party People* follows the career of Tony Wilson, a cantankerous, egomaniacal television journalist turned music impresario whose record label, Factory Records, helped launch the careers of New Order and the Happy Mondays, among other groups. "I utterly love this film," Boyce admitted to Ebert. "It's a hymn to Manchester, and to Tony Wilson who is reviled and laughed at in Manchester for being pretentious and pompous. I think in these times being pretentious is sort of heroic, and I hope the film makes that case for him."

*Hilary and Jackie,* directed by Anand Tucker, concerns the emotionally charged relationship between renowned cellist Jacqueline du Pre and her sister, Hilary. In the words of *New York Times* critic Stephen Holden, "this study of two gifted sisters who are so close they can literally read each other's minds is an astoundingly rich and subtle exploration of sibling rivalry and the volcanic collisions of love and resentment, competitiveness and mutual dependence that determine their lives."

In *Millions,* Boyce tells the story of a young boy who discovers a fortune in cash. When thieves toss a bag of loot off a passing train, it is picked up by Damien, a sweet, naïve fourth grader who obsesses over the patron saints, patterning his life after theirs. Damien's older brother, Anthony, convinces his sibling that the money—more than 20,000 British pounds—must be spent immediately before the nation converts to the Euro. "There's plenty of excitement as the deadline approaches and the brothers' secret becomes known," wrote *School Library Journal* critic Steven Engelfried of the novel. As London *Guardian* reviewer Adèle Geras observed, "the main joy of the novel . . . is Damian's voice. We see everything through his eyes, and his account of what's going on is funny, direct and very often moving."

The film version of *Millions* also earned strong praise. *Salon.com* contributor Stephanie Zacharek called it "an incredibly sweet-tempered picture about the human impulse toward generosity." Discussing his decision to adapt his screenplay as a young-adult novel, Boyce explained to London *Telegraph Online* contributor that the film's director, Danny Boyle, initially encouraged him in his dream of writing for children. "I'd already made every wrong move possible while working out the screenplay," Boyce admitted in his interview. "So by the time I sat down to write the book I was really confident of the story. I finished the novel while we were shooting the film, so I could wander round the set and talk to my characters, which was fantastic. I mean, "Narnia" series author [C.S. Lewis] could never go and ask Aslan's view on anything."

Boyce's second teen novel, *Framed,* was inspired by the author's visits to London's National Gallery of Art, as well as the stories of how Britain's art treasures were hidden in mines below the gallery to keep them out of German hands during World War II. Another inspiration, an art theft in Scotland, serves as the central focus of the novel. In *Framed* nine-year-old Dylan Hughes lives with his family in Manod, Wales, where they operate the Snowdonia Oasis Auto Marvel. Life changes for everyone in Manod when, in response to widespread flooding in London, a convoy of trucks appears, carrying artworks from the National Gallery to a nearby slate quarry for temporary storage. Gradually, the art caretakers begin to reach out to Manod's residents, and the presence of great works of art bolster's the sagging spirits of the town. However, the mood is threatened by Dylan's younger sister, who plots to improve her family's lot by stealing several works of art. "Boyce's signature daffiness plays hilarity and pathos off each other with not one wrong note," concluded a *Kirkus Reviews* writer in a review of *Framed.* While *Booklist* critic Cindy Dobrez described the novel as "a quieter book" than Boyce's Carnegie Medal-winning debut, the critic nonetheless predicted that teens who share a belief in "the importance of art will be charmed." *Framed* features the "same charm and deadpan humor" as *Millions,* according to *School Library Journal* contributor Connie Tyrrell Burns, and in the London *Guardian* Philip Ardagh wrote that Boyce's characters are compelling and endearing, and his "lightness of touch is a delight." "I don't know how hard Frank Cottrell Boyce finds it to write," Ardagh concluded, "but he makes it seem easy, which is the mark of a true master."

Though the lure of Hollywood remains strong, Boyce continues to work in the smaller, less-lucrative British film industry. As the screenwriter once jokingly told Ebert, "I'm not sure that I'm that successful! I think I've probably let others do all the moving and shaking for me. Living far away from London may have something to do with it. People hesitate about calling you down to meetings so you never get sacked. Maybe people don't want to sack someone who's got so many mouths to feed!"

## Biographical and Critical Sources

*PERIODICALS*

*Booklist,* August, 2004, Cindy Dobrez, review of *Millions,* p. 1932; September 1, 2006, Cindy Dobrez, review of *Framed,* p. 125.

*Guardian* (London, England), March 13, 2004, Adèle Geras, "Holly, Lolly, and Searching for Saint Maureen," review of *Millions;* September 24, 2005, Philip Ardagh, review of *Framed.*

*Kirkus Reviews,* July 1, 2004, review of *Millions,* p. 626; August 1, 2006, review of *Framed,* p. 982.

*New York Times,* May 3, 1996, Stephen Holden, "A Femme Fatale Who Takes Her Calling Literally"; November 26, 1997, Janet Maslin, "Dangers and Jitters of Life in

Sarajevo"; December 30, 1998, Stephen Holden, "Discordant Concerto, Played upon Two Hearts"; April 20, 2001, Stephen Holden, "In the Accents of Thomas Hardy, a Tale of the Gold-Hungry Old West"; July 13, 2001, Lawrence Van Gelder, review of *Pandaemonium*; August 9, 2002, Elvis Mitchell, Megalomania as an Unembarrassed Art Form"; August 6, 2004, A.O. Scott, "A Future More Nasty, Because It's So Near"; March 11, 2005, Manohla Dargis, "Before Soaring Imagination Is Grounded by Convention."

*School Library Journal,* October, 2004, Steven Engelfried, review of *Millions,* p. 158; August, 2006, Connie Tyrell Burns, review of *Framed,* p. 116.

*ONLINE*

*Chicago Sun Times Online,* http://rogerebert.suntimes.com/ (March 13, 2005), "*Millions* Writer Wins 'Lottery.'"

*HarperCollins Web site,* http://www.harpercollinschildrens.com/ (August 28, 2007), "Frank Cottrell Boyce."

*Salon.com,* http://www.salon.com/ (March 11, 2005), Stephanie Zacharek, review of *Millions.*

*Telegraph Online* (London, England), http://www.telegraph.co.uk/arts/ (October 7, 2005), "A Writer's Life: Frank Cottrell Boyce."

* * *

# BRIGHT, Paul 1949-

## Personal

Born 1949, in Welwyn, Hertfordshire, England. *Education:* Studied engineering and materials science.

## Addresses

*Home and office*—Spain.

## Career

Author. Employed at a chemical company.

## Awards, Honors

Practical Pre-School Silver Award, 2003, for *Under the Bed;* Stockport School's Book Award shortlist, Stockport Metropolitan Borough Council, 2007, for *I'm Not Going out There!*

## Writings

*Quiet!,* illustrated by Guy Parker-Rees, Orchard Books (New York, NY), 2003.

*Under the Bed,* illustrated by Ben Cort, Good Books (Intercourse, PA), 2004.

*Nobody Laughs at a Lion!,* illustrated by Matt Buckingham, Good Books (Intercourse, PA), 2005.

*I Am Not Going out There!,* illustrated by Ben Cort, Good Books (Intercourse, PA), 2006.

## Sidelights

Paul Bright began his writing career creating stories for his own children, and he has continued to do even now that his children are far too old for bedtime tales. The majority of Bright's picture-book texts are geared for preschool-aged audiences and focus on universal childhood themes such as fear and individuality. In *Nobody Laughs at a Lion!,* for example, a clumsy lion is discouraged when he finds that other jungle animals have talents he does not possess. The lion is unable to climb trees as quickly as the monkeys, and he cannot run as fast as the cheetah. When the lion tries to outdo the jungle animals at contests that draw on their individual talents, he fails miserably and is laughed at. When the lion roars, however, he finally realizes that he, too, has a talent others cannot match. A *Kirkus Reviews* critic deemed Bright's jungle tale "a simple but fun read."

Bright's rhyming text takes center stage in *I'm Not Going out There!,* one of several titles that feature artwork by Ben Cort. In *I'm Not Going out There!* a young boy hides under his bed and vehemently declares that he will not come out. As a host of scary characters are described—everything from witches to monsters and ghosts—each creature appears, but becomes so frightened of the thing that has terrified the boy that it joins him in his under-the-box-spring refuge. Ultimately, the terror reveals itself: it is the boy's little sister, busy having a temper tantrum. Praising Cort's "bold and colorful" illustrations, Maren Ostergard wrote in *School Library Journal* that *I'm Not Going out There!* is "a rhyming tale with a twist," and a *Kirkus Reviews* writer cited the book's "bouncy rhymes, bright colors and . . . entertaining punch line." A second *Kirkus Reviews* writer deemed *Under the Bed* another successful collaboration between author and illustrator, writing that the "soothing" bedtime tale is enlivened by "Bright's vivid imagery and Cort's grand detonations of color."

## Biographical and Critical Sources

*PERIODICALS*

*Kirkus Reviews,* May 15, 2004, review of *Under the Bed,* p. 488; May 15, 2005, review of *Nobody Laughs at a Lion,* p. 585; September 15, 2006, review of *I'm Not Going out There!,* p. 947.

*Library Media Connection,* January, 2004, review of *Quiet!,* p. 56.

*School Library Journal,* December, 2003, Andrea Tarr, review of *Quiet!,* p. 104; August, 2004, Sheilah Kosco, review of *Under the Bed,* p. 84; November, 2006, Maren Ostergard, review of *I'm Not Going out There!,* p. 84.

*School Librarian,* winter, 2003, review of *Quiet!,* p. 185; winter, 2003, review of *Under the Bed,* p. 185; spring, 2006, Derek Lomas, review of *Nobody Laughs at a Lion,* p. 17; winter, 2006, Joyce Banks, review of *I'm Not Going out There!,* p. 181.

*ONLINE*

*World Book Day Web site,* http://www.worldbookday.com/ (August 6, 2007).*

* * *

# BROOKS, Erik 1972-

## Personal

Born 1972, in Madison, WI; married; wife's name Sarah. *Education:* Carleton College, B.A. (studio art), and teacher's license, 1994.

## Addresses

*Home*—P.O. Box 731, Winthrop, WA 98862. *E-mail*—brooks@methownet.com.

## Career

Author and illustrator of children's books. Carleton College, Northfield, MN, cross-country and track coach. Participant at writing conferences; visiting author/illustrator at numerous schools.

## Member

Society of Children's Book Writers and Illustrators, Children's Literature Network, Methow Arts, Methow Print Arts.

## Awards, Honors

New York City Public Library 100 Titles for Reading and Sharing, and Bank Street College of Education Best Books designation, both 2005, both for *Monkey Business* by Shirley Climo; International Reading Association Children's Choices designation, 2001, for *The Practically Perfect Pajamas;* Society of Midland Authors Award for Children's Fiction, 2004, for *Octavius Bloom and the House of Doom;* New Jersey Blue Hen Book Award nomination, 2006, for *Slow Days, Fast Friends.*

## Writings

*SELF-ILLUSTRATED*

*The Practically Perfect Pajamas,* Winslow Press (New York, NY), 2000.

*Octavius Bloom and the House of Doom,* Albert Whitman (New York, NY), 2003.

*Slow Days, Fast Friends,* Albert Whitman (Morton Grove, IL), 2005.

*ILLUSTRATOR*

Shirley Climo, *Monkey Business: Stories from around the World,* Henry Holt (New York, NY), 2005.

Aimee Garn, *The Scritchy Little Twitchell Sisters,* Pretty Please Press, 2005.

Betsy Byars, *Boo's Dinosaur,* Holt (New York, NY), 2006.

Deb Vanesse, *Totem Tale: A Tall Story from Alaska,* Sasquatch Books (Seattle, WA), 2006.

Emme Aronson, *What Are You Hungry For?,* HarperCollins (New York, NY), 2007.

Betsy Byars, Betsy Duffey, and Laurie Myers, *Dog Diaries: Secret Writings of the WOOF Society,* Holt (New York, NY), 2007.

## Sidelights

Children's book author and illustrator Erik Brooks has always been passionate about art, so much so, in fact, that he decided to write his first children's book in order to have something to illustrate. When the result, *The Practically Perfect Pajamas,* was picked up by a publisher, Brooks began to consider a career as a writer as well as an illustrator, and the success of his second effort, *Octavius Bloom and the House of Doom,* confirmed that this notion was a good one. In addition to his work as an author/illustrator, which has also produced the picture book *Slow Days, Fast Friends,* Brooks also illustrates texts by other writers, including *Monkey Business: Stories from around the World* by Shirley Climo and *Boo's Dinosaur* by Betsy Byars. When asked why he likes being an author and illustrator, Brooks explained to an interviewer for the Winslow Press Web site: "Because I like to think that I am making a difference to the kids reading my stories."

Children are taught a valuable lesson in *The Practically Perfect Pajamas:* Always be true to yourself. In the story, a polar bear named Percy Orlando Leonard Alexander Reginald Bear loves to wear colorful pajamas. There is only one problem: Percy gets teased by all the other polar bears for his unusual garb. Desperate to fit in, Percy decides to sacrifice his favorite pajamas in hopes of being accepted. Although his plan works and the teasing stops, Percy soon finds himself missing his brightly colored jammies and reconsidering his decision. While longing for his forbidden PJs, the polar bear meets Aurora the fox, and she inspires Percy to follow his own fashion muse and take pride in his individuality. While a reviewer for *Publishers Weekly* found Brooks's illustrations to be overly "cartoonish," in *Booklist* Connie Fletcher described the conclusion of *The Practically Perfect Pajamas* as a "satisfying resolution to a story that every child can identify with."

In a rhyming text, *Octavius Bloom and the House of Doom* tells the story of young and adventurous Octavius Bloom as he tries to solve the mystery surround-

***Erik Brooks tells the story of an unusual friendship in his self-illustrated picture book* Slow Days, Fast Friends.** (Illustration © 2005 by Erik Brooks. Reproduced by permission.)

ing a suspicious-looking shed in his neighborhood. The shed belongs to Priscilla O'Moore, a mysterious, witch-like woman who lives at the very end of a dead-end street. After his classmates warn him about the scary noises they have heard coming from the shed, and describe things they have seen—like a zombie's hand—brave Octavius sets out to find out exactly what is going on. Suspense builds for readers as he bravely enters the shed to uncover the truth, and the surprise that awaits the boy as well as young readers, is ultimately revealed in Brooks's colored-pencil and watercolor cartoon illustrations. Linda Ludke commented in *School Library Journal* that Brooks's artwork is "imaginatively detailed, and the mysterious shadows visible through the shed's windows build suspense."

A cheetah named Howard meets Quince the sloth in *Slow Days, Fast Friends.* In a story drawn from Brooks's interest in running—in addition to his work in children's books, he coaches both track and cross country—the cheetah becomes frustrated when an injury to his leg forces him to take life slow. However, when he falls into step with the slow-moving Quince, Howard learns to see the world in a new way, and gains a new friend in the process. Praising Brooks for his ability to include "expressive animal faces" in his cartoon art, JoAnn Jonas added in her *School Library Journal* review that *Slow Days, Fast Friends* is a "simple story [that] conveys several complex messages about friendship, healing, and perspective."

Brooks's work as an illustrator has earned him critical praise from several reviewers. Appraising his artwork for *Monkey Business, Horn Book* contributor Margaret A. Bush wrote that the "congenial humor" to be found in Brooks's "richly colored scenes" pairs well with the fourteen stories in Climo's collection, making the book an "attractive sampling of folk literature." A *Kirkus Reviews* writer described the book's pencil-and-watercolor art as "full of action," and in *School Library Journal* Suzanne Myers Harold wrote that Brooks's images "capture the myriad cultures and creatures represented" in Climo's "entertaining" anthology of monkey tales. According to another *Kirkus Reviews* contributor, the illustrator's contribution of "warm" drawings to *Boo's Dinosaur* "extend the text" of Byars' beginning chapter book "and provide ample visual cues" to the author's humorous brother-and-sister tale.

## Biographical and Critical Sources

*PERIODICALS*

*Booklist,* May 15, 2000, Connie Fletcher, review of *The Practically Perfect Pajamas,* p. 1747; May 15, 2005, John Peters, review of *Monkey Business: Stories from around the World,* p. 1654.

*Bulletin of the Center for Children's Books,* November, 2006, Deborah Stevenson, review of *Boo's Dinosaur,* p. 117.

*Horn Book,* July-August, 2005, Margaret A. Bush, review of *Monkey Business,* p. 481.

*Kirkus Reviews,* May 15, 2005, review of *Monkey Business,* p. 585; September 15, 2006, review of *Boo's Dinosaur,* p. 948.

*Publishers Weekly,* May 8, 2000, review of *The Practically Perfect Pajamas,* p. 221.

*School Library Journal,* May, 2000, Barbara Buckley, review of *The Practically Perfect Pajamas,* p. 132; June, 2003, Lina Ludke, review of *Octavius Bloom and the House of Doom,* p. 96; June, 2005, Suzanne Myers Harold, review of *Monkey Business,* p. 585; January, 2006, JoAnn Jonas, review of *Slow Days, Fast Friends,* p. 93; September, 2006, Adrienne Furness, review of *Boo's Dinosaur,* p. 160; June, 2007, Terrie Dorio, review of *Dog Diaries: Secret Writing of the WOOF Society,* p. 92.

*ONLINE*

*Children's Literature Network,* http://www.childrensliteraturenetwork.org/ (February 5, 2004), "Erik Brooks."

*Erik Brooks Home Page,* http://www.erikbrooks.com (August 17, 2007).

*Winslow Press Web site,* http://www.winslowpress.com/ (February 5, 2004), "Erik Brooks."*

## BULLA, Clyde R. 1914-2007 (Clyde Robert Bulla)

*OBITUARY NOTICE—* See index for *SATA* sketch: Born January 9, 1914, near King City, MO; died May 23, 2007, in Warrensburg, MO. Author. Bulla was an award-winning author of children's books. Growing up on a farm, he attended a one-room school but later dropped out in order to help his family at home. He continued schooling through correspondence courses to earn his high school diploma and also began writing. Working on stories late at night, he managed to sell some of them to magazines for extra income to support his family. His first book, *These Bright Young Dreams,* was published in 1941. A novel for adults, the work earned him no money because his publisher went out of business. From 1942 until 1947, Bulla worked as a columnist and linotype operator at the *Tri-County News* in King City. A friend suggested he try his hand at a children's book, and so Bulla penned the nonfiction *The Donkey Cart* (1946). Over sixty books would follow, many of them drawing on American history, such as *Squanto, Friend of the White Men* (1954), *Lincoln's Birthday* (1966), and *Charlie's House* (1983). He also wrote modern tales such as *The Chalk Box Kid* (1987) and instructional works such as *A Tree Is a Plant* (1960; revised edition, 2000). During the 1950s, he collaborated with Lois Lenski to write a series of song books; Bulla composed the music and Lenski wrote lyrics. Among his many honors, the author won outstanding juvenile book by a Southern California author from the Authors Club of Los Angeles in 1961 for *Benito,* a 1971 Christopher Award for *Pocahontas and the Strangers,* and the Southern California Council on Children's Literature award for distinguished contribution, the Sequoyah Children's Book Award, and the South Carolina Children's Book Award, all for *Shoeshine Girl.*

*OBITUARIES AND OTHER SOURCES:*

*BOOKS*

Bull, Clyde R., *A Grain of Wheat: The Story Begins,* Godine (Boston, MA), 1985.

*PERIODICALS*

*Los Angeles Times,* May 27, 2007, p. B12.

*Washington Post,* May 29, 2007, p. B6.

* * *

## BULLA, Clyde Robert

See BULLA, Clyde R.

# C

## CABRERA, Jane 1968-

### Personal

Born July 30, 1968, in Berkhamsted, England; daughter of Bernard and Jill Johnson; married Julian Cabrera (a writer and disc jockey), August 29, 1995. *Education:* Watford College of Art, higher national diploma (in graphic design; with distinction). *Politics:* "Green." *Hobbies and other interests:* Environmental activism, travel, nature crafts, mural painting, cooking, country walks, socializing with friends.

### Addresses

*Home*—London, England. *Office*—The Drawing Room, Panther House, 38 Mount Pleasant, London WCIX 40P, England.

### Career

Illustrator and author. *Apollo Arts and Antiques* (magazine), art director, 1989-91; freelance graphic designer, with clients including British Broadcasting Corporation Children's Books, Reed Children's Books, Dorling Kindersley, HarperCollins, Tiger Print (design group), and HIT Entertainment PLC, 1991-98; freelance illustrator, beginning 1997. Speaker on children's book design and illustration at schools in England.

### Member

Amnesty International, Greenpeace, Friends of the Earth.

### Writings

*SELF-ILLUSTRATED; FICTION FOR CHILDREN*

*Cat's Colors,* Dial (New York, NY), 1997.
*Dog's Day,* Reed (London, England), 1998, Orchard Books (New York), 2000.
*Panda Big and Panda Small,* DK Publishing (New York, NY), 1998.
*Rory and the Lion,* DK Publishing (New York, NY), 1999.
*Over in the Meadow,* Holiday House (New York, NY), 2000.
*Old Mother Hubbard,* Holiday House (New York), 2001.
*Bear's Good Night,* Candlewick Press (Cambridge, MA), 2002.
*Monkey's Playtime* (pop-up book), Candlewick Press (Cambridge, MA), 2002.
*The Polar Bear and the Snow Cloud,* Macmillan (London, England), 2002, published as *The Lonesome Polar Bear,* Random House (New York, NY), 2003.
*If You're Happy and You Know It!: A Sing-along Action Book,* Gullane Children's (London, England), 2003, Holiday House (New York, NY), 2005.
*The Pram Race,* Macmillan (London, England), 2004.
*The Creaky Noise,* Simon & Schuster (New York, NY), 2004.
*Mummy Carry Me Please!,* Gullane Children's (London, England), 2004, published as *Mommy, Carry Me Please!,* Holiday House (New York, NY), 2006.
(Adaptor) *Ten in the Bed,* Holiday House (New York, NY), 2006.
*Cat's Cuddles,* Gullane (London, England), 2006, published as *Kitten's Cuddles,* Holiday House (New York, NY), 2007.
*Buttercup's Baby Bird* ("Fairy Folk of Leafy Wood" series), Scholastic (London, England), 2007.
*Fern's Holiday* ("Fairy Folk of Leafy Wood" series), Scholastic (London, England), 2007.

*ILLUSTRATOR; FICTION FOR CHILDREN*

Joyce Dunbar, *Eggday,* David & Charles (London, England), 1999.
Sally Crabtree and Roberta Mathieson, *My Sister's Hair,* Random House (New York, NY), 2001.

*OTHER*

*Reader's Digest Complete Drawing Course,* David & Charles (London, England), 2003.

Contributor of illustrations to travel magazine.

## Sidelights

Environmentally conscious children's book author and illustrator Jane Cabrera left behind a career in graphic design to pursue her love of writing and illustration. At age twenty-nine she was credited by *Books* magazine with "breaking the mould" when it comes to illustrating picture books for preschoolers. In addition to illustrating books like *Eggday* by Joyce Dunbar, Cabrera has also written and illustrated many original children's stories, among them *Cat's Colors, The Lonesome Polar Bear,* and *Mommy, Carry Me Please!* She has also created as well as updated art for picture-book versions of the childhood songs *Over in the Meadow, Ten in the Bed,* and *If You're Happy and You Know It!: A Sing-along Action Book.* Praising Cabrera's easy-to-read story about a small polar bear cub looking for a new friend, *School Library Journal* contributor Genevieve Gallagher noted that *The Lonesome Polar Bear* is a "charming picture book" enhanced by colorful illustrations full of "depth and texture."

Animals figure prominently in many of Cabrera's books, and these engaging creatures lead children into learning. *Cat's Colors* finds a finicky feline perusing ten different colors in order to select a favorite; in this brightly colored book children not only count along with the likeable kitten, but also learn color names. Cabrera's song adaptation in *Over in the Meadow* similarly helps children by presenting finger-paint-style illustrations of bunnies, goldfish, and turtles clustered together for easy counting. The last two pages provide a chance for learning to be reinforced as readers locate and count the correct groups of animals as they are lined up. Cabrera's large, clear illustrations for *Over in the Meadow* depict an open field bathed in warm sunlight, and a reviewer for *Publishers Weekly* stated that her fresh variation on the popular nursery rhyme format "offers an appealing and energetic landscape of boldly applied colors." In *School Library Journal* Jean Gaffney commented of Cabrera's work that the "movement and energy conveyed in her illustrations enhance the rhyme, and listeners may be inspired to act out the animals or chime in."

***Jane Cabrera mixes a winsome character, simple, rounded shapes, and soothing colors in her self-illustrated picture book* The Lonesome Polar Bear.** (Illustration © 2002 by Jane Cabrera. Reproduced by permission of Macmillan Children's Books, London. Reproduced in the U.S. by permission of Random House Children's Books, a division of Random House, Inc.)

*Eggday* provides readers with a useful lesson about animals and competition, as main character Dora the duck declares the following day to be Eggday: All barnyard animals will compete to see who can lay the best egg. Giving egg-laying a sincere try, with a series of effortful oinks, neighs, and bleats many of the animals acknowledge that they do not have the ability to lay an egg. Finally, Hetty the hen steps in to put an end to these futile efforts. She explains that not every animal is capable of laying eggs and gives each animal an egg to decorate instead. Excited about their creations, the farm animals race back to show Dora what they have done, and are ultimately greeted with a wonderful surprise. A reviewer for *Publishers Weekly* complimented Cabrera's "eye-catching artwork," as well as her knack for covering the pages from top to bottom with "vibrant colors that seem infused with the spring sunshine." Ilene Cooper noted in *Booklist* that Cabrera's style artfully resembles children's finger paints and added that her "bright pictures exude playfulness and good cheer."

Cabrera's nursery-rhyme adaptation of *If You're Happy and You Know It!* was praised by *Booklist* critic Hazel Rochman as "perfect for the lap-sit crowd" on the strength of its "bright, exuberant" animal characters. Marge Loch-Wouters also praised the artistic adaptation, writing in *School Library Journal* that Cabrera's use of "brush strokes gives texture" to the monkey, elephant, giraffe, and other characters.

An original story by Cabrera, *Kitty Cuddles* finds Kitty deciding which among her many friends is the best partner for hugging. Noting the illustrator's "trademark" use of "eye-catching" bold color, Loch-Wouters added that the book's "animal friends are rendered with a verve" that energizes the simple text. In *Booklist* Cooper dubbed the book "awfully cute" due to its "charming" naive-styled art. Another original story by Cabrera contains an oft-heard plea. *Mommy, Carry Me Please!* focuses on the many ways animal young are portaged by their parents, from arms to teeth to comfy pouch. The artist's "breezy, blocky, and bold animals" carry the show, according to Loch-Wouters, while a *Kirkus*

***Of all Cabrera's engaging animal characters, none are more appealing than the mother and child featured in* Mommy, Carry Me Please!** (Illustration © 2004 by Jane Cabrera. Reproduced by permission of Holiday House, Inc.)

*Reviews* writer concluded of *Mommy, Carry Me Please!* that the book's "vibrant" colors and "kid-appealing artwork . . . will keep the focus on the Mommy-child interaction."

Cabrera, who works in a studio in London, continues to take on new creative projects, all with a central purpose. As she once told *SATA:* "My main passion is the environment. I am very concerned for the future of our planet and that of the children on it. I'm involved in a lot of green groups and . . . feel it's time to put people and nature before profits, before it's too late. My husband and I try to live a low-impact lifestyle as much as it's possible within a big city.

"My ambition is to produce children's environmental books. Not only would the stories be environmental, but the production would be too—from recycled/sustainable paper, to non-toxic inks, and the production workers would be treated ethically.

"My other hobbies include mural painting for toddlers' bedrooms, life drawing, long country walks, and cooking and eating. (I'm a vegetarian of fourteen years and a big fan of organic food.) I also enjoy reading; collecting children's books; making mobiles, picture frames, blinds, etc., from collected nature finds (driftwood, leaves, and even broken pottery and nineteenth-century clay pipes from the River Thames); but my main hobby is socializing with my friends!"

## Biographical and Critical Sources

*PERIODICALS*

*Booklist,* April 1, 1999, Ilene Cooper, review of *Eggday,* p. 1420; February 1, 2000, Hazel Rochman, review of *Over in the Meadow,* p. 1026, and Ilene Cooper, review of *Dog's Day,* p. 1028; September 1, 2001, Hazel Rochman, review of *Old Mother Hubbard,* p. 111; February 15, 2005, Hazel Rochman, review of *If You're Happy and You Know It!: A Sing-along Action Book,* p. 1081; October 1, 2006, Julie Cummins, review of *Ten in the Bed,* p. 56; February 15, 2007, Ilene Cooper, review of *Kitty's Cuddles,* p. 83.

*Books,* June, 1997, review of *Cat's Colors,* p. 21.

*Bulletin of the Center for Children's Books,* July, 1997, Elizabeth Bush, review of *Cat's Colors,* pp. 388-389; May, 2000, review of *Over in the Meadow,* p. 310; November, 2001, review of *Old Mother Hubbard,* p. 96.

*Children's Book Review,* August, 1997, review of *Cat's Colors,* p. 158.

*Horn Book,* May 1999, review of *Eggday,* p. 313.

*Kirkus Reviews,* January 15, 1997, review of *Cat's Colors,* p. 138; September 1, 2001, review of *Old Mother Hubbard,* p. 1287; February 1, 2005, review of *If You're Happy and You Know It!,* p. 174; February 15, 2006, review of *Mommy, Carry Me Please!,* p. 179; September 15, 2006, review of *Ten in the Bed,* p. 948.

*Publishers Weekly,* April 21, 1997, review of *Cat's Colors,* p. 70; February 22, 1999, review of *Eggday,* p. 93; January 31, 2000, review of *Over in the Meadow,* p. 105; March 20, 2000, review of *Top Dog,* p. 94; June 3, 2002, review of *Bear's Good Night,* p. 91.

*School Librarian,* August, 1997, review of *Cat's Colors,* p. 130.

*School Library Journal,* May, 1997, Melissa Hudak, review of *Cat's Colors,* p. 93; December, 1999, Janet M. Bair, review of *Rory and the Lion,* p. 88; March, 2000, Linda Ludke, review of *Dog's Day,* p. 189; April, 2000, Jean Gaffney, review of *Over in the Meadow,* p. 92; January, 2002, Linda M. Kenton, review of *Old Mother Hubbard,* p. 116; February, 2002, Jane Marino, review of *My Sister's Hair,* p. 97; January, 2004, Genevieve Gallagher, review of *The Lonesome Polar Bear,* p. 95; March, 2005, Blair Christolon, review of *If You're Happy and You Know It!,* p. 191; February, 2006, Marge Loch-Wouters, review of *Mommy, Carry Me Please!,* p. 94; September, 2006, Martha Simpson, review of *Ten in the Bed,* p. 161; March, 2007, Marge Loch-Wouters, review of *Kitty Cuddles,* p. 152.*

* * *

# CANTONE, AnnaLaura

## Personal

Married.

## Addresses

*Home and office*—Milan, Italy. *E-mail*—info@annalauracantone.com.

## Career

Illustrator.

## Illustrator

Brigitte Weninger, *Zara Zebra Counts,* North-South Books (New York, NY), 2002.

Brigitte Weninger, *Zara Zebra Draws,* North-South Books (New York, NY), 2002.

Brigitte Weninger, *Zara Zebra Gets Dressed,* North-South Books (New York, NY), 2002.

(With Sophie Fatus and Anna De Carlo) *Prima di Natale,* Nuages, 2002.

Brigitte Weninger, *Zara Zebra's Busy Day,* North-South Books (New York, NY), 2002.

Beatrice Masini, *The Wedding Dress Mess,* Watson-Guptill Publications (New York, NY), 2003.

Emily Jenkins, *My Favorite Thing (according to Alberta),* Atheneum Books for Young Readers (New York, NY), 2004.

Alan Madison, *Pecorino's First Concert,* Atheneum Books for Young Readers (New York, NY), 2005.

Alan Madison, *Pecorino Plays Ball,* Atheneum Books for Young Readers (New York, NY), 2006.

Barbara Veit, *Who Stole Little Snail's House?,* North-South Books (New York, NY), 2007.

Pippa Goodhart, *Three Little Ghosties,* Bloomsbury Children's Books (New York, NY), 2007.

Also illustrator of books published in Italian.

## Sidelights

Italian illustrator AnnaLaura Cantone has a penchant for creating illustrations with a humorous flair. She has contributed images to children's books by a number of authors, among them Brigitte Weninger's picture-book series about a spunky young zebra, Alan Madison's *Pecorino's First Concert* and *Pecorino Plays Ball,* and Emily Jenkins' *My Favorite Thing (according to Alberta).*

In her art, Cantone often works in mixed media, and this technique allows her to accentuates her whimsical style. In creating her illustrations, she incorporates textiles and other fibers, as well as photographs, into the backdrop for her pen-and-ink and acrylic art. Her illustrations for Madison's "Pecorino" series have been cited by critics for their unusual but engaging and humorous qualities. Mary Elam, reviewing *Pecorino's First Concert* for *School Library Journal,* wrote that Cantone's "mixed-media pen-and-paint illustrations . . . add whimsy to descriptive text." In the same periodical, Roxanne Burg wrote of *Pecorino Plays Ball* that Cantone's "acrylic, pen, and collage illustrations add to the general silliness" of the story and highlight Madison's determined main character with over-exaggerated features.

*My Favorite Thing* also incorporates Cantone's illustrations, which a *Publishers Weekly* reviewer dubbed both "imaginative" and "zippy." In the book, a young girl named Alberta goes through a list of things she likes and dislikes, and ultimately declares herself to be her most favorite thing. In line with Jenkins' text, Cantone portrays Alberta as a "a squat, bossy presence," noted a *Publishers Weekly* critic. In a review of *My Favorite Thing* for *Horn Book,* Christine M. Heppermann praised Cantone's comical images and noted that the picture book's "idiosyncratic rundown [of favorite things is] depicted in humorously manic mixed-media cartoons."

## Biographical and Critical Sources

*PERIODICALS*

*Booklist,* February 1, 2006, GraceAnne A. DeCandido, review of *Pecorino Plays Ball,* p. 56.

*Horn Book,* July-August, 2004, Christine M. Heppermann, review of *My Favorite Thing (according to Alberta),* p. 439.

*Kirkus Reviews,* May 15, 2004, review of *My Favorite Thing,* p. 493; June 15, 2005, review of *Pecorino's First Concert,* p. 43; January 1, 2006, review of *Pecorino Plays Ball,* p. 43.

*Publishers Weekly,* July 12, 2004, review of *My Favorite Thing,* p. 63; August 8, 2005, review of *Pecorino's First Concert,* p. 234.

*School Library Journal,* September, 2004, Roxanne Burg, review of *My Favorite Thing,* p. 169; August, 2005, review of *Pecorino's First Concert,* p. 102; March, 2006, Roxanne Burg, review of *Pecorino Plays Ball,* p. 198.

*ONLINE*

*AnnaLaura Cantone Home Page,* http://www.annalauracantone.com (August 6, 2007).

*Bloomsbury Web site,* http://www.bloomsbury.com/ (August 6, 2007), "AnnaLaura Cantone."

*Simon & Schuster Web site,* http://www.simonsays.com/ (August 6, 2007), "AnnaLaura Cantone."*

*  *  *

# CARRIS, Joan 1938-
# (Joan Davenport Carris)

## Personal

Born August 18, 1938, in Toledo, OH; daughter of Roy (a sales manager) and Elfrid (an artist) Davenport; married Barr Tupper Carris (in data processing), December 28, 1960; children: Mindy, Leigh Ann, Bradley. *Education:* Iowa State University, B.S. (English/speech, 1960; Hollins University, M.A. (children's literature); Duke University, teaching credentials. *Religion:* Protestant. *Hobbies and other interests:* Walking, playing tennis and bridge.

## Addresses

*Home and office*—Box 231, 48 Princeton Ave., Rocky Hill, NJ 08553. *Agent*—Dorothy Markinko, McIntosh & Otis, Inc., 310 Madison Ave., New York, NY 10017. *E-mail*—nsb@joancarrisbooks.com.

## Career

Educator and author. High school English teacher in Nevada, IA, 1960-61; high school teacher of French, speech, and English in Des Moines, IA, 1963-65; private English tutor in Princeton, NJ, 1974—; author, 1977—. Duke University, instructor in graduate-level writing. Commentator for Public Radio East. Member, New Jersey Council for Children's Literature.

## Member

National League of American Pen Women (president of Princeton, NJ, branch, 1980-84), Society of Children's Book Writers and Illustrators, Children's Book Guild of Washington, DC (former president), Rocky Hill Community Group (member of executive board, 1974-78).

## Awards, Honors

Outstanding Science Book designation, *Science and Children* magazine, 1984, for *Pets, Vets, and Marty Howard;* Iowa Children' Choice Award, Iowa Educational Media Association, 1984, Tennessee Readers Award, 1985, and Young Hoosier Book Award, Indiana Media Educators, 1986, all for *When the Boys Ran the House;* New York Readers Award, Ethical Culture School, 1985, for *Witch-Cat.*

## Writings

*FOR CHILDREN*

*The Revolt of 10-X,* Harcourt (New York, NY), 1980.

*When the Boys Ran the House,* Harper (New York, NY), 1982.

*Pets, Vets, and Marty Howard* (sequel to *When the Boys Ran the House*), illustrated by Carol Newsom, Harper (New York, NY), 1984.

*Witch-Cat* (fantasy), illustrated by Beth Peck, Harper (New York, NY), 1984.

*Rusty Timmons' First Million,* illustrated by Kim Mulkey, Harper (New York, NY), 1985.

*Hedgehogs in the Closet* (sequel to *Pets, Vets, and Marty Howard*), Harper (New York, NY), 1988.

*Aunt Morbelia and the Screaming Skulls,* illustrated by Doug Cushman, Little, Brown (Boston, MA), 1990.

*The Greatest Idea Ever,* illustrated by Carol Newsom, Lippincott (Philadelphia, PA), 1990.

*A Ghost of a Chance,* illustrated by Paul Henry, Little, Brown (Boston, MA), 1992.

*Howling for Home,* illustrated by Judith Mitchell, Little, Brown (Boston, MA), 1992.

*Stolen Bones,* illustrated by Stephen Marchesi, Little, Brown (Boston, MA), 1993.

*Beware the Ravens, Aunt Morbelia,* Little, Brown (Boston, MA), 1995.

*Ghost of a Chance,* Coastal Carolina Press (Wilmington, NC), 2003.

*Welcome to the Bed and Biscuit,* illustrated by Noah Z. Jones, Candlewick Press (Cambridge, MA), 2006.

*OTHER*

(With Michael R. Crystal) *SAT Success: Peterson's Guide to English and Math Skills for College Entrance Examinations* (study guide), Peterson's Guides (Princeton, NJ), 1982, revised edition with William R. McQuade, 1987.

*Peterson's Success with Words,* Peterson's Guides (Princeton, NJ), 1987, fourth edition, 2004.

(With Michael R. Crystal and William R. McQuade) *Peterson's Panic Plan for the SAT,* Peterson's Guides (Princeton, NJ), 1990, sixth edition, Thomson/Peterson's (Laurenceville, NJ), 2002.

*SAT Word Flash: The Quick Way to Build Verbal Power for the New SAT—and Beyond,* Peterson's Guides (Princeton, NJ), 1993, fifth edition published as *In-a-Flash Vocabulary,* Thomson/Peterson's (Laurenceville, NJ), 2004.

Also author of "Tremendous Trifles" (humor column), in *Princeton Spectrum* and *Trenton Times,* 1977-81. Contributor to periodicals, including *Better Homes and Gardens* and *Think.*

## Adaptations

*Witch-Cat* was adapted for film as part of the Columbia Broadcasting System (CBS-TV) *Story Hour Special,* 1985, and was adapted for audiocassette, read by Ruth Ann Phimister, Recorded Books, 2001.

## Sidelights

Gearing her children's books for readers from age six through the mid-teens, writer and educator Joan Carris creates fast-moving stories that feature likeable characters and plots that often feature elements of fantasy. "We have a responsibility to be entertaining . . . ," Carris explained to Jacksonville, North Carolina *Daily News* interviewer Joe Miller in discussing her work as a children's writer. "The reason I read and read and read is that I have fun. Kids deserve the same chance."

Carris's elementary-grade mystery *A Ghost of a Chance* finds a twelve year old searching for the lost treasure of Blackbeard the pirate during a family vacation in coastal North Carolina. *Aunt Morbelia and the Screaming Skulls* and *Beware the Ravens, Aunt Morbelia* combine mystery and comedy as they chronicle the adventures of a preteen, the boy's best friends, and his eccentric aunt. In *Witch-Cat* a magical feline finds that its assignment—to help a twelve-year-old girl recognize her abilities as a witch—presents a daunting challenge. Noting that the book features "nicely placed clues" and "daffy characters," *Booklist* contributor Chris Sherman wrote that *Beware the Ravens, Aunt Morbelia* also contains "enough chills to please middle-grade readers."

Dubbed a "sweetly satisfying" and "reassuring tale of family life" by a *School Library Journal* critic, *Welcome to the Bed and Biscuit* takes place in an animal shelter, where a kindly elderly veterinarian named Grampa Bender cares for an assortment of creatures, including Gabby the mynah bird, Ernest the mini-pig, and Milly the orange cat. When a Scottie puppy that has barely survived a house fire arrives at the shelter and requires a lot of the veterinarian's time, Milly feels jealous and neglected. When the cat disappears without warning, Gabby and Ernest must track down their missing friend and convince her that she is still important to Grampa. Praising the pencil-and-watercolor illustrations by Noah Z. Jones, a *Kirkus Reviews* writer predicted that Carris's "easy" chapter-book text will appeal to young animal lovers, and in *School Library Journal* Elizabeth Bird described *Welcome to the Bed and Biscuit* as a "remarkably sweet beginning chapter book" with "gentle humor."

Carris once noted: "I discovered the vast number of things I couldn't do pretty early in life. I couldn't do a handstand, jump rope past 'pepper,' skate without bloodying my entire body, or dance. I thought I might have to take my mother to college with me so that she could continue doing my hair—a feat I'd never managed alone.

***A veterinarian's cat deals with her jealousy with the help of good friends in Joan Carris's elementary-grade chapter book* Welcome to the Bed and Biscuit.** (Illustration © 2006 by Noah Z. Jones. Reproduced by permission of the publisher, Candlewick Press, Inc., Cambridge, MA.)

"Just as I was about to declare myself a washout, I discovered that I could understand literature, really understand it. I could diagram sentences and spell—of all things. Moreover, I could write an analytical essay in English class, and some God-sent professor would read it aloud, or even publish it in a literary magazine. What a relief. Even my French was passable, and in a feeble way I can still communicate and read that sonorous language descended from Latin, my all-time favorite.

"Now that I am older, I am still involved with language, and my love for it grows, even though it *is* tricky to work those old spelling medals into a cocktail-party conversation.

"My impetus for writing was the glut of English teachers in the field at the time I wanted to return to teaching. There was no place for me—I'd been gone ten long years (whomping up three children) and it was too long. In a snit, I plunked my typewriter on the dining room table and said I'd try my hand at the only other possibility: education through writing for young people. But

I didn't want to lure people to reading in the traditional way. I wanted to do it through humor, with as much warmth as I could transfer to paper, with that always-difficult goal of making readers laugh and say 'ah, yes' at the same time.

"Trying to teach young people to love and emulate good English is behind everything I do. For that reason I began teaching Scholastic Aptitude Test (SAT) preparation classes. In class we discuss old myths, the fascinating stories behind words, the power words have to take us anywhere we want to go. Out of this class has grown a book. I have a hunch it will be much like a house I would build—full of faults that get discovered only after I take possession.

"Writing children's books is my delight. If I can create even one character who truly comes to life, I'll feel immense satisfaction. And there will never be enough time for all the stories I want to tell about the kids who are like my kids, like the ones next door, like me when I was a kid. It is the hardest work I have ever done, the loneliest, the least rewarding financially, and the most frustrating.

"I wouldn't change it for anything."

## Biographical and Critical Sources

*PERIODICALS*

*Booklist,* March 15, 1992, Randy Meyer, review of *A Ghost of a Chance,* p. p. 1357; May 1, 1993, Carolyn Phelan, review of *Stolen Bones,* p. 1588; February 1, 1994, review of *Hedgehogs in the Closet,* p. 1010; December 15, 1994, Chris Sherman, review of *Beware the Ravens, Aunt Morbelia,* p. 752; October 1, 2006, Ilene Cooper, review of *Welcome to the Bed and Biscuit,* p. 56.

*Bulletin of the Center for Children's Books,* March, 1981, review of *The Revolt of 10-X,* p. 128; November, 1984, review of *Pets, Vets, and Marty Howard,* p. 42; March, 1986, review of *Rusty Timmons' First Million,* p. 123; November, 1989, review of *Just a Little Ham,* p. 88; June, 1992, review of *A Ghost of a Chance,* p. 256.

*Daily News* (Jacksonville, NC), November 15, 2006, Joe Miller "Writer Meeting a Responsibility."

*Horn Book,* December, 1980, Anna A. Flowers, review of *The Revolt of 10-X,* p. 640.

*Kirkus Reviews,* September 15, 2006, review of *Welcome to the Bed and Biscuit,* p. 948.

*Publishers Weekly,* August 18, 1987, review of *Rusty Timmons' First Million,* p. 82; December 11, 1987, review of *Hedgehogs in the Closet,* p. 65; May 25, 1992, review of *A Ghost of a Chance,* p. 55.

*School Library Journal,* February, 1983, Virginia Marr, review of *When the Boys Ran the House,* p. 74; September, 1984, Mavis D. Arizzi, review of *Witch-Cat,* p. 114; November, 1984, Kathleen Brachmann, review of *Pets, Vets, and Marty Howard,* p. 122; February, 1986, Richard Luzer, review of *Rusty Timmons' First Million,* p. 81; March, 1988, Bonnie L. Raasch, review of *Hegehogs in the Closet,* p. 186; February, 1990, Martha Rosen, review of *Just a Little Ham,* p. 88; June, 1990, Bonnie L. Raasch, review of *The Greatest Idea Ever,* p. 117; April, 1992, review of *A Ghost of a Chance,* p. 112; March, 1993, Lynnea McBurney, review of *Howling for Home,* p. 171; April, 1993, Connie Tyrrell Burns, review of *Stolen Bones,* p. 117; October, 2006, Elizabeth Bird, review of *Welcome to the Bed and Biscuit,* p. 103.

*Voice of Youth Advocates,* February, 1981, review of *The Revolt of 10-X,* p. 28; February, 1985, review of *Pets, Vets, and Marty Howard,* p. 323; December, 1985, review of *Rusty Timmons' First Million,* p. 318; October, 1992, review of *A Ghost of a Chance,* p. 221.

*ONLINE*

*Joan Carris Home Page,* http://www.joancarrisbooks.com (August 17, 2007).*

* * *

## CARRIS, Joan Davenport
## See CARRIS, Joan

* * *

## CHAPRA, Mimi

### Personal

Born in Havana, Cuba; married. *Hobbies and other interests:* Hiking.

### Addresses

*Home and office*—212 W. Highland Ave., Philadelphia, PA 19118.

### Career

Author.

### Writings

*Amelia's Show-and-Tell Fiesta/Amelia y la fiesta de muestra y cuenta,* illustrated by Martha Avilés, HarperCollins (New York, NY), 2004.

*Sparky's Bark/El ladrido de Sparky,* illustrated by Viví Escrivá, HarperCollins (New York, NY), 2006.

### Sidelights

Mimi Chapra was born in Havana, Cuba, and came to the United States as a young child. As an author, she writes immigrant stories that explore the experiences of children assimilating to a new country and language. Chapra's bilingual stories include *Amelia's Show-and-Tell Fiesta/Amelia y la fiesta de muestra y cuenta,* in which readers share a Cuban girl's excitement as she prepares for the show-and-tell session at her new American school. Amelia proudly wears her native fiesta dress on show-and-tell day, but when she arrives at school she realizes that she misunderstood the teacher's directions and was only to bring a small item to share with her class. At first the girl is embarrassed, but with encouragement from her teacher and classmates Amelia talks about her dress and Cuban culture. A critic for *Kirkus Reviews* regarded *Amelia's Show-and-Tell Fiesta* as "sweet-tempered and inviting," noting that Chapra "zeroes in on a common emotion, while also introducing Amelia's Cuban culture."

In *Sparky's Bark/El ladrido de Sparky* a young girl's enthusiasm about leaving her home in Cuba and visiting American relatives in Ohio turns to trepidation. Arriving in Ohio, Lucy finds it difficult to overcome the language barrier that exists between her and her relatives. She is even more disappointed when she finds that she cannot even communicate with the family dog, Sparky. Things begin to change, however, when a friendly cousin teaches Lucy some simple American phrases and helps the girl ease into the new culture. In *Booklist,* Stella Clark acknowledged Chapra's picture book for its "simple, firmly delineated message about language and culture."

## Biographical and Critical Sources

*PERIODICALS*

*Booklist,* May 1, 2006, Stella Clark, review of *Sparky's Bark/El ladrido de Sparky,* p. 88.

*Kirkus Reviews,* May 15, 2004, review of *Amelia's Show-and-Tell Fiesta/Amelia y la fiesta de muestra y cuenta,* p. 489; June 1, 2006, review of *Sparky's Bark/El ladrido de Sparky,* p. 570.

*Publishers Weekly,* September 4, 2006, review of *Sparky's Bark/El ladrido de Sparky,* p. 67.

*School Library Journal,* September, 2004, Ann Welton, review of *Amelia's Show-and-Tell Fiesta/Amelia y la fiesta de muestra y cuenta,* p. 195; June, 2006, Maria Otero-Boisvert, review of *Sparky's Bark/El ladrido de Sparky,* p. 142

*ONLINE*

*HarperCollins Web site,* http://www.harpercollins.com/ (August 7, 2007).*

* * *

# CHARLES, Veronika Martenova

## Personal

Born in Prague, Czechoslovakia; immigrated to Canada. *Education:* Ryerson University, B.A. (applied arts); Ontario College of Art and Design, degree; York University, M.A. (folklore), 2006.

## Addresses

*Home and office*—Toronto, Ontario, Canada. *E-mail*—veronikacharles@yahoo.ca.

## Career

Author and illustrator of children's books. Former teen pop recording artist in eastern Europe; worked as an interior designer and art director; freelance author and illustrator, beginning 1991.

## Member

Writers' Union of Canada.

## Awards, Honors

Amelia Frances Howard-Gibbon Illustrators Award finalist, 1993, and Bank Street College of Education Children's Book of the Year designation, 1994, both for *The Crane Girl;* Canadian Children's Book Centre (CCBC) Our Choice designation, 1995, for *Hey! What's That Sound?,* 1998, for *Necklace of Stars,* 2001, for *Don't Open the Door!,* and 2002, for *Maiden of the Mist;* Storytelling World Award Honor book, 2002, for *Maiden of the Mist;* Governor General's Award finalist, 2006, and ASPCCA Henry Bergh Children's Book Award finalist, CCBC Our Choice designation, KIND Children's Book Award Honor Book designation, and Sigurd F. Oloson Award for Nature Writing, all 2007, and Rocky Mountain Book Award finalist, 2008, all for *The Birdman.*

## Writings

*FOR CHILDREN*

(And illustrator) *The Crane Girl,* Orchard Books (New York, NY), 1992.

(And illustrator) *Hey! What's That Sound?,* Stoddart (Toronto, Ontario, Canada), 1994.

(And illustrator) *Necklace of Stars,* Stoddart Kids (Toronto, Ontario, Canada), 1996.

(And illustrator) *Stretch, Swallow, and Stare,* Stoddart Kids (Toronto, Ontario, Canada), 1999.

(Reteller and illustrator) *Maiden of the Mist: A Legend of Niagara Falls,* Stoddart Kids (Toronto, Ontario, Canada), 2001.

*The Birdman,* illustrated by Annouchka Gravel Galouchko and Stéphan Daigel, Tundra Books (Plattsburgh, NY), 2006.

*"EASY-TO-READ SPOOKY TALES" SERIES; FOR CHILDREN*

*Don't Open the Door!,* illustrated by Leanne Franson, Stoddart Kids (Toronto, Ontario, Canada), 2000, illustrated by David Parkins, Tundra Books (Toronto, Ontario, Canada), 2007.

*Don't Go into the Forest!,* illustrated by Leanne Franson, Stoddart Kids (Toronto, Ontario, Canada), 2001, illustrated by David Parkins, Tundra Books (Toronto, Ontario, Canada), 2007.

*Don't Go near the Water!,* illustrated by Leanne Franson, Stoddart Kids (Toronto, Ontario, Canada), 2002, illustrated by David Parkins, Tundra Books (Toronto, Ontario, Canada), 2007.

*Don't Go in There!,* illustrated by David Parkins, Tundra Books (Plattsburgh, NY), 2007.

*Don't Walk Alone at Night!,* illustrated by David Parkins, Tundra Books (Plattsburgh, NY), 2007.

*Don't Talk to Strangers!,* illustrated by David Parkins, Tundra Books (Plattsburgh, NY), 2008.

*Don't Touch That!,* illustrated by David Parkins, Tundra Books (Plattsburgh, NY), 2008.

*Don't Forget!,* illustrated by David Parkins, Tundra Books (Plattsburgh, NY), 2008.

*Don't Eat That!,* illustrated by David Parkins, Tundra Books (Plattsburgh, NY), 2008.

*Don't Enter the House!,* illustrated by David Parkins, Tundra Books (Plattsburgh, NY), 2008.

*ILLUSTRATOR*

Gail E. Gill, *There's an Alligator under My Bed,* Three Trees Press (Toronto, Ontario, Canada), 1984.

Maria R. Plant, *Robin and the Rainbow,* Three Trees Press (Toronto, Ontario, Canada), 1985.

Marion Mineau, *The Flowers,* Black Moss Press (Toronto, Ontario, Canada), 1988.

Laurel Dee Gugler, *Casey's Carousel,* Black Moss Press (Toronto, Ontario, Canada), 1989.

## Sidelights

Veronika Martenova Charles creates stories for children that are inspired by her own travels around the world as well as by her fascination with the stories and folklore of many lands. In her books, which include *Maiden of the Mist: A Legend of Niagara Falls, The Crane Girl,* and *The Birdman,* as well as her her "Easy-to-Read Spooky Tales" series for beginning readers, Charles weaves multicultural details into both folktale retellings and original stories, all reflecting her positive outlook. Her first self-illustrated picture book, a retelling of a story set in Japan and titled *The Crane Girl,* was praised by a *Publishers Weekly* contributor who cited its "poignance and . . . timeless universality," as well as its "skillfully rendered setting." From Japan, Charles transports readers to the Andes mountains of Ecuador in *Necklace of Stars,* which finds a boy who has captured mythical golden ducks now confronting a difficult decision. In addition to praising Charles' artwork as "dreamlike and luminescent," a *Resource Links* contributor cited the author/illustrator for her ability to blend "history and tradition."

Charles developed an interest in both art and music while growing up in Prague, Czechoslovakia. After her art studies were curtailed, the teenager focused on music and, through her talent and determination, found success in a Western-style pop band formed with a friend. As an entertainer, Charles toured throughout Europe in addition to visits in the rest of the Soviet Union. Stopping in Newfoundland, Canada, on her way home from performing in Cuba—a Cold War ally of the then-USSR—Charles decided to defect. She decided to make English-speaking Canada her new home, and learned her new language by reading novels, and worked a variety of jobs while also earning several college degrees.

***Veronika Martenova Charles' picture book* The Birdman, *based on a true story, features award-winning illustrations by Anouchka Gravel and Stéphan Daigle.*** (Illustration © 2006 by Anouchka Gravel Galouchka and Stephán Daigle. Reproduced by permission.)

Charles' award-winning picture book *The Birdman* was inspired by a newspaper article the author read, and this article motivated her to take a trip to Calcutta to investigate the story for herself. In the story, a tailor named Noor Nobi is emotionally crushed by the accidental death of his three children. Wandering the streets of Calcutta, homeless and alone, the distraught man eventually finds himself in a bustling marketplace. There he sees a caged and frightened bird, which he purchase with the very last of his money. Caring for the bird helps Nobi focus on something other than his sadness, and by the time the bird is strong enough to fly away, the man has come to terms with his loss. Returning to his tailor shop, Nobi continues to dedicate himself to healing injured birds, and ultimately gains respect for his caring. In her *Booklist* review, Gillian Engberg praised *The Birdman*, noting Charles' "vivid, poetic text" and her "focus . . . on the uplifting message that acts of kindness can ease grief." Engberg also cited the "lavish" and award-winning illustrations by Annouchka Gravel Galouchko and Stéphan Daigle, while a *Kirkus Reviews* writer concluded that the book's richly toned paintings "combine with the theme of the story to lift the reader's spirit."

In her "Easy-to-Read Spooky Tales" chapter-book series, which include *Don't Go in There!, Don't Go into the Forest!, Don't Go Near the Water!,* and *Don't Open the Door!,* Charles' young characters engage in activities that allow them to share scary stories based on actual tales from around the world. In *Don't Open the Door!,* for example, the young narrator invites friends Leon and Marcos to his home for a sleep-over. Soon the supervising parent has to leave, and the boys are told not to open the door to strangers. While left alone, the friends take turns telling scary stories about the downfall of people who have ignored such sound advice. Ultimately, they successfully scare each other into staying away from the door. *Don't Go Near the Water!* takes a similar tack, as the imaginative boys conjure up new versions of three traditional tales about the downfall of walking too near the banks of a local, fast-moving creek. As an added feature of each book, Charles leaves the last story told open-ended and invites the reader to create his or her own ending. In her afterwords to each book in the series, Charles explains the origins of each story she has included, noting that they are drawn from diverse cultures. Reviewing *Don't Go into the Forest!,* which finds the boys staying at a woodland cottage, a *Resource Links* contributor praised the book's "captivating" text, and added that Charles' "skillful combination of comedy and horror might also be a draw for reluctant readers."

## Biographical and Critical Sources

*PERIODICALS*

*Booklist,* April 15, 2001, Ilene Cooper, review of *Don't Open the Door!,* p. 1568; October 1, 2006, Gillian Engberg, review of *The Birdman,* p. 57.

*Kirkus Reviews,* August 15, 2006, review of *The Birdman,* p. 837.

*Publishers Weekly,* March 29, 1993, review of *The Crane Girl,* p. 54.

*School Library Journal,* September, 2001, Karen Scott, review of *Don't Open the Door!,* p. 1568; January, 2002, Susan Weitz, review of *Maiden of the Mist: A Legend of Niagara Falls,* p. 116; December, 2006, Alexa Sandmann, review of *The Birdman,* p. 95.

*Resource Links,* February, 1997, review of *Necklace of Stars,* p. 110; October, 1999, review of *Stretch, Swallow, and Stare,* pp. 2-3; June, 2001, Evette Signarowski, review of *Don't Go into the Forest!,* p. 9; December, 2006, Denise Parrott, review of *The Birdman,* p. 2; April, 2007, Elaine Rospad, review of *Don't Open the Door!,* p. 13.

*ONLINE*

*Canadian Review of Materials Online,* http://www.umanitoba.ca/cm/ (October, 1992), Gillian Martin Noonan, review of *The Crane Girl.*

*Tundra Books Web site,* http://www.tundrabooks.com/ (August 27, 2007), "Veronika Martenova Charles."

* * *

# CHOLDENKO, Gennifer 1957-

## Personal

Born October 20, 1957, in Santa Monica, CA; daughter of Jimmy (a business executive) and Ann (a physical therapist) Johnson; married Jacob Brown; children: Ian Brown, Kai Brown. *Education:* Brandeis University, B.A. (English and American literature; cum laude); Rhode Island School of Design, B.F.A. (illustration).

## Addresses

*Home*—San Francisco Bay area, CA. *E-mail*—choldenko@earthlink.net.

## Career

Writer. Worked in various jobs, including horseback riding instructor for seeing-and hearing-impaired children.

## Awards, Honors

New York Library Top 100 Book designation, Cuyahoga County Library Best Book selection, and National Parenting Center Seal of Approval, all 1997, all for *Moonstruck;* California Book Award Silver Medal for Young Adults, and International Reading Association/Children's Book Council (CBC) Children's Choice, all for *Notes from a Liar and Her Dog;* Newbery Honor Book designation, Carnegie Medal shortlist, American Library Association Notable Book designation, New York Public Library Books for the Teen Age inclusion, CBC/National Council for Social Studies Notable Social Studies Trade Book designation, Special Needs Award (UK), Beatty Award, California Library Association, Judy Lopez Honor Award, Northern California Book Award, and Parents' Choice Silver Medal, all 2005, and California Young Readers Medal, Garden State Teen Book Award, and Keystone State Reading Association Young-adult Book Award, all 2007, all for *Al Capone Does My Shirts.*

## Writings

*PICTURE BOOKS*

*Moonstruck: The True Story of the Cow Who Jumped over the Moon,* illustrated by Paul Yalowitz, Hyperion (New York, NY), 1997.

***Gennifer Choldenko*** (Photograph by Pat Stroud. Courtesy of Gennifer Choldenko.)

*How to Make Friends with a Giant,* illustrated by Amy Walrod, Putnam (New York, NY), 2006.

*Louder, Lili,* illustrated by S.D. Schindler, Putnam (New York, NY), 2007.

*MIDDLE-GRADE NOVELS*

*Notes from a Liar and Her Dog,* Putnam (New York, NY), 2001.

*Al Capone Does My Shirts,* Putnam's (New York, NY), 2004.

*If a Tree Falls at Lunch Period,* Harcourt (Orlando, FL), 2007.

Choldenko's books have been translated into several languages, including Chinese, French, German, Japanese, Korean, and Spanish.

## Adaptations

*Notes from a Liar and Her Dog* was adapted for audiocassette, Listening Library, 2001. *Al Capone Does My Shirts* was adapted for audiocassette, Recorded Books, 2004. *If a Tree Falls at Lunch Period* was adapted for audiocassette, Recorded Books, 2007.

## Sidelights

Selling her first book manuscript to a publisher at age thirty-three, Gennifer Choldenko has gone on to become an award-winning author of both picture books for young children and novels for middle-grade readers. In her fast-paced novels, Choldenko focuses on serious topics that range from chronic lying to autism, but makes them seem fresh through her light, witty touch. Featuring both her characteristic humor and her offbeat perspective, Choldenko's novel *Al Capone Does My Shirts* earned her the prestigious 2005 Newbery Honor Book designation, one of several honors accorded the book. Crediting her father, an unpublished but passionate writer, for inspiring her own efforts as an author, Choldenko added on her home page: "It took me a long time to . . . be willing to take the risks necessary to pursue a career as a writer."

Choldenko was born in Santa Monica, California, in the late 1950s, the youngest in a family that included four boisterous children. As a child, her first love was horses, and her second was writing and making up stories. Choldenko's interests turned to poetry in high school, but during her years as a student at Brandeis University she returned to prose and graduated *cum laude* with a dual major in American literature and English (the school did not yet offer a major in creative writing). Later, she earned an illustration degree from the prestigious Rhode Island School of Design, where she produced her first picture-book text, *Moonstruck: The True Story of the Cow Who Jumped over the Moon*

Aided by illustrations created by Paul Yalowitz, *Moonstruck* sheds new light on the perplexing line "And the cow jumped over the moon," which has puzzled generations of listeners, young and old like. In Choldenko's version, the rhyme's narrator—a horse—explains that the black-and-white bovine in question accomplished the high-flying task after training with a group of agile horses that regularly made the leap into the night sky to skim the top of the moon and return to Earth. Calling the picture book "a giggle from beginning to end," a *Publishers Weekly* contributor noted that the author "clearly had fun setting tradition on its ear, and her glee is evident throughout." In her review of Choldenko's debut for *Booklist,* Ilene Cooper dubbed *Moonstruck* "fractured and funny" and called it "a fun read-aloud—and a tribute to hard work."

Although Choldenko has focused predominately on middle-grade novels since writing *Moonstruck,* she returned to the picture-book format in *How to Make Friends with a Giant,* which features cartoon illustrations by Amy Walrod. In this humorous tale, Jake worries that he is too short until he makes a friend of Jacomo, the new boy who moves next door. While Jake is short for his young age, Jacomo is practically a giant. Watching Jacomo deal with the jokes and frustrations of his first-grade classmates over his clumsy strength and cumbersome size, Jake encourages and protects his new friend, in the process learning to accept his own differences as well. In *Horn Book* Christina M. Hepperman dubbed *How to Make Friends with a Giant* a "perceptive portrait of . . . friendship," in which the author shows that "the best way to get over your own insecurities is to help someone else with theirs." A *Kirkus Reviews* writer also praised the story and found young Jake to be an "inventive" friend, while in *School Library Journal* Grace Oliff described Choldenko's book as "a quirky tale of two opposites."

*Notes from a Liar and Her Dog,* Choldenko's first novel for middle-grade readers, introduces preteen narrator Antonia "Ant" MacPherson, a middle sibling who finds herself constantly on the outs with her two perfect sisters: "Your Highness Elizabeth" and "Katherine the Great." Because her relationship with her parents is equally strained, Ant's only confidants are a Chihuahua named Pistachio and her best friend Harrison, an artist who is obsessed with poultry. As a way to mask her unhappiness, the sixth grader embroiders her life with elaborate falsehoods until a perceptive teacher helps her come to terms with her own role in her difficult family relationship. Noting that Choldenko "vividly captures the feelings of a middle child torn between wanting to be noticed and wanting to be invisible," a *Publishers Weekly* contributor called *Notes from a Liar and Her Dog* a "funny and touching novel." Reviewing the book for *School Library Journal* Connie Tyrrell Burns dubbed Ant's narration "humorous, tongue-in-cheek, and as irreverent as her independent heroine," and *Booklist* critic Susan Dove Lempke called Choldenko's story "funny, moving, and completely believable."

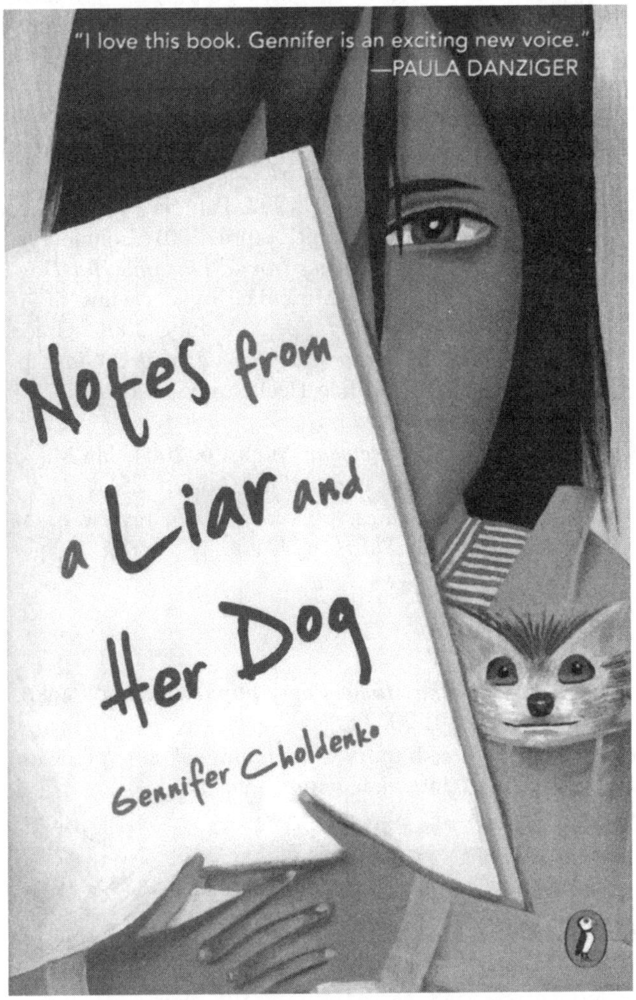


***Cover of Choldenko's middle-grade novel* Notes from a Liar and Her Dog, *featuring artwork by Mark Ulriksen.*** (Illustration © 2001 by Mark Ulriksen. Reproduced by permission of Puffin Books, a division of Penguin Putnam Books for Young Readers.)

In *Al Capone Does My Shirts* Choldenko returns to middle-grade angst, this time by exploring the trauma of moving to a new home. Set in 1935, the novel introduces twelve-year-old Moose Flanagan. Moose is less than enthused when he learns that his family is moving to Alcatraz, an island prison. In order to afford his autistic sister Natalie's tuition at a special school in San Francisco, Moose's dad is working as a prison guard on the island, guarding infamous criminals like mobster Al Capone. Moose has to leave his winning baseball team behind to make the move, and he feels that his sacrifice has gone unnoticed. Now he sees very little of his busy father, and his mom is almost totally involved with Natalie's illness and education. A new confidante is found in the warden's daughter, Piper, a feisty new friend who leads Moose into mischief as he learns to accept his family's situation and appreciate his parents' sacrifices.

In *Booklist* Ed Sullivan praised *Al Capone Does My Shirts* as a "warm, engaging coming-of-age story," and a *Publishers Weekly* contributor described the book as "fast-paced and memorable," citing Choldenko's ability to create "unusual characters and plot lines." According to School Library Journal reviewer Miranda Doyle, the story is "told with humor and skill," and Paula Rohrlick wrote in *Kliatt* that the author couches with in her story a "sensitive portrait of autism and how it affects a family." In *Kirkus Reviews* a writer noted that Choldenko's "pacing is exquisite" and deemed *Al Capone Does My Shirts* a "great read," a view that was shared by the Newbery awards committee in deeming the book a Newbery Honor Book.

*Al Capone Does My Shirts* was inspired by a newspaper article Choldenko read that discussed Alcatraz's evolution from prison to museum. It also discussed the little-known fact that, during its years as a prison, the island was home to the families of prison guards and officials. While researching her book, Choldenko served as a docent on Alcatraz island, immersing herself in the history of the institution, its inmates, and the prison support staff. She also took inspiration from her own sister, Gina, who suffered from autism. The book's title comes from a joke Moose and Piper make about the prison's famous inmate and his prison jobs. Capone worked in the prison laundry during his stay on Alcatraz, and military personnel stationed in San Francisco during World War II used to make a similar joke: "Al Capone does my shorts."

Also taking place in California, *If A Tree Falls at Lunch Period* takes readers to an exclusive middle school

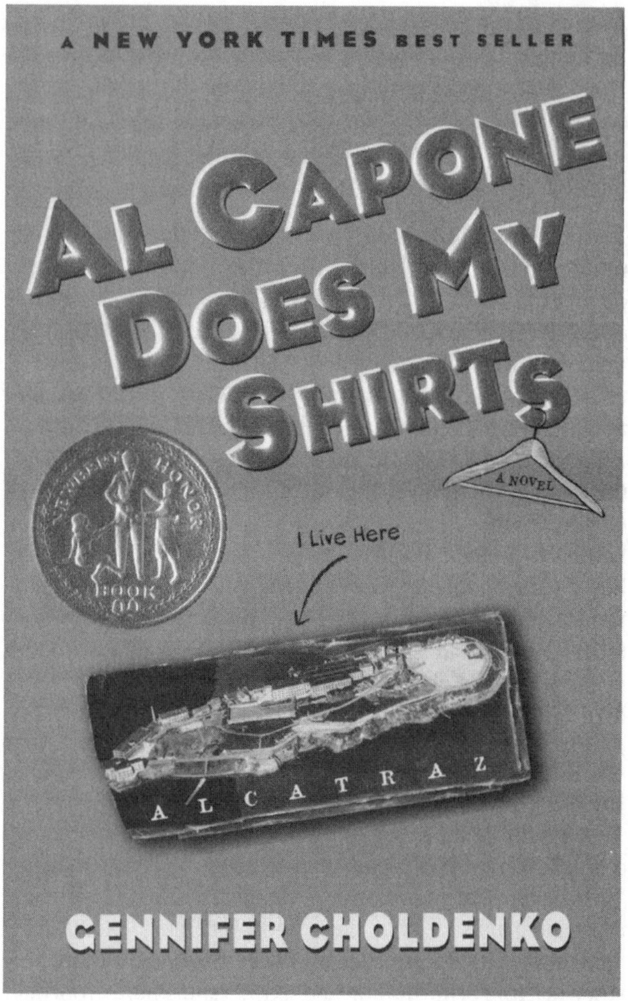


***Choldenko's award-winning novel* Al Capone Does My Shirts *finds a preteen living in very unusual—and very humorous—circumstances.*** (Puffin Books, 2004. Used by permission of Puffin Books, a division of Penguin Putnam Books for Young Readers.)

where the friendship between two seventh graders is explored. Overweight Kirsten is the daughter of a doctor, and her weight is the result of dealing with many stresses in her tension-fraught family. Walker, a scholarship student and one of only three African-American students at Mountain School, was raised by a single mom; he misses his old friends and does not share many of the experiences of his fellow students. In her novel, Choldenko tells her story through two alternating narratives: Kirstin's first-person drama as well as a third-person overview of Walker's struggle to fit in. According to *Horn Book* contributor Susan Dove Lempke, *If a Tree Falls at Lunch Period* "explores themes of racism and wealth with subtlety and insight," while a *Kirkus Reviews* writer noted that "Choldenko's talent for characters and conversation brings the two voices instantly to life." While the *Kirkus Reviews* critic suggested the novel's value in sparking "book-club or classroom discussion," *School Library Journal* critic Lillian Hecker cited *If a Tree Falls at Lunch Period* for its "sparkling characterization and touches of humor."

## Biographical and Critical Sources

*PERIODICALS*

*Booklist,* March 1, 1997, Ilene Cooper, review of *Moonstruck: The True Story of the Cow Who Jumped over the Moon,* p. 1169; April 15, 2001, Susan Dove Lempke, review of *Notes from a Liar and Her Dog,* p. 1550; February 1, 2004, Ed Sullivan, review of *Al Capone Does My Shirts,* p. 976.

*Horn Book,* March-April, 2005, "Newbery Medal," p. 235; September-October, 2006, Christine M. Heppermann, review of *How to Make Friends with a Giant,* p. 563; July-August, 2007, Susan Dove Lempke, review of *If a Tree Falls at Lunch Period.*

*Kirkus Reviews,* March 1, 2004, review of *Al Capone Does My Shirts,* p. 220; June 1, 2006, review of *How to Make Friends with a Giant,* p. 570; August 15, 2007, review of *If a Tree Falls at Lunch Period.*

*Kliatt,* March 1, 2004, review of *Al Capone Does My Shirts,* p. 220.

*Publishers Weekly,* February 10, 1997, review of *Moonstruck,* p. 83; May 14, 2001, review of *Notes from a Liar and Her Dog,* p. 82; July 7, 2003, review of *Notes from a Liar and Her Dog,* p. 74; February 2, 2004, review of *Al Capone Does My Shirts,* p. 78; August 7, 2006, review of *How to Make Friends with a Giant,* p. 58; July 15, 2007, review of *If a Tree Falls at Lunch Period,* p. 167.

*School Library Journal,* April, 1997, Patricia Pearl Doyle, review of *Moonstruck,* p. 91; April, 2001, Connie Tyrrell Burns, review of *Notes from a Liar and Her Dog,* p. 139; March, 2004, Miranda Doyle, review of *Al Capone Does My Shirts,* p. 203; July, 2006, Grace Oliff, review of *How to Make Friends with a Giant,* p. 70; August, 2007, Lillian Hecker, review of *If a Tree Falls at Lunch Period.*

*Times Educational Supplement,* August 6, 2004, Jan Mark, review of *The Rock and a Hard Case,* p. 25.

*Voice of Youth Advocates,* February, 2005, review of *Al Capone Does My Shirts,* p. 441.

*ONLINE*

*Gennifer Choldenko Home Page,* http://www.choldenko.com (August 1, 2007).

*Quercus Web site,* http://www.windingoak.com/quercus/ (July, 2006), interview with Choldenko.

* * *

# CIRRONE, Dorian

## Personal

Female; children: two. *Education:* Received B.A. and M.A.; coursework toward Ph.D.

## Addresses

*Home and office*—Davie, FL. *E-mail*—dcirrone@aol.com.

## Career

Writer.

## Awards, Honors

Amelia Bloomer Listee for Feminist Fiction, and New York Public Library Best Books for the Teen Age selection, both 2006, both for *Dancing in Red Shoes Will Kill You.*

## Writings

*Dancing in Red Shoes Will Kill You,* HarperCollins (New York, NY), 2005.

*The Missing Silver Dollar* ("Lindy Blues" mystery series), illustrated by Liza Woodruff, Marshall Cavendish (New York, NY), 2006.

*The Big Scoop* ("Lindy Blues" mystery series), illustrated by Liza Woodruff, Marshall Cavendish (New York, NY), 2006.

*Prom Kings and Drama Queens,* HarperCollins (New York, NY), 2008.

Poetry anthologized in *I Invited a Dragon to Dinner,* Philomel, 2002; and *Milk of Almonds: Italian American Women Writers on Food and Culture,* Feminist Press, 2003. Short fiction included in *Sports Shorts,* Darby Creek, 2005. Contributor of poetry and essays to periodicals, including *Parting Gifts, Paterson Literary Review,* and *FEMSPEC.*

## Sidelights

Before Dorian Cirrone decided to be a writer, she planned to become a ballet dancer and teacher. Although she remembers enjoying writing from third grade on, "the thought of actually being a writer never occurred to me," she wrote on her home page. While working as a dance instructor during college, Cirrone came up with the idea behind her first novel and filed it away for the future. Between the novel's inspiration and creation, she spent time as a journalist, attended graduate school, and also had two children. It was while working on an uncompleted Ph.D. dissertation that Cirrone came across the line, from a Margaret Atwood poem, that made the plot threads connect: "dancing in red shoes will kill you." That moment "everything fell together," Cirrone recalled to Cynthia Leitich-Smith for *Cynsations* online. "I wrote the first five chapters over a period of about nine months, and the rest a short time after." After passing the manuscript to an agent, Cirrone's novel *Dancing in Red Shoes Will Kill You* found a publisher in six weeks. Although she enjoys writing for all ages, Cirrone especially enjoys writing for children and young adults because of how much books meant to her as a child. She still remembers the love she had for the books *Ballet Shoes* and *Dancing Shoes* by Noel Streatfeild.

*Dancing in Red Shoes Will Kill You* is the story of sixteen-year-old Kayla, a ballet student who is denied a part she feels she deserves because her breasts are too large. While Kayla struggles with the decision whether or not to get breast-reduction surgery in order to continue in ballet, an issue of censorship over a feminist art project crops up at her high school. In addition, a picture of red dance slippers, accompanied by text that reads "Dancing in red shoes will kill you," begins appearing all over school. An allusion to the fairy tale "The Red Shoes"—a tale of pride that could also be read as a story about curtailing women's rights—drives the story and also helps Kayla reevaluate her own self-image. "Cirrone is an author to watch," concluded *School Library Journal* contributor Susan Riley after reading *Dancing in Red Shoes Will Kill You.* Noting that while the novelist's story contains humor, it also deals with serious issues involving censorship and feminism, Claire Rosser wrote in *Kliatt* that "it's terrific to have a cast of characters so talented, smart, and socially responsible." Jennifer Mattson, reviewing the novel for *Booklist,* commented that "Cirrone's debut novel convincingly portrays teens' repartee with the ever-fertile issues of gender politics and self-expression." A *Publishers Weekly* contributor maintained that "the mystery and its resolution . . . raise thought-provoking questions about cultural expectations for girls and women."

Turning her focus to slightly younger readers, Cirrone's "Lindy Blues" mystery series for middle-grade readers features an industrious fourth grader who produces her own neighborhood news show, taped on a camcorder by her brother. In *The Missing Silver Dollar* Lindy investigates the disappearance of a coin on a slow news day, while *The Big Scoop* finds her tackling the mystery of a disappearing ice cream shop. "Tuned-in kids will enjoy Lindy's inventiveness as she scoops some really local news," wrote a *Kirkus Reviews* contributor in an appraisal of *The Missing Silver Dollar.* A *Kirkus Reviews* contributor praised Lindy as "a spunky, likable heroine who thinks on her feet and truly embodies an entrepreneurial spirit."

*Prom Kings and Drama Queens* is the story of sixteen-year-old Emily Bennet, who has three desires: to go to the prom with Brian Harrington, to become editor of her school newspaper, and to take the world by storm. Emily gets close to Brian by becoming a matchmaker for his eccentric grandmother. She gets even closer to becoming editor when she and her journalistic competitor, Daniel Cummings, partner up to write an exposé of the excesses of prom. Emily's two worlds begin to collide when she must choose between going to the prom with Brian and keeping her word to Daniel to stage an alternative fundraiser prom.

***Dorian Cirrone's elementary-grade mystery* The Missing Silver Dollar, *features illustrations by Liza Woodruff.*** (Marshall Cavendish, 2006. Illustration © 2006 by Liza Woodruff. Reproduced by permission.)

## Biographical and Critical Sources


*PERIODICALS*

*Booklist,* January 1, 2005, Jennifer Mattson, review of *Dancing in Red Shoes Will Kill You,* p. 844; May, 2006, Hope Morrison, review of *The Missing Silver Dollar,* p. 394.

*Bulletin of the Center for Children's Books,* February, 2005, Deborah Stevenson, review of *Dancing in Red Shoes Will Kill You,* p. 247.

*Children's Bookwatch,* October, 2006, review of *The Big Scoop.*

*Kirkus Reviews,* January 1, 2005, review of *Dancing in Red Shoes Will Kill You,* p. 50; March 1, 2006, review of *The Missing Silver Dollar,* p. 227; September 15, 2006, review of *The Big Scoop,* p. 949.

*Kliatt,* January, 2005, Claire Rosser, review of *Dancing in Red Shoes Will Kill You,* p. 8.

*Publishers Weekly,* March 14, 2005, review of *Dancing in Red Shoes Will Kill You,* p. 68; March 6, 2006, review of *Dancing in Red Shoes Will Kill You,* p. 77.

*School Library Journal,* February, 2005, Susan Riley, review of *Dancing in Red Shoes Will Kill You,* p. 132; September, 2006, Rachael Vilmar, review of *The Missing Silver Dollar,* p. 164; October, 2006, Adrienne Furness, review of *The Big Scoop,* p. 103.

*Voice of Youth Advocates,* June, 2005, Cass Kvenild, review of *Dancing in Red Shoes Will Kill You,* p. 126.

*ONLINE*

*Cynsations,* http://cynthialeitichsmith.blogspot.com/ (September 22, 2005), Cynthia Leitich Smith, interview with Cirrone.

*Dorian Cirrone Home Page,* http://www.doriancirrone.com (August 6, 2007).

*HarperCollins Web site,* http://www.harpercollinschildrens.com/ (August 6, 2007), "Dorian Cirrone."


* * *

# CLARK, Joan 1934-

## Personal

Born October 12, 1934, in Liverpool, Nova Scotia, Canada; daughter of W.I. and Sally MacDonald; married Jack Clark (a geotechnical engineer), 1958; children: Tim, Tony, Sara. *Education:* Acadia University, B.A. (English), 1957; attended University of Alberta, 1960.

## Addresses

*Home*—6 Dover Place, St. John's, Newfoundland A1B 2P5, Canada. *Office*—c/o Writers' Union of Canada, 24 Ryerson Ave., Toronto M5T 2P3, Canada. *E-mail*—joan.clark@nl.rogers.com.

## Career

Writer. Teacher in Sussex, New Brunswick, Canada, 1957-58, Edmonton, Alberta, Canada, 1960-61, Calgary, Alberta, 1962-63, and Dartmouth, Nova Scotia, Canaa, 1969-70. Co-founder and co-editor of *Dandelion* (magazine), 1974-81.

## Member

Writers' Union of Canada, PEN International, Writers' Guild of Alberta (president, 1983-84), Writers' Alliance of Newfoundland and Labrador.

## Awards, Honors

Alberta Book Award, 1983; Alberta Culture Award, 1985; Canadian Library Association Book of the Year for Children runner-up, 1986, for *Wild Man of the Woods;* Canada Council "B" Award, 1988; Governor General's Fiction Award shortlist, 1989; W.H. Smith/Books Canada Award shortlist, 1989; Canadian Authors Association Award for Fiction, 1989, for *The Victory of*

*Geraldine Gull;* Geoffrey Bilson Award for Historical Fiction, Canadian Children's Book Centre, 1995, and Mr. Christie's Book Award, Christie Brown & Co., 1996, both for *The Dream Carvers;* honorary doctor of letters, Sir Wilfred Grenfell University, 1998; Vicky Metcalf Award, 1999; Geoffrey Bilson Award, 2003, for *The Word for Home;* IMPAC Award longlist, 2006, for *An Audience of Chairs.*

## Writings

*FOR YOUNG PEOPLE*

*Girl of the Rockies,* illustrated by Douglas Philips, Ryerson Press (Toronto, Ontario, Canada), 1968.
*Thomasina and the Trout Tree,* illustrated by Ingeborg Hiscox, Tundra Books (Toronto, Ontario, Canada), 1971.
*The Hand of Robin Squires,* illustrated by William Taylor and Mary Cserepy, Clarke, Irwin (Toronto, Ontario, Canada), 1977.
*The Leopard and the Lily* (fable), illustrated by Velma Foster, Oolichan Books (Lantzville, British Columbia, Canada), 1984.
*Wild Man of the Woods,* Penguin Books Canada (Markham, Ontario, Canada), 1985.
*The Moons of Madeleine,* Viking Kestrel (Markham, Ontario, Canada), 1987.
*The Dream Carvers,* Viking (Toronto, Ontario, Canada), 1995.
*Leaving Home,* illustrated by Cherrisa Bonine, Your Book, 1996.
*The Word for Home,* Viking (Toronto, Ontario, Canada), 2002.
*Snow,* illustrated by Kady McDonald Delton, Vintage Canada (Toronto, Ontario, Canada), 2006.

Author's books have been translated into Braille, as well as into several languages, including French, Italian, and German.

*OTHER*

*From a High Thin Wire* (short stories), NeWest Press (Edmonton, Ontario, Canada), 1982.
*The Victory of Geraldine Gull* (adult novel), Macmillan of Canada (Toronto, Ontario, Canada), 1988.
*Swimming toward the Light* (short stories), Macmillan of Canada (Toronto, Ontario, Canada), 1990.
*Eiriksdottir: A Tale of Dreams and Luck* (adult novel), Macmillan of Canada (Toronto, Ontario, Canada), 1994.
*Latitudes of Melt* (adult novel), Knopf (Toronto, Ontario, Canada), 2000, Soho (New York, NY), 2002.
*An Audience of Chairs* (adult novel), Knopf (Toronto, Ontario, Canada), 2005.

Work included in anthologies, including *CBC Anthology, Alberta Anthology, Doublebound, Glass Canyons, Calgary Stories,* and *Prairie Fire.* Contributor of short stories to periodicals, including *Canadian Fiction, Waves, Dalhousie Review, Saturday Night, Journal of Canadian Fiction,* and *Wascana Review.*

## Adaptations

Several books by Clark have been adapted for audiobook.

## Sidelights

Award-winning Canadian writer Joan Clark populates her historical fiction with young heroes and heroines who are confronted with realistic personal challenges as well as adventures of the kind often encountered in myth and folklore. While researching her novels, picture books, and short stories, Clark draws factual elements from the historical record and structures her story around them, integrating these facts so that they do not disrupt the momentum of the tale. As Clark explained in an essay for *Canadian Children's Literature,* she is "guided by the words that the Icelandic novelist, Halldor Laxness, wrote in *Christianity in Glacier,* '. . . the closer you try to approach history through facts, the deeper you sink into fiction.'"

Clark did not begin her work as a writer until after she married and moved from eastern Canada to Winisk, in northern Ontario. She began by writing poetry, and continued to do so after another move, this time to Calgary, in the prairies of Alberta. "I like the energy in the West," Clark explained in an interview with Nancy Robb for *Quill & Quire.* "It was very much the frontier, while the Maritimes were very traditional—and enclosed. Just walking down the street in Halifax, or any of the small towns I lived in, you can see the leaves leaning overhead, and you're kind of in a tunnel. It was almost like I was breaking out when I went west. Anything was possible."

After her move west, Clark moved into fiction. Her first book for young readers, *Girl of the Rockies,* is the story of a girl and a bear cub in the mountains. "I just naturally slid into the young girl's point of view," the author recalled to Robb. After scribbling out a rough draft, she bought a typewriter and finished the manuscript, sending it off to Ryerson Press, where it was quickly accepted. "I was so surprised when *Girl of the Rockies* was published, but I could see the glaring flaws," she added in her *Quill & Quire* interview. "That's when I knew I was serious about writing."

At the beginning of her career, Clark also raised her three children, and "there were long periods when I couldn't write at all," as she recalled to Robb. Like many working women, she sometimes found herself dealing with the tension created by the conflicts she felt between being a mother and being a writer. "I was always a bit too tired, and I thought that to be a good writer, I should do it full-time," she explained to Robb. "But I knew I had my priorities straight."

As her children grew older and more independent, Clark became more active in the publishing world. In 1974 she became a co-founding editor of *Dandelion,* a literary magazine to which she contributed for seven years. At the same time, her writing career flourished with such novels as *The Hand of Robin Squires, Wild Man of the Woods,* and *The Moons of Madeleine.* Based on historical accounts of searches for treasure on Oak Island off the coast of Nova Scotia between 1795 and 1971, *The Hand of Robin Squires* follows the adventures of nineteen-year-old Robin Squires as he travels from England to Oak Island with his uncle Edward after his father's death. Robin's father had invented a pump to use in mine shafts during flooding, and Edward wants his nephew to construct one of these, to be used in conjunction with a huge vault on Oak Island where the man plans to hide the Spanish treasure he seized during the battle of Vigo Bay. Robin's "first-person narration invites immediate reader-identification and his blend of visual detail, conversations, and action creates a sense of time present," maintained John Smallbridge in *Canadian Children's Literature.* Smallbridge added that "each chapter advances the plot significantly and contains sufficient foreshadowing and suspense to impel the reader to finish the book 'at one sitting.'"

*Wild Man of the Woods* and *The Moons of Madeleine* were originally conceived as one story. However, in recognizing how differently boys and girls handle conflict, Clark opted to break the tale into two separate books which focus on cousins who travel to each other's homes for the summer. In *Wild Man of the Woods* Stephen leaves Calgary to visit his aunt, uncle, and cousin Louie in the Rocky Mountain town of Inverary. Madeleine, Louie's sister, visits Stephen's family in Calgary, and her experiences are detailed in *The Moons of Madeleine.* For both children, the summer is filled with experiences that cause them to gain in maturity. Stephen deals with being bullied through the use of a mythical mask which brings about a violent result. Madeleine, on the other hand, copes with her beloved grandmother's illness, as well as with her own confused adolescent feelings, during an escape to the cave of the First Woman and an introduction to the continuity of the circle of life. In a *Canadian Children's Literature Annual* review of both *Wild Man of the Woods* and *The Moons of Madeleine,* Barbara Michasiw pointed out that Clark's coming-of-age novels "are self-contained, and the truths the protagonists discover are profoundly different; but each complements the other." "For both cousins," the critic added, "the month will bring experience, testing, a symbolic death, and a rebirth into a new stage of maturity."

Taking readers further back in time, *The Dream Carvers* centers around the kidnapping of fourteen-year-old Thrand as the teen accompanies his father from their Greenland home to Leif Ericsson's colony on the northern tip of Newfoundland. Captured by the Osweet people to replace a young man of the tribe who was killed by the Greenlanders, Thrand first tries to escape, but eventually adapts to his new culture and comes to respect the traditions and lifestyle of the Osweet. "On the whole, Clark uses and invents from her source material with skill and tact," observed Frances Frazer in the *Canadian Children's Literature Annual.* Describing *The Dream Carvers* as "an exciting adventure story," *Quill & Quire* contributor Barbara Greenwood cited Clark's use of "language that is poetic and reflective."

In Clark's middle-grade novel *The Word for Home,* fourteen-year-old Sadie Morin attempts to provide her younger sister Flora with a sense of family after the girls' mother dies and their widowed geologist father leaves them in Mrs. Hatch's boarding house in 1920s Newfoundland. As it becomes clear that Mr. Morin will not be returning from his prospecting adventure, Mrs. Hatch becomes increasingly severe in her treatment of the sisters. Fortunately, Sadie develops several close and empowering friendships at school and also gains academic recognition. When the decision is made to transfer the sisters to a local orphanage, Sadie is able to deal with the circumstances with emotional clarity and confidence. In addition to noting the novel's value as a window into life as it was lived in post-World War I Newfoundland, *Resource Links* reviewer Victoria Pennell added that *The Word for Home* can be "read and enjoyed for the wonderful story it tells."

Geared for younger readers, Clark's picture book *Snow* transports readers to a winter in the north, where a boy named Sammy watches the snow pile up around his family's house every day for almost a month. Surveying the scene from the roof of his house each day as the deep snows melt, Sammy allows his imagination to conjure up a magical world under the fields of rising snow, his daydreams brought to life in illustrations by Kady MacDonald Denton. In *Resource Links,* Isobel Lang described *Snow* as "lyrical, imaginative and repetitive, full of fun and dreams," and Maryann H. Owen noted that Denton's highly textured, mixed-media illustrations "deftly reveal the various possibilities that Sammy ponders."

While *Girl of the Rockies* marked the start of Clark's career as a respected writer for young readers, the author has also penned novels and short stories for adults, and many of her stories have appeared in magazines and anthologies. Sharing its setting with Clark's young-adult novel *The Dream Carvers,* the historical novel *Eiriksdottir: A Tale of Dreams and Luck* focuses on Freydis Eiriksdottir, the illegitimate daughter of Eirik the Red. In 1015 Freydis organizes an expedition to Leifsbudir, the Viking outpost in Newfoundland that has been established by her brother, Leif Eiriksson. Determined that luck and good fortune will be hers, Freydis endures many hardships during her journey, and these hardships continue even after she settles in her new home. "With the characters and conditions of the voyage very firmly established, Clark diversifies both plot and narrative, bringing the adventure to life," maintained Kathleen Hickey in *Quill & Quire.* Eva Tihanyi, in a review of the novel for *Books in Canada,* concluded that *Eiriksdottir* "is a meditation on the nature of the human spirit, its courage and treachery, its quest for material wealth and sensory adventure, but above all, its quest for meaning of its own self."

Another adult novel, *Latitudes of Melt,* also takes Newfoundland as its setting, but moves the action forward to the first decades of the twentieth century. As the story starts, a fisherman discovers an abandoned infant nestled in a basket left on the ice. Named Aurora, the child is taken in and raised by the fisherman's family. She grows up to marry Tom, a lighthouse keeper, and raise two children. The marriage of Aurora and Tom is the focus of the first part of the story, while the personal travails of their grown son and daughter figure prominently in successive chapters of Clark's multigenerational novel.The action of *Latitudes of Melt,* which also moves from present to past and from Canada to Ireland as Aurora's granddaughter Sheila searches for her grandmother's roots. Describing Clark's story as "as subtle as the working of water on ice," *Booklist* contributor Neal Wyatt added that *Latitudes of Melt* "exposes the daily struggle to build a life and cope with its inevitable dissolution." In *Publishers Weekly,* a critic concluded that "Aurora's story will please those with an interest in northerly lands and Titanic mythmaking."

Clark's penchant for historical fiction is something the author herself cannot fully explain. "While I am conceiving a story, be it historical or not, I seldom understand why I am attracted to it," she commented in *Canadian Children's Literature.* "Part of the process of writing the story is figuring out the attraction. I like to think this adds to the mysteriousness, the indefinable quality of a story, that which helps lift it from the page. The reason for writing any story, amorphous as the initial impulse might be, is simply that it is there. The fact that the impulse (or, if you like, inspiration) comes from the past makes it no less real."

## Biographical and Critical Sources

*PERIODICALS*

*Booklist,* January 1, 2002, Neal Wyatt, review of *Latitudes of Melt,* p. 806.

*Books in Canada,* December, 1985; September, 1994, Eva Tihanyi, "Heroic Quests," pp. 48-49.

*Bulletin of the Center for Children's Books,* November, 2006, Deborah Stevenson, review of *Snow,* p. 118.

*Canadian Children's Literature Annual,* number 14, 1979, John Smallbridge, "Two Mysteries: Pirate Treasure and Wisdom," pp. 73-75; number 50, 1988, Barbara Michasiw, review of *Wild Man of the Woods* and *The Moons of Madeleine,* pp. 86-87; winter, 1991, pp. 238-240; number 83, 1996, Joan Clark, "What Is History?," pp. 78-81; winter, 1995, Frances Frazer, review of *The Dream Carvers,* p. 80.

*Growing Point,* January, 1980, pp. 3619-3623.

*Junior Bookshelf,* April, 1980, p. 79.

*Kirkus Reviews,* December 1, 2001, review of *Latitudes of Melt,* p. 1624; August 15, 2006, review of *Snow,* p. 837.

*Library Journal,* January, 2002, Joshua Cohen, review of *Latitudes of Melt,* p. 149.

*Maclean's,* June 27, 1988, pp. 52-53.

*Publishers Weekly,* January 28, 2002, review of *Latitudes of Melt,* p. 272.

*Quill & Quire,* December, 1985, p. 30; December, 1986, Nancy Robb, interview with Clark, pp. 12-13; May, 1988, p. 26; June, 1990, p. 30. May, 1994, Kathleen Hickey, review of *Eiriksdottir: A Tale of Dreams and Luck,* pp. 22-23; March, 1995, Barbara Greenwood, review of *The Dream Carvers,* p. 75.

*School Library Journal,* September, 1986, p. 132; September, 2006, Maryann H. Owen, review of *Snow,* p. 164.

*Resource Links,* February, 2002, Victoria Pennell, review of *The Word for Home,* p. 9; October, 2005, review of *The Hand of Robin Squires,* p. 31; November, 2006, Deborah Stevenson, review of *Snow,* p.118; February, 2007, Isobel Lang, review of *Snow,* p. 2.*

* * *

# CLEMENT, Janet

## Personal

Born in Washington, DC; children: Michael, Bradley, Robert. *Education:* Florida State University, B.S. (education). *Hobbies and other interests:* Scrap booking, genealogy research.

## Addresses

*Home and office*—Clearwater, FL. *E-mail*—clement-rodriguez@janet-and-al.com.

## Career

Author. Temple Ahavat Shalom, Palm Harbor, FL, early childhood director, 1987-96; Coordinated Child Care of Pinellas, Inc., provider consultant, 2000—. Member, Pinellas Advocates for Children and Families.

## Member

Society of Children's Book Writers and Illustrators.

## Writings

*Jewish Alphabet,* illustrated by Albert G. Rodriguez, Pelican Publishing (Gretna, LA), 2006.

## Sidelights

Janet Clement's goals as a writer are to share her love of reading, promote early literacy, and through her Judaic children's books foster appreciation of her Jewish

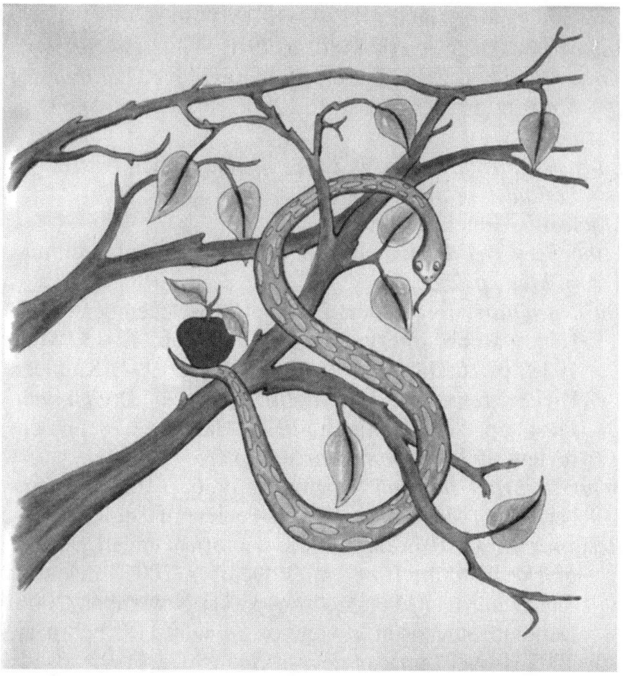

***Janet Clement draws on her Jewish heritage to create an unusual abecedarium in* Jewish Alphabet, *featuring artwork by Albert G. Rodriguez.*** (Illustration © 2006 by Janet Clement and Albert G. Rodriguez. Reproduced by permission.)

faith. In her debut book *Jewish Alphabet,* which features illustrations by Clement's fiancée, Albert G. Rodriguez, she utilizes the letters of the Anglo alphabet to introduce young readers to Jewish culture. In addition to being a children's book author, Clement offers training and technical assistance through her position as a provider consultant for Pinellas County's central agency for child care to providers of child care serving children from infancy through school age.

*Jewish Alphabet* describes the customs and traditions of Jewish culture. For instance, Clement uses the letter "K" to describe "Kiddush, a prayer over wine" and the letter "L" to detail "latkes fried 'til crisp and yummy." The text of *Jewish Alphabet* uses both rhyming verse and prose to elaborate on some of the Jewish symbols and concepts. Although a *Kirkus Reviews* critic described the book as a "hodgepodge of information," a *Children's Bookwatch* online reviewer praised *Jewish Alphabet* as a work for young readers that "celebrates aspects of Jewish religion and culture."

Clement told *SATA:* "I especially love picture books. Picture books allow enormous opportunity for both the writer and the illustrator to create a work that will enable children to develop crucial literacy skills. Vocabulary acquisition in the early years has significant implications and connection to later school success."

Clement usually envisions her concept as an illustrated work before she even begins to sit down to write. "Usually the writing and the illustration of a picture book is a very separate experience," she explained. "Manuscripts are often fully edited and completed before an illustrator is ever assigned to a project. A good illustrator must be more than just a good artist: he or she must be able to grasp the vision of the writer." Discussing her collaboration with Rodriguez, Clement noted: "Not having the capability to illustrate my own stories, I am so fortunate to be able to work collaboratively with Al during the entire writing process as my manuscripts take shape. His artistic talent and the ability to illustrate are true gifts." The couple continue working on children's-book projects, both Judaic and secular.

## Biographical and Critical Sources

*BOOKS*

Clement, Janet, *Jewish Alphabet,* Pelican Publishing (Gretna, LA), 2006.

*PERIODICALS*

*Kirkus Reviews,* September 15, 2006, review of *Jewish Alphabet,* p. 949.

*School Library Journal,* December, 2006, Heidi Estrin, review of *Jewish Alphabet,* p. 120.

*ONLINE*

*Children's Book Watch Online,* http://www.midwestbookreview.com/ (February, 2007), review of *Jewish Alphabet.*

*Janet Clement Home Page,* http://www.janet-and-al.com (August 9, 2007).

*Pelican Publishing Web site,* http://www.pelicanpub.com/ (August 9, 2007), "Janet Clement and Albert G. Rodriguez."

* * *

# COLLIER, Kristi

## Personal

Born in New Castle, IN. *Education:* Indiana University—Bloomington, B.A., M.S. *Hobbies and other interests:* Running, cheering her daughter's sports teams, gardening, hunting for unicorns.

## Addresses

*Home and office*—Louisville, KY. *E-mail*—readermail@collierbooks.com.

## Career

Writer, educator, and mental-health and school counselor.

## Awards, Honors

Josette Frank Award for Fiction, Best Children's Book of the Year citation, *Smithsonian,* and International Reading Association/Children's Book Council Notable Book designation, all 2002, all for *Jericho Walls.*

## Writings

*Jericho Walls,* Henry Holt (New York, NY), 2002.
*Throwing Stones,* Henry Holt (New York, NY), 2006.

## Sidelights

Becoming a writer was third on the list of career goals for Kristi Collier while growing up. "I desperately wanted to become the Queen of Narnia," the young-adult novelist and educator wrote on her home page, referencing C.S. Lewis's classic "Chronicles of Narnia" novel series. "When it didn't look like that was going to happen, I considered becoming a hobbit. I decided to become a writer as a last resort." Collier wrote a puppet play in fifth grade, and wrote her first novel (unpublished) between fifth and sixth grade. Getting one of her works published soon became her biggest challenge. "I needed a great deal of practice and wrote nine never-to-be-published novels . . . and many, many freelance magazine articles before starting work on my first book," she explained. That first book, *Jericho Walls,* earned Collier critical praise as well as the Josette Frank Award for Fiction.

In *Jericho Walls,* readers are transported to the 1950s, where Josephine struggles to find a place to fit in while conforming to her preacher father's expectations for her. As Josephine encounters the unwritten race rules practiced in her southern community, she decides that there are things more important than fitting in. "Jo's struggle for individualism and her love of adventure will echo readers' own feelings," predicted *School Library Journal* contributor Susan Cooley, and a *Kirkus Reviews* contributor wrote that *Jericho Walls* "breathes life into an important era in US history." According to a *Publishers Weekly* "Collier creates a compelling narrative voice in Jo Clawson." While noting the story might seem didactic at times, Anne O'Malley wrote in *Booklist* that "readers will care about Jo and the tough choices she faces." Betty Carter explained in *Horn Book* that although Collier's story is somewhat predictable, "Jo's rejection of the weight of racism" illuminates the book's "realistic, but seldom articulated, Southern setting."

*Throwing Stones* is set in a different era of U.S. history. The year is 1923, and Andy, a promising high school basketball player, joins his school's varsity team. Andy's place on the team reminds him of his brother, a star basketball player who died while fighting during World War I. While Andy struggles with his grief over losing his brother, he also competes with a fellow team member for the star position as well as the affection of a certain girl. Andy ends up getting sidelined after his effort to impress her results in an accident, but this tragedy proves to be a blessing in disguise when the teen discovers an aptitude for journalism. While noting that plot and subplots in *Throwing Stones* might cause confusion, *Booklist* contributor Carolyn Phelan felt that "Collier weaves them into an involving novel with a full, varied cast of convincing characters." Also noting the novel's character development, Myrna Marler wrote in *Kliatt* that "Andy matures from a somewhat flawed protagonist to a more mature, generous hero."

## Biographical and Critical Sources

*PERIODICALS*

*Booklist,* April 1, 2002, Anne O'Malley, review of *Jericho Walls,* p. 1318; September 1, 2006, Carolyn Phelan, review of *Throwing Stones,* p. 115.
*Bulletin of the Center for Children's Books,* September, 2002, review of *Jericho Walls,* p. 10.
*Horn Book,* July-August, 2002, Betty Carter, review of *Jericho Walls,* p. 456.
*Kirkus Reviews,* April 15, 2002, review of *Jericho Walls,* p. 564; September 15, 2006, review of *Throwing Stones,* p. 949.
*Kliatt,* November, 2006, Myrna Marler, review of *Throwing Stones,* p. 6.
*Publishers Weekly,* April 15, 2002, review of *Jericho Walls,* p. 65.
*School Library Journal,* April, 2002, Susan Cooley, review of *Jericho Walls,* p. 142; November, 2006, M. Heather Campbell, review of *Throwing Stones,* p. 132.
*Voice of Youth Advocates,* June, 2002, review of *Jericho Walls,* p. 115.

*ONLINE*

*Kristi Collier Home Page,* http://www.collierbooks.com (August 6, 2007).

* * *

# COTE, Nancy

## Personal

Married; husband's name Mike; children: Melissa, Kate, John. *Education:* University of Massachusetts—Dartmouth, B.F.A. (painting).

## Addresses

*Home and office*—31 Avon St., Somerset, MA 02726. *E-mail*—nancycote@comcast.net.

## Career

Artist and illustrator. Also teaches at Rhode Island School of Design. Speaker at conferences. *Exhibitions:* Work included in Society of Illustrators Original Art '98 exhibit at Museum of American Illustration, and in group illustration exhibits throughout southeastern MA and RI.

## Member

Society of Children's Book Writers and Illustrators, Freelance Artists Network.

*Nancy Cote* (Courtesy of Nancy Cote.)

## Awards, Honors

Children's Book Council/International Reading Association (CBC/IRA) Notable Children's Trade Book designation, 1995, for *Fireflies, Peach Pies, and Lullabies; Smithsonian* Notable Book for Children designation, Florida Reading Association Children's Book Award, both 1997, both for *The Borrowed Hanukkah Latkes;* Society of School Librarians International Honor Book designation, and American Booksellers Association Pick-of-the-List designation, both 1998, both for *The Can-Do Thanksgiving;* Oppenheim Toy Portfolio Gold Seal Award, 2000, for *When I Feel Angry;* Oppenheim Toy Portfolio Gold Seal Award, and Sidney Taylor Notable Book designation, both 2004, both for *Mrs. Greenberg's Messy Hanukkah.*

## Writings

*SELF-ILLUSTRATED*

*Palm Trees,* Four Winds Press (New York, NY), 1993.
*Flip-flops,* Albert Whitman (Morton Grove, IL), 1998.
*It Feels like Snow!,* Boyds Mills Press (Honesdale, PA), 2003.
*It's All about Me!,* G.P. Putnam's Sons (New York, NY), 2005.
*Jackson's Blanket,* G.P. Putnam's Sons (New York, NY), 2008.

*ILLUSTRATOR*

Sharon Phillips Denslow, *Woollybear Good-bye,* Four Winds Press (New York, NY), 1994.
Amy Hest, *Ruby's Storm,* Four Winds Press (New York, NY), 1994.
Virginia Kroll, *Fireflies, Peach Pies, and Lullabies,* Simon & Schuster (New York, NY) 1995.
Linda Glaser, *The Borrowed Hanukkah Latkes,* Albert Whitman (Morton Grove, IL), 1997.
Marion Hess Pomeranc, *The Can-do Thanksgiving,* Albert Whitman (Morton Grove, IL), 1998.
Abby Levine, *Gretchen Groundhog, It's Your Day!,* Albert Whitman (Morton Grove, IL), 1998.
Sarah Marwil Lamstein, *I Like Your Buttons!,* Albert Whitman (Morton Grove, IL), 1999.
Cornelia Maude Spelman, *When I Feel Angry,* Albert Whitman (Morton Grove, IL), 2000.
Leslie Kimmelman, *Round the Turkey: A Grateful Thanksgiving,* Albert Whitman (Morton Grove, IL), 2002.
Leslie Kimmelman, *Happy Fourth of July, Jenny Sweeney!,* Albert Whitman (Morton Grove, IL), 2003.
Linda Glaser, *Mrs. Greenberg's Messy Hanukkah,* Albert Whitman (Morton Grove, IL), 2004.
Virginia Kroll, *Jason Takes Responsibility,* Albert Whitman (Morton Grove, IL), 2005.
Pat Brisson, *Tap-Dance Fever,* Boyds Mills Press (Honesdale, PA), 2005.
Teresa Bateman, *Hamster Camp: How Harry Got Fit,* Albert Whitman (Morton Grove, IL), 2005.
Virginia Kroll, *Honest Ashley,* Albert Whitman (Morton Grove, IL), 2006.
Lori Anne Ries, *Mrs. Fickle's Pickles,* Boyds Mills Press (Honesdale, PA), 2006.
Virginia Kroll, *Good Neighbor Nicholas,* Albert Whitman (Morton Grove, IL), 2006.
Virginia Kroll, *Good Citizen Sarah,* Albert Whitman (Morton Grove, IL), 2007.
Virginia Kroll, *Makayla Cares about Others,* Albert Whitman (Morton Grove, IL), 2007.
Lacy Finn Borgo, *Big Mama's Baby,* Boyds Mills Press (Honesdale, PA), 2007.

Also illustrator of numerous educational books, including *The Bossy Pig* by Marie Brown, *Going the Right Way* by Meish Goldish, *Pink Milk* by Barbara A. Donovan, *Corn Bread for Everyone!* by Mary Atkinson, and *Joy's Trip to the Toy Shop* by Debbie O'Brien.

## Sidelights

Illustrator and author Nancy Cote has provided the artwork for picture books by such award-winning writers as Virginia Kroll and Cornelia Maude Spelman. She has also published a number of self-illustrated works, among them the critically acclaimed *It's All about Me!* Cote developed an interest in drawing at an early age, and she later majored in painting at the University of Massachusetts—Dartmouth. After starting a family, she discovered the world of children's literature and began working in that medium. On her home page, Cote explained: "I've never lost the emotional ties to my own childhood and still feel very connected to that spirit."

***Cote's colorful images bring to life a budding friendship in Sarah Marwil Lamstein's picture book* I Like Your Buttons!** (Illustration © 1999 by Nancy Cote. Reproduced by permission.)

In Cote's debut work, *Palm Trees,* a young African-American girl named Millie spends the morning happily styling her unruly mop of hair. When good friend Renee compares Millie's new hairdo to a pair of palm trees, Millie begins to sulk, but her mood brightens as the friends begin experimenting with even-more outrageous coiffures. "Cote's dexterous, frisky pastels display sunny facial expressions and carefree gestures," a *Publishers Weekly* contributor remarked. *Flip-flops,* another self-illustrated title by Cote, centers on Penny, a young girl who stubbornly resists a trip to the beach, then loses one of her cherished sandals. With the help of some new friends, Penny finds several ways to enjoy the day, using her lone flip-flop as a shovel and a boat. According to *Booklist* contributor Ilene Cooper, Cote's "art executed in gouache and colored pencil is lively and upbeat."

An elderly woman with an uncanny ability to predict the weather is the subject of *It Feels like Snow!,* Cote's third solo effort. Though Alice realizes that her throbbing bones and tingling nose mean bad weather is on its way, her neighbors continually dismiss the warning signs. When a blizzard hits, though, Alice invites the apologetic crowd to her home to relax in front of a warm fire. "The story line is fresh and original with a repetitive structure that works," observed Martha Topol in a review of *It Feels like Snow!* for *School Library Journal.* Cote's "cartoony illustrations give Alice an eager smile, whimsical wardrobe . . . and a menagerie of pets," concluded a reviewer in *Publishers Weekly.*

Another self-illustrated work, *It's All about Me!* concerns a young boy's rocky adjustment to his new baby brother. Cote's portrait "of a loving, caring family is told through simple rhyming language and lively gouache and watercolor-pencil artwork," observed *School Library Journal* critic Linda Staskus. The book was also praised as "a wonderfully sweet look at the challenges and benefits of adding children to the family" by a *Kirkus Reviews* contributor.

In addition to her self-illustrated works, Cote has illustrated more than twenty educational and trade books. *When I Feel Angry,* written by Cornelia Maude Spelman, helps early readers deal with often frustrating situations. According to *School Library Journal* critic Joy Fleishhacker, "Cote's vibrant paintings skillfully convey the feelings of the characters and add significantly to the child appeal." One of several titles Cote has illustrated for the "The Way I Act" series by Virginia Kroll, *Honest Ashley* focuses on a procrastinator who is tempted to cheat on a school assignment. In this work, "Cote's acrylic paintings ably illustrate" the tale, according to *Booklist* reviewer Kathy Broderick.

Author Linda Glaser collaborated with Cote on two works about a popular Jewish holiday. In *The Borrowed Hanukkah Latkes,* a young girl named Rachel convinces her kindly elderly neighbor, Mrs. Greenburg, to join Rachel's family for dinner. *Booklist* contributor Carolyn Phelan wrote of this work that Cote's "bright, jovial illustrations move to a rhythm of their own, delighting with repeated lines and patterns." In an award=winning sequel, *Mrs. Greenberg's Messy Hanukkah,* Rachel tries to help her neighbor prepare a special dinner, with disastrous results. "Mixed-media folksy paintings of wintry scenes often with blue-toned backdrops illustrate the humorous and often predictable predicaments Rachel creates," a *Kirkus Reviews* critic noted.

In Pat Brisson's tall tale *Tap-Dance Fever,* Annabelle Applegate drives the people of Fiddler's Creek crazy with her nonstop tapping, until her dancing helps tame the town's rattlesnakes. Phelan praised Cote's watercolor-and-gouache illustrations for this work, noting that the illustrator's contribution "is varied in composition, exaggerated in characterization, and exuberant in spirit." Teresa Bateman's *Hamster Camp: How Harry Got Fit,* in which a junk-food junkie is transformed into a hamster and learns the benefits of exercise and good eating habits, also features "Cote's friendly color illustrations," which "add to the positive message of this story," according to Staskus.

Cote told *SATA:* "Ever since I can remember, I have been either drawing or late for something. I find myself constantly being sidetracked by the infinite beauty around me. I've always needed to see, feel, and breathe

***Cote takes on the role of both author and illustrator in the child-centered picture book* It's All about Me!** (Illustration © 2005 by Nancy Cote. Reproduced by permission of G.P. Putnam's Sons, a division of Penguin Putnam Books for Young Readers.)

***Cote's art pairs well with Leslie Kimmelman's engaging story in the 2003 picture book* Happy 4th of July, Jenny Sweeney!** (Albert Whitman & Company, 2003. Illustration © 2003 by Nancy Cote. All rights reserved. Reproduced by permission.)

in everything in sight which keeps me moving at a rather slow pace. I never realized how sense-oriented I was until I became an adult and part of a very fast-paced world. Nevertheless, I've managed to continue to absorb everything in my path.

"I had never thought about writing or illustrating children's books while growing up. It was when I had a family of my own that I discovered this world of immense creative possibility. I literally read thousands of books to my children and was convinced that I wanted to express myself through this medium. Having majored in painting in college it was a natural progression for me to tie the two life experiences together. As a mom, I had endless inspiration and insight into the world of children. In many ways I've never lost the emotional ties to my own childhood and feel very connected to these sensations. Working as a full-time author/illustrator just reinforces my conviction that you can achieve any goal that you have 'even though you may get distracted along the way!'"

## Biographical and Critical Sources

*PERIODICALS*

*Booklist,* March 1, 1994, Kay Weisman, review of *Ruby's Storm,* p. 1270; December 15, 1995, Susan Dove Lempke, review of *Fireflies, Peach Pies, and Lullabies,* p. 708; September 1, 1997, Carolyn Phelan, review of *The Borrowed Hanukkah Latkes,* p. 139; May 15, 1998, Ilene Cooper, review of *Flip-flops,* p. 1631; November 1, 1998, Ilene Cooper, review of *The Can-do Thanksgiving,* p. 505; December 1, 1998, Ilene Cooper, review of *Gretchen Groundhog, It's Your Day!,* p. 671; August, 1999, Ilene Cooper, review of *I Like Your Buttons!,* p. 2064; March 15, 2000, Marta Segal, review of *When I Feel Angry,* p. 1390; September 15, 2002, Helen Rosenberg, review of *Round the Turkey: A Grateful Thanksgiving,* p. 245; May 15, 2003, Karen Hutt, review of *Happy Fourth of July, Jenny Sweeney!,* p. 1672; September 15, 2004, Stephanie Zvirin, review of *Mrs. Greenberg's Messy*

*Hanukkah,* p. 249; March 1, 2005, Carolyn Phelan, review of *Tap-Dance Fever,* p. 1201; May 15, 2005, Julie Cummins, review of *Hamster Camp: How Harry Got Fit,* p. 1662; December 15, 2005, Gillian Engberg, review of *It's All about Me!,* p. 49; June 1, 2006, Kathy Broderick, review of *Honest Ashley,* p. 87.

*Bulletin of the Center for Children's Books,* April, 1999, review of *I Like Your Buttons!,* p. 284.

*Childhood Education,* winter, 2003, Liane Troy, review of *It Feels like Snow!,* p. 91.

*Horn Book,* September-October, 1993, Ellen Fader, review of *Palm Trees,* p. 633; Jeannine M. Chapman, review of *Mrs. Greenberg's Messy Hanukkah,* p. 659.

*Kirkus Reviews,* July 15, 2002, review of *Round the Turkey,* p. 1035; March 15, 2003, review of *Happy Fourth of July, Jenny Sweeney!,* p. 470; November 1, 2004, review of *Mrs. Greenberg's Messy Hanukkah,* p. 1049; September 15, 2005, review of *It's All about Me!,* p. 1023; October 15, 2006, review of *Mrs. Fickle's Pickles,* p. 1078.

*Publishers Weekly,* March 29, 1993, review of *Palm Trees,* p. 54; October 6, 1997, review of *The Borrowed Hanukkah Latkes,* p. 52; September 28, 1998, review of *The Can-do Thanksgiving,* p. 50; November 23, 1998, review of *Gretchen Groundhog, It's Your Day!,* p. 66; November 17, 2003, review of *It Feels like Snow!,* p. 64;

*School Library Journal,* December, 1994, Ruth Semrau, review of *Woollybear Good-bye,* p. 73; October, 1997, Jane Marino, review of *The Borrowed Hanukkah Latkes,* p. 38; July, 1998, Lisa Falk, review of *Flip-flops,* p. 72; September, 1998, Anne Knickerbocker, review of *The Can-do Thanksgiving,* p. 179; January, 1999, Sally R. Dow, review of *Gretchen Groundhog, It's Your Day!,* p. 97; December, 1999, Kimberlie Monteforte, review of *Happy Fourth of July, Jenny Sweeney!,* p. 102; April, 2000, Joy Fleishhacker, review of *When I Feel Angry,* p. 115; September, 2002, Genevieve Gallagher, review of *Round the Turkey,* p. 195; July, 2003, Linda M. Kenton, review of *Happy Fourth of July, Jenny Sweeney!,* p. 100; November, 2003, Martha Topol, review of *It Feels like Snow!,* p. 91; March, 2005, Be Astengo, review of *Tap-Dance Fever,* p. 168; July, 2005, Linda Staskus, review of *Harry Hamster,* p. 64; December, 2005, Linda Staskus, review of *It's All about Me!,* p. 107; January, 2006, Sandra Welzenbach, review of *Jason Takes Responsibility,* p. 104; March, 2006, Maura Bresnahan, review of *Honest Ashley,* p. 194.

*ONLINE*

*Freelance Artists Network Web site,* http://www.freelanceartistsnetwork.com/ (July 20, 2007), "Nancy Cote."

*Nancy Cote Home Page,* http://www.nancycote.com (July 20, 2007).

* * *

## CRAVATH, Lynne Avril
## See CRAVATH, Lynne W.

## CRAVATH, Lynne W. 1951-
## (Lynne Avril, Lynne Avril Cravath)

### Personal

Born March 6, 1951, in Miles City, MT; daughter of Walter B. and Mary Lou Woodcock; married Jay Cravath (a teacher), September 7, 1975; children: Chloe, Jeff. *Education:* University of Montana, B.A. (art; with high honors). *Politics:* Democrat. *Religion:* Episcopalian.

### Addresses

*Home and office*—10438 S. 45th Place, Phoenix, AZ 85044-1139. *Agent*—Bernadette Szost, Portfolio Solutions, 136 Jameson Hill Rd., Clinton Corners, NY 12514. *E-mail*—lynneavril@cox.net.

### Career

Children's book illustrator. Chico Chism Chicago Blues Band, bass player. *Exhibitions:* Work exhibited at Paulina Miller Studio, Phoenix, AZ; and Society of Illustrators, New York, NY.

### Member

Society of Children's Book Writers and Illustrators.

### Awards, Honors

Society of School Librarians International Honor Book designation, for *Love, Ruby Valentine;* Children's Book Council honor; Oppenheim Toy Portfolio designation.

### Illustrator

Debbie Driscoll, *Three Two One Day,* Simon and Schuster (New York, NY), 1994.

Tony Geiss, *My Little Teddy Bear: A Jewelry Book,* Random House (New York, NY), 1994.

Natalie Standiford, *Brave Maddie Egg,* Random House (New York, NY), 1995.

Margaret Yatsevitch Phinney, *Will You Play with Us?,* Mondo (Greenvale, NY), 1995.

Ellen Weiss and Mel Friedman, *The Plug at the Bottom of the Lake, and Other Wacky Camp Stories,* HarperCollins (New York, NY), 1996.

Ellen Weiss and Mel Friedman, *The Flying Substitute,* HarperCollins (New York, NY), 1996.

Allan Trusell-Cullen, *No Singing Today,* Mondo (Greenvale, NY), 1996.

Linda Tracey Brandon, *The Little Flower Girl,* Random House (New York, NY), 1997.

Alice Lyne, *A, My Name Is . . . ,* Whispering Coyote Press (Boston, MA), 1997.

*A Poem a Day* (poetry anthology), Scholastic (New York, NY), 1997.

JoAnn Vandine, *Play Ball,* Mondo (Greenvale, NY), 1997.

Sharon Dennis Wyeth, *Tomboy Trouble,* Random House (New York, NY), 1998.

Patricia Reilly Giff, *Kidnap at the Catfish Café* (first book in "Minnie and Max" series), Viking (New York, NY), 1998.

Patricia Reilly Giff, *Mary Moon Is Missing* (second book in "Minnie and Max" series), Viking (New York, NY), 1998.

Stuart J. Murphy, *The Penny Pot,* HarperCollins (New York, NY), 1998.

Sheila Kelly Welch, *Little Prince Know-It-All,* Golden Books (New York, NY), 1998.

*Over the River and Through the Wood* (musical board book), HarperCollins (New York, NY), 1998.

Margaret Holtschlag and Carol Trojanowski, *Button Crafts,* Random House (New York, NY), 1999.

Bettina Lang, *The Royal Diner,* Scholastic (New York, NY), 1999.

Phillis Gershator, *Tiny and Bigman,* Marshall Cavendish (New York, NY), 1999.

Sarah Albee, *Cool School,* Golden Books (New York, NY), 1999.

Stuart J. Murphy, *Spunky Monkeys on Parade,* HarperCollins (New York, NY), 1999.

B.G. Hennessy, *One Little, Two Little, Three Little Pilgrims,* Viking (New York, NY), 1999.

P.J. Petersen, *I Hate Weddings,* Dutton (New York, NY), 2000.

Joan Holub, *Light the Candles: A Hanukkah Lift-the-Flap Book,* Puffin (New York, NY), 2000.

Gloria Whelan, *Welcome to Starvation Lake,* Random House (New York, NY), 2000.

*My First Action Rhymes* (anthology of songs and rhymes), HarperCollins (New York, NY), 2000.

Mary Ann Hoberman, *The Two Sillies,* Harcourt/Gulliver (San Diego, CA), 2000.

Stuart J. Murphy, *Shark Swimathon,* HarperCollins (New York, NY), 2001.

Gloria Whelan, *Rich and Famous in Starvation Lake,* Random House (New York, NY), 2001.

Joan Holub, *Pizza That We Made,* Viking/Puffin (New York, NY), 2001.

Bob Hartman, *Granny Mae's Christmas Play,* Augsburg (Minneapolis, MN), 2001.

Marsha Hayles, *He Saves the Day,* Putnam (New York, NY), 2001.

Gloria Whelan, *Are There Bears in Starvation Lake?,* Random House (New York, NY), 2002.

Patricia Rae Wolff, *A New Improved Santa,* Orchard (New York, NY), 2002.

Teresa Bateman, *The Princesses Have a Ball,* Albert Whitman (Morton Grove, IL), 2002.

Gloria Whelan, *A Haunted House in Starvation Lake,* Random House (New York, NY), 2003.

Craig Kee Strete, *The Rattlesnake Who Went to School,* Putnam (New York, NY), 2004.

Robert Lopshire, *Big Max and the Mystery of the Missing Giraffe,* HarperCollins (New York, NY), 2004.

Kin Platt, *Big Max and the Mystery of the Missing Giraffe,* HarperCollins (New York, NY), 2005.

Gail Saltz, *Amazing You!: Getting Smart about Your Private Parts,* Dutton (New York, NY), 2005.

(Under name Lynne Avril Cravath) Laurie Friedman, *Love, Ruby Valentine,* Carolrhoda (Minneapolis, MN), 2006.

(Under name Lynne Avril Cravath) Barbara Abercrombie, *The Show-and-Tell Lion,* Margaret K. McElderry Books (New York, NY), 2006.

(Under name Lynne Avril Cravath) Jean Cassels, *The Twelve Days of Christmas in Louisiana,* Sterling Publishing (New York, NY), 2007.

(Under name Lynne Avril) Susan Middleton Elya, *Oh No, Gotta Go Number Two,* Putnam (New York, NY), 2007.

Gail Saltz, *Changing You: A Guide to Body Changes and Sexuality,* Dutton (New York, NY), 2007.

(Under name Lynne Avril) Catherine Stier, *If I Ran for President,* Albert Whitman (Morton Grove, IL), 2007.

*"FLOWER GIRLS" SERIES; ILLUSTRATOR*

Kathleen Leverich, *Daisy,* HarperCollins (New York, NY), 1997.

Kathleen Leverich, *Heather,* HarperCollins (New York, NY), 1997.

Kathleen Leverich, *Rose,* HarperCollins (New York, NY), 1997.

Kathleen Leverich, *Violet,* HarperCollins (New York, NY), 1997.

## Sidelights

A popular illustrator of books for children, Lynne W. Cravath finds inspiration for her lighthearted cartoon-style art in the everyday things that happen all around her. Sometimes published under the names Lynne Avril or Lynne Avril Cravath, her work has appeared in a wide variety of picture books, from Stuart J. Murphy's *The Penny Pot* and *Shark Swimathon* to Barbara Abercrombie's *The Show-and-Tell Lion* and Gail Saltz's humorous nonfiction title *Amazing You!: Getting Smart about Your Private Parts.* Gloria Whelan, Kathleen Leverich, Patricia Reilly Giff, Mary Ann Hoberman, Craig Kee Strete, Joan Holub, and Teresa Bateman have also had their texts brought to life in Cravath's art. As Ilene Cooper wrote in a *Booklist* review of *The Show-and-Tell Lion,* Abercrombie's "simple, heartfelt tale gets a boost from [Cravath's] . . . imaginative, wonderfully child-friendly artwork." In the same periodical, Catherine Andronik wrote that the illustrator's contribution to *Shark Swimathon,* rendered "in swimming-pool hues, feature amusing details and an interesting assortment of sharks," Sandra Welzenbach similarly noted in her *School Library Journal* review of Strete's *The Rattlesnake Who Went to School* that Cravath's "flowing illustrations . . . beg readers to look more closely at the details as they enter the [narrator's] . . . imaginary world."

A counting book for small children, Murphy's *The Penny Pot* finds a little girl collecting pennies so she can accumulate enough money to have her face painted at the school festival. ok, "Cravath's colorful cartoon illustrations match the story's playful tone," commented Lauren Peterson in a *Booklist* review of the picture book, while in *School Library Journal* Marty Abbott

*Lynne W. Cravath specializes in creating whimsical picturebook characters, a pair ofwhich star in Mary Ann Hoberman's* **The Two Sillies.** (Illustration © 2000 by Lynne Avril Cravath. Reprinted by permission of Harcourt, Inc. This material may not be reproduced in any form or by any means without the prior written permission of the publisher. )

Goodman praised Cravath for depicting "life-size, authentic-looking coins" and "multiethnic children." Another counting book by Murphy, *Spunky Monkeys on Parade,* contains "vividly costumed, energetically parading" monkeys, according to *Booklist* contributor Ellen Mandel. As Anne Knickerbocker noted of the same book in *School Library Journal,* each illustration "suggests plenty of movement and excitement."

History and intercultural cooperation are the lessons of *One Little, Two Little, Three Little Pilgrims,* a picture book by B.G. Hennessy that features Cravath's art. The book plays on a familiar rhyme to show the activities of young North American pilgrims as they join with Wampanoag children to prepare a dinner to celebrate the harvest: the celebration still commemorated as Thanksgiving. Cravath's illustrations are full of "authentic detail," remarked Peterson, the *Booklist* critic adding that Cravath includes notes about her research for the book. Another culture, that of the West Indies, provides the setting for *Tiny and Bigman.* Featuring a story by Phillis Gershator, the picture book follows the adventures of a large, strong woman named Miss Tiny. Capable of great physical feats, Miss Tiny is also intimidating to men, but she ultimately finds love with a slim little man named Mr. Bigman. Together, the two defy traditional gender roles and become happily married parents: he cooks, she does carpentry, and Tiny ultimately protects the couple's house during a hurricane. Cravath's paintings present an "exuberant" and "lively portrayal of Caribbean life," noted Shelle Rosenfeld in *Booklist,* while a *Publishers Weekly* reviewer dubbed the illustrator's works "bold and cheery."

Cravath has contributed her talents to a pair of mysteries by Giff: *Kidnap at the Catfish Café* and *Mary Moon Is Missing.* The central character in both stories is young detective Minnie, an orphan who lives with her older brother, Catfish Café owner Orlando. With the help of her black cat Max, Minnie sets about solving mysteries. *Kidnap at the Catfish Café* takes Minnie through several sleuthing assignments, while *Mary Moon Is Missing* focuses on the hunt for a prize pigeon that is stolen just before a big pigeon race. Cravath illustrates both books with pen-and-ink drawings, and in *School Library Journal,* Janie Schomberg concluded that this artistic contribution to *Mary Moon Is Missing* "add[s] to the enjoyment."

Adventures of the imagination make up the story of *He Saves the Day* by Marsha Hayles. Here a little boy imagines himself performing all sorts of heroic deeds as he plays with various toys: an airplane and a car, among many others. Eventually, though, the boy gets into a fix and needs his mother to save him. "The exuberant art creates both the reality (a summer backyard scene) and the flights of fancy," commented Martha Topol in a review of *He Saves the Day* for *School Library Journal.* Cravath "does a good job" of showing how toys "can launch greater imaginative leaps," concluded a *Kirkus Reviews* contributor of the illustrator's work.

In *The Princesses Have a Ball* Teresa Bateman and Cravath collaborate on an updated version of the traditional fairy tale about the twelve dancing princesses. In Bateman's text, readers learn that the princesses have worn out their shoes rapidly not by dancing, but by playing basketball, an activity they worry that their father, the king, will not approve of. Ultimately, a helpful cobbler makes each princess her own pair of athletic shoes, and when the king discovers his dozen daughters' secret, he enjoys their basketball games so much that he signs on as their referee. Cravath's illustrations have "amusing anachronistic features" and "just the right look," remarked Bina Williams in a *School Library Journal* review of *The Princesses Have a Ball.* The humorously "animated illustrations . . . tell the story visually for prereaders," added Lauren Peterson in *Booklist,* and a *Publishers Weekly* critic praised Cravath for including "shots from odd angles and cute visuals for the grown-ups."

In Laurie Frieman's *Love, Ruby Valentine,* Cravath's lighthearted watercolor art is paired with a Valentine's Day tale about a young girl and her pet bird. Excited by the upcoming holiday, Ruby makes cards and cookies for her friends. When she grows exhausted with the preparations, the girl then falls asleep and misses the special day altogether. In *Kirkus Reviews* a critic praised Cravath's "engaging" illustrations, calling the picture

***Cravath teams up with author Teresa Bateman to give a contemporary spin to a traditional tale in* The Princesses Have a Ball.** (Albert Whitman and Company, 2002. Illustration © 2002 by Lynne Avril Cravath. Reproduced by permission.)

book a "Valentine's offering as sweet as candy." The "pastel watercolor-and-collage illustrations are fill of humor and convey Ruby's joy and industriousness," wrote Linda Staskus in her review of *Love, Ruby Valentine* for *School Library Journal.*

"I have a friend who says that all my characters are just myriad little self-portraits of myself," Cravath once told *SATA.* "In a sense, that's probably true. We can only paint what we know, and we paint the world the way we want to see it. As an illustrator, exposure to all types of people and events in the world around you is very important, along with a good sense of humor. Watching people—their characteristics, clothing, etc.—I carry around a sketchbook at all times and try not to be too obvious about scribbling down a stranger's best and worst features. Animals seem more oblivious to it."

Although her own experiences raising her children, traveling, and talking to people continue to fuel much of her art, Cravath has also drawn inspiration from other artists, such as Ludwig Bemelmans, who created the "Madeline" books, and Charlotte Voake. In addition to pencil and pen, her preferred medium is an opaque water color known as gouache. Its advantages, Cravath once told *SATA,* include rich color and versatility: "you can make it very opaque, or you can add water or acrylic medium to make it transparent." What's more, she added, "It's a very forgiving medium. If you make a mistake, you can lift it out or paint over it."

## Biographical and Critical Sources

*PERIODICALS*

*Booklist,* December 15, 1998, Lauren Peterson, review of *The Penny Pot,* p. 753; September 1, 1999, Lauren Peterson, review of *One Little, Two Little, Three Little Pilgrims,* p. 148; October 15, 1999, Shelle Rosenfeld, review of *Tiny and Bigman,* p. 452; December 1, 1999, Ellen Mandel, review of *Spunky Monkeys on Parade,* p. 708; December 1, 2000, Lauren Peterson, review of *The Two Sillies,* p. 721; February 1, 2001, Catherine Andronik, review of *Shark Swimathon,* p. 1058; November 1, 2002, Lauren Peterson, review of *The Princesses Have a Ball,* p. 504; March 15, 2003, Carolyn Phelan, review of *Are There Bears in Starvation Lake?,* p. 1328; August, 2004, Hazel Rochman, review of *The Rattlesnake Who Went to School,* p. 1948; September 15, 2006, Ilene Cooper, review of *The Show-and-Tell Lion,* p. 65.

*Horn Book,* July-August, 2005, Lauren Adams, review of *Amazing You!: Getting Smart about Your Private Parts,* p. 491.

*Kirkus Reviews,* February 15, 2002, review of *He Saves the Day,* p. 258; August 15, 2002, review of *The Princesses Have a Ball,* p. 1215; November 1, 2002, review of *A New Improved Santa,* p. 1627; June 1, 2006, review of *The Show-and-Tell Lion,* p. 567; September 1, 2006, review of *Love, Ruby Valentine,* p. 903.

*Publishers Weekly,* October 11, 1999, review of *Tiny and Bigman,* p. 75; March, 2001, Melinda Piehler, review of *Shark Swimathon,* p. 239; September 24, 2001, review of *Granny Mae's Christmas Play,* p. 50; July 15, 2002, review of *The Princesses Have a Ball,* p. 74; July, 2004, Sandra Welzenbach, review of *The Rattlesnake Who Went to School,* p. 88; October 9, 2006, review of *Love, Ruby Valentine,* p. 55.

*School Library Journal,* December, 1998, Marty Abbott Goodman, review of *The Penny Pot,* pp. 111-112; January, 1999, Janie Schomberg, review of *Mary Moon Is Missing,* p. 88; September, 1999, Adele Greenlee, review of *One Little, Two Little, Three Little Pilgrims,* p. 183; December, 1999, Anne Knickerbocker, review of *Spunky Monkeys on Parade,* p. 108; March, 2001, Melinda Piehler, review of *Shark Swimathon,* p. 239; April, 2002, Martha Topol, review of *He Saves the Day,* p. 110; October, 2002, Mara Alpert, review of *A New Improved Santa,* p. 65; December, 2002, Bina Williams, review of *The Princesses Have a Ball,* p. 84; July, 2006, Grace Oliff, review of *The Show-and-Tell Lion,* p. 68; November, 2006, Linda Staskus, review of *Love, Ruby Valentine,* p. 92.

*ONLINE*

*Lynn Avril Cravath Home Page,* http://www.lynneavril.com (August 27, 2007).*

# D-E

## DANDI
See MACKALL, Dandi Daley

* * *

## DAVIES, Nicola 1958-
(Stevie Morgan)

### Personal
Born May 3, 1958, in Birmingham, England; daughter of William Howard Davies and Beryl Rona Morgan; married Mark Harrison, July 21, 1984 (divorced December 19, 1997); children: Joseph, Gabriel. *Education:* Kings College, Cambridge, degree (zoology; with honours). *Hobbies and other interests:* Films, cartoons.

### Addresses
*Home*—Holkworthy, Somerset, England. *Agent*—Lizzy Kremer, David Higham Associates, 5-8 Lower John St., Golden Square, London W1F 9HA, England. *E-mail*—nicola.davies@btinternet.com.

### Career
Freelance broadcaster and writer. British Broadcasting Corporation, London, England, researcher for Natural History Unit, then host of *The Really Wild Show.* Freelance author. Bath Spa University College, Bath, England, associate lecturer in creative writing.

### Awards, Honors
*Boston Globe-Horn Book* Nonfiction Honor, for *Surprising Sharks;* Branford Boase Award shortlist, 2006, for *Home;* Blue Peter Book Award shortlist, 2006, for *Poop.*

### Writings

*FOR CHILDREN*

*Wild about Dolphins,* Candlewick Press (Cambridge, MA), 2001.

*Poop: A Natural History of the Unmentionable,* illustrated by Neal Layton, Candlewick Press (Cambridge, MA), 2004.

*Ice Bear: In the Steps of the Polar Bear,* illustrated by Gary Blythe, Candlewick Press (Cambridge, MA), 2005.

*Home* (novel), Walker (London, England), 2005.

*Extreme Animals: The Toughest Creatures on Earth,* illustrated by Neal Layton, Candlewick Press (Cambridge, MA), 2006.

*White Owl, Barn Owl,* illustrated by Michael Foreman, Walker (London, England), 2007.

*What's Eating You?: Parasites—The Inside Story,* illustrated by Neal Layton, Candlewick Press (Cambridge, MA), 2007.

Also author of television scripts.

*"READ AND WONDER" SERIES; FOR CHILDREN*

*Big Blue Whale,* illustrated by Nick Maland, Candlewick Press (Cambridge, MA), 1997.

*Bat Loves the Night,* illustrated by Sarah Fox-Davies, Candlewick Press (Cambridge, MA), 2001.

*One Tiny Turtle,* illustrated by Jane Chapman, Candlewick Press (Cambridge, MA), 2001.

*Surprising Sharks,* illustrated by James Croft, Candlewick Press (Cambridge, MA), 2003.

*"KINGFISHER YOUNG KNOWLEDGE" SERIES; FOR CHILDREN*

*Birds,* Kingfisher (Boston, MA), 2003.

*Oceans and Seas,* Kingfisher (Boston, MA), 2004.

*Deserts,* Kingfisher (Boston, MA), 2005.

*FOR ADULTS; UNDER PSEUDONYM STEVIE MORGAN*

*Delphinium Blues,* Hodder & Stoughton (London, England), 1999.

*Fly away Peter,* Flame (London, England), 1999.

*Checking Out,* Hodder & Stoughton (London, England), 2002.

Columnist for London *Independent;* contributor to periodicals.

## Adaptations

*Poop* was the basis of an exhibition staged at the Rothchilds Museum, 2005.

## Sidelights

Trained as a zoologist and working for several years as a television host for England's British Broadcasting Corporation (BBC), Nicola Davies is known for her ability to introduce the natural world and its fascinating creatures to picture-book audiences. Her works, which include *One Tiny Turtle, Wild about Dolphins, Bat Loves the Night,* and *Extreme Animals: The Toughest Creatures on Earth,* as well as the humorous *Poop: A Natural History of the Unmentionable,* pair an engaging text with interesting facts, sparking young readers' interests in topics ranging from zoology and oceanography to ecology. Noting that "Davies has a poet's touch with metaphor," *Bulletin of the Center for Children's Books Online* essayist Carolyn LaMontagne added that in all the author's work "narration and exposition flow together to create ideal books for young children eager to learn more about the natural world." While many of Davies' books for children feature both a simple story and useful information, she has also moved into fiction with the children's novel *Home.*

Davies' many interests are evident in *Big Blue Whale,* part of the "Read and Wonder" series and a look at one of Earth's most majestic animals. In the book Davies presents facts and anecdotes ranging from the texture of the blue whale's skin to its diet. "Conversational text and soft, crosshatched pen-and-ink illustrations ebb and flow in a fluid look at the largest mammal ever to inhabit the earth," noted a *Kirkus Reviews* critic, the reviewer adding that Davies' "unassuming book is teeming with new discoveries upon each rereading." Ellen Fader, writing in *Horn Book,* maintained that *Big Blue Whale* "offers young readers exactly what they want to know about this magnificent animal." In her *Booklist* review, Ellen Mandel predicted that *Big Blue Whale* "will definitely satisfy youngsters' curiosity."

Other books Davies has contributed to the "Read and Wonder" series include *Bat Loves the Night, One Tiny Turtle,* and *Surprising Sharks.* Featuring illustrations by Sarah Fox-Davies, *Bat Loves the Night* follows a pipistrelle bat as she embarks for an evening of hunting insects and darting through the landscape, using her internal sonar as a guide. Through her simple story, Davies helps young children understand that a seemingly frightening creature such as a bat is in fact a dedicated parent and an exciting participant in the after-dark world, as well as a helpful consumer of mosquitoes. In *One Tiny Turtle,* the life cycle of an elusive loggerhead turtle unfolds through text and drawings, from the turtle's hatching and first dangerous toddle across the beach to the ocean, to her months hiding in a clump of driftwood, to her triumphant return, thirty years later, to the beach where she first hatched. Davies shows how loggerheads are able to travel thousands of miles through ocean currents and, by some unerring instinct, return to the location of their births. In *Booklist* Gillian Engberg called *Bat Loves the Night* "an enticing picture book," and *School Library Journal* critic Cynde Marcengill cited Davies for her "excellent writing." A *Publishers Weekly* critic praised the same work for its "enigmatic beauty" in both prose and illustration. Reviewing *One Tiny Turtle,* a *Publishers Weekly* critic noted the author's "accomplished storytelling," while a *Reading Teacher* reviewer dubbed the work "an outstanding read-aloud book." Hazel Rochman, reviewing *One Tiny Turtle* for *Booklist,* wrote that Davies' "simple, lyrical words . . . convey . . . astonishing facts."

In *Surprising Sharks* Davies works with illustrator James Croft to help dispel the shark's fearsome reputation as a predator of human beings. In what *Horn Book* contributor Danielle J. Ford described as "informative yet humorous writing," the author joins with the illustrator to show that shark species come in many different sizes and shapes. In her text, Davies also assures young readers that only three of the 500-odd species of sharks have actually been known to attack people. Reviewing the work for *Booklist,* Todd Morning called *Surprising Sharks* "solid nonfiction on a popular subject," and Lynda Ritterman wrote in her *School Library Journal* review that the book's "interesting facts . . . should help this title make a splash." "Rarely do author and illustrator complement each other as perfectly as in this undersea jewel," concluded a *Kirkus Reviews* contributor.

A childhood fascination with dolphins led Davies to pursue a career in zoology, and as a young adult she worked with dolphin study teams in Newfoundland and the Indian Ocean. Her book *Wild about Dolphins* recounts her experiences during those expeditions while also introducing readers to dolphin anatomy, behavior, and ecology. Patricia Manning, reviewing the book for *School Library Journal,* suggested that youngsters "will find themselves entranced by the eager enthusiasm that pours from the pages." In *Booklist,* Ilene Cooper deemed *Wild about Dolphins* "energetic" and concluded that children interested in the marine mammals "will page through this with glee."

In *White Owl, Barn Owl* Davies weaves interesting facts about owl pellets, territorial avian behavior, and a long list of barn-owl facts within her story about a young child who helps Grandfather puts a nest-box high in an oak tree hear the family home. Checking the box one spring evening, the two are greeted by a pair of large owl eyes peering out into the dusk. Davies' "poetic, sensory" text will inspire readers' "interest in these intriguing animals," according to *Booklist* contributor Gil-

***Naturalist and author Nicola Davies mixes an entertaining story with useful facts in books such as* Bat Loves the Night, *featuring paintings by Sarah Fox-Davies.*** (Illustration © 2001 by Sarah Fox Davies. Reproduced by permission of the publisher, Candlewick Press, Inc., Cambridge, MA on behalf of Walker Books Ltd., London.)

lian Engberg. Betty Carter wrote in her *Horn Book* review of the work that Davies' many facts "smoothly complement the story," and each part of the book—fictional story and nonfiction reference—can be read independently." Citing illustrator Michael Foreman's "lovely watercolor and pastel paintings," Margaret Bush predicted in her *School Library Journal* review that *White Owl, Barn Owl* "will be enjoyed widely for personal reading" as well as research.

In what Rochman described as a "chatty, funny text," *Extreme Animals* introduces readers to a variety of creatures, all of which are capable of surviving in conditions that would kill most humans. Davies takes readers from harsh deserts and the dark depths of the sea to the sulfurous surface of volcanoes and the frigid polar regions, locations where cold-blooded frogs, water-toting camels, sulfur-eating microorganisms, and other creatures make quite comfortable homes. In her text, Davies compares these hardy critters with the weakling homo sapiens, adding an element of humor to a work that Rochman predicted would make biology "exciting" for young students. Another picture book that combines fact and fiction, *Ice Bear: In the Steps of the Polar Bear* takes a closer look at one of these hardy creatures through the fictional narrative of an Inuit. Praising illustrator Gary Blythe for contributing "impressionistic oil paintings of stunning polar settings," *Booklist* reviewer Jennifer Mattson deemed *Ice Bear* an "inviting" work, and Amelia Jenkins praised Davies' "quiet, thoughtful book" for treating polar bears as animals rather than anthropomorphized creatures.

In *Poop,* a subject of perennial fascination to many children is discussed openly. Grounding her description of the whys, wheres, and hows of animal defecation in scientific terms, Davies posits poop as the ultimate in recycling. She also includes an intriguing list of "Poop Facts," and further engages readers with humorous chapter headings that *School Library Journal* contributor Blair Christolon predicted would "bring a smile to many faces." In *Kirkus Reviews* a contributor deemed *Poop* a "breezy introduction" to the many facts—including uses—for the surprisingly useful substance, and Betty Carter noted in *Horn Book* that *Poop* takes its subject "out of the sewers and into the scientific community where it belongs." Expressing appreciation that the book features illustrations rather than photographs, Cooper noted that artist Neal Layton's characteristically "clever ink-and-watercolor cartoons go for big laughs," and a *Publishers Weekly* contributor wrote that the book's "slap-dash cartoons mine the scatological humor of the subject."

Although Davies has also produced several novels for adults under the pseudonym Stevie Morgan, she does most of her writing for young readers.She also teaches creative writing at the college level. As she once told *SATA:* "I am interested in communication: communication about zoology, about science and about how we as humans experience and interpret our existence. I'm convinced that art and science are all part of the same picture and can contribute enormously to each other. It's the crossovers and combinations of fields of interest that motivate me in life and work."

*Gary Blythe's stunning paintings for* **Ice Bear** *give added appeal to Davies' fact-filled study of the polar bear and its habitat.* (Illustration © 2005 by Gary Blythe. Reproduced by permission of the publisher Candlewick Press, Inc., Cambridge, MA on behalf of Walker Books Ltd., London.)

***Poop: A Natural History of the Unmentionable,* Davies' fact-filled study of an unusual topic, is given an appealing levity by cartoonist Neal Layton.** (Illustration © 2004 by Neal Layton. Reproduced by permission of the publisher Candlewick Press, Inc., Cambridge, MA on behalf of Walker Books Ltd., London.)

## Biographical and Critical Sources

*PERIODICALS*

*Booklist,* September 1, 1997, Ellen Mandel, review of *Big Blue Whale,* p. 128; September 1, 2001, Gillian Engberg, review of *Bat Loves the Night,* p. 114; November 1, 2001, Ilene Cooper, review of *Wild about Dolphins,* p. 471; December 1, 2001, Hazel Rochman, review of *One Tiny Turtle,* p. 656; October 15, 2003, Todd Morning, review of *Surprising Sharks,* p. 413; October 15, 2004, Ilene Cooper, review of *Poop: A Natural History of the Unmentionable,* p. 400; December 1, 2005, Jennifer Mattson, review of *Ice Bear: In the Steps of the Polar Bear,* p. 55; December 1, 2006, Hazel Rochman, review of *Extreme Animals: The Toughest Creatures on Earth,* p. 58; May 15, 2007, Gillian Engberg, review of *White Owl, Barn Owl,* p. 53.

*Bulletin of the Center for Children's Books,* October, 1997, review of *Big Blue Whale,* p. 48; October, 2001, review of *Wild about Dolphins,* p. 53; November, 2001, review of *One Tiny Turtle,* p. 99; December, 2001, review of *Bat Loves the Night,* p. 135; February, 2004, Karen Coats, review of *Surprising Sharks,* p. 227; November, 2004, Deborah Stevenson, review of *Poop,* p. 118.

*Horn Book,* May-June, 1997, Ellen Fader, review of *Big Blue Whale,* pp. 338-339; January-February, 2004, Danielle J. Ford, review of *Surprising Sharks,* p. 99; September-October, 2004, Betty Carter, review of *Poop,* p. 605; January-February, 2006, Betty Carter, review of *Ice Bear,* p. 97; January-February, 2007, Danielle J. Ford, review of *Extreme Animals,* p. 81; July-August, 2007, Betty Carter, review of *White Owl, Barn Owl,* p. 411.

*Kirkus Reviews,* June 1, 1997, review of *Big Blue Whale,* pp. 871-872; August 1, 2001, review of *Bat Loves the Night,* p. 1120; September 15, 2003, review of *One Tiny Turtle,* p. 1210; September 15, 2003, review of *Surprising Sharks,* p. 1173; August 15, 2004, review of *Poop,* p. 804; November 15, 2005, review of *Ice Bear,* p. 1230; August 15, 2006, review of *Extreme Animals,* p. 838.

*New York Times Book Review,* March 10, 2002, review of *Bat Loves the Night,* p. 20.

*Publishers Weekly,* August 13, 2001, review of *One Tiny Turtle,* p. 312; November 12, 2001, "Natural Wonders," p. 62; August 30, 2004, review of *Poop,* p. 55.

*Reading Teacher,* October, 2002, Cyndi Giorgis and Nancy J. Johnson, "Living Creatures," p. 200; November, 2002, review of *One Tiny Turtle,* p. 257.

*School Library Journal,* September, 2001, Cynde Marcengill, review of *Bat Loves the Night,* p. 187; October, 2001, Patricia Manning, review of *Wild about Dolphins,* p. 182; December, 2001, Margaret Bush, review of *One Tiny Turtle,* p. 120; October, 2003, Lynda Ritterman, review of *Surprising Sharks,* p. 148; December, 2004, Blair Christolon, review of *Poop,* p. 128; June, 2005, Kathy Piehl, review of *Deserts,* p. 136; February, 2006, Amelia Jenkins, review of *Ice Bear,* p. 95; December, 2006, Cynde Suite, review of *Extreme Animals,* p. 161; July, 2007, Margaret Bush, review of *White Owl, Barn Owl,* p. 89.

*ONLINE*

*Bulletin of the Center for Children's Books Online,* http://bbcb.lis.uiuc.edu/ (February 1, 2004), Carolyn LaMontagne, "Nicola Davies."

*Candlewick Press Web site,* http://www.candlewick.com/ (December 9, 2003), "Nicola Davies."

*David Higham Associates Web site,* http://www.davidhigham.co.uk/ (August 27, 2007), "Nicola Davies."*

* * *

## "DINO" DON LESSEM
## See LESSEM, Don

* * *

## DOTLICH, Rebecca Kai 1951-

### Personal

Born Rebecca Kay Thomson, July 10, 1951, in Indianapolis, IN; daughter of John and Charlotte Thompson; married; husband's name Steve; children: one son, one daughter. *Education:* Attended Indiana University, Bloomington.

### Addresses

*Home*—IN. *E-mail*—rebeccakai@aol.com.

### Career

Writer. Formerly worked as a library staffer, in real estate, and in public relations.

### Awards, Honors

International Reading Association Children's Choice designation, and Indiana Best Read-Aloud designation, both 1998, both for *Lemonade Sun;* Oppenheim Toy Portfolio Gold Award, and Ten Best Books for Babies designation, both 2000, both for *Away We Go!;* Bank Street College of Education Best Children's Book designation, and Subaru SB & F Prize for Excellence in Science Books, AAAS/Subaru, both 2007, both for *What Is Science?*

### Writings

*POETRY*

*Sweet Dreams of the Wild: Poems for Bedtime,* illustrated by Katharine Dodge, Wordsong/Boyds Mills Press (Honesdale, PA), 1996.

*Lemonade Sun; and Other Summer Poems,* illustrated by Jan Spivey Gilchrist, Wordsong/Boyds Mills Press (Honesdale, PA), 1998.

*When Riddles Come Rumbling: Poems to Ponder,* illustrated by Karen Dugan, Wordsong/Boyds Mills Press (Honesdale, PA), 2001.

*In the Spin of Things: Poetry of Motion,* illustrated by Karen Dugan, Wordsong/Boyds Mills Press (Honesdale, PA), 2003.

*Over in the Pink House: New Jump Rope Rhymes,* illustrated by Melanie Hall, Wordsong/Boyds Mills Press (Honesdale, PA), 2004.

(With J. Patrick Lewis) *Castles: Old Stone Poems,* illustrated by Dan Burr, Wordsong/Boyds Mills Press (Honesdale, PA), 2006.

*CONCEPT BOOKS*

*What Is Square?,* illustrated by Maria Ferrari, HarperFestival (New York, NY), 1999.

*What Is Round?,* illustrated by Maria Ferrari, HarperFestival (New York, NY), 1999.

*What Is Triangle?,* illustrated by Maria Ferrari, HarperFestival (New York, NY), 2000.

*Away We Go!,* illustrated by Dan Yaccarino, HarperFestival (New York, NY), 2000.

*PICTURE BOOKS*

*A Family like Yours,* illustrated by Tammie Lyon, Boyds Mills Press (Honesdale, PA), 2002.

*Mama Loves,* illustrated by Kathryn Brown, HarperCollins (New York, NY), 2004.

*Grandpa Loves,* illustrated by Kathryn Brown, HarperCollins (New York, NY), 2005.

*What Is Science?,* illustrated by Sachiko Yoshikawa, Holt (New York, NY), 2006.

*Peanut and Pearl's Picnic Adventure* (reader), illustrated by R.W. Alley, HarperCollins (New York, NY), 2007.

Contributor to periodicals, including *Ladybug, Click, Storyworks, ASK!, Highlights, Turtle, Humpty Dumpty, Creative Classroom,* and *Teaching K-8.* Poetry represented in anthologies, including Paul Janeczko, editor, *A Kick in the Head: An Everyday Guide to Poetic Forms,* Candlewick Press; Janeczko, editor, *Hey, You!* HarperCollins; Jack Prelutsky, editor, *The 20th-Century Children's Poetry Treasury,* Knopf; Prelutsky, editor, *Read a Rhyme, Write a Rhyme,* Knopf; Lee Bennett Hopkins, editor, *A Pet for Me,* HarperCollins; Hopkins, editor, *Halloween Howls: Holiday Poetry,* HarperCollins; Hopkins, *Valentine Hearts: Holiday Poetry,* HarperCollins; Hopkins, editor, *Christmas Presents: Holiday Poetry,* HarperCollins; Hopkins, editor, *Climb into My Lap,* Simon & Schuster; Hopkins, editor, *School Supplies: A Book of Poems,* Simon & Schuster; Hopkins, editor, *Yummy! Eating through the Day,* Simon & Schuster; Hopkins, editor, *Marvelous Math,* Simon & Schuster; Hopkins, *Spectacular Science,* Simon & Schuster; Hopkins, editor, *Wonderful Words,* Simon &

Schuster; Hopkins, *Got Geography!* Greenwillow; Hopkins, editor, *Days to Celebrate: A Full Year of Poetry, People, Fascinating Facts, and More,* Greenwillow; and Hopkins, editor, *My America: A Poetry Atlas of the U.S.,* Simon & Schuster.

## Sidelights

Even before she realized she wanted to be a writer, Rebecca Kai Dotlich understood the importance words would play in her life. "I remember pouring over the words to the lyrics from my parent's favorite songs. This was far more important to me than the music," she explained on the Embracing the Child Web site. A middle child, Dotlich grew up in suburban Indiana, comfortably wedged between older brother Curtis and younger sister Beth. In high school she was officially dubbed a poet after a poem she had written made one of her teachers cry. New inspirations for writing came in college, when Dotlich attended Indiana University, Bloomington. There, as she admitted on her home page, "My only real interest was in classes that celebrated the written word: creative writing, poetry, and even the history of song lyrics. As long as I was involved with words on paper, I was content."

After college came marriage, and motherhood, and exposure to the books that would inspire Dotlich to write for children. "I began to read fairy tales, picture books, and poetry to sleepy bodies at night, or during cranky afternoons," she recalled on her home page. "I woke up early and stayed up late, just so I could write. . . . Many afternoons were spent in the backyard with lunch boxes, reading stacks of books. Life doesn't get much better." After years of practice, rejection, study, and rewriting, Dotlich's poetry found its way into magazines. Then, in 1995, her first book-length manuscript, *Sweet*

***Rebecca Kai Dotlich mixes realism and fantasy in her energetic paintings for Jan Spivey Gilchrist's*** **Lemonade Sun, and Other Summer Poems.** (Boyds Mills Press, 2000. Illustration © 1998 by Jan Spivey Gilchrist. Reproduced by permission.)

*Dreams of the Wild: Poems for Bedtime,* was picked up by Boyds Mills Press, beginning Dotlich's award-winning career as a respected poet for children.

*Sweet Dreams of the Wild: Poems for Bedtime,* collects night-themed poetry featuring an assortment of wild animals and their sleeping habits. Susan Dove Lempke, reviewing the book for *Booklist,* praised the "soothing, rhythmic poems" in the collection and noted Dotlich's ability to convey a "quiet, tender mood." Another verse collection, *When Riddles Come Rumbling: Poems to Ponder,* finds twenty-nine everyday objects described in a rhyming text designed to help readers guess each poem's subject. "Children will enjoy these riddle poems either one-on-one or in a group setting," predicted Cathie Reed in *School Library Journal.*

*In the Spin of Things: Poetry of Motion* collects twenty-three free-verse poems about the actions of every-day objects, from ice cubes to pencil sharpeners. Sally R. Dow, writing in *School Library Journal,* found the poems "imaginative," and *Booklist* contributor Hazel Rochman noted that "reading aloud these short rhythmic lines will make kids find poetry in ordinary things." *Over in the Pink House: New Jump Rope Rhymes* finds children, rather than objects, in motion. A *Kirkus Re-*

***Dotlich joins J. Patrick Lewis in creating the anthology* Castles: Old Stone Poems, *a work enhanced by Dan Burr's detailed art.*** (Wordsong Press, 2006. Illustration © 2006 by Dan Burr. Reproduced by permission.)

*views* contributor wrote that Dotlich's verse collection "ably captures" the "timeless, folkloric quality" of traditional skipping-rope rhymes and dubbed the collection a "winning combination of infectious rhythms and easy-to-learn rhymes." Dow wrote of the poems that "each one has a lighthearted, whimsical quality," and Rochman noted that *Over in the Pink House* "makes words a part of play."

Dotlich collaborated with fellow children's book author J. Patrick Lewis on *Castles: Old Stone Poems.* The verses in this work each focus on a different part of a castle and also bring castles to life. "Dreamers will latch on to the poems and pictures," wrote a *Kirkus Reviews* contributor, the reviewer adding that a timeline is also included for young historians. Gillian Engberg, writing in *Booklist,* recommended *Castles* "for classroom exercises that show how poetry can help bring history into the present."

In addition to her poetry, Dotlich has written several picture books and concept books for very young readers. In *What Is Round?* her rhyming text accompanies photographs of round objects which toddlers are likely to encounter. Each entry takes "just the right amount of time to hold a young child's attention," according to *Booklist* contributor Kathy Broderick. *Away We Go,* which introduces children to different forms of transportation, is "a direct, joyful way to teach words, colors, [and] movements," according to Rochman, while Martha Topol noted in *School Library Journal* that "the catchy phrase 'Away we go!' will have listeners chanting along" with the rollicking text.

Dotlich presents basic concepts of science in her picture book *What Is Science?* "This title will be enjoyed by newly independent readers, or will ignite excitement in a group," wrote Lynda Ritterman in her *School Library Journal* review of the book. A *Kirkus Reviews* contributor described the title as "a child-friendly introduction to the huge, and sometimes daunting, realm of science."

In *A Family like Yours* Dotlich looks at how families are alike and how they are different in many different settings and situations. "This delightful offering is a welcome departure from stories about family groupings," wrote a *Kirkus Reviews* contributor. *Mama Loves* focuses on the relationship between a mother pig and her daughter. "This sweet story in rhyme works without becoming sappy," concluded Roxanne Burg in her *School Library Journal* review, and a *Kirkus Reviews* contributor found the tale "comforting and gentle." Ilene Cooper, writing in *Booklist,* predicted that Dotlich's "charmer . . . will easily resonate with little ones." *Grandpa Loves* share a similar theme as it explores the relationship between a grandparent and grandchild. *School Library Journal* contributor Sheilah Kosco deemed *Grandpa Loves* to be "a wonderful and touching tribute."

## Biographical and Critical Sources

*PERIODICALS*

*Booklist,* January 1, 1996, Susan Dove Lempke, review of *Sweet Dreams of the Wild: Poems for Bedtime,* p. 839; July, 1999, Kathy Broderick, review of *What Is Round?,* p. 1950; September 1, 2000, Hazel Rochman, review of *Away We Go!,* p. 121; November 1, 2001, Hazel Rochman, review of *When Riddles Come Rumbling: Poems to Ponder,* p. 472; April 1, 2003, Hazel Rochman, review of *In the Spin of Things: Poetry of Motion,* p. 1408; March 1, 2004, Ilene Cooper, review of *Mama Loves,* p. 1204; May 1, 2004, Hazel Rochman, review of *Over in the Pink House: New Jump Rope Rhymes,* p. 1560; June 1, 2005, Ilene Cooper, review of *Grandpa Loves,* p. 1821; September 15, 2006, Carolyn Phelan, review of *What Is Science?,* p. 63; October 1, 2006, Gillian Engberg, review of *Castles: Old Stone Poems,* p. 51.

*Kirkus Reviews,* March 15, 2002, review of *A Family like Yours,* p. 409; February 15, 2003, review of *In the Spin of Things,* p. 304; February 1, 2004, review of *Mama Loves,* p. 131; March 15, 2004, review of *Over in the Pink House,* p. 267; August 15, 2006, review of *What Is Science?,* p. 839; October 1, 2006, review of *Castles,* p. 1018.

*Publishers Weekly,* March 1, 1999, review of *What Is Round?,* p. 71; February 26, 2001, review of *Lemonade Sun,* p. 88; March 15, 2004, review of *Mama Loves,* p. 73.

*School Library Journal,* April, 1999, Susan Marie Pitard, review of *What Is Round?,* p. 113; November, 2000, Martha Topol, review of *Away We Go!,* p. 113; Ellen Heath, review of *What Is a Triangle?,* p. 140; October, 2001, Cathie Reed, review of *When Riddles Come Rumbling,* p. 182; July, 2002, Lisa Gangemi Kropp, review of *A Family like Yours,* p. 106; March, 2003, Sally R. Dow, review of *In the Spin of Things,* p. 216; August, 2004, Sally R. Dow, review of *Over in the Pink House,* p. 130; December, 2004, Roxanne Burg, review of *Mama Loves,* p. 106; May, 2005, Sheilah Kosco, review of *Grandpa Loves,* p. 80; October, 2006, Jill Heritage Maza, review of *Castles,* p. 179; November, 2006, Lynda Ritterman, review of *What Is Science?,* p. 119.

*Voice of Youth Advocates,* February, 2007, Tina Frolund, review of *Castles,* p. 550.

*ONLINE*

*Boyds Mills Press Web site,* http://www.boydsmillspress.com/ (August 6, 2007), "Rebecca Kai Dotlich."

*Embracing the Child Web site,* http://www.embracingthechild.org/ (August 6, 2007), interview with Dotlich.

*Rebecca Kai Dotlich Home Page,* http://www.rebeccakaidotlich.com (August 6, 2007).

* * *

# ESCRIVÁ, Viví

## Personal

Born in Spain.

## Addresses

*Home*—Spain.

## Career

Children's book illustrator and author.

## Writings

*SELF-ILLUSTRATED*

*El príncipe de las ranas,* Laredo Publishing (Beverly Hills, CA), 1995.

*El amigo de Olmo,* Laredo Publishing (Beverly Hills, CA), 1995, translated as *Olmo and the Dragon,* 1997.

*ILLUSTRATOR*

Joles Sennell, *El bosque encantado,* Espasa-Calpe (Madrid, Spain), 1988.

Alma Flor Ada, *La sorpresa de Mamá,* Santillana (Compton, CA), 1991, translated by Rosalma Zubizarreta as *A Surprise for Mother Rabbit,* 1992.

Alma Flor Ada, *Como nacio el arco iris,* Santillana (Compton, CA), 1991 translated by Bernice Randall as *How the Rainbow Came to Be,* 1991.

Alma Flor Ada, *La hamaca de la vaca, o, Un amigo más,* Santillana (Compton, CA), 1991 translated by Rosalma Zubizarreta as *In the Cow's Backyard,* 1991.

Alma Flor Ada, *El susto de los fantasmas,* Santillana (Compton, CA), 1991, translated by Rosalma Zubizarreta as *What Are Ghosts Afraid Of?,* 1991.

Alma Flor Ada, *No fui yo,* Santillana (Compton, CA), 1992, translated by Rosalma Zubizarreta as *It's Not Me,* 1992.

Alma Flor Ada, *El papalote,* Santillana (Compton, CA), 1992, translated by Rosalma Zubizarreta as *The Kite,* 1992.

Alma Flor Ada, *Olmo y la mariposa azul,* Laredo Publishing (Torrance, CA), 1992.

Alma Flor Ada, *Pavo para la cena de Gracias?,* Santillana (Compton, CA), 1993, translated by Rosalma Zubizarreta as *Turkey for Thanksgiving? No, Thanks!,* 1993.

Cecilia Avalos, reteller, *The Goat Who Wouldn't Sneeze,* Scot Foresman (Glenview, IL), 1993.

Alma Flor Ada, *Rosa alada,* Santillana (Compton, CA), 1993, translated by Rosalma Zubizarreta as *A Rose with Wings,* 1993.

Alma Flor Ada, *El pañuelo de seda,* Laredo Publishing (Torrance, CA), 1993.

Alma Flor Ada, *La piñata vaía,* Santillana (Compton, CA), 1993, translated by Rosalma Zubizarreta as *The Empty Piñata,* 1993.

Alma Flor Ada, *No quiero derretirme!,* Santillana (Compton, CA), 1993, translated by Rosalma Zubizarreta as *I Don't Want to Melt!,* 1993.

Alma Flor Ada, *La jaula dorada,* Santillana (Compton, CA), 1993, translated by Rosalma Zubizarreta as *The Golden Cage,* 1993.

Alma Flor Ada, *Después de la tormenta,* Santillana (Compton, CA), 1993, translated by Rosalma Zubizarreta as *After the Storm,* 1993.

Diana Noonan, reteller, *The Farmer's Journey,* Celebration Press (Glenview, IL), 1996.

Hilda Perera, *Rana ranita,* translated by Janet Sklar as *Froggie Froggette,* Lectorum Publications (New York, NY), 1997.

Joan Fallon and Arlene Feltenstein, *Will the New Baby Be Bigger than Me?,* Laredo Publishing (Beverly Hills, CA), 1998.

Paz Rodero, *The Storyteller/El cuentista,* Laredo Publishing (Beverly Hills, CA), 1998.

Alma Flor Ada, *Ima extraña visita,* Santillana (Compton, CA), 1999, translated by Rosalma Zubizarreta as *Strange Visitors,* 1999.

Alma Flor Ada, *Me gustaria tener,* Santillana (Compton, CA), 1999.

Maria Isabel Tiera, *The Coconut Flan,* Houghton Mifflin (Boston, MA), 2001.

Alma Flor Ada and F. Isabel Campoy, *Uno, dos, tres: Dime quín eres!/One, Two, Three: Who Is It?,* Alfaguara Infantil, 2002.

Alma Flor Ada and F. Isabel Campoy, *A New Home for the Seven Little Kids,* Santillana (Compton, CA), 2002, translated as *El nuevo hogar de los siete cabritos,* 2002.

Diana Star Helmer, *The Cat Who Came for Tacos,* Albert Whitman (Morton Grove, IL), 2003.

Alma Flor Ada, *Coral y espuma: Abecedario del mar,* Espasa Calpe Mexicana, 2003.

Alma Flor Ada and F. Isabel Campoy, selectors, *Pío Peep!: Traditional Spanish Nursery Rhymes,* HarperCollins (New York, NY), 2003.

Mimi Chapra, *Sparky's Bark/El ladrido de Sparky,* Katherine Tegan Books (New York, NY), 2006.

Ginger Foglesong Guy, *My School/Mi escuela,* HarperFestival (New York, NY), 2006.

Ginger Foglesong Guy, *My Grandma/Mi abuelita,* HarperFestival (New York, NY), 2007.

Also illustrator of picture books published in Spain.

## Sidelights

Viví Escrivá's celebrated watercolors have graced the pages of picture books by several authors, among them Alma Flor Ada, Mimi Chapra, Ginger Foglesong Guy, and F. Isabel Campoy. Her work with Ada is perhaps best known, and includes *Pío Peep!: Traditional Spanish Nursery Rhymes.* Praising Escrivá's work for Guy's bilingual picture book *My School/Mi escuela,* a *Kirkus Reviews* writer noted that the artist's pictures, rendered in "warm watercolors, [are] busy with detail" and feature "children of various ethnicities." A resident of Spain, Escrivá is widely known to young children in her own country, where her art appears in numerous Spanish-language books, several of which feature her original stories.

In a review of *Pío Peep!, School Library Journal* reviewer Ann Welton praised the collaboration between Ada and Escrivá, dubbing the work a "wonderful, reassuring lap book." "Escriva's watercolor and colored-pencil illustrations use brilliant hues and detail to reconstruct a young child's world," the critic added. "Warm colors and Latin American motifs contribute to the cultural interest" of Diana Star Helmer's *The Cat Who Came for Tacos,* according to *School Library Journal* critic Rosalyn Pierini, in describing another "lighthearted tale" featuring Escrivá's colorful art.

Another book pairing Escrivá's art with a lighthearted story is Mimi Chapra's *Sparky's Bark/El ladrido de Sparky.* This bilingual picture book finds a little girl visiting her American relatives. The girl is from Latin America, and life in Ohio feels very strange and uncomfortable until a perceptive cousin translates some simple objects that both cultures share, including a pet dog and its bark. Escrivá's colorful artwork "combines realism and cartoon," explained a *Kirkus Reviews* contributor, noting the "accentuated roundness" that characterizes the artist's rendering of human characters. In *Booklist,* Stella Clark wrote of *Sparky's Bark* that Escrivá's "appealing" illustrations add to Chapra's "simple . . . message about language and culture." An equally positive appraisal of the work was offered by Maria Otero-Boisvert, who in *School Library Journal* deemed the watercolor illustrations "delightful and detailed," making *Sparky's Bark* "a solid choice for storytimes"

## Biographical and Critical Sources

*PERIODICALS*

*Booklist,* February 15, 2002, Isabel Schon, review of *A New Home for the Seven Little Kids,* p. 1022; September 1, 2003, Ilene Cooper, review of *¡Pío Peep!: Traditional Spanish Nursery Rhymes,* p. 126; May 1, 2006, Stella Clark, review of *Sparky's Bark/El ladrido de Sparky,* p. 88; January 1, 2007, Carolyn Phelan, review of *My Grandma/Mi abuelita,* p. 114.

*Bulletin of the Center for Children's Books,* June, 2003, review of *¡Pío Peep!,* p. 388.

*Kirkus Reviews,* April 15, 2003, review of *¡Pío Peep!,* p. 603; June 1, 2006, review of *Sparky's Bark/El ladrido de Sparky,* p. 570, and review of *My School/Mi escuela,* p. 572.

*Publishers Weekly,* May 26, 1997, review of *Froggie Froggette,* p. 85; September 4, 2006, review of *Sparky's Bark/El ladrido de Sparky,* p. 67.

*School Library Journal,* August, 1990, review of *Una extraña visita,* p. 172; November, 1991, Valentin Porras, review of *Como nacio el arco iris,* p. 153; July, 2003, Ann Welton, review of *¡Pío Peep!,* p. 121; September, 2003, Rosalyn Pierini, review of *The Cat Who Came for Tacos,* p. 179; June, 2006, Maria Otero-Boisvert, review of *Sparky's Bark/El ladrido de Sparky,* p. 142; June, 2007, Linda Staskus, review of *My Grandma/Mi abuelita,* p. 100.*

# F

## FAILING, Barbara Larmon

### Personal

Married; children: one son. *Education:* Elizabethtown College, graduate; Arcadia University, M.A. *Hobbies and other interests:* Going to the beach, playing games.

### Addresses

*Home*—Cape Cod, MA. *E-mail*—barbara@barbaralarmonfailing.com.

### Career

Elementary school teacher for twenty years, retired, 1998; writer.

### Writings

*Lasso Lou and Cowboy McCoy,* illustrated by Tedd Arnold, Dial Books for Young Readers (New York, NY), 2003.

### Biographical and Critical Sources

*PERIODICALS*

*Bulletin of the Center for Children's Books,* October, 2003, Deborah Stevenson, review of *Lasso Lou and Cowboy McCoy,* p. 57.

*School Library Journal,* October, 2003, Shelley B. Sutherland, review of *Lasso Lou and Cowboy McCoy,* p. 118.

*ONLINE*

*Barbara Larmon Failing Web site,* http://www.barbaralarmonfailing.com (August 27, 2007).*

## FATUS, Sophie 1957-

### Personal

Born 1957, in Boulogne-sur-Seine, France; immigrated to Italy, c. 1981. *Education:* École des Beaux Arts (Paris, France), graduated, 1980.

### Addresses

*Home*—Florence, Italy. *Agent*—Advocate Art Agency, 39 Church Rd., Wimbledon Village, London SW19 5DQ, England.

### Career

Artist and illustrator. *Exhibitions:* Works exhibited throughout Europe.

### Writings

*SELF-ILLUSTRATED*

(Reteller) *I tre porcellini,* Fatatrac (Florence, Italy), 1983.

*Il brutto anatroccolo,* Fatatrac (Florence, Italy), 1987.

*Biancaneva e i sette nani,* Fatatrac (Florence, Italy), 1988.

*L'arca di Noè,* Fatatrac (Florence, Italy), 1989.

*Domani nasce un fatrellino,* Fatatrac (Florence, Italy), 1990.

*Domani vado a scuola,* Fatatrac (Florence, Italy), 1990.

(Reteller) *Cenerentola,* Fatatrac (Florence, Italy), 1990.

*Cappuccetto Rosso,* Fatatrac (Florence, Italy), 1991.

*Hansel e Gretel,* Fatatrac (Florence, Italy), 1991.

*Il principe ranocchio,* Fatatrac (Florence, Italy), 1991.

*Ali Babà e i guaranta ladroni,* Fatatrac (Florence, Italy), 1992.

*Stego ha fame,* Giunti Editore, 1993.

*Brachio ha sonno,* Giunti Editore, 1993.

*Pelle d'asino,* Fatatrac (Florence, Italy), 1994.

*Rana Boccuccia,* Giunti Editore, 1995.

*Il lupo ei 7 capretti,* Fatatrac (Florence, Italy), 1995.

(Reteller) *Pinocchio e la balena,* Fatatrac (Florence, Italy), 1995.

(Reteller) *Pinocchio, il gatto e la volpe,* Fatatrac (Florence, Italy), 1997.

*Pollicino,* Fatatrac (Florence, Italy), 1997.

(Reteller) *Sindbad il marinaio,* Fatatrac (Florence, Italy), 1997.

(Reteller) *Pinocchio e Mangiafoco,* Fatatrac (Florence, Italy), 1998.

*La principessa sul piscello,* Fatatrac (Florence, Italy), 1999.

*Il cavallino e il fiume,* Carthusia, 1999.

*Per milo dimmi il vero,* Fatatrac (Florence, Italy), 2001.

*Rana boccuccia,* Giunti Editore, 2002.

*A tutto gatto,* Fatatrac (Florence, Italy), 2003.

*White Night,* Nuages, 2007.

*Here We Go round the Mulberry Bush* (with audio CD by Fred Penner), Barefoot Books (Cambridge, MA), 2007.

*Bugia!,* Fatatrac (Florence, Italy), 2007.

Author/illustrator of other books published in Italian, including *Ciuffettino, Pinocchio e il cane Melampo,* and *Guarda quo, guarda là,* all published by Fatatrac.

Author's books have been translated into Spanish.

*"SILLY SHAPES" BOARD BOOKS; SELF-ILLUSTRATED*

*Stripes,* Abbeville Kids (New York, NY), 1997.

*Squares,* Abbeville Kids (New York, NY), 1997.

*Spots,* Abbeville Kids (New York, NY), 1997.

*Holes,* Abbeville Kids (New York, NY), 1997.

*ILLUSTRATOR*

Matteo Faglia, *Il gatto con stivali,* Fatatrac (Florence, Italy), 1983.

Nicoletta Condignola, *La bella addornmentata,* Fatatrac (Florence, Italy), 1984.

Nicoletta Condignola, *È Natale,* Fatatrac (Florence, Italy), 1986.

Matteo Faglia, *L'usignolo dell'imperatore,* Fatatrac (Florence, Italy), 1990.

Matteo Faglia, reteller, *I musicanti di Brema,* Fatatrac (Florence, Italy), 1992.

Matteo Faglia, reteller, *Le tre caravelle,* Fatatrac (Florence, Italy), 1992.

Matteo Faglia, reteller, *La lampada di Aladino,* Fatatrac (Florence, Italy), 1993.

Matteo Faglia, reteller, *Gli abiti nuovi dell'imperatore,* Fatatrac (Florence, Italy), 1993.

Matteo Faglia, reteller, *Raperonzollo,* Fatatrac (Florence, Italy), 1993.

Nicoletta Codignola, reteller, *Alice ne paese delle meraviglie,* Fatatrac (Florence, Italy), 1996.

Nicoletta Codignola, reteller, *Perseo e il mostro Medusa,* Fatatrac (Florence, Italy), 1998.

Nicoletta Codignola, reteller, *La sirenetta,* Fatatrac (Florence, Italy), 1998.

Nicoletta Codignola, reteller, *Ulisse nell'isola dei ciclopi,* Fatatrac (Florence, Italy), 1999.

Matteo Faglia, *Buon compleanno, ho tre anní!,* Giunti Gruppo (Florence, Italy), 1999, translated as *Happy Birthday, I'm Three,* Kane/Miller (La Jolla, CA), 2001.

Hugh Lupton, reteller, *The Story Tree: Tales to Read Aloud,* Barfoot Books (New York, NY), 2001.

Nicoletta Codignola, reteller, *Orfeo e Euridice,* Fatatrac (Florence, Italy), 2002.

Nicoletta Codignola, reteller, *Il gigante egoista,* Fatatrac (Florence, Italy), 2002.

Nicoletta Codignola, reteller, *La postrella e lo spazzacamino,* Fatatrac (Florence, Italy), 2002.

(With AnnaLaura Cantone and Anna De Carlo) *Prima di Natale,* Nuages, 2002.

Sandra Ann Horn, reteller, *Babushka,* Barefoot Books (Cambridge, MA), 2002.

Hugh Lupton, *Riddle Me This!: Riddles and Stories to Challenge Your Mind,* Barefoot Books (Cambridge, MA), 2003.

Nicoletta Codignola, reteller, *L'asino d'oro e il bastone castigamatti,* Fatatrac (Florence, Italy), 2004.

*Guai a chi mi chiama passerotto! I diritti dei bambini in ospedale,* Fatatrac (Florence, Italy), 2004.

Fraziella Favaro, *Il cavallino e il fiume. Una storia dalla Cina,* Carthusia, 2004.

Joyce Dunbar, *The Love-Me Bird,* Orchard Books (New York, NY), 2004.

Baron Baptiste, *My Daddy Is a Pretzel: Yoga for Parents and Kids,* Barefoot Books (Cambridge, MA), 2004.

Margaret Read MacDonald, *The Farmyard Jamboree,* Barefoot Books (Cambridge, MA), 2005.

Margaret Read MacDonald, *A Hen, a Chick, and a String Guitar,* Barefoot Books (Cambridge, MA), 2005.

Giusi Quarenghi, *Dove comincia l'arcobaleno,* Panini Franco Cosimo, 2005.

Jemina Lumley, *The Journey Home from Grandpa's,* Barefoot Books (Cambridge, MA), 2006.

Berti M. Cristina and Elena Torre, *Gli indovinelli della principessa Turandot,* ETS, 2006.

Angela McAllister, *Just like Sisters,* Atheneum Books (New York, NY), 2006.

Fran Parnell, reteller, *The Barefoot Book of Monsters!,* Barefoot Books (Cambridge, MA), 2006.

Carrie Weston, *If a Chicken Stayed for Supper,* Simon & Schuster UK (London, England), 2006, Holiday House (New York, NY), 2007.

Alma Flor Ada, *One More Friend,* Harcourt (Orlando, FL), 2007.

Aleksandr Puskin, *Il pescioli d'oro* (with audio CD), Fabbri, 2007.

## Sidelights

Sophie Fatus is an author and illustrator whose colorful, child-friendly paintings have made her beloved by young children as well as parents, teachers, and critics in her native Italy. In 2000 her work also became sought after by English-language publishers, and authors such as Alma Flor Ada, Angela McAllister, and Fran Parnell have had their stories brought to life in Fatus's images. Original, self-illustrated books by Fatus that are also

***Italian author and illustrator Sophie Fatus gives readers some subtle clues in her art for Hugh Lupton's* Riddle Me This!** (Barefoot Books, 2003. Illustration © 2006 by Sophie Fatus. Reproduced by permission.)

available in English-language versions include the "Silly Shapes" board books—*Stripes, Spots, Holes,* and *Squares*—in which she collects a whimsical assortment of unusual but related objects. *Stripes,* for example, portrays everything from striped socks to a zebra, while *Spots* depicts a ladybug, a giraffe, and even a banana. In a review of the illustrator's contribution to another English-language text, Sandra Ann Horn's *Babushka,* a *Kirkus Reviews* praised Fatus's engaging artistic style, writing that her "enchanting acrylic paintings employ a stylized, folk-art style using flattened . . . perspectives" and "jewel-bright tones." Bringing to life a familiar rhyme, her illustrated version of *Here We Go round the Mulberry Bush* was described by *School Library Journal* contributor Blair Christolon as a "multicultural treat" designed to "encourage creative movement as well as creativity" in young storyhour fans.

In her colorful illustrations for Joyce Dunbar's *The Love-Me Bird,* Fatus's "cheery," flower-filled pastel images "perfectly match this whimsical tale with wisdom at its heart," according to *Booklist* reviewer Connie Fletcher. Internationally known yoga instructor Baron Baptiste's picture book *My Daddy Is a Pretzel: Yoga for Parents and Kids* benefits from what *Booklist* contributor Gillian Engberg described as "cheery, tropical-colored paintings [that] reinforce a sunny mood," while Fatus's artwork for Carrie Weston's humorous *If a Chicken Stayed for Supper* features "glowing colors and simplified shapes" and "combine[s] a naive look with a sense of form that is sophisticated yet very accessible," according to *Booklist* critic Carolyn Phelan. Dubbed "a charming celebration of friendship" by *School Library Journal* contributor Elaine Lesh Morgan, *Just like Sisters* pairs a story by Angela McAllister with Fatus's "endearing paintings" which, featuring textured backdrops and cartoon characters, "are funny and filled with affection."

## Biographical and Critical Sources

*PERIODICALS*

*Booklist,* October 1, 2001, Kathy Broderick, review of *The Story Tree: Tales to Read Aloud,* p. 321; December 15, 2002, Lauren Peterson, review of *Babushka,* p. 764; December 1, 2003, Hazel Rochman, review of *Riddle Me This!: Riddles and Stories to Challenge Your Mind,* p. 663; February 15, 2004, Connie Fletcher, review of *The Love-Me Bird,* p. 1062; October 15, 2004, Gillian Engberg, review of *My Daddy Is a Pretzel: Yoga for Parents and Kids,* p. 409; March 15, 2007, Carolyn Phelan, review of *If a Chicken Stayed for Supper,* p. 55; June 1, 2007, Carolyn Phelan, review of *Here We Go round the Mulberry Bush,* p. 76.

*Kirkus Reviews,* November 1, 2002, review of *Babushka,* p. 1619; April 15, 2005, review of *A Hen, a Chicken, and a String Guitar,* p. 477; May 15, 2006, review of *Just like Sister,* p. 521; March 1, 2007, review of *If a Chicken Stayed for Supper,* p. 234.

*Publishers Weekly,* March 10, 1997, review of "Silly Shapes" series, p. 67; December 15, 2003, review of *The Love-Me Bird,* p. 46; April 2, 2007, review of *If a Chicken Stayed for Supper,* p. 56.

*School Library Journal,* October, 2002, Eva Mitnick, review of *Babushka,* p. 59; September, 2003, Bina Williams, review of *The Barefoot Book of Monsters!,* p. 204; January, 2004, Sally R. Dow, review of *The Love-Me Bird,* p. 97; April, 2004, Cynde Suite, review of *Riddle Me This!,* p. 139; January, 2005, Joyce Adams Burner, review of *My Daddy Is a Pretzel,* p. 85; May, 2004, Kathleen Whalin, review of *A Hen, a Chick, and a String Guitar,* p. 111; June, 2005, Elaine Lesh Morgan, review of *Just like Sisters,* p. 121; March, 2007, Susan Moorhead, review of *If a Chicken Stayed for Supper,* p. 190.

*ONLINE*

*Bibliotecafossano Web site,* http://www.bibliotecafossano.it/ (September 25, 2003), "Sophie Fatus."*

* * *

# FERGUSON, Alane 1957-

## Personal

Born February 8, 1957, in Cumberland, MD; daughter of Edward (an aerospace engineer) and Gloria (a children's author) Skurzynski; married Ronald Ferguson (a sales and marketing professional), October 11, 1980; children: Kristin Ann, Daniel Edward, Katherine Alane. *Education:* Attended Westminster College and University of Utah. *Politics:* "Environmentalist." *Religion:* Lutheran.

## Addresses

*Home*—1460 Conifer Trail, Elizabeth, CO 80107. *E-mail*—aferguson@alaneferguson.com.

## Career

Writer.

## Awards, Honors

Edgar Allan Poe Award, Mystery Writers of America, 1990, Belgium Children's Choice Award, and International Reading Association Young-Adult Choice citation, all for *Show Me the Evidence;* Children's Crown Classic citation, 1990, for *Cricket and the Crackerbox Kid;* New York Public Library Books for the Teen Age designation, and American Library Association Recommended Book for Reluctant Young-Adult Reader designation, both 1992, both for *Overkill;* Edgar Allan Poe Award nomination, 1994, for *Poison,* 1997, for *Wolf Stalker,* 2007, for *The Christopher Killer;* Indiana Hoozer Award, 2002, for *Cliffhanger,*

## Writings

*FOR CHILDREN*

*That New Pet!,* illustrated by Catherine Stock, Lothrop (New York, NY), 1987.
*Show Me the Evidence,* Bradbury (New York, NY), 1989.
*Cricket and the Crackerbox Kid,* Bradbury (New York, NY), 1990.
*The Practical Joke War,* Bradbury (New York, NY), 1991.
*Stardust,* Bradbury (New York, NY), 1993.
*Tumbleweed Christmas,* illustrated by Tom Sully, Bradbury (New York, NY), 1995.
(With mother, Gloria Skurzynski) *Mystery of the Spooky Shadow,* illustrated by Jeffrey Lindberg, Troll (Mahwah, NJ), 1996.
*Secrets,* Simon & Schuster (New York, NY), 1997.

Contributor to anthologies, including *See You in September,*1995, and *Night Terrors,* 1996.

*YOUNG-ADULT NOVELS*

*Overkill,* Bradbury (New York, NY), 1992.
*Poison,* Bradbury (New York, NY), 1994.
*The Angel of Death: A Forensic Mystery,* Sleuth (New York, NY), 2006.
*The Christopher Killer: A Forensic Mystery,* Sleuth (New York, NY), 2006.
*The Circle of Blood: A Forensic Mystery,* Sleuth (New York, NY), 2007.

*"MYSTERIES IN OUR NATIONAL PARKS" SERIES; MIDDLE-GRADE NOVELS*

(With Gloria Skurzynski) *Wolf Stalker,* National Geographic Society (Washington, DC), 1997.
(With Gloria Skurzynski) *Rage of Fire,* National Geographic Society (Washington, DC), 1998.
(With Gloria Skurzynski) *Cliff Hanger,* National Geographic Society (Washington, DC), 1999.
(With Gloria Skurzynski) *Deadly Waters,* National Geographic Society (Washington, DC), 1999.
(With Gloria Skurzynski) *Ghost Horses,* National Geographic Society (Washington, DC), 2000.
(With Gloria Skurzynski) *The Hunted,* National Geographic Society (Washington, DC), 2000.
(With Gloria Skurzynski) *Valley of Death,* National Geographic Society (Washington, DC), 2002.
(With Gloria Skurzynski) *Escape from Fear,* National Geographic Society (Washington, DC), 2002.
(With Gloria Skurzynski) *Out of the Deep,* National Geographic Society (Washington, DC), 2002.
(With Gloria Skurzynski) *Over the Edge,* National Geographic Society (Washington, DC), 2002.
(With Gloria Skurzynski) *Running Scared,* National Geographic Society (Washington, DC), 2002.
(With Gloria Skurzynski) *Buried Alive,* National Geographic Society (Washington, DC), 2003.
(With Gloria Skurzynski) *Night of the Black Bear,* National Geographic Society (Washington, DC), 2007.

## Sidelights

Alane Ferguson began her writing career in the mid-1980s with the picture book *That New Pet!* While she has written other picture books during her busy career as an author, she has become best known for her middle-grade novels and teen mysteries such as *Overkill* and *The Christopher Killer: A Forensic Mystery.* In addition, Ferguson collaborates with her writer mom Gloria Skurzynski on the "Mysteries in Our National Parks" series, which follow the adventures of the Landon family as Mrs. Landon's job as a wild-animal veterinarian and Mr. Landon's profession as a photographer draw ten-year-old Ashley Landon and older brother Jack into numerous page-turning adventures. In *Cliff Hanger,* in which the Landons track a killer cougar through Mesa Verde National Part, the coauthors "do a fine job of integrating lots of material into an exciting story," according to *Booklist* contributor Ilene Cooper. Fans of the "Mysteries in Our National Parks" series can also follow the Landons on a vacation to Hawaii's Volcanoes National Park in *Rage of Fire.* The holiday turns south when a stalker looms, and the "tense, exciting chase scene [that results] will keep readers on the edge of their seats," predicted *Booklist* contributor Lauren Peterson. *Buried Alive,* another book in the series,

***Ferguson joins mother Gloria Skurzynski in writing* Wolf Stalker, *a "National Parks Mystery" novel featuring artwork by Greg Harlin.*** (Illustration © 1997 by Greg Harlin. Reproduced by permission of National Geographic Society.)

"stands alone as a suspenseful survival story" about the family's adventures in Alaska's Denali National Park, according to *School Library Journal* critic Yapha Nussbaum Mason.

"All through my childhood I talked nonstop to my parents, my four sisters, and to my dolls," Ferguson once told *SATA*. "I always loved communicating but never wanted to commit my thoughts to the page. To me, ideas were fluid and needed to be unfettered by pen and paper. That conviction dogged me throughout my adolescence and well into adulthood. But when my oldest daughter was less than thrilled at the announcement of the upcoming birth of my second child, I decided to comfort her on paper. *That New Pet!,* a picture book, was born right along with my son. And so was my desire to write." *That New Pet!* tells the story of the disruptions that can occur to the lives of family pets when a new baby comes into a family's life. The book was praised by *Horn Book* contributor Ethel R. Twichell as a story full of "good nature and good humor." Another picture book, *Tumbleweed Christmas,* finds a boy and his mother driving across the desert on the way to a holiday get-together. When their car breaks down and they find themselves stranded at a run-down hotel, the boy makes the best of things and celebrates a desert Christmas with a tree crafted from a tumbleweed.

Ferguson turns to young teens in her second book, the novel *Show Me the Evidence.* Here Janaan, a teen from a conservative Arab family, is understandably shaken when her baby brother dies of Sudden Infant Death Syndrome (SIDS). Within six months, two other babies with whom Janaan has had contact also die, and when the teen is accused of murder, she is joined by best friend Lauren in her effort to unravel the mystery and prove her innocence. Reviewing the novel, Roger Sutton wrote in the *Bulletin of the Center for Children's Books* that Ferguson's "story is convincing, the emotions intense, and the suspense exceptionally well maintained."

The joys and strains of growing friendships is one of the themes addressed in Ferguson's middle-grade novel *Cricket and the Crackerbox Kid.* In this story, only-child Cricket Winslow makes a much-needed friend in Dominic, a "crackerbox kid" from the wrong side of town. The two remain friends until they discover that Treasure, a dog Cricket has rescued from the pound, is actually Dominic's recently lost pet. A trial and a jury of fellow fifth graders must now decide the ownership of the dog while Cricket grapples with the question of whether something that is lawful is therefore morally right. Reviewing the novel, Carolyn K. Jenks wrote in *Horn Book* that the two main characters—who "interact in friendship, anger, and sorrow—are honest and believable, as is their love for one beautiful Springer spaniel."

Readers can enjoy a lighthearted look at sibling rivalry in *The Practical Joke War,* as middle child Taffy discovers that her friend Susan is actually interested in Taffy's older brother, Russell. As the two girls work out their complex relationship, Taffy, Russell, and younger brother Eddy engage in an all-out war of pranks and practical jokes, complete with shifting alliances, shaving cream, and precariously perched buckets of water. In *School Library Journal,* Todd Morning praised *The Practical Joke War* for "accurately portray[ing] . . . the rough-and-tumble of family life." Also geared for middle-grade readers, *Stardust* focuses on preteen actress Haley Loring who plays a character on a popular television sitcom. After growing out of the role, Haley and her family move to a small town where the girl adopts Samantha's tough-talking persona as a way to fit in with her new sixth-grade class. Ultimately, Haley learns that she can "dare to be herself, and find real friends," as Susan W. Hunter noted in a review of *Stardust* for *School Library Journal.*

Ferguson first turned the corner from straight fiction to mystery/thriller with *Show Me the Evidence* and fol-

**Tumbleweed Christmas, *Alane Ferguson's picture book about a boy who makes the best out of a lonely holiday on the road, features illustrations by Tom Sully.*** (Illustration © 1996 by Tom Sully. All rights reserved. Reprinted by permission of Simon & Schuster Books for Young Readers, an imprint of Simon & Schuster Children's Publishing Division.)

lowed it up with 1992's *Overkill.* In the award-winning *Overkill* high-school senior Lacey Brighton is preoccupied with the emotional ups and downs surrounding her parents' divorce and her rocky relationship with her older sister. The teen finally seeks the help of a therapist when she begins experiencing violent nightmares. In one dream Lacey stabs her best friend Celeste, and when Celeste is subsequently found dead Lacey is arrested for the crime. During her effort to prove her innocence, Lacey learns the ins and outs of the criminal justice system and also discovers the extent of her friends' loyalty. According to Patricia Gosda, in a review of *Overkill* for *Voice of Youth Advocates,* "the tension builds until the identity of the killer is revealed in a neat, satisfying conclusion."

Set in Silverton, Colorado, *The Christopher Killer* focuses on another high-school senior, in this case Cameryn Mahoney, whose work as a part-time assistant to her coroner father draws her into murder. During an autopsy of a friend, Cammie and her father realize that the murder is the work of a serial killer who leaves a St. Christopher medal on each of his—or her—victims. Determined to bring closure to her friend's death, the teen takes on the task of tracking down the killer, but in the process positions herself as a potential fifth victim. In *Booklist* Stephanie Zvirin commented on the novel's "vivid autopsy scenes," and added that "Cammie's energy and chutzpa . . . propel the story." While Heather M. Campbell wrote in her *School Library Journal* review of *The Christopher Killer* that Ferguson's "story line . . . is as engaging as it is implausible," the critic added that readers will remain transfixed by the fast-moving narrative due to the many "well-researched scientific tidbits sprinkled throughout the text."

Cammie returns in *The Angel of Death: A Forensic Mystery.* When popular English teacher Brad Oakes arrives in her father's morgue in a body bag, the victim of a horrific death, the teen attempts to track down the killer. Her efforts to follow the forensic clues to the murderer are balanced by issues arising in her personal life: her growing emotional bond with Kyle, the high-school classmate who discovered the body, as well as her mixed feelings with regard to an upcoming reunion with the mom she hardly knows. In *The Angel of Death* "the macabre and the melodramatic run neck and neck," observed Zvirin, the critic dubbing Ferguson's novel a "page-turner." In *School Library Journal* Lynn Evarts complimented the author for her competent research into forensic methods and predicted that even reluctant readers would "enjoy the [novel's] fast pace and . . . suspense."

Ferguson once told *SATA:* "A good bit of the energy I once flung around in spoken words is now committed to paper. As I travel to schools across the country, I see many students whose own communication stops exactly where mine used to: in talking to friends. I try to convert them. If there is a satisfaction beyond my own storytelling, it is the opportunity to stoke the writing fire in others. The pure fun of creating characters and worlds is catching, and the rewards are permanent."

*Cover of Ferguson's forensic mystery* **The Christopher Killer,** *in which a high-school sleuth tracks down the killer of her favorite teacher.* (Illustration © 2006 by Jiho Sohn. Reproduced by permission of Sleuth Viking, a division of Penguin Putnam Books for Young Readers.)

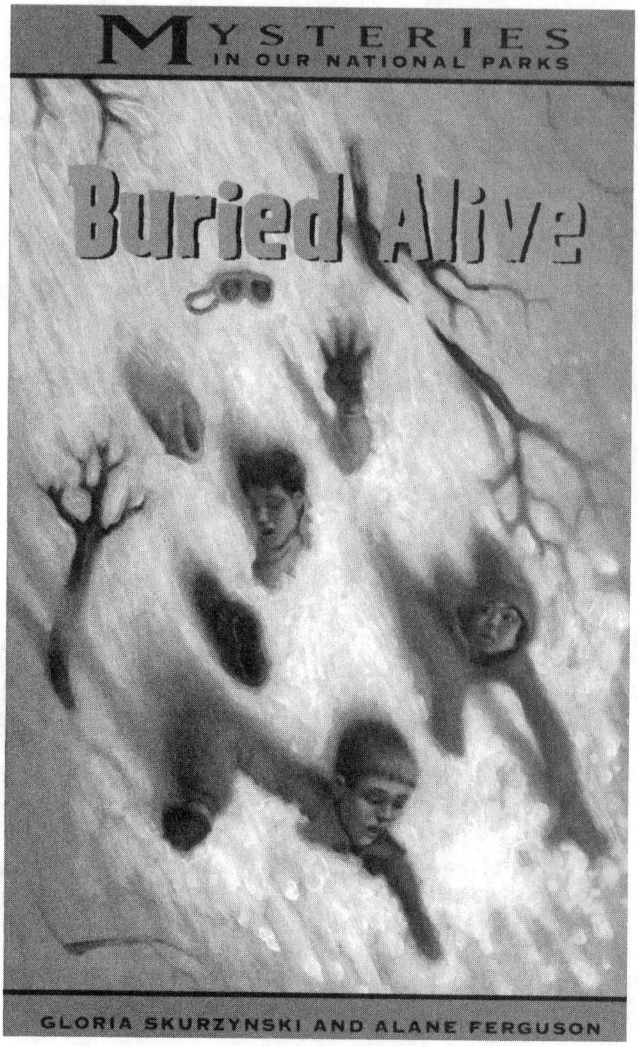


*Cover of* **Buried Alive,** *a novel by the mother-daughter team of Ferguson and Skurzynski, featuring artwork by Loren Long.* (Illustration © 2003 by Loren Long. Reproduced by permission of National Geographic Society.)

## Biographical and Critical Sources

*PERIODICALS*

*Booklist,* January 1, 1993, Stephanie Zvirin, review of *Overkill,* p. 801; May 15, 1993, Deborah Abbott, review of *Stardust,* p. 1692; April 15, 1999, Ilene Cooper, review of *Cliff-hanger,* p. 1532; June 1, 2000, Anne O'Malley, review of *The Hunted,* p. 1898; December 1, 2000, Denise Wilms, review of *Ghost Horses,* p. 821; July 1, 2006, Stephanie Zvirin, review of *The Christopher Killer: A Forensic Mystery,* p. 48; February 15, 2007, Stephanie Zvirin, review of *The Angel of Death: A Forensic Mystery,* p. 73.

*Bulletin of the Center for Children's Books,* April, 1989, Roger Sutton, review of *Show Me the Evidence,* p. 193; July, 1991, review of *The Practical Joke War,* p. 261; April, 1993, review of *Stardust,* p. 246; November, 1996, review of *Tumbleweed Christmas,* p. 96; July, 1997, review of *Secrets,* p. 393.

*Horn Book,* December, 1986, Ethel R. Twichell, review of *That New Pet!,* p. 732; July-August, 1990, Carolyn K. Jenks, review of *Cricket and the Crackerbox Kid,* p. 453.
*Kirkus Reviews,* April 15, 1993, p. 527.
*New York Times Book Review,* January 18, 1987, p. 28.
*Publishers Weekly,* December 12, 1986, review of *That New Pet!,* p. 51; February 24, 1989, review of *Show Me the Evidence,* p. 236; November 21, 1994, review of *Poison,* p. 78; September 30, 1996, review of *Tumbleweed Christmas,* p. 90; Nay 12, 1997, review of *Secrets,* p. 76.
*School Library Journal,* March, 1987, Dana Pinizzotto, review of *That New Pet!,* p. 143; March, 1989, David Thomson Gale, review of *Show Me the Evidence,* p. 198; March, 1990, Nancy P. Reeder, review of *Cricket and the Crackerbox Kid,* p. 217; June, 1991, Todd Morning, review of *The Practical Joke War,* p. 102; January, 1993, Alice Casey Smith, review of *Overkill,* p. 130; June, 1993, Susan W. Hunter, review of *Stardust,* p. 105; January, 1995, Lisa Dennis, review of *Poison,* p. 105; March, 1996, Susan W. Hunter, review of *See You in September,* p. 218; October, 1996, Jane Marino, review of *Tumbleweed Christmas,* p. 35; July, 1997, Nancy Schimmel, review of *Secrets,* p. 93; January, 1998, Marlene Gawron, review of *Wolf Stalker,* p. 114; July, 1998, Janet Gillen, review of *Rage of Fire,* p. 99; May, 1999, Jana R. Fine, review of *Cliff-hanger,* p. 130; October, 1999, Linda L. Plevak, review of *Deadly Waters,* p. 158; August, 2000, Janet Gillen, review of *The Hunted,* p. 190; November, 2000, Ann Cook, review of *Ghost Horses,* p. 162; December, 2003, Yapha Mussbaum Mason, review of *Buried Alive,* p. 151; August, 2006, Heather M. Campbell, review of *The Christopher Killer,* p. 118; September, 2006, Lynn Evarts, review of *The Angel of Death,* p. 204.
*Voice of Youth Advocates,* April, 1993, Patricia Gosda, review of *Overkill,* p. 24.

*ONLINE*

*Alane Ferguson Home Page,* http://www.alaneferguson.com (August 27, 2007).
*Childrenslit.com,* http://www.childrenslit.com/ (August 27, 2007), "Alane Ferguson."*

* * *

# FORTUNE, Eric

## Personal
Male. *Education:* Columbus College of Art and Design, graduated.

## Addresses
*Office*—517 E. Tompkins St., Columbus, OH 43202.

## Career
Illustrator and painter. *Exhibitions:* Works exhibited in Spectrum show, 2005, and Society of Illustrators shows, 2005, 2006.

## Awards, Honors
Best of Show award, Blue Cube Art of Illustration competition.

## Illustrator
James Howe, *Bunnicula Meets Edgar Allan Crow,* Atheneum (New York, NY), 2006.
Jodi Lynn Anderson, *May Bird among the Stars,* Atheneum (New York, NY), 2006.
Anne Ursu, *The Shadow Thieves* ("Cronus Chronicles" series), Atheneum (New York, NY), 2007.
Anne Ursu, *The Siren Song* ("Cronus Chronicles" series), Aladdin (New York, NY), 2007.

Contributor of illustrations to periodicals, including *Spectrum 11.*

## Biographical and Critical Sources

*PERIODICALS*

*Booklist,* March 1, 2006, Holly Koelling, review of *The Shadow Thieves,* p. 94.
*Bulletin of the Center for Children's Books,* May, 2006, Karen Coats, review of *The Shadow Thieves,* p. 426.
*Horn Book,* March-April, 2006, Anita L. Burkam, review of *The Shadow Thieves,* p. 197.
*Kirkus Reviews,* March 1, 2006, review of *The Shadow Thieves,* p. 241; September 15, 2006, review of *May Bird among the Stars,* p. 945.
*School Library Journal,* April, 2006, Lisa Marie Williams, review of *The Shadow Thieves,* p. 149; February, 2007, Elaine E. Knight, review of *Bunnicula Meets Edgar Allan Crow,* p. 118.
*Tribune Books* (Chicago, IL), February 26, 2006, Mary Harris Russell, review of *The Shadow Thieves,* p. 7.
*Washington Post Book World,* May 28, 2006, Elizabeth Ward, review of *The Shadow Thieves,* p. 11.

*ONLINE*

*Art Department Blog,* http://igallo.blogspot.com/ (August 15, 2007), interview with Fortune.
*Donna Rosen Artists Representative Web site,* http://www.donnarosenartists.com/ (August 17, 2007), "Eric Fortune."

* * *

# FRASIER, Debra 1953-

## Personal
Born April 3, 1953, in Vero Beach, FL; daughter of George (stepfather; in marine sales) and Mildred (an artist) Bunnell; married James V. Henkel (an artist/photographer), March 17, 1984; children: Calla Virginia

***Debra Frasier*** (Photograph by James Henkel. Reproduced by permission.)

Frasier-Henkel. *Education:* Florida State University, B.S., 1976; attended Penland School of Crafts, 1976-81, and Humphrey Institute, University of Minnesota, 1988-89.

## Addresses

*Home*—Minneapolis, MN. *Agent*—Virginia Knowlton, Curtis Brown, Ltd., 10 Astor Pl., New York, NY 10003. *E-mail*—DebFra@aol.com.

## Career

Author and illustrator. Project CAST, Tallahassee, FL, director of visual-arts department, 1974-75; artist-in-education program participant, beginning 1976; artist-in-residence at Penland School, 1981-83, and Department of Community Services, City of St. Paul, MN, 1989; sculptor-in-residence at American Cultural Center and Cité des Arts, Paris, France, 1986-87. National spokesperson, Read with a Child Campaign, 1997. Lecturer at conferences and workshops and at schools and universities. *Exhibitions:* Works exhibited in solo and group shows throughout North America and in Switzerland. Sculpture projects incorporated in cities throughout the United States, 1981-86.

## Member

Society of Children's Book Writers and Illustrators.

## Awards, Honors

National Endowment for the Arts project grant, 1980; Parents' Choice Illustrators Gold Award, *Hungry Mind Review* Book of Distinction honor, NSTA-CBC Outstanding Science Trade Book for Children designation, Notable Children's Trade Book in Language Arts designation, and Notable Children's Trade Book in the Field of Social Studies, all 1991, all for *On the Day You Were Born;* American Booksellers Association (ABA) Booksellers Association Pick of the List designation, and American Graphics Society honor list citation, both 1992, both for *The Animal That Drank up Sound;* ABA Pick of the Lists designation, 1994, for *We Got Here Together;* Carnegie Medal for Best Children's Video, American Library Association, 1997, for *On the Day You Were Born;* ABA Pick of the Lists designation, National Parenting Publication honor, Minnesota Book Award, and Southeast Booksellers Association Children's Book Gold Award, all 1999, all for *Out of the Ocean;* International Reading Association Children's Choice and Teacher's Choice honors, both 2000, both for *Miss Alaineus.*

## Writings

*SELF-ILLUSTRATED*

*On the Day You Were Born,* Harcourt (New York, NY), 1991, published with musical CD, 2005, board-book edition, Red Wagon Books (New York, NY), 2006.

*Out of the Ocean,* Harcourt (New York, NY), 1997.

*Miss Alaineus: A Vocabulary Disaster,* Harcourt (New York, NY), 2000.

*The Incredible Water Show,* Harcourt (Orlando, FL), 2004.

*A Birthday Cake Is No Ordinary Cake,* Harcourt (Orlando, FL), 2006.

Adaptor, with others, of stage version of *On the Day You Were Born,* produced 1992, and Braille edition in which visual illustrations are paired with tactile counterparts.

Author's work has been translated into Spanish, Japanese, and Portuguese.

*ILLUSTRATOR*

William Stafford, *The Animal That Drank up Sound,* Harcourt (New York, NY), 1992.

Kim R. Stafford, *We Got Here Together,* Harcourt (New York, NY), 1994.

Richard Lewis, *In the Space of the Sky,* Harcourt (San Diego, CA), 2002.

## Adaptations

*On the Day You Were Born* was adapted as a symphony with a score composed by Steve Heitzeg, an animated video featuring the symphony as soundtrack, and an audiobook.

## Sidelights

Debra Frasier is an artist and animator as well as the author and illustrator of unique award-winning picture books for children. Each of her self-illustrated books, which include *On the Day You Were Born, Miss Alaineus: A Vocabulary Disaster,* and *The Incredible Water Show,* features Frasier's characteristic cut-paper collage art and creative approach to an illuminating subject. In addition to her own books, Frasier has also created art for texts by other writers. In reviewing her brightly colored contribution to Richard Lewis's picture book *In the Space of the Sky,* a *Kirkus Reviews* writer exclaimed that Frasier's "collages of cut paper . . . are dazzling," and *Booklist* contributor Ilene Cooper concluded that the "abstract beauty" of her "intricate cut-paper" images successfully brings to life Lewis's rhyming ode to the vast universe.

Frasier was born and raised in Vero Beach, Florida, where her family has lived since her great grandfather helped to lay out the streets in 1911. "Vero Beach faces the Atlantic Ocean," Frasier once told *SATA,* "and I grew up looking out at the great curved line made where the ocean meets the sky. Summers were my favorite time and often my brother and I would crawl into bed with our bathing suits hidden under our pajamas so we did not have to waste time changing for the beach the following morning! Swimming and walking the beaches were our daytime pastimes, along with collecting shells, drawing with mangrove seeds, and building sand castles and forts out of driftwood. Around fourth grade I discovered books, and began reading with a passion. I remember keeping a flashlight under my pillow so I could creep into the bathroom to read at night."

***Frazier mixes her engaging illustrations with a whimsical story full of wordplay in* Miss Alaineus.** (Illustration © 2002 by Debra Frasier. Reprinted by permission of Harcourt, Inc. This material may not be reproduced in any form or by any means without the prior written permission of the publisher.)

"I loved art from the beginning," Frasier also recalled. "My mother is an artist and she was always collecting shells and bits of surf-worn glass to glue into collaged pictures. She also painted on driftwood and taught me how to paint canvas when I was about twelve." Frasier nurtured her love of art and studied textiles in college. "I studied batik, an ancient wax resist process, with the idea of designing for interiors," she explained. "But, upon graduation, I gave a final party that changed my life—I staged a giant puppet show in my backyard, drafting all of my neighbors into an improvised version of the story of Persephone. I loved making the characters and figuring out the staging, and that led to years of building large, outdoor puppet pageants." Her outdoor pageants have integrated fabrics, words, and even wind; her sixty-foot puppets have danced on a North Carolina mountaintop, and an exhibit called "Windwalk" led viewers through an outdoor trail lined with thousands of strips of cloth blowing in the breeze, interspersed with quotes about the wind.

Frasier has devoted a great deal of time to introducing art to children in the classroom through artist-in-the-schools programs in Minneapolis and elsewhere. One of her programs, titled "Walk around the World," integrates art, storytelling, and academic material into a unified curriculum "where art plays a major part in the learning process rather than its usual minor role," as she told *SATA.* Students are asked to use factual information *and* their imagination to understand how people in other countries live. The experience is "aimed at tolerance," Frasier told Mike Steele for the Twin Cities, Minnesota *Star Tribune.* "The geography, architecture, [and] languages [we study] are different from [the children's] experience. Instead of being afraid of that, they learn to enjoy the differences."

A desire to explore the ways children understand the world gave Frasier the idea of writing a book, and her experiences during a difficult pregnancy provided the motivation. "I hoped my baby would be born safe and sound, and, while I was hospitalized, I began the notes for the book, *On the Day You Were Born,*" she recalled. "I wanted to write about all the things that would welcome my child if she could just get here. I started making notes of things that defied boundaries, that were everywhere and could be counted on to welcome all children. After my daughter was born, I began writing those notes into a manuscript. All of the illustrations were made with cut paper. I was influenced by the work of Matisse and the clear, clean shapes in Japanese textiles."

*On the Day You Were Born* was praised by Steele as "exceptionally simple and marvelously deep," and "a welcome to the world and to each reader's place in it."

The book's poetic text describes the welcome that the sun, the trees, the moon, and other natural forces extend to every newborn child. Frasier pairs her text with bold paper cutout illustrations that vividly portray this welcome and depict children of all colors dancing in the natural world. Michele Landsberg, writing in *Entertainment Weekly,* declared that the award-winning book "will make each child feel linked to planet Earth in a thrillingly personal way," and a *Publishers Weekly* reviewer deemed the work a "paean to nature and to birth."

Frasier's self-illustrated picture book *Out of the Ocean* celebrates her childhood experiences beachcombing with her mother. "As in *On the Day You Were Born,* the layout is inventive and effective, whether cradling the text or propelling readers on to the next page," remarked Liza Bliss in a review of the work for *School Library Journal.* In *Out of the Ocean* Frasier combines collages of photographs and cut-paper shapes with a poetic text emphasizing the wonder and joy of collecting the ocean's sights and sounds as well as more material delights such as sea glass and the proverbial message in a bottle. The book concludes with a journal offering factual details about some of the objects depicted in the story. "Frasier . . . has made a kind of mixed-media naturalist's diary of the beach in front of her house" that is "very low-tech and quite endearing," attested Penelope Green in a *New York Times Book Review* appraisal. *Out of the Ocean* was likewise recognized by other reviewers as a moving tribute to the spiritual solace to be gained from an awareness of the natural world. "The value of this treasure hunter's appreciation is in the notion that real 'treasure' is in the looking," observed a contributor to *Kirkus Reviews.*

In *Miss Alaineus* a fifth grader named Sage mis-hears and misunderstands one of her vocabulary words. Her error leads to a humbling catastrophe in front of the entire class. Described by *School Library Journal* contributor Steve Engelfried as a work "celebrating the fun and the tricky nature of words and their meanings,"

*Frasier's self-illustrated picture book* On the Day You Were Born *uses a poetic text and dramatic art to introduce children to a complex subject.* (Illustration © 1991 by Debra Frasier. Reprinted by permission of Harcourt, Inc. This material may not be reproduced in any form or by any means without the prior written permission of the publisher.)

***A young chef takes the responsibility for creating a very special cake for someone's very special day in Frasier's self-illustrated* A Birthday Cake Is No Ordinary Cake.** (Illustration © 2006 by Debra Frasier. Reprinted by permission of Harcourt, Inc. This material may not be reproduced in any form or by any means without the prior written permission of the publisher. )

*Miss Alaineus* grew out of Frasier's desire to make a story about a mistake carrying someone to a new place. As the author/illustrator once recalled, "My daughter confessed to me one night when she was nine years old that she had just figured out that miscellaneous was not a person . . . Miss Alaineus! I couldn't stop thinking about that marvelous mistake!" Praising the volume, Carolyn Phelan praised Frasier's "highly visual, first-person story," while *School Library Journal* reviewer Karen Land noted that Sage's "ability to . . . remake [her misunderstanding] . . . into a positive experience is a valuable lesson."

The passage of time is Frasier's focus in *A Birthday Cake Is No Ordinary Cake,* a picture book that features Frasier's characteristic brightly colored collage art. In the simple story, a baker assembles a cake over the period of a year, and ingredients include a dozen full moons, snowflakes, the shadows of migrating birds, and a years' worth of sunrises. Praising the book's unique and thought-provoking premise, Helen Foster James wrote in *School Library Journal* that *A Birthday Cake Is No Ordinary Cake* "blends a melodic, metaphorical look of nature with scientific topics" addressed in Frasier's informative text. Another scientific topic is the focus of *The Incredible Water Show,* which follows a fifth-grade class as they create a play that dramatizes Earth's water cycle and the effects of pollution on the planet. Lynda Ritterman praised the book, citing its "snappy text, jazzy picture, and upbeat tone" in her *School Library Journal* review.

## Biographical and Critical Sources

*PERIODICALS*

*Booklist,* April 15, 1998, Susan Dove Lempke, review of *Out of the Ocean,* p. 1451; September 15, 2000, Carolyn Phelan, review of *Miss Alaineus: A Vocabulary Disaster,* p. 240; May 1, 2002, Ilene Cooper, review of *In the Space of the Sky,* p. 1534.

*Entertainment Weekly,* April 5, 1991, Michele Landsberg, "Happy Birthdays," pp. 72-73.

*Five Owls,* March-April, 1991, review of *On the Day You Were Born.*

*Kirkus Reviews,* March 1, 1998, review of *Out of the Ocean,* p. 337; April 1, 2002, review of *In the Space of Sky,* p. 495; August 1, 2004, review of *The Incredible Water Show,* p. 741; August 14, 2006, review of *A Birthday Cake Is No Ordinary Cake,* p. 840.

*New York Times Book Review,* July 19, 1998, Penelope Green, review of *Out of the Ocean,* p. 24; March 11, 2001, review of *Miss Alaineus,* p. 26.

*Publishers Weekly,* February 15, 1991, review of *On the Day You Were Born*; March 22, 1991, review of *On the Day You Were Born,* p. 79; April 1, 2002, review of *In the Space of the Sky,* p. 81.

*School Library Journal,* June, 1991, Eve Larkin, review of *On the Day You Were Born,* p. 76; August, 1998, Liza Bliss, review of *Out of the Ocean,* p. 139; September, 2000, Karen Land, review of *Miss Alaineus,* p. 197; May, 2002, Wendy Lukehart, review of *In the Space of the Sky,* p. 120; June, 2004, Steven Engelfried, review of *Miss Alaineus,* p. 56; December, 2004, Lynda Ritterman, review of *The Incredible Water Show,* p. 106; October, 2006, Helen Foster James, review of *A Birthday Cake Is No Ordinary Cake,* p. 134.

*Star Tribune* (Twin Cities, MN), March 17, 1991, Mike Steele, "In Book and Play, Debra Frasier Celebrates Life," pp. F1, F7.

*ONLINE*

*Debra Frasier Home Page,* http://www.debrafrasier.com (June 10, 2007).*

# G-I

## GARZA, Carmen Lomas 1948-

### Personal

Born 1948, in Kingsville, TX. *Ethnicity:* "Mexican." *Education:* Texas Arts and Industry University, B.S., 1972; Juarez-Lincoln/Antioch Graduate School, M.Ed., 1973; San Francisco State University, M.A., 1981.

### Addresses

*Home and office*—P.O. Box 881683, San Francisco, CA 94188-1683. *E-mail*—lasecretaria@carmenlomasgarza.com.

### Career

Artist and illustrator. Worked variously as an administrative assistant and curator. *Exhibitions:* Solo exhibitions staged at San Jose Museum of Art, San Jose, CA; Hirschhorn Museum and Sculpture Garden, Smithsonian Institution, Washington, DC; and Whitney Museum of American Art, New York, NY.

### Awards, Honors

Texas Bluebonnet Award, Texas Library Association, 1990, for *Family Pictures*; Tomás Rivera Mexican-American Children's Book Award, 1996-97; Pura Belpré Honor Book designation, American Library Association, 1990, for *Family Pictures,* 1997, for *In My Family,* and 2000, for *Magic Windows*; *Skipping Stones* magazine Book Award, and Américas Award Honor Book, both 2000, both for *Magic Windows;* Carmen Lomas Garza Primary Center named by Los Angeles Unified School District Board, 2007.

### Writings

*Family Pictures/Cuadros de familia* (picture book), Children's Book Press (San Francisco, CA), 1990, reprinted, 2005.

***Carmen Lomas Garza*** (Courtesy of Children's Book Press. )

*A Piece of My Heart/Pedacito de mi corazon: The Art of Carmen Lomas Garza,* New Press (New York, NY), 1994.

*In My Family/En mi familia* (picture book), Children's Book Press (San Francisco, CA), 1996.

*Magic Windows/Ventanas magicas* (picture book), Children's Book Press (San Francisco, CA), 1999.

*Making Magic Windows: Creating Papel Picado/Cut-Paper Art with Carmen Lomas Garza,* Children's Book Press (San Francisco, CA), 1999.

### Sidelights

Texas-born artist Carmen Lomas Garza is committed to celebrating the history and culture of the Mexican-American community of the southern United States. Garza taught herself the tenets of art and drawing at a young age and was heavily influenced by the artwork of her mother and grandmother. As she noted in the artist

***Artist Garza draws on memories of her large, close-knit family to create the intriguing bilingual picture book* Family Pictures/Cuadros de familia.** (Children's Book Press, 2005. Illustration © 1990, 2005 by Carmen Lomas Garza. Reproduced by permission.)

statement on her home page, she was encouraged by the 1960s Chicano movement to devote her creativity "to the depiction of special and everyday events in the lives of Mexican Americans." As an artist, Garza is well celebrated in the Mexican-American community in addition to being known nationally; she has also created commissioned works for the San Francisco International Airport and the San Francisco Water Department.

Garza's self-illustrated books for children, which include *In My Family/En mi familia, Magic Windows/ Ventanas magicas,* and *Family Pictures/Cuadros de familia,* are based on the artist's memories of growing up in South Texas. Garza often depicts close family members, such as her mother, grandmother, and grandfather, tending to daily household chores. For instance, in *Magic Windows* Garza portrays her grandfather watering his garden while her mother is in the kitchen, cooking. The illustrations for *Magic Windows* are designed to make the reader feel as if they are glimpsing family scenes through stained-glass windows. *Family Pictures* also highlights the family setting and includes paintings with "rich detail"—as noted by Kent Anderson and Ken Marantz of *School Arts*—for its ability to portray "family bonds and vital community support." Annie Ayres, writing in *Booklist,* described *In My Family* as a "family album" that "shares the artist's memories of the Hispanic cultural experience."

## Biographical and Critical Sources

*PERIODICALS*

*Booklist,* November 1, 1996, Annie Ayres, review of *In My Family/En mi familia,* p. 503; May 1, 1999, Annie Ayres, review of *Magic Windows/Ventanas magicas,* p. 1592; March 15, 2000, review of *Magic Windows,* p. 1342.

*Booklinks,* January-February, 2006, April Whatley Bedford and Roxane Cuellar, review of *In My Family,* p. 25.
*Horn Book,* November-December, 1996, Maria B. Salvadore, review of *In My Family,* p. 760.
*Publishers Weekly,* February 22, 1999, "Window of Creative Opportunity," p. 97.
*School Arts,* May-June, 1995, Kent Anderson and Ken Marantz, review of *Family Pictures/Cuadros de familia,* p. 42; September, 2005, Rebecca J. Martin, review of *Family Pictures,* p. 60.
*School Library Journal,* November, 1996, Rose Zertuche Trevino, review of *In My Family,* p. 134.
*Skipping Stones,* March-April, 1997, Dick Keis, review of *In My Family,* p. 7; May-August, 2000, Beth Erfurth, review of *Magic Windows,* p. 7.
*Texas Monthly,* June, 1994, review of *A Piece of My Heart/ Pedacito de mi corazon: The Art of Carmen Lomas Garza,* p. 80.

*ONLINE*

*Carmen Lomas Garza Home Page,* http://www.carmenlomasgarza.com (August 9, 2007).
*San Jose Museum of Art Web site,* http://www.sjmusart.org/ (August 9, 2007), "Carmen Lomas Garza."

* * *

# HELLARD, Susan

## Personal

Born in England. *Education:* Earned degree (graphics).

## Addresses

*Home and office*—North London, England. *Agent*—Arena Works, 31 Eleanor Rd., London E15 4AB, England.

## Career

Illustrator, beginning 1978.

## Writings

*SELF-ILLUSTRATED*

*How to Be Popular with Your Pet,* Piccadilly Press (London, England), 1984.
(Adaptor) *Billy Goats Gruff,* Piccadilly Press (London, England) 1986.
(Adaptor) Hans Christian Andersen, *The Ugly Duckling,* Putnam (New York, NY), 1987.
(Adaptor) *Froggie Goes A-Courting,* Putnam (New York, NY), 1988.
(Adaptor) *This Little Piggy,* Putman (New York, NY), 1989.
*Time to Get Up,* Piccadilly Press (London, England), 1989, Putnam (New York, NY), 1990.
*Eleanor and the Babysitter,* Little, Brown (Boston, MA), 1991.
*Baby Tiger,* Piccadilly Press (London, England), 1999.
*Baby Panda,* Piccadilly Press (London, England), 1999.
*Baby Lemur,* Holt (New York, NY), 1999.
*Baby Elephant,* Piccadilly Press (London, England), 2000.

*ILLUSTRATOR; FOR CHILDREN*

Sam McBratney, *Zesty,* Hamilton (London, England), 1984.
Anita Harper, *It's Not Fair!,* G.P. Putnam's (New York, NY), 1986.
Barbara Iresom, *Fighting in Break, and Other Stories,* Faber & Faber (London, England), 1987.
Sandy Asher, *Where Do You Get Your Ideas?: Helping Young Writers Begin,* Walker (New York, NY), 1987.
Anita Harper, *Just a Minute!,* Putnam (New York, NY), 1987.
Kathy Henderson, *Don't Interrupt!,* Barron's (New York, NY), 1988.
Anita Harper, *What Feels Best?,* Putnam (New York, NY), 1988.
Dick King-Smith, *Friends and Brothers,* Mammoth (London, England), 1989.
Sylvia Woods, *Now Then, Charlie Robinson,* Puffin (London, England), 1989.
Jill Tomlinson, *The Gorilla Who Wanted to Grow Up,* Mammoth (London, England), 1990.
Jill Tomlinson, *The Cat Who Wanted to Go Home,* Mammoth (London, England), 1990.
Terrance Dicks, *Teacher's Pet,* Piccadilly Press (London, England), 1990.
Paul Sidey, *The Dinosaur Diner, and Other Poems,* Piccadilly Press (London, England), 1990.
Jill Tomlinson, *Penguin's Progress,* Mammoth (London, England), 1991.
Jill Tomlinson, *The Hen Who Wouldn't Give Up,* Mammoth (London, England), 1991.
Gwen Grant, *Little Blue Car,* Orchard Books (London, England), 1991.
Jill Tomlinson, *The Aardvark Who Wasn't Sure,* Mammoth (London, England), 1991.
Jill Tomlinson, *The Otter Who Wanted to Know,* Methuen (London, England), 1992.
Jill Tomlinson, *The Owl Who Was Afraid of the Dark,* Methuen (London, England), 1992.
Elizabeth Gouge, *I Saw Three Ships,* Lion (London, England), 1992.
Lucy Coats, *One Hungry Baby: A Bedtime Counting Rhyme,* Orchard Books (London, England), 1992, Crown (New York, NY), 1994.
Mary Hooper, *Spook Spotting,* Walker (London, England), 1993.
Ken Adams, *Samson Superslug,* Lion (London, England), 1993.
Linda Newbery, *The Marmalade Pony,* Hippo (London, England), 1994.
Elizabeth Laird, *Stinker Muggles and the Dazzle Bug,* Collins (London, England), 1995.

Terrance Dicks, *Harvey to the Rescue,* Piccadilly (London, England), 1995.

Phil Roxbee Cox, *Nightmare at Mystery Mansion,* Usborne (London, England), 1995.

W.J. Corbett, *Hamish: Climbing Father's Mountain,* Hodder (London, England), 1995.

Julie Hope and John Hope, *Christmas Carols for Cats,* HarperCollins (New York, NY), 1996.

Terrance Dicks, *Harvey and the Beast of Bodmin,* Piccadilly (London, England), 1996.

Terrance Dicks, *Harvey on Holiday,* Piccadilly (London, England), 1996.

Stan Cullimore, *George's Gang in Trouble,* Piccadilly Press (London, England), 1996.

(With Amanda Hall) Richard Brown and Kate Ruttle, selectors, *A Mosquito in the Cabin* (poems), Cambridge University Press (Cambridge, England), 1996.

Terrance Dicks, *Harvey and the Swindlers,* Piccadilly Press (London, England), 1997.

Terrance Dicks, *Harvey Goes to School,* Piccadilly Press (London, England), 1997.

Bernard Ashley, *Flash,* Orchard (London, England), 1997.

Mary Hooper, *Spooks Ahoy!,* Walker (London, England), 1997.

Julie Hope and John Hope, *Nursery Rhymes for Cats,* Bantam (London, England), 1998.

Mary Hooper, *The Great Twin Trick,* Walker (London, England), 1999.

Julie Hope and John Hope, *Christmas Crackers for Cats,* Bantam (London, England), 2000.

Mary Hooper, *Spook Summer,* Walker (London, England), 2001.

Kate Lum, *Princesses Are Not Quitters!,* Bloomsbury (London, England), 2002, Bloomsbury Children's Books (New York, NY), 2003.

Giles Andreae, *My Grandson Is a Genius!,* Bloomsbury Children's Books (New York, NY), 2003.

Irena Green, *You Can Do It, Stanley,* Corgi Pups (London, England), 2004.

Belinda Hollyer, *She's All That!: Poems about Girls,* Kingfisher (London, England), 2005, Kingfisher (Boston, MA), 2006.

Louise Baum, *The Mouse Who Braved Bedtime,* Bloomsbury Children's Books (New York, NY), 2006.

Angela McAllister, *Take a Kiss to School,* Bloomsbury Children's Books (New York, NY), 2006.

Bel Mooney, *Who Loves Mr Tubs?,* Egmont (London, England), 2006.

*"T.R. BEAR" SERIES; ILLUSTRATOR*

Terrance Dicks, *Enter T.R.,* Piccadilly (London, England), 1985, Barrons's (New York, NY), 1988.

Terrance Dicks, *T.R. Goes to School,* Piccadilly (London, England), 1985, Barron's (New York, NY), 1988.

Terrance Dicks, *T.R.'s Day Out,* Piccadilly (London, England), 1985.

Terrance Dicks, *T.R. Afloat,* Piccadilly Press (London, England), 1986.

Terrance Dicks, *T.R.'s Hallowe'en,* Piccadilly Press (London, England), 1986, Barron's (New York, NY), 1988.

Terrance Dicks, *T.R.'s Festival,* Piccadilly Press (London, England), 1987.

Terrance Dicks, *T.R.'s Big Game,* Piccadilly Press (London, England), 1987.

Terrance Dicks, *T.R. Goes to Hollywood,* Piccadilly Press (London, England), 1988.

Terrance Dicks, *T.R. Goes Skiing,* Piccadilly Press (London, England), 1988.

Terrance Dicks, *T.R. Down Under,* Piccadilly Press (London, England), 1989.

Terrance Dicks, *T.R. in New York,* Piccadilly Press (London, England), 1989.

Terrance Dicks, *T.R. Bear at the Zoo,* Piccadilly Press (London, England), 1990.

*"RHYMES WITH ME" SERIES: ILLUSTRATOR*

Tony Bradman, *Play Time,* MacDonald (London, England), 1985.

Tony Bradman, *At the Park,* Macdonald (London, England), 1985.

Tony Bradman, *Let's Pretend,* Macdonald (London, England), 1985.

Tony Bradman, *Hide and Seek,* Macdonald (London, England), 1985.

*"DILLY THE DINOSAUR" SERIES; ILLUSTRATOR*

Tony Bradman, *Dilly the Dinosaur,* Piccadilly Press (London, England), 1986, Viking Kestrel (New York, NY), 1987.

Tony Bradman, *Dilly Visits the Dentist,* Piccadilly Press (London, England), 1986, published as *Dilly Goes to the Dentist,* Viking Kestrel (New York, NY), 1987.

Tony Bradman, *Dilly's Muddy Day,* Mammoth (London, England), 1986, published as *Dilly Gets Muddy!,* 1999.

Tony Bradman, *Dilly and the Horror Film,* Piccadilly Press (London, England), 1987, Viking Kestrel (New York, NY), 1989.

Tony Bradman, *Dilly and the Tiger,* Piccadilly Press (London, England), 1988.

Tony Bradman, *Dilly: The Worst Day Ever,* Piccadilly Press (London, England), 1988.

Tony Bradman, *Dilly Tells the Truth,* Viking Kestrel (New York, NY), 1988.

Tony Bradman, *Dilly-Dinosuar, Superstar,* Piccadilly Press (London, England), 1989.

Tony Bradman, *Dilly and the Ghost,* Piccadilly Press (London, England), 1989.

Tony Bradman, *Dilly Goes on Holiday,* Piccadilly Press (London, England), 1990.

Tony Bradman, *Dilly Speaks Up,* Piccadilly Press (London, England), 1990, Viking (New York, NY), 1991.

Tony Bradman, *Dilly the Angel,* Piccadilly Press (London, England), 1990, published as *Dilly at the Funfair,* Mammoth (London, England), 1999.

Tony Bradman, *Dilly's Birthday Party,* Piccadilly Press (London, England), 1991.

Tony Bradman, *Dilly and the Big Kids,* Piccadilly Press (London, England), 1991, published as *Dilly to the Rescue,* 1999.

Tony Bradman, *Dilly and His Swamp Lizard,* Piccadilly Press (London, England), 1991.

Tony Bradman, *Dilly Goes to School,* Mammoth (London, England), 1992.

Tony Bradman, *Dilly and the Pirates,* Piccadilly Press (London, England), 1992.

Tony Bradman, *Dilly Goes Swamp Wallowing,* Mammoth (London, England), 1993.

Tony Bradman, *Dilly Dinosaur, Detective,* Heinemann (London, England), 1994.

Tony Bradman, *Dilly and the Tiger, and Other Stories,* Dean (London, England), 1994.

Tony Bradman, *Dilly and the Vampire,* Heinemann (London, England), 1995, published as *Dilly Saves the Day,* 1999.

*Dilly and the Goody-Goody,* Mammoth (London, England), 1996.

*Dilly and the Cup Final,* Mammoth (London, England), 1997, published as *Dilly and the School Report,* Egmont Children's (London, England), 2001.

*Dilly Breaks the Rules,* Mammoth (London, England), 1999.

*Dilly and the Gold Medal,* Mammoth (London, England), 1999.

Tony Bradman, *Dilly and the School Play,* Egmont Children's (London, England), 2002.

*"WOODSIDE SCHOOL STORIES" SERIES; ILLUSTRATOR*

Jean Ure, *The Fright,* Orchard (London, England), 1988.

Jean Ure, *Loud Mouth,* Orchard (London, England), 1988.

Jean Ure, *Soppy Birthday,* Orchard (London, England), 1988.

*"FAMOUS CHILDREN" SERIES: ILLUSTRATOR*

Ann Rachlin, *Bach,* Barron's (New York, NY), 1992.

Ann Rachlin, *Handel,* Barron's (New York, NY), 1992.

Ann Rachlin, *Haydn,* Barron's (New York, NY), 1992.

Ann Rachlin, *Mozart,* Barron's (New York, NY), 1992.

Ann Rachlin, *Brahms,* Barron's (New York, NY), 1993.

Ann Rachlin, *Chopin,* Barron's (New York, NY), 1993.

Ann Rachlin, *Schumann,* Barron's (New York, NY), 1993.

Ann Rachlin, *Tchaikovsky,* Barron's (New York, NY), 1993.

Ann Rachlin, *Schubert,* Gollancz (London, England), 1993, Barron's (New York, NY), 1994.

Ann Rachlin, *Beethoven,* Gollancz (London, England), 1993, Barron's (New York, NY), 1994.

Tony Hart, *Toulouse-Lautrec,* Gollancz (London, England), 1993, Barron's (New York, NY), 1994.

Tony Hart, *Michelangelo,* Gollancz (London, England), 1993, Barron's (New York, NY), 1994.

Tony Hart, *Leonardo da Vinci,* Barron's (New York, NY), 1994.

Tony Hart, *Picasso,* Barron's (New York, NY), 1994.

*"CAMBRIDGE READING" SERIES; ILLUSTRATOR*

June Crebbin, *Nibbles,* Cambridge University Press (Cambridge, England), 1997.

June Crebbin, *Apples!,* Cambridge University Press (Cambridge, England), 1997.

June Crebbin, *Wrigglebottom,* Cambridge University Press (Cambridge, England), 1997.

June Crebbin, *The Flying Football,* Cambridge University Press (Cambridge, England), 1997.

June Crebbin, *The Puppy Chase,* Cambridge University Press (Cambridge, England), 1997.

June Crebbin, *Granny's Teeth,* Cambridge University Press (Cambridge, England), 1997.

*"JENNY DALE'S KITTENS" SERIES; ILLUSTRATOR*

Jenny Dale, *Star the Snowy Kitten,* Macmillan Children's (London, England), 1999, Aladdin (New York, NY), 2001.

Jenny Dale, *Nell the Naughty Kitten,* Macmillan Children's (London, England), 1999, Aladdin (New York, NY), 2001.

Jenny Dale, *Bob the Bouncy Kitten,* Macmillan Children's (London, England), 1999, Aladdin (New York, NY), 2000.

Jenny Dale, *Patch the Perfect Kitten,* Macmillan Children's (London, England), 2000, Aladdin (New York, NY), 2001.

Jenny Dale, *Colin the Clumsy Kitten,* Aladdin (New York, NY), 2000.

Jenny Dale, *Felix the Fluffy Kitten,* Aladdin (New York, NY), 2000.

Jenny Dale, *Leo the Lucky Kitten,* Macmillan Children's (London, England), 2000.

Jenny Dale, *Lucy the Lonely Kitten,* Macmillan Children's Books (London, England), 2000.

Jenny Dale, *Snuggles the Sleepy Kitten,* Macmillan Children's (London, England), 2001.

Jenny Dale, *Pip the Prize Kitten,* Macmillan Children's (London, England), 2001.

Jenny Dale, *Sid the Speedy Kitten,* Macmillan Children's (London, England), 2001.

Jenny Dale, *Poppy the Posh Kitten,* Macmillan Children's (London, England), 2001.

*"JENNY DALE'S PUPPIES" SERIES; ILLUSTRATOR*

Jenny Dale, *Spike the Special Puppy,* Macmillan Children's (London, England), 2000.

Jenny Dale, *Merlin the Magic Puppy,* Macmillan Children's (London, England), 2000.

Jenny Dale, *Snowy the Surprise Puppy,* Macmillan Children's (London, England), 2000, Scholastic (New York, NY), 2005.

*"JENNY DALE'S BEST FRIENDS" SERIES; ILLUSTRATOR*

Jenny Dale, *Bubble and Squeak,* Macmillan Children's (London, England), 2001, Scholastic (New York, NY), 2005.

Jenny Dale, *Crumble and Custard,* Macmillan Children's (London, England), 2001.

Jenny Dale, *Banger and Mash,* Macmillan Children's (London, England), 2001.
Jenny Dale, *Lily at the Beach,* Macmillan Children's (London, England), 2001.
Jenny Dale, *Lily Finds a Friend,* Macmillan Children's (London, England), 2001.
Jenny Dale, *Amber and Alfie,* Macmillan Children's (London, England), 2002.
Jenny Dale, *Snowflake and Sparkle,* Macmillan Children's (London, England), 2002.
Jenny Dale, *Bramble and Berry,* Macmillan Children's (London, England), 2002.
Jenny Dale, *Skipper and Sky,* Macmillan Children's (London, England), 2002.
Jenny Dale, *Pogo and Pip,* Macmillan Children's (London, England), 2002.
Jenny Dale, *Carrot and Clover,* Macmillan Children's (London, England), 2002.
Jenny Dale, *Blossom and Beany,* Macmillan Children's (London, England), 2002, Scholastic (New York, NY), 2004.
Jenny Dale, *Hattie and Henry,* Macmillan Children's (London, England), 2003.
Jenny Dale, *Lottie and Ludo,* Macmillan Children's (London, England), 2003.

*"MARVIN REDPOST" SERIES; ILLUSTRATOR*

Louis Sachar, *Marvin Redpost, Class President,* new edition, Bloomsbury Children's Books (London, England), 2004.
Louis Sachar, *Is He a Girl?,* Bloomsbury Children's Books (London, England), 2004.
Louis Sachar, *Marvin Redpost—Why Pick on Me?,* Bloomsbury Children's Books (London, England), 2004.
Louis Sachar, *Marvin Redpost, Kidnapped at Birth,* Bloomsbury Children's Books (London, England), 2004.
Louis Sachar, *Super Fast, out of Control!,* new edition, Bloomsbury Children's (London, England), 2005.

*ILLUSTRATOR; OTHER*

Anita Naik, *Single Again: Living Alone and Liking It,* Piccadilly Press (London, England), 1992.
Vida Adamoli, *You and Your Cat: The Ultimate Relationship,* Piccadilly (London, England), 1994.

## Biographical and Critical Sources

*PERIODICALS*

*Children's Bookwatch,* December, 2006, reviews of *The Mouse Who Braved Bedtime.*
*Horn Book,* November, 1995, review of *Chopin,* p. 774; November, 1995, review of *Tchaikovsky,* p. 774.
*Kirkus Reviews,* September 15, 2006, review of *The Mouse Who Braved Bedtime,* p. 946.
*Publishers Weekly,* February 9, 1990, review of *Time to Get Up,* p. 58; April 26, 1991, review of *Eleanor and the Babysitter,* p. 59; March 27, 2006, "Advice and Inspiration for Girls," p. 81.
*School Arts,* May-June, 2006, Ken Marantz, review of *Leonardo da Vinci,* p. 57.
*School Library Journal,* August, 1994, review of *Toulouse-Lautrec,* p. 151; August, 1994, Shirley Wilton, review of *Leonardo da Vinci,* p. 151; August, 1994, Shirley Wilton, review of *Michelangelo,* p. 151; August, 1994, Shirley Wilton, review of *Picasso,* p. 151; January, 2000, Michele Snyder, review of *Baby Lemur,* p. 104; July, 2006, Jill Heritage, review of *She's All That!: Poems about Girls,* p. 120; October, 2006, Tamara E. Richman, review of *The Mouse Who Braved Bedtime,* p. 102.
*Times Educational Supplement,* September 25, 1992, Philippa Davidson, review of *Mozart, Bach, Handel,* and *Hayden,* p. 12; July 5, 1996, review of *George's Gang in Trouble,* p. 6; September 20, 1996, review of *Dilly and the Goody-Goody,* p. 16; September 20, 1996, review of *Dilly and the Vampire,* p. 16.

*ONLINE*

*Arena Works Web site,* http://www.arenaworks.com/ (August 21, 2007), "Susan Hellard."
*Bloomsbury USA Web site,* http://www.bloomsburyusa.com/ (August 17, 2006), "Susan Hellard."*

* * *

# INGMAN, Bruce 1963-

## Personal

Born 1963, in Liverpool, England; son of a dressmaker; married; children: Alvie (daughter). *Education:* Attended Nottingham Trent University and Royal College of Art.

## Addresses

*Home*—London, England.

## Career

Author and illustrator. Teacher at art colleges.

## Awards, Honors

National Art Library Illustration Award, 1995, and Mother Goose Award, 1996, both for *When Martha's Away;* Victoria and Albert Second Prize for Book Illustration (jointly with Simone Lia), 2004.

## Writings

*SELF-ILLUSTRATED*

*When Martha's Away,* Houghton Mifflin (Boston, MA), 1995.

*Lost Property,* Methuen (London, England), 1997, Houghton Mifflin (Boston, MA), 1998.
*A Night on the Tiles,* Methuen (London, England), 1998, Houghton Mifflin (Boston, MA), 1999.
*Bad News! I'm in Charge,* Candlewick Press (Boston, MA), 2003.

*ILLUSTRATOR*

Sean Taylor, *Boing!,* Candlewick Press (Cambridge, MA), 2004.
Kate Feiffer, *Double Pink,* Simon & Schuster (New York, NY), 2005.
Allan Ahlberg, *The Runaway Diner,* Candlewick Press (New York, NY), 2006.
Allan Ahlberg, *Previously,* Candlewick Press (New York, NY), 2007.

Contributor of illustrations to periodicals, including *Vogue* and London *Sunday Times.*

## Sidelights

British author and illustrator Bruce Ingman is the creator of several picture books for young children. As an illustrator, he is known for mixing gestured line drawings with collage elements and interesting graphic images, all washed with vibrant colors. Beginning his picture-book career in 1996 with the award-winning *When Martha's Away,* Ingman has gone on to write and illustrate several more picture books, as well as creating art for texts by authors such as Kate Feiffer, Sean Taylor, and Allan Ahlberg.

In his award-winning first book, *When Martha's Away,* Ingman follows a cat named Lionel on its rounds during a day left at home alone. While Martha, his young caretaker, believes the cat sleeps each day away, Lionel in fact keeps current on world news, cooks himself fancy lunches, and entertains the female cats in the neighborhood, all while keeping up his reputation for shiftlessness. Reviewers remarked not only on Ingman's story but also on his illustrations. Calling *When Martha's Away* "a keen debut," Ilene Cooper wrote in *Booklist* that Ingman's "art has a childlike feel that readers of all ages will respond to." Reviewing the book for *School Library Journal,* Kathy Mitchell claimed that "the bold, uncluttered illustrations . . . define objects quite nicely and are pleasing to the eye," and a *Kirkus Reviews* critic predicted that *When Martha's Away* "will inspire laughs out loud from all readers, no matter what their ages."

Lionel makes an encore appearance in *A Night on the Tiles,* a book that reveals what happens when the clever cat is supposedly fast asleep on Martha's bed. Instead of snoozing, the feline waits until his owner falls asleep before beginning his own event-packed evening. During the moonlight hours, the nocturnal Lionel attends classes at the Cat Academy, has his whiskers trimmed at Jean-Pierre's, and watches a movie with a female friend before returning home in time to resume his on-the-bed posture. Reviewers again commented favorably on Ingman's artwork, a *Publishers Weekly* critic noting that the author/illustrator's "exuberant use of wonderfully balanced color fields and quick-flowing, quirkily expressive line drawings" exudes "a celebratory, happy energy."

Misplaced objects are the featured attraction in Ingman's *Lost Property,* a book described by a *Publishers Weekly* contributor as a "winning successor to his debut." Strangely, things seem to go missing in Maurice's house, everything from his father's dry-cleaning stub to bathroom towels to car keys. As readers observe, Mac, the family dog, is a nearby presence every time a family member realizes that one thing or another is not where he or she left it. "Details of the family mess will make kids laugh," predicted *Booklist* reviewer Hazel Rochman, while a *Kirkus Reviews* critic suggested that *Lost Property* "works best as inspiration for children to put together their own scenes of comic domestic turmoil."

In his self-illustrated picture book *Bad News! I'm in Charge!* Ingman "once again wields delectably artless acrylics and a wicked sense of humor," according to a *Publishers Weekly* contributor. When Danny discovers a document that makes him the ruler of the land, he sets

***Bruce Ingman brings a modernistic and whimsical flair to his self-illustrated picture books, which include* Lost Property.** (Illustration © 1997 by Bruce Ingman. Reprinted by permission of Houghton Mifflin Company. All rights reserved.)

***Sean Taylor's simple text in* Boing! *is given added meaning in Ingman's thought-provoking graphic images.*** (Illustration © 2004 by Bruce Ingman. Reproduced by permission of the publisher, Candlewick Press, Inc., Cambridge, MA on behalf of Walker Books Ltd., London.)

about making changes to the parental rules. Along with ordering that French fries be served at every meal, Danny decrees that all schoolchildren can bring their pets to class, making the day more fun. As the work piles up and distasteful but necessary tasks remain undone, readers learn the downside to a child being in charge via a story that a *Kirkus Reviews* writer dubbed "gleeful." "Ingman's illustrations will likely charm all ages," a *Publishers Weekly* contributor noted of *Bad News! I'm in Charge!,* citing the "delightful unfinished elements" in the book's "intriguing compositions."

As an illustrator, Ingman "paints the dynamic action" of Sean Taylor's humorous picture book, *Boing!,* in postmodern paintings "with a reckless elan," according to a *Publishers Weekly* reviewer. The story of a man with rubber legs, *Boing!* pairs Taylor's slapstick storyline about a trampoline artist with acrylic paintings that *Booklist* contributor Michael Cart deemed "a suitable match for this simple but zany tale." One of several collaborations between Ingman and Ahlberg, *The Runaway Diner* inspired *School Library Journal* contributor Linda Ludke to write that the illustrator's "naive drawings of the stick-legged sausage and his fellow runaways will elicit giggles." In Ahlberg's lighthearted story, a hungry boy is startled when the components of his dinner—the silverware and dishes as well as every pea and carrot—suddenly become individual creatures with names and leap off the table and out the door. Ingman's "childlike" illustrations for *The Runaway Diner* "are expressively and colorfully detailed," concluded a *Kirkus Reviews* writer, describing the work as a "madcap riff . . . for primary-grade readers."

## Biographical and Critical Sources

*PERIODICALS*

*Booklist,* January 1, 1996, Ilene Cooper, review of *When Martha's Away,* p. 845; April 15, 1998, Hazel Rochman, review of *Lost Property,* p. 1452; April 1, 1999, GraceAnne A. DeCandido, review of *A Night on the Tiles,* p. 1420; April 1, 2003, Hazel Rochman, review of *Bad News! I'm in Charge!,* p. 1402; August, 2004, Michael Cart, review of *Boing!,* p. 1946.

*Bulletin of the Center for Children's Books,* June, 2003, review of *Bad News! I'm in Charge!,* p. 406.

*Kirkus Reviews,* September 15, 1995, review of *When Martha's Away,* p. 1352; February 18, 1998, review of *Lost Property,* p. 268; February 15, 1999, review of *A Night on the Tiles,* p. 300; March 15, 2003, review of *Bad News! I'm in Charge!,* p. 469; June 15, 2004, review of *Boing!,* p. 582; October 15, 2005, review of *Double Pink,* p. 1136; September 15, 2006, review of *The Runaway Diner,* p. 945.

*Publishers Weekly,* October 23, 1995, review of *When Martha's Away,* p. 67; March 16, 1998, review of *Lost Property,* p. 63; February 15, 1999, review of *A Night on the Tiles,* p. 107; March 10, 2003, review of *Bad News! I'm in Charge!,* p. 71; July 12, 2004, review of *Boing!,* p. 63; November 7, 2005, review of *Double Pink,* p. 72; October 2, 2006, review of *The Runaway Diner,* p. 61.

*School Library Journal,* December, 1995, Kathy Mitchell, review of *When Martha's Away,* p. 81; April, 1998, Jackie Hechkopf, review of *Lost Property,* p. 100; March, 1999, Joy Fleishhacker, review of *A Night on the Tiles,* p. 176; August, 2003, Liza Graybill, review of *Bad News! I'm in Charge!,* p. 129; August, 2004, Shawn Brommer, review of *Boing!,* p. 96; November, 2005, Catherine Threadgill, review of *Double Pink,* p. 90; December, 2006, Linda Ludke, review of *The Runaway Diner,* p. 94.

*ONLINE*

*Picture Book Quarterly,* http://www.pbq.com/ (May 8, 2002), interview with Ingman.

*Walker Books Web site,* http://www.walkerbooks.co.uk/ (August 15, 2007), "Bruce Ingman."*

# J-K

## JAMES, Curtis E.

### Personal

Male. *Education:* Pratt Institute, B.F.A., M.F.A (fine art).

### Addresses

*Office*—210 W. 146th St., Ste. CB, New York, NY 10039. *E-mail*—cjsstudio@aol.com.

### Career

Illustrator.

### Awards, Honors

Silver Plate Award, U.S. House of Representatives; Albany Museum Purchase Award; Gold Key Award, Savannah College; Merit Award, Atlanta College of Arts; Outstanding Artist Award, Georgia State Board of Education.

***A young girl's painful experiences as a minority student in public school is captured by Curtis E. James in his artwork for Doreen Rappaport's* The School Is Not White!** (Illustration © 2005 by Curtis E. James. Reprinted by permission of Hyperion Books for Children.)

## Illustrator

Joyce Carol Thomas, editor, *Linda Brown, You Are Not Alone: The Brown v. Board of Education Decision,* Jump at the Sun/Hyperion Books for Children (New York, NY), 2003.

Doreen Rappaport, *The School Is Not White!: A True Story of the Civil Rights Movement,* Jump at the Sun/Hyperion Books for Children (New York, NY), 2005.

Doreen Rappaport, *Freedom Ship,* Jump at the Sun/Hyperion Books for Children (New York, NY), 2006.

## Sidelights

Artist and illustrator Curtis E. James has created artwork for a variety of media and magazine companies, including E Entertainment, CNN, *Essence,* and *Ebony.* As an illustrator, James has also contributed artwork to children's books that focus on African-American history, such as the anthology *Linda Brown, You Are Not Alone: The Brown v. Board of Education Decision* and Doreen Rappaport's picture books *The School Is Not White: A True Story of the Civil Rights Movement* and *Freedom Ship.*

*Freedom Ship* is the story of Robert Smalls, a mulatto slave who abducted the Confederate steamership *Planter* in 1862. As the appointed pilot of the *Planter,* Smalls and his allies in the ship's crew seized the steamship and transported the enslaved black women and children aboard to freedom while also trading the ship and its ammunition to Union forces. Smalls eventually went on to serve several terms in the U.S. House of Representatives. Hazel Rochman, reviewing *Freedom Ship* in *Booklist,* acknowledged James' "handsome illustrations" and his capability to portray Smalls' heroic story. The artwork for *Freedom Ship* was also recognized by Julie R. Ranelli, who in *School Library Journal* wrote that the book's "realistic chalk-pastel drawings" aptly capture "the secrecy of the families' nighttime escape, while the facial features and body language express urgency." A *Kirkus Reviews* critic commented that, "overall," the illustrations for *Freedom Ship* are "attractively designed."

## Biographical and Critical Sources

*PERIODICALS*

*Booklist,* December 1, 2003, Gillian Engberg, review of *Linda Brown, You Are Not Alone: The Brown v. Board of Education Decision,* p. 658; February 1, 2005, John Green, review of *The School Is Not White!: A True Story of the Civil Rights Movement,* p. 976; October 1, 2006, Hazel Rochman, review of *Freedom Ship,* p. 60.

*Horn Book,* July-August, 2005, Joanna Rudge Long, review of *The School Is Not White!,* p. 489.

*Kirkus Reviews,* August 1, 2005, review of *The School Is Not White!,* p. 857; August 15, 2006, review of *Freedom Ship,* p. 850.

*Publishers Weekly,* December 8, 2003, review of *Linda Brown, You Are Not Alone,* p. 62; September 12, 2005, review of *The School Is Not White!,* p. 67.

*School Library Journal,* January, 2004, Kelly Czarnecki, review of *Linda Brown, You Are Not Alone,* p. 161; October, 2004, Mary N. Oluonyn, review of *Linda Brown, You Are Not Alone,* p. 68; September, 2005, Holly T. Sneeringer, review of *The School Is Not White!,* p. 195; November, 2006, Julie R. Ranelli, review of *Freedom Ship,* p. 108.

*ONLINE*

*Curtis E. James Home Page,* http://www.curtisejames.com (August 9, 2007).

* * *

# JONES, Noah Z.

## Personal

Married Diane Jones (a children's librarian). *Education:* Pacific Northwest College of Art, degree (illustration).

## Addresses

*Home and office*—Camden, ME. *E-mail*—noah@noahzjones.com.

## Career

Illustrator and animator. FableVision, Boston, MA, animator.

## Awards, Honors

Oppenheim Toy Portfolio Gold Award, 2006, for *Not Norman* by Kelly Bennett.

## Illustrator

Kelly Bennett, *Not Norman: A Goldfish Story,* Candlewick Press (Cambridge, MA), 2005.

Joan Carris, *Welcome to the Bed and Biscuit,* Candlewick Press (Cambridge, MA), 2006.

Lisa Moser, *The Monster in the Backpack,* Candlewick Press (Cambridge, MA), 2006.

Maribeth Boelts, *Those Shoes,* Candlewick Press (Cambridge, MA), 2007.

## Sidelights

Noah Z. Jones is an author/illustrator/animator who draws all sorts of wacky oddities out of his New Jersey home. After taking part in a monster-drawing contest in the fifth grade—and placing fourth out of five contestants—Jones realized that he wanted to create art for a living.

After attending several art schools, Jones found himself working at FableVision, a Boston-based animation studio. He swiftly moved up the ranks from lowly animator to creative director where he headed up award-winning projects for clients such as Nickelodeon, the Public Broadcasting System, and Houghton Mifflin. Bidding farewell to the big city. As an illustrator, Jones has created art for *Not Norman: A Goldfish Story* by Kelly Bennett and *Welcome to the Bed and Biscuit* by Joan Carris, among others.

Jones' work is often acknowledged for its fun, upbeat mood. In *Not Norman* the illustrator uses digital art to bring to life Bennett's story about a little boy and his pet gold fish. *School Library Journal* reviewer Grace Oliff compared the "clear lines and vibrant colors" of Jones' illustrations to the works of Japanese illustrator Taro Gomi. Jones' stylistic artwork for *Not Norman* was also credited with carrying the weight of the story by a *Kirkus Reviews* critic who wrote that the book's "bold art" "give[s] the rather bald text the warmth to teach that appearances are rarely the whole truth."

In his work for *Welcome to the Bed and Biscuit* Jones' evocative line illustrations have been applauded for their combination of simplicity and humor. Carris's gentle story focuses on jealousy and centers on an animal shelter run by a kindly man named Grampa Bender. In *Booklist* Ilene Cooper noted that Jones' "simple line illustrations break up the text" and allow beginning readers to fully comprehend the story. Elizabeth Bird, writing in *School Library Journal,* noted that *Welcome to the Bed and Biscuit* has "more than its fair share of amusing illustrations and gentle humor."

## Biographical and Critical Sources

*PERIODICALS*

*Booklist,* February 15, 2005, Carolyn Phelan, review of *Not Norman: A Goldfish Story,* p. 1082; October 1, 2006, Ilene Cooper, review of *Welcome to the Bed and Biscuit,* p. 56.

*Horn Book,* November-December, 2006, review of *The Monster in the Backpack,* p. 721.

*Kirkus Reviews,* February 1, 2005, review of *Not Norman,* p. 173; September 15, 2006, review of *Welcome to the Bed and Biscuit,* p. 948.

*Publishers Weekly,* March 21, 2005, review of *Not Norman,* p. 50.

*School Library Journal,* March, 2005, Grace Oliff, review of *Not Norman,* p. 166; August, 2006, Laura Scott, review of *The Monster in the Backpack,* p. 94; October, 2006, Elizabeth Bird, review of *Welcome to the Bed and Biscuit,* p. 103.

*ONLINE*

*Fablevision Web site,* http://www.fablevision.com/ (August 9, 2007), "Noah Z. Jones."

*Noah Z. Jones Home Page,* http://www.noahzjones.com (August 9, 2007).

# KENAH, Katharine 1949-

## Personal

Born April 15, 1949; married; children: one son, two daughters.

## Addresses

*Home*—Granville, OH.

## Career

Children's book author. Formerly worked in scientific research.

## Awards, Honors

Bank Street College of Education Best Children's Books of the Year designation, 2005, for *The Best Seat in Second Grade.*

## Writings

*PICTURE BOOKS*

*Eggs over Easy,* illustrated by Maxie Chambliss, Dutton (New York, NY), 1993.

*The Dream Shop,* illustrated by Peter Catalanotto, HarperCollins (New York, NY), 2002.

*The Best Seat in Second Grade* ("I Can Read" series), illustrated by Abby Carter, HarperCollins (New York, NY), 2005.

*The Best Teacher in Second Grade* ("I Can Read" series), illustrated by Abby Carter, HarperCollins (New York, NY), 2005.

*The Best Chef in Second Grade* ("I Can Read" series), illustrated by Abby Carter, HarperCollins (New York, NY), 2007.

*NONFICTION; "EXTREME READERS" SERIES*

*Wild Weather,* McGraw-Hill (Columbus, OH), 2004.

*Animals Day and Night,* McGraw-Hill (Columbus, OH), 2004.

*Undercover Creatures,* McGraw-Hill (Columbus, OH), 2004.

*Tiny Terrors,* McGraw-Hill (Columbus, OH), 2004.

*Space Mysteries,* McGraw-Hill (Columbus, OH), 2004.

*The Bizarre Body,* McGraw-Hill (Columbus, OH), 2004.

*Predator Attack!,* McGraw-Hill (Columbus, OH), 2004.

*Nature's Amazing Partners,* McGraw-Hill (Columbus, OH), 2004.

*Destructive Earth,* McGraw-Hill (Columbus, OH), 2004.

*Weird and Wacky Plants,* McGraw-Hill (Columbus, OH), 2005.

*Fantastic Planet,* McGraw-Hill (Columbus, OH), 2005.

*Creatures of the Deep,* McGraw-Hill (Columbus, OH), 2005.

***Cover of Katharine Kenah's* Amazing Creations, *an elementary-grade history of the wonders of the ancient world.*** (School Specialty Publishing, 2007. Reproduced by permission.)

*Big Beasts,* School Specialty Publishing (Columbus, OH), 2006.

*Amazing Creations,* School Specialty Publishing (Columbus, OH), 2006.

*Amazing Journeys,* School Specialty Publishing (Columbus, OH), 2007.

*"LITHGOW PALOOZA READERS" SERIES*

*Zippety Zoo,* School Specialty Publishing (Columbus, OH), 2005.

*A Den, a Tree, a Nest Is Best,* School Specialty Publishing (Columbus, OH), 2006.

*Slither, Slide, Hop, and Run,* School Specialty Publishing (Columbus, OH), 2006.

## Sidelights

Raised on an oceanographic observatory, Katharine Kenah has a strong interest in the physical sciences, Earth's plant and animal life, and the environment. Kenah worked for several years as a scientific research before turning to writing, and her first book, *Eggs over Easy,* was published in 1993. Although it would be several more years before Kenah returned to children's books with *The Dream Shop,* she has continued to write picture-book texts, and has also create science-related book series' for beginning readers. Her "Extreme Readers" series includes the titles *Animals Day and Night, Weird and Wacky Plants, Amazing Creations,* and *Destructive Earth,* and she has also contributed several titles to the "I Can Read" series and the lighthearted "Lithgow Palooza Readers" library.

*The Dream Shop,* which features illustrations by Peter Catalanotto, follows a girl named Pip as she takes a trip to a strange dream store after falling asleep. Amid shelves of dreams and nightmares of all sorts, a pajama-clad Pip meets her cousin Joseph, and Joseph helps her corral the dragon the two discover while exploring the surreal establishment. Noting Kenah's use of vivid, evocative language, *School Library Journal* contributor Gay Lynn Van Vleck wrote that the story "gloriously journeys" through the human "subconscious, and encourages consideration of our power over nighttime fears." A *Publishers Weekly* critic cited Kenah's "imagery-charged prose" and concluded that in *The Dream Shop* author and illustrator "give readers a window-shopping tour that's worth the trip."

Kenah's contribution to the "I Can Read" series include *The Best Seat in Second Grade, The Best Teacher in Second Grade,* and *The Best Chef in Second Grade.* Chock full of puns and other wordplay, each book focuses on one student in Mr. Hopper's second-grade classroom; in the first volume, for example, Sam decides to bring the class hamster, George Washington, on a class field trip to a science museum, with humorous results. *The Best Teacher in Second Grade* finds Luna inspiring her classmates to create a circus of stars on the school's Family Night, while *The Best Chef in Second Grade* follows the visit of a popular chef to Mr. Hopper's class, and the pot-luck that is planned in the chef's honor. A *Kirkus Reviews* writer dubbed *The Best Teacher in Second Grade* "a school story that shines," and Hazel Rochman wrote in *Booklist* that Kenah's "lively chapter book" presents "a nice take on the outsider story." Gloria Koster also commended the author in *School Library Journal,* writing that "the character development and opportunity for inferential thinking" in Kenah's story make *The Best Teacher in Second Grade* "more substantial than many" readers for the early elementary grades.

## Biographical and Critical Sources

*PERIODICALS*

*Booklist,* August, 2005, Kay Weisman, review of *The Best Seat in Second Grade,* p. 2039; June 1, 2006, Hazel Rochman, review of *The Best Teacher in Second Grade,* p. 84.

*Bulletin of the Center for Children's Books,* December, 1993, review of *Eggs over Easy,* p. 124; October,

2006, Deborah Stevenson, review of *The Best Teacher in Second Grade,* p. 78.

*Kirkus Reviews,* December 1, 2001, review of *The Dream Shop,* p. 1685; June 15, 2005, review of *The Best Seat in Second Grade,* p. 684; June 15, 2006, review of *The Best Teacher in Second Grade,* p. 634.

*Publishers Weekly,* December 10, 2001, review of *The Dream Shop,* p. 70.

*School Library Journal,* March, 1994, Ruth Semrau, review of *Eggs over Easy,* p. 200; January, 2002, Gay Lynn Van Vleck, review of *The Dream Shop,* p. 104; October, 2005, review of *The Best Seat in Second Grade,* p. 40; July, 2006, Gloria Koster, review of *The Best Teacher in Second Grade,* p. 80; July, 2006, Gloria Koster, review of *The Best Teacher in Second Grade,* p. 80.*

* * *

## KONING, Hans 1921-2007 (Hans Koningsberger)

*OBITUARY NOTICE—* See index for *SATA* sketch: Born July 12, 1921, in Amsterdam, Netherlands; died April 13, 2007, in Easton, CT. Author. Koning was best known as a novelist but also wrote works of history and travel. As World War II approached, he fled the Netherlands for England, joining the British Liberation Army. After the war, he returned home and edited a weekly newspaper. In 1950, he moved briefly to Indonesia, where he hosted a radio show for a year. Traveling by Dutch freighter, he immigrated to the United States and settled in New York City. Koning began his career as a freelance writer, initially publishing under his real surname of Koningsberger. His first books were *Modern Dutch Painting: An Introduction* (1955; 3rd edition, 1960) and the young-adult novel *The Golden Keys* (1956). He continued writing such novels as *An American Romance* (1960), *A Walk with Love and Death* (1961), and *The Revolutionary* (1967) under this name, as well as translating books, writing travel works, and publishing the play *Hermione* (1963). Finding his name often misspelled, he changed it to the simpler Koning by 1972. Under the new name, he released titles such as *Death of a Schoolboy* (1974) and his popular-but-controversial history *Columbus: His Enterprise: Exploding the Myth* (1976). In the latter work, Koning accused Columbus and his followers of brutalizing native peoples. Although Koning wrote fiction to entertain, he believed that the best novels, like his nonfiction, also contain a message about the world's injustices. He had a bent for social activism himself, forming the group Resist during the Vietnam War. His more-recent works include the novels *America Made Me* (1979) and *De Witt's War* (1983), and the nonfiction *The Conquest of America: How the Indian Nations Lost Their Continent* (1993) and *Pursuit of a Woman on the Hinge of History* (1998). Several of Koning's novels were adapted to film, including *A Walk with Love and Death* (1969), *The Revolutionary* (1970), *Death of a Schoolboy* (1991), and *The Petersburg-Cannes Express* (2003).

*OBITUARIES AND OTHER SOURCES:*

*PERIODICALS*

*Chicago Tribune,* April 22, 2007, section 4, p. 6.

*New York Times,* April 18, 2007, p. A25.

*Washington Post,* April 23, 2007, p. B6.

* * *

## KONINGSBERGER, Hans
See KONING, Hans

* * *

## KRISHNASWAMI, Uma 1956-

### Personal

Born June 27, 1956, in New Delhi, India; daughter of V. (an Indian government official) and Vasantha (a homemaker) Krishnaswami; married Sumant Krishnaswamy; children: Nikhil Krishnaswamy (son). *Ethnicity:* "Asian Indian." *Education:* University of New Delhi (India), B.A. (political science), 1975, M.A. (social work), 1977; University of Maryland—College Park, M.A. (counseling), 1982. *Religion:* Hindu. *Hobbies and other interests:* Gardening, birdwatching, reading.

### Addresses

*Home*—Aztec, NM. *E-mail*—uma@umakrishnaswami.com.

### Career

Author and educator. LEAP, Inc., Silver Spring, MD, rehabilitation counselor, 1981-86; Epilepsy Foundation of America, Landover, MD, employment specialist/program administrator, 1986-88; University of Maryland, College Park, project coordinator in special education department, 1988-97; freelance writer, 1997—. Leader of workshops, teacher of online writing courses for *Writers on the Net,* and codirector of Bisti Writing Project (local site of National Writing Project). Writer-in-residence, Aztec Ruins National Monument.

### Member

Society of Children's Book Writers and Illustrators, Authors Guild, Children's Book Guild of Washington, DC, PEN West/PEN New Mexico.

### Awards, Honors

Young Readers Award, *Scientific American,* 1997, for *The Broken Tusk;* International Reading Association Notable Book for a Global Society designation, for *Naming Maya;* Bank Street College of Education Best Book designations; CCBC Choice honors.

***Uma Krishnaswami*** (Photograph © 2003 by Nikhil Krishnaswamy. Reproduced by permission.)

## Writings

*FOR CHILDREN*

(Reteller) *Stories of the Flood,* illustrated by Birgitta Saflund, Roberts Rinehart Publishers (Niwot, CO), 1994.

(Reteller) *The Broken Tusk: Stories of the Hindu God Ganesha,* illustrated by Maniam Selven, Linnet Books (North Haven, CT), 1996.

(Reteller) *Shower of Gold: Girls and Women in the Stories of India,* illustrated by Maniam Selven, Linnet Books (North Haven, CT), 1999.

*Yoga Class* (nonfiction), illustrated by Stephanie Roth, Bebop Books (New York, NY), 2000.

*Hello Flower* (picture book), illustrated by Stephanie Roth, Bebop Books (New York, NY), 2002.

*Holi* (nonfiction), Children's Press (New York, NY), 2003.

*Chachaji's Cup* (picture book), illustrations by Soumya Sitarman, Children's Book Press (San Francisco, CA), 2003.

*Monsoon* (picture book), illustrated by Jamel Akib, Farrar, Straus & Giroux (New York, NY), 2003.

*Naming Maya* (novel), Farrar, Straus & Giroux (New York, NY), 2004.

*The Happiest Tree: A Yoga Story* (picture book), illustrated by Ruth Jeyaveeran, Lee & Low (New York, NY), 2005.

*The Closet Ghosts* (picture book), illustrated by Shiraaz Bhabha, Children's Book Press (San Francisco, CA), 2006.

*Bringing Asha Home* (picture book), illustrated by Jamel Akib, Lee & Low (New York, NY), 2006.

*Remembering Grandpa* (picture book), illustrated by Layne Johnson, Boyds Mills Press (Honesdale, PA), 2007.

*OTHER*

*Beyond the Field Trip: Teaching and Learning in Public Places* (for teachers), Linnet Professional Publications (North Haven, CT), 2002.

Contributor of poems and stories to children's magazines, including *Highlights for Children, Cricket, Ladybug, Spider,* and *Skipping Stones,* and adult magazines, including *Bulletin of the Society of Children's Book Writers and Illustrators, Tumbleweeds, Bookbird,* and *Writer's Carousel.* Contributor of book reviews to *Children's Literature.*

## Sidelights

Writer and teacher Uma Krishnaswami credits her son, Nikhil, with inspiring her to become a children's book author. Drawing on her Asian-Indian heritage, Krishnaswami writes in a variety of genres and gears her work for many age levels. In *Stories of the Flood, The Broken Tusk: Stories of the Hindu God Ganesha,* and *Shower of Gold: Girls and Women in the Stories of India* she retells traditional tales from around the world. Honing her storytelling skills with these anthologies, Krishnaswami quickly made the move to original stories, winning critical praise for picture books such as *Chachaji's Cup, The Happiest Tree: A Yoga Story,* and *Bringing Asha Home.*

Krishnaswami was born in New Delhi, India, and traveled throughout the Indian subcontinent, including Wellington, the southern Nilgiri Hills, Delhi, Pune in western India, and the mountains of Himachal Pradesh. "A Remington manual typewriter is responsible for my entry into the writing life," she once recalled to *SATA.* "My father owned it when I was a child in India. . . . With its squat silhouette, it is the VW Beetle of typewriters. It has the clean sharp smell of inky ribbon, and when you strike the keys, the metal letters fly up to hit that ribbon and place an imprint on the paper. You never have to figure out how to turn it on." As a grade-school child, Krishnaswami wrote sequels to books she liked, such as the original "Winnie the Pooh" stories she read while perched in her favorite reading spot, a banyan tree.

"Between the ages of five and eleven, I hammered those keys as if I was possessed," Krishnaswami wrote on her home page in describing her development as a writer. "I took a brief detour in an experiment with Wall Writing (green crayon on wall), but quickly learned that was not the way to get grownups to appreciate creativity. So I remained true to that typewriter. I wrote stories and typed them up. I stapled them together and hid them in drawers and bookcases with warnings that read 'Danger' and 'Enter at Your Own Risk.' At ten, I began sending my writing off to magazines. At thirteen, my first poem was published in *Children's World,* a children's magazine begun in India by a farsighted man named Shankar who drew cartoons and believed in kids. I don't remember that much about that poem, except that it tried very hard to sound grown-up. But I do remember the thrill of seeing my name in print."

Despite her early publishing success, Krishnaswami's ambitions changed as she grew older. Enrolling at the University of New Delhi, she earned a master's degree in social work. Married, she and her husband immigrated to the United States, where she earned a second master's degree in counseling. Raising her family while working as a counselor and as a program administrator for special-education programs, she once again felt inspired to write creatively. In an interview with Cynthia Leitich-Smith for *Children's Literature Resources,* Krishnaswami recalled her return to writing, noting: "It was all a lark at first. My first book [*Stories of the Flood*] was a collection of stories I began writing for my son to read to him." In the process of researching the tales, she talked to people and pored over microfiches and documents at museum and university libraries. "I submitted it because my husband said he thought I should, so I was quite surprised when it got accepted as soon as it did, with only three rejections, one of them a personal one. So I had a relatively painless entrance into publication."

In *Stories of the Flood* Krishnaswami retells nine tales that focus on the worldwide flood which occurs in many ancient sagas, among them an ancient Sumerian tale and obscure Asian, North American, and African stories. While describing these stories as "short and readable with few obscure words," *School Library Journal* contributor Nancy Menaldi-Scanlan took issue with the lack of sources provided in the book. Krishnaswami corrected this omission corrected in her second story collection, *The Broken Tusk.*

*The Broken Tusk* contains stories about Ganesha, the Hindu god of new beginnings who has the head of an elephant. In addition to documenting her sources in this work, Krishnaswami includes a pronunciation guide and glossary. *The Broken Tusk* attracted the attention of reviewers, among them *Booklist* contributor Ilene Cooper, who remarked on the rarity of finding a Hindu folktale collection geared toward middle-grade readers. In *Kirkus Reviews* a critic deemed the volume "elegant and eminently readable," as well as a "vital addition" to library collections on non-European cultures. Janice M. Del Negro, writing in the *Bulletin of the Center for Children's Books,* suggested that *The Broken Tusk* "would be very useful as part of an introduction to Hindu culture," a view echoed by Patricia Lothrop-Green in *School Library Journal.*

In *Shower of Gold,* published in 1999, Krishnaswami focuses on stories with female protagonists. Here she collects and retells tales from Hindu and Buddhist mythology, ancient literature, and legends, all of which feature women as central characters. Because the heroines act differently than many of the heroines of Western fairytales, readers might find the stories in this "worthy" collection "intriguing," a *Kirkus Reviews* contributor noted, while Carol Fazioli concluded in her *School Library Journal* review that *Shower of Gold* is a "wonderful collection" that would serve as "a fine addition to any library."

With her 2002 book *Hello Flower,* Krishnaswami moved into picture books, a genre where she has won fans and gained critical accolades with books such as *Chachaji's Cup, The Happiest Tree, The Closet Ghosts,* and *Bringing Asha Home. Chachaji's Cup* deals with the 1947 partitioning of India into two countries, a move that created the nation of Pakistan. In Krishnaswami's story, a young boy named Neel enjoys listening to Great-uncle Chachaji's enchanting stories about Hindu gods, and then is told a somber tale about Chachaji's childhood experience as a refuge. Following the partition, Chachaji and his family were forced to relocate within the new boundary of India, and could only bring what they could carry. While others laughed at Chachaji's mother for bringing along a teacup, she replied that if the fragile drinking vessel could survive the journey, then so could she. Pointing out that the partitioning of India is presented in a manner easily understandable to children in *Chachaji's Cup, School Library Journal* critic Nancy Palmer claimed that Krishnaswami's de-

**Bringing Asha Home,** ***Krishnaswami's gentle story about an interracial adoption is brought to life in Jamel Akib's evocative art.*** (Illustration © 2006 by Jamel Akib. All rights reserved. Reproduced by permission of Lee & Low Books, Inc.)

*Featuring art by Ruth Jeyaveeran, Krishnaswami's* **The Happiest Tree** ***finds a young girl gaining self-confidence as she masters yoga.*** (Illustration © 2005 by Ruth Jeyaveeran. Reproduced by permission of Lee & Low Books, Inc.)

piction of young Neel "lends immediacy and a warm family feeling to this graceful story." A *Publishers Weekly* critic also praised the book, writing that "the author smoothly handles the issues of loss, alienation, and assimilation" in her gentle tale.

Another young boy is the focus of *Bringing Asha Home,* which finds eight-year-old Arun awaiting the arrival of his adopted sister from India, excited that he will now have a sibling with whom to celebrate Rakhi Day. Praising the book for presenting a biracial family, a *Kirkus Reviews* writer also cited Krishnaswami's "warm, clear text." Life in India is brought to life in *Monsoon,* as Jamel Akib's "richly colored illustrations" provide a backdrop to Krishnaswami's "lyrical" story about a girl and her family awaiting the start of the country's monsoon rains, according to a *Kirkus Reviews* writer.

The author tells a multigenerational story in *Remembering Grandpa,* in which young Daysha helps her widowed Grandma deal with the first anniversary of her beloved Grandpa's death, and in *The Happiest Tree* yoga helps eight-year-old Meena gain the coordination and confidence she needs to perform in an upcoming performance of a play about Red Riding Hood. In *School Library Journal* Laura Scott described *Remembering Grandpa* as a "beautiful story of remembrance," and Gillian Engberg wrote in *Booklist* that *The Happiest Tree* features a "warm, encouraging story about overcoming challenges." "Krishnaswami occasionally dabs the text [of *The Happiest Tree*] with Hindi words and expressions," observed *School Library Journal* reviewer Be Astengo, the critic noting that the exotic vocabulary gives the story "a delightful Indian flavor."

Another story featuring a young girl of Indian descent, *The Closet Ghosts* finds Anu conquering her fears of a suspicious closet in her bedroom in a new home by drawing on the power of Hanuman, the monkey god. Calling *The Closet Ghosts* a "delightful story," Nancy

Menaldi-Scanlan added in her *School Library Journal* review that, despite its "familiar theme," Krishnaswami's "upbeat" tale benefits from "the addition of Hindu mythology and the twist of having the protagonist herself discover a way out of her dilemma." In *Kirkus Reviews,* a critic cited Shiraaz Bhabha's "color-drenched" illustrations and recommended the picture book as "a unique tale that is worthy of a wide audience."

Krishnaswami addresses older readers in *Naming Maya,* a middle-grade novel. Here a preteen leaves her home in New Jersey to stay with her mother's family in Chennai, India following her parents' divorce and the death of her grandfather. Through Maya's narration, readers gain a sense of everyday life in hot, dusty, yet beautiful southern India. With the help of a cousin and the family housekeeper, Kamala Mami, Maya grows up in many ways during her visit, learning to deal with her anger at her divorced parents and also build strong, loving relationships with her Indian relatives. Praising the story's "memorable" setting, a *Kirkus Reviews* writer noted that Krishnaswami's "language is lush and Maya's observations are piercingly honest," while Engberg cited the author's use of "rich, poetic imagery" in her insightful story.

In addition to her writing, Krishnaswami teaches writing to young students at the Aztec Ruins National Monument, and also helps direct an affiliate of the National Writing Project. An outgrowth of her work as an educator, *Beyond the Field Trip: Teaching and Learning in Public Places* assists teachers in making the most of learning opportunities.

## Biographical and Critical Sources

*PERIODICALS*

*Booklist,* February 1, 1995, Janice Del Negro, review of *Stories of the Flood,* p. 1001; October, 1, 1996, Ilene Cooper, review of *The Broken Tusk: Stories of the Hindu God Ganesha,* pp. 335-336; October 1, 1999, Stephanie Zvirin and Ilene Cooper, review of *The Broken Tusk,* p. 373; March 15, 2003, Hazel Rochman, review of *Chachaji's Cup,* p. 1332; May 1, 2003, Gillian Engberg, review of *Holi,* p. 1062; September 1, 2003, Abby Nolan, review of *Monsoon,* p. 129; April 1, 2004, Gillian Engberg, review of *Naming Maya,* p. 1363; October 1, 2005, Gillian Engberg, review of *The Happiest Tree: A Yoga Story,* p. 63; October 15, 2006, Linda Perkins, review of *Bringing Asha Home,* p. 54.

*Bulletin of the Center for Children's Books,* October, 1996, Janice M. Del Negro, review of *The Broken Tusk,* p. 66; May, 1999, review of *Shower of Gold: Girls and Women in the Stories of India,* p. 319; June, 2003, review of *Chachaji's Cup,* p. 408; January, 204, Deborah Stevenson, review of *Monsoon,* p. 196; June, 2004, Hope Morrison, review of *Naming Maya,* p. 424.

*Daily Times* (Ottawa, IL), March 19, 2002, Verlie Hutchens, "Exploring the World with Uma Krishnaswami."

*Kirkus Reviews,* June 15, 1996, review of *The Broken Tusk;* March 1, 1999, review of *Shower of Gold,* p. 377; April 1, 2003, review of *Chachaji's Cup,* p. 535; October 1, 2003, review of *Monsoon,* p. 1226; March 15, 2004, review of *Naming Maya,* p. 272; August 15, 2006, review of *The Happiest Tree,* p. 917; April 1, 2006, review of *The Closet Ghosts,* p. 350; August 15, 2006, review of *Bringing Asha Home,* p. 845.

*Publishers Weekly,* April 21, 2003, review of *Chachaji's Cup,* p. 62; November 24, 2003, review of *Monsoon,* p. 63; April 19, 2004, review of *Naming Maya,* p. 62.

*School Library Journal,* February, 1995, Nancy Menaldi-Scanlan, review of *Stories of the Flood,* p. 99; July, 1997, Patricia Lothrop-Green, review of *The Broken Tusk,* p. 107; August, 1999, Carol Fazioli, review of *Shower of Gold,* pp. 173-174; June, 2003, Nancy Palmer, review of *Chachaji's Cup,* p. 110; December, 2003, Liza Graybill, review of *Monsoon,* p. 118; June, 2004, Laurie von Mehren, review of *Naming Maya,* p. 145; November, 2005, Be Astengo, review of *The Happiest Tree,* p. 96; June, 2006, Nancy Menaldi-Scanlan, review of *The Closet Ghosts,* p. 120; November, 2006, Julie R. Ranelli, review of *Bringing Asha Home,* p. 98; April, 2007, Laura Scott, review of *Remembering Grandpa,* p. 110.

*Scientific American,* December, 1997, Phylis Morrison and Philip Morrison, review of *The Broken Tusk,* p. 124.

*Skipping Stones,* November, 1999, review of *Shower of Gold,* p. 32.

*Voice of Youth Advocates,* February, 2002, Deborah L. Dubois, review of *Beyond the Field Trip: Teaching and Learning in Public Places,* p. 467.

*ONLINE*

*Children's Literature Resources Online,* http://www.cynthialeitichsmith.com/ (March 12, 2003), Cynthia Leitich-Smith, interview with Krishnaswami.

*Uma Krishnaswami Home Page,* http://www.umakrishnaswami.com (August 27, 2007).

* * *

# KURTZ, Katherine 1944-
# (Katherine Irene Kurtz)

## Personal

Born October 18, 1944, in Coral Gables, FL; daughter of Fredrick Harry Kurtz (an electronics technician) and Margaret Frances Carter (a paralegal); married Scott Roderick MacMillan (an author and producer), March 9, 1983; children: Cameron Alexander Stewart. *Education:* University of Miami, B.S., 1966; University of California—Los Angeles, M.A., 1971. *Religion:* Episcopalian.

## Addresses

*Home*—1417 N. Augusta St., Staunton, VA 24401. *Agent*—Russell Galen, Scovil, Chichak, Galen Literary Agency, 381 Park Ave. S., New York, NY 10016.

***Katherine Kurtz*** (Photograph by Beth Gwinn. Reproduced by permission.)

## Career

Writer. Los Angeles Police Department, Los Angeles, CA, instructional technologist, 1969-81.

## Member

Authors Guild, Authors' League, Science-Fiction and Fantasy Writers' of America.

## Awards, Honors

Edmund Hamilton Memorial Award, 1977, for *Camber of Culdi;* Balrog Award, 1982, for *Camber the Heretic;* named dame of Military and Hospitaller Order of St. Lazarus of Jerusalem, and companion of Royal House of O'Conor; dame grand officer of Imperial Order of Emperor Menelik II of Ethiopia.

## Writings

*"DERYNI" FANTASY SERIES*

*Deryni Rising,* Ballantine (New York, NY), 1970, revised, Ace (New York, NY), 2004.

*Deryni Checkmate,* Ballantine (New York, NY), 1972, revised, Ace (New York, NY), 2005.

*High Deryni,* Ballantine (New York, NY), 1973, reprinted, Ace (New York, NY), 2007.

*Camber of Culdi* ("Legends of Camber of Culdi" cycle), Ballantine (New York, NY), 1976.

*Saint Camber* ("Legends of Camber of Culdi" cycle), Ballantine (New York, NY), 1978.

*Camber the Heretic* ("Legends of Camber of Culd," cycle), Ballantine (New York, NY), 1981.

*The Bishop's Heir* ("Histories of King Kelson" cycle), Ballantine (New York, NY), 1984.

*The King's Justice* ("Histories of King Kelson" cycle), Ballantine (New York, NY), 1985.

*The Chronicles of the Deryni* (includes *Deryni Rising, Deryni Checkmate,* and *High Deryni*), Science Fiction Book Club, 1985.

*The Quest for Saint Camber* ("Histories of King Kelson" cycle), Ballantine (New York, NY), 1985.

*The Harrowing of Gwynedd* ("Heirs of St. Camber" cycle), Ballantine (New York, NY), 1985.

*The Deryni Archives* (stories), Ballantine (New York, NY), 1986.

*Deryni Magic: A Grimoire,* Del Rey (New York, NY), 1991.

*King Javan's Year* ("Heirs of St. Camber" cycle), Ballantine (New York, NY), 1992.

*The Bastard Prince* ("Heirs of St. Camber" cycle), Ballantine (New York, NY), 1994.

(Compiler and editor, with Robert Reginald) *Codex Derynianus: Being a Comprehensive Guide to the Peoples, Places, and Things of the Derynye and the Human Worlds of the XI Kingdoms,* Borgo Press (San Bernardino, CA), 1998, second edition, Underwood Books (Nevada City, CA), 2005.

*King Kelson's Bride,* Ace (New York, NY), 2000.

(Editor) *Deryni Tales: An Anthology,* Ace (New York, NY), 2002.

*In the King's Service,* Ace (New York, NY), 2003.

*Childe Morgan,* Ace (New York, NY), 2006.

*"ADEPT" FANTASY SERIES; WITH DEBORAH TURNER HARRIS*

*The Adept,* Ace (New York, NY), 1991.

*Death of an Adept,* Ace (New York, NY), 1992.

*The Lodge of the Lynx,* Ace (New York, NY), 1992.

*The Templar Treasure,* Ace (New York, NY), 1993.

*Dagger Magic,* Ace (New York, NY), 1995.

*OTHER*

*Lammas Night* (novel), Ballantine (New York, NY), 1983, hardcover edition, Severn, 1986.

*The Legacy of Lehr* (science-fiction novel), Walker (New York, NY), 1986.

(Editor) *Tales of the Knights Templar,* Warner (New York, NY), 1995.

*Two Crowns for America,* Bantam (New York, NY), 1996.

(With Deborah Turner Harris) *The Temple and the Stone,* Warner (New York, NY), 1998.

(Editor) *On Crusade: More Tales of the Knights Templar,* Warner (New York, NY), 1998.

*St. Patrick's Gargoyle,* Ace (New York, NY), 2001.

(With Deborah Turner Harris) *The Temple and the Crown,* Warner (New York, NY), 2001.

(Editor) *Crusade of Fire: Mystical Tales of the Knights Templar,* Warner (New York, NY), 2002.

Contributor of stories to anthologies, including *Flashing Swords No. 4,* edited by Lin Carter, Dell (New York, NY), 1977; *Hecate's Cauldron,* edited by Susan Shwartz, DAW (New York, NY), 1982; *Nine Visions,* edited by Andrea LaSonde Melrose, Seabury Press (New York, NY), 1983; *Moonsinger's Friends,* edited by Shwartz, Bluejay, 1985; *Once upon a Time,* edited by Lester del Rey and Risa Kessler, Ballantine (New York, NY), 1991; *Crafter I,* edited by Bill Fawcett and Christopher Stasheff, Ace (New York, NY), 1991; *Gods of War,* edited by Fawcett, Baen (New York, NY), 1992; and *Battlestation II,* edited by Fawcett and Stasheff, Ace, 1992. Contributor of stories to periodicals, including *Fantasy Book.*

Kurtz's works have been translated into Dutch, German, Italian, Polish, Swedish, Japanese, Spanish, and Romanian.

## Sidelights

Katherine Kurtz's love of history has helped to shape the medieval worlds she crafts in her fantasy novels, as well as the plots of her books set in twentieth-century England and Scotland. Her "Deryni" fantasy series, composed of four base trilogies plus additional novels, focuses on the land of Gwynedd in the Eleven Kingdoms, a world based on medieval Wales. There the Deryni, a race of beings with unusual psychic powers, struggle against persecution by humans and attempt to preserve their powers and their culture. In a review of *The Quest for Saint Camber,* a *Publishers Weekly* critic dubbed Kurtz "queen of the proliferating fantasy subgenre that adds a magical element to dynastic historical romances." Kurtz's ability to weave historical detail with themes of magic and sorcery has made her books popular with both adults and young adults, prompting a *Publishers Weekly* contributor to crown Kurtz "a master of epic fantasy." In addition to her fantasy novels, Kurtz has also produced the thriller *Lammas Night,* edited several fiction anthologies, authored a science-fiction novel, and, with Deborah Turner Harris, has written the popular "Adept" series of contemporary mysteries. Comparing Kurtz to British fantasy writer J.R.R. Tolkien in her approach to her imaginary world, a *St. James Guide to Fantasy Writers* essayist commented that Kurtz's "magic is well realized, [her] . . . characters much better drawn than in most modern fantasies, and, for anyone with a romantic interest in the Middle Ages, [her "Deryni"] saga will inevitably have a great deal of fascination."

Born in 1944, in Coral Gables, Florida, during a hurricane, Kurtz once recalled her first moments on Earth to *SATA* as "a whirlwind entry into the world which I like to think was a portent of exciting things to come." Kurtz began her love affair with books at an early age, and as a fourth grader she discovered her first science-fiction novel, *Lodestar.* "After that, no science fiction book in any library was safe from eye-tracking by 'The Kurtz,'" she recalled. After graduating from high school, Kurtz earned her B.S. in chemistry at the University of Miami. "My tastes always leaned toward humanities rather than hard science," she nonetheless explained. "It was during my undergraduate years at the University of Miami that I consciously fell in love with history, and it was to history that I returned when I decided, after one year of medical school, that I would rather write about medicine than practice it." In 1971 she graduated from the University of California—Los Angeles, with an M.A. in English history. "More important than the piece of pa-

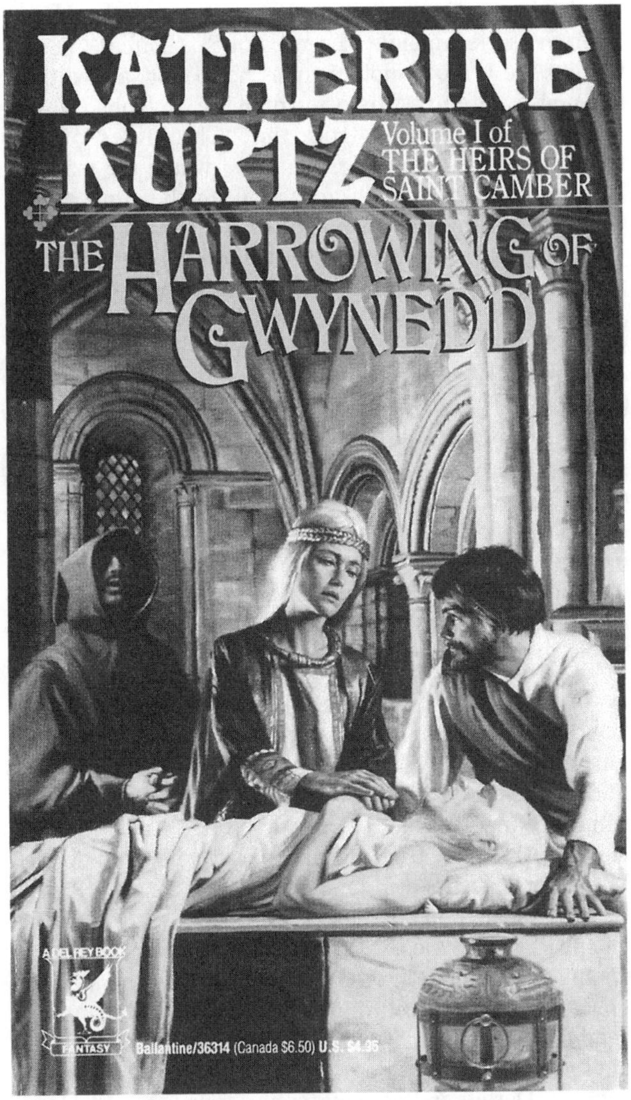


*Cover of Kurtz's 1989 novel* **The Harrowing of Gwynedd,** *featuring an illustration by Michael Herring.* (Del Rey Books, 1989. Reproduced by permission of Del Rey Books, a division of Random House, Inc.)

per," Kurtz explained, "was the formal knowledge of the medieval and renaissance world that I gained and the sharpening of research skills which would stand me in good stead as I continued writing medievally set fantasy."

Kurtz wrote what would become the first six "Deryni" novels in her spare time while working for the Los Angeles Police Department as a technical writer and curriculum designer. Ten years later, in 1980, she embarked on her full-time career as a fiction writer. "I can't imagine a more satisfying life than to be making a living doing what I love," she admitted to *SATA.* "Far too few people get the opportunity to do that, and especially at a relatively young age."

The first "Deryni" novel, *Deryni Rising,* was published in 1970. The first installment in the three-volume "Chronicles of the Deryni" cycle, it introduces readers to the kingdom of Gwynedd, the culture of which is laced with magic. The other three-volume cycles in the "Deryni" series include "Legends of St. Camber," which follows the life of a nobleman as he is first sainted then deemed a heretic; "Histories of King Kelson," which continues the events from the "Chronicles of the Deryni"; and "Heirs of St. Camber," where the magical kingdom suffers a dark age between the time of St. Camber and the rise to power of King Kelson. While *Voice of Youth Advocates* contributor Diane G. Yates expressed personal dismay that in the second part of the "Heirs of St. Camber" cycle, *King Javan's Year,* "so many of the characters . . . lose their lives in an unceasing struggle with the forces of evil," she added that the novel "is beautifully written, and should appeal to teens as well as adults." In *The Bastard Prince,* the concluding volume in "Heirs of St. Camber," the efforts of the heir to the throne "reflects the atmospheric gloom of a dark and secret land, full of treachery and cruelty but shot through with light and a promise of hope," in the opinion of a *Publishers Weekly* contributor, the critic also praising Kurtz for her ability to sustain tension and create vivid characters.

*In the King's Service* begins a new three-volume "Deryni" cycle, this time taking readers back to the time of King Kelson's grandfather, King Donal Haldane. Following the tragic death of a bastard son who was being groomed to be protector to Prince Brion, Deryni heiress Alyce de Corwyn and her toddler son Alaric Morgan are destined to take on the task. Fearing Prince Brion's succession, Bishop de Nore focuses his efforts on spearheading the extermination of the Deryni among the human population of Gwynedd. *Childe Morgan* continues the story, which finds Alyce and her human husband Kenneth Morgan raising Alaric to fulfill his destiny as protector. Problems arise when the power shifts between Deryni and human, forcing four-year-old Alaric to accept his responsibilities early. Calling *In the King's Service* an "exquisitely detailed" fantasy novel, a *Publishers Weekly* contributor added that readers are pulled along by characters who "follow . . . paths strewn with danger, difficulties, misjudgments—and the 'agonizing possibility' of death." Kurtz's "meticulous recreation of a medieval world" in *Childe Morgan* provides the novel "a sumptuous background," according to Jackie Cassada in *Library Journal,* and *Booklist* reviewer Frieda Murray deemed the novel "a vital continuation of the ["Deryni"] saga."

In addition to the "Deryni" novels, Kurtz has made what she terms "several literary forays outside the medieval world of the Eleven Kingdoms." Her historical thriller *Lammas Night* takes place in England during World War II. As Kurtz once explained to *SATA:* "British folk tradition has it that England has been saved from invasion more than once by the magical intervention of those appointed to guard her, Napoleonic and Armada times being cited as two specific examples. Less-well-known tradition has it that similar measures were employed to keep Hitler from invading Britain during that fateful summer of 1940, with its sagas of Dunkirk and the Battle of Britain. Whether or not what was done actually had any effect we will never know for certain, but the fact remains that Hitler never did invade, even though he was poised to do so for many months. *Lammas Night* is the story of how and why that might have been."

Together with fellow author Deborah Turner Harris, Kurtz has written several volumes in the "Adept" series. Set in the twentieth century, the novels features members of a secret, three-member brotherhood known as the Adept: former members of the ancient Knights Templar who, now based in Scotland, have sworn to uphold cosmic laws in their reincarnated form. In *The Templar Treasure,* the trio search for the treasured Seal of Solomon, only to discover a host of horrors. And in *Dagger Magic,* the Adept must foil efforts by a reincarnated Tibetan magician to gain absolute power by way of a collection of ancient texts confiscated by the Nazis decades ago and now discovered to exist in a German U-boat hidden in a cave along the northern coast of Ireland. "The plot, though somewhat convoluted, has a

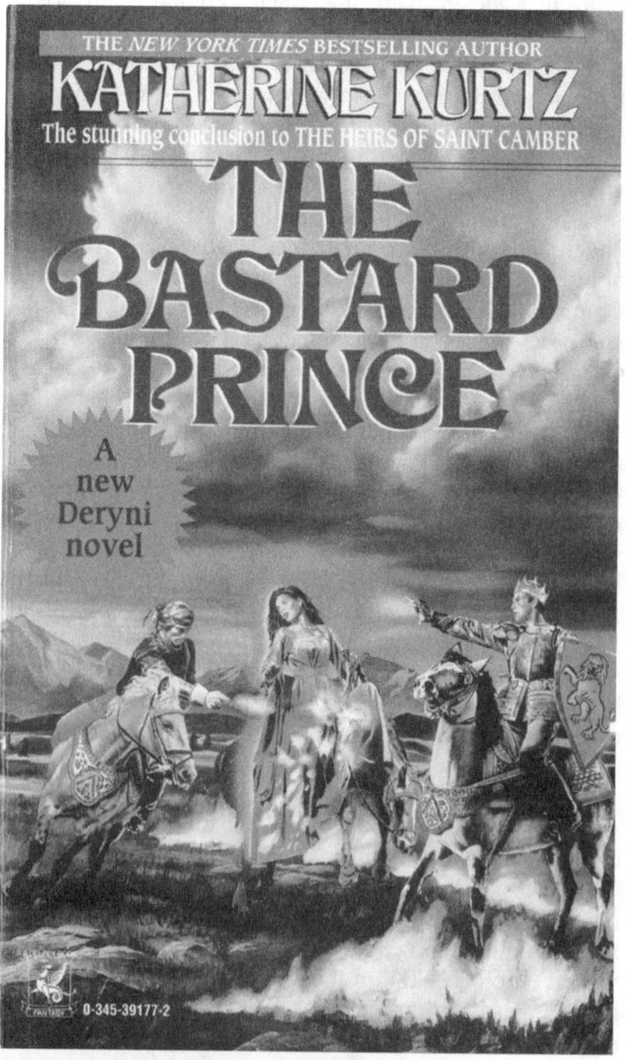


*Cover of* **The Bastard Prince,** *a novel in Kurtz's "Deryni" series featuring artwork by Edwin Herder.* (Copyright ©1994 by Katherine Kurtz. Reproduced by permission of Del Rey Books, a division of Random House, Inc.)

***Kurtz collaborates with Deborah Turner Harris on* The Temple and the Stone, *a novel featuring artwork by Greg Call.*** (Illustration © 1999 by Warner Books, Inc. Reproduced by permission.)

Wangerian intensity and a profound moral message chillingly told," maintained *Voice of Youth Advocates* contributor Mary Anne Hoebeke in her review of *Dagger Magic.*

Other works by Kurtz include the science-fiction novels *The Legacy of Lehr,* several collections of short stories focusing on the Knights Templar, the young-adult fantasy *St. Patrick's Gargoyle,* and an historical novel set during the American Revolutionary War, titled *Two Crowns for America.* Positing an alternate history, in *Two Crowns for America* Kurtz shows what would have happened had America adopted a monarchy, with factional Jacobites and Freemasons attempting to crown their preferred king while an occult Master has a plan of his own for the new country's future. Calling the novel an "engrossing and elegant tale," *Booklist* reviewer Roland Green praised its author for her "vivid portrayals" of such characters as Prince Charles Edward Stuart, otherwise known as Bonnie Prince Charlie, George Washington, and Benjamin Franklin. *St. Patrick's Gargoyle,* which *Booklist* contributor Ray Olson predicted would become a "Christmas perennial," finds a guardian gargoyle and a member of the Knights of Malta determined to find those responsible for vandalizing Ireland's famed St. Patrick's Cathedral in the days before Christmas. The novel was described by a *Publishers Weekly* contributor as a "light, sentimental fantasy" that combines Celtic history and a tour of the ancient city of Dublin.

Kurtz has several interests outside history and writing, although, as she noted, "most of them do tend to relate to my writing or medieval background in some way." A voracious reader, she tackles history, religion, and other books related to her research, while saving time to dip into "the occasional Brother Cadfael mystery for fun." Other hobbies take her away from the printed page; as Kurtz explained: "I delight in counted cross-stitch embroidery and needlepoint, will occasionally crochet, but am totally indifferent to knitting. I can sew just about anything, including medieval costumes and horse bardings." Together with her husband, whom she met at a Scottish country dance in Santa Monica, California, she restored an historic country house which they bought in County Wicklow, Ireland, in 1986. They have since moved to an even older and equally historic house in Virginia.

## Biographical and Critical Sources

*BOOKS*

Clarke, Boden, and Mary A. Burgess, *The Work of Katherine Kurtz: An Annotated Bibliography and Guide,* Borgo Press (San Bernardino, CA), 1993.

*St. James Guide to Fantasy Writers,* St. James Press (Detroit, MI), 1996.

*St. James Guide to Science Fiction Writers,* 4th edition, St. James Press (Detroit, MI), 1996.

*PERIODICALS*

*Booklist,* May 1, 1994, Roland Green, review of *The Bastard Prince,* p. 1583; February 1, 1996, Roland Green, review of *Two Crowns for America,* p. 920; December 1, 1996, Roland Green, review of *Death of an Adept,* p. 643; February 1, 2001, Ray Olson, review of *St. Patrick's Gargoyle,* p. 1042; April 15, 2001, Roland Green, review of *The Temple and the Crown,* p. 1540; May 1, 2002, Roland Green, review of *Deryni Tales: An Anthology,* p. 1513; November 1, 2002, Roland Green, review of *Crusades of Fire: Mystical Tales of the Knights Templar,* p. 480; October 15, 2003, Frieda Murray, review of *In the King's Service,* p. 399; November 1, 2006, Frieda Murray, review of *Childe Morgan,* p. 35.

*Kirkus Reviews,* April 1, 1998, review of *On Crusade,* p. 452.

*Kliatt,* September, 1995, Judith H. Silverman, review of *Tales of the Knights Templar,* p. 23.

*Library Journal,* June 15, 2000, Jackie Cassada, review of *King Kelson's Bride,* p. 121; February 15, 2001, review of *St. Patrick's Gargoyle,* p. 205; June 15, 2002, Jackie Cassada, review of *Deryni Tales,* p. 100; November 15, 2003, Jackie Cassada, review of *In the King's Service,* p. 101; November 15, 2006, Jackie Cassada, review of *Childe Morgan,* p. 62.

*Publishers Weekly,* April 10, 1972, p. 60; July 9, 1973, p. 48; May 31, 1976, p. 197; September 11, 1978, review of *Saint Camber,* p. 77; September 25, 1981, review of *Camber the Heretic,* p. 87; September 21, 1984, review of *The Bishop's Heir,* p. 92; August 8, 1986 review of *The Quest for Saint Camber,* p. 58; September 26, 1986, review of *The Legacy of Lehr,* p. 69; December 2, 1988, review of *The Heirs of Saint Camber,* p. 48; December 21, 1990, review of *Deryni Magic,* p. 50; February 8, 1991, review of *The Adept,* p. 54; June 21, 1993, review of *The Templar Treasure,* p. 102; May 23, 1994, review of *The Bastard Prince,* p. 82; November 27, 1995, review of *Two Crowns for America,* pp. 52-53; April 13, 1998, review of *On Crusade,* p. 57; July 27, 1998, review of *The Temple and the Stone,* pp. 58-59; May 29, 2000, review of *King Kelson's Bride,* p. 57; January 1, 2001, review of *St. Patrick's Gargoyle,* p. 72; October 20, 2003, review of *In the King's Service,* p. 39; October 9, 2006, review of *Childe Morgan,* p. 41.

*School Library Journal,* January, 1985, review of *The Bishop's Heir,* p. 92; February, 1986, Betsy Shorb, review of *The King's Justice,* p. 103; November, 1986, review of *The Deryni Archives,* p. 116; December, 1986, Betsy Shorb, review of *The Quest for Saint Camber,* p. 126; January, 1990, Annette Demeritt, review of *The Harrowing of Gwynedd,* p. 128; September, 1991, review of *The Adept,* p. 298; September, 1992, review of *The Lodge of the Lynx,* p. 29; November, 19995, review of *Dagger Magic,* p. 141.

*Voice of Youth Advocates,* December, 1986, p. 238; April, 1987, p. 38; August, 1989, p. 166; April, 1993, Diane G. Yates, review of *King Javan's Year,* p. 42; October, 1993, Faye H. Gottschall, review of *The Templar Treasure,* p. 230; October, 1995, Mary Anne Hoebeke, review of *Dagger Magic,* p. 234.

*ONLINE*

*Katherine Kurtz Home Page,* http://www.deryni.net (August 20, 2007).

* * *

## KURTZ, Katherine Irene

See KURTZ, Katherine

* * *

## KVASNOSKY, Laura McGee 1951-

### Personal

Born January 27, 1951, in Sacramento, CA; daughter of Harvey C. (a newspaper publisher) and Helen (a comptroller) McGee; married John Kvasnosky (a public relations executive), December 16, 1972; children: Timothy John, Noelle Helen. *Education:* Occidental College, B.A., 1973, studied writing with Jane Yolen at Centrum (Port Townsend, WA), 1994; studied illustration with Keith Baker at School of Visual Concepts (Seattle, WA). *Hobbies and other interests:* Gardening, cross-country skiing, hiking.

### Addresses

*Home and office*—801 NW Culbertson Dr., Seattle, WA 98177. *E-mail*—laura@lmkbooks.com.

### Career

Writer and illustrator. University of Washington—Extension, Seattle, founding instructor in certificate program in writing for children, 2000-01; Vermont College MFA Program in Writing for Children and Young People, member of faculty, 2001—. Graphic designer and proprietor of one-person design shop, Seattle, WA, beginning 1980. Society of Children's Book Writers and Illustrators, edited regional newsletter, 1992-94. Northwest Girlchoir, member of board of directors, 1992-96.

### Awards, Honors

Best Books selection, *Parents* magazine, 1995, for *See You Later, Alligator;* Pick of the Lists selection, American Booksellers Association, 1996, for *A Red Wagon Year* by Kathi Appelt; Society of Children's Book Writers and Illustrators Golden Kite Honor, Oppenheim Best Book Gold Award, and Notable Book designation, American Library Association, all 1999, all for *Zelda and Ivy;* Oppenheim Best Book Gold Award, for *Zelda and Ivy One Christmas;* Theodor Seuss Geisel Award, 2007, for *Zelda and Ivy: The Runaways.*

### Writings

*SELF-ILLUSTRATED*

*Pink, Red, Blue, What Are You?,* Dutton (New York, NY), 1994.

*One, Two, Three, Play with Me,* Dutton (New York, NY), 1994.

*See You Later, Alligator,* Harcourt (San Diego, CA), 1995.

*Mr. Chips!,* Farrar, Straus & Giroux (New York, NY), 1996.

*Zelda and Ivy,* Candlewick Press (Cambridge, MA), 1998.

*Zelda and Ivy and the Boy Next Door,* Candlewick Press (Cambridge, MA), 1999.

*Zelda and Ivy One Christmas,* Candlewick Press (Cambridge, MA), 2000.

*Frank and Izzy Set Sail,* Candlewick Press (Cambridge, MA), 2004.

*Zelda and Ivy: The Runaways,* Candlewick Press (Cambridge, MA), 2006.

*ILLUSTRATOR*

Florence Page Jaques, *There Once Was a Puffin,* Dutton (New York, NY), 1995.
Kathi Appelt, *A Red Wagon Year,* Harcourt (San Diego, CA), 1996.
Libby Hough, *If Somebody Lived Next Door,* Dutton (New York, NY), 1997.

Contributor of illustrations to poetry collection *This Place I Know: Poems of Comfort,* edited by Georgia Heard.

*OTHER*

*What Shall I Dream?,* illustrated by Judith Byron Schachner, Dutton (New York, NY), 1996.
*One Lucky Summer* (chapter book), Dutton (New York, NY), 2002.

## Sidelights

Known for her gentle humor both in text and illustrations, Laura McGee Kvasnosky is the author and/or illustrator of picture books such as *See You Later, Alligator* and *Frank and Izzy Set Sail,* as well as beginning readers in the "Zelda and Ivy" series. Particularly popular, her "Zelda and Ivy" books follow the adventures of two "true-to-life little fox sisters," as Ilene Cooper described the fictional siblings in a *Booklist* review. While Kvasnosky's simple texts and vibrant gouache illustrations have won her numerous fans among the storybook set, she has also attracted older elementary-grade audiences with her children's novel *One Lucky Summer,* in which a pair of ten year olds are brought together by their interest in a flying squirrel.

"I come from a long line of California newspaper writers," Kvasnosky once told *SATA.* "Perhaps we feel a genetic urge to organize a story as a way to understand life. Being part of [a larger] family also affects what I choose to write about. I'm the middle of five kids. In many ways my childhood was like growing up in a summer camp. My mother even put name tags in our underwear.

"Three things happened in third grade that led me to become a writer and illustrator. First, we moved, so I was a new kid at school. As an outsider looking in, I developed observation skills. Second, I made up tremendous stories (lies) in hopes of attracting friends, thus developing a keen understanding of the blend of fact and fiction that a good, 'believable'story requires. Third, my reading improved to the point where I could really read. I became (and still am) a bookworm.

"I began my work career at the age of eight, sharpening pencils for my editor-father. Over the years, I contributed in the advertising and editorial departments of his newspaper, too. When my children were small, I created over 10,000 bakers clay Christmas ornaments in my kitchen. Then, in 1980, I started my own graphic design firm. I decided to go for a lifelong dream of publishing a children's book when I turned forty."

Kvasnosky's first published books for children were the self-illustrated board books *One, Two, Three, Play with Me* and *Pink, Red, Blue, What Are You?,* both published in 1994. Featuring short, rhyming phrases and bright pictures that introduce colors and numbers, these works also employ various groupings of children or animals to illustrate learning concepts; In *Pink, Red, Blue, What Are You?,* for example, animals define themselves by their color, temperament, and sometimes even their scent. A *Publishers Weekly* reviewer dubbed Kvasnosky's board books "simple, fun and effective," and in *School Library Journal* Linda Wicher wrote that the author/illustrator's "sketched figures are full of movement and wit."

In *See You Later, Alligator* a group of young reptiles begin the day deposited by their parents at River Bottom School. In a text filled with reptilian plays on words, Kvasnosky conveys the "upbeat" side of parent-child separation, according to *School Library Journal* contributor Nancy Seiner. In *Booklist,* April Judge concluded that, while "slight," *See You Later, Alligator* "will tickle the funny bones of young listeners."

Other picture books by Kvasnosky include *What Shall I Dream?,* featuring illustrations by Judith Byron Schachner, as well as the self-illustrated *Mr. Chips!* and *Frank and Izzy Set Sail.* Described as "a lovely bedtime story" by *School Library Journal* contributor Judith Constantinides, *What Shall I Dream?* takes readers into the world of young Prince Alexander, who worries over what to dream. His royal family uses their power and influence to summon Dream Brewers, Dream Weavers, and Dream Sweepers to assist him, but when the dreams these masters concoct prove unsatisfying, it is the shrewd observation of the humble nursemaid that saves the day. *Mr. Chips!* focuses on the affectionate bond between a dog and a young girl named Ellie. In this instance, the dog, Mr. Chips, disappears for several days, just before his little companion moves with her family to a new house in another. Although the dog's disappearance might worry young animal lovers, all ends well for girl and pet. "Stories about lost pets who manage to find their families despite vast distances are always touching, and this one is no exception," asserted a *Kirkus Reviews* critic, and in *School Library Journal* Marianne Saccardi called *Mr. Chips!* "a heartwarming story" in which "Kvasnosky's cartoon art is bright and appropriately childlike." Lauren Peterson, reviewing the same title in *Booklist,* called *Mr. Chips!* "a heartwarming story."

Kvasnosky's colorful artwork brings to life her lighthearted story about appreciating differences in *Frank and Izzy Set Sail.* Frank, a brown bear, and Izzy, a rabbit, decide to go on a camping trip to a nearby island. For Frank, the trip will be quite a change, because he is

***In* Frank and Izzy Set Sail *Laura McGee Kvasnosky tells a story about how differences can strengthen true friendship.*** (Illustration © 2004 by Laura McGee Kvasnosky. Reproduced by permission of the publisher, Candlewick Press, Inc., Cambridge, MA.)

a homebody at heart and likes nothing better than to be at home, playing his ukulele. Adventurous Izzy can't wait, however, and can't wait for the new adventures she is sure the two will encounter. To make Frank comfortable, Izzy brings the things from his home that she knows her friend would miss, and Frank's slow, methodical nature comes in handy when trouble arises. In *Booklist* Ilene Cooper noted that Kvasnosky's "underlying message . . . comes across subtly" in the simple story. Writing that the author/illustrator's gouache paintings give the tale "a quiet, non-threatening atmosphere," a *Publishers Weekly* reviewer added that the "easygoing, give-and-take friendship" between the two fictional friends "provides an example for any age." The illustrations in *Frank and Izzy Set Sail* capture the ways the characters' "budding relationship allows them to grow and learn from each other," wrote a *Kirkus Reviews* writer, and in *School Library Journal* Andrea Tarr praised Kvasnosky's "colorful" paintings as "full of charming details that are perfect for poring over."

Kvasnosky's "Zelda and Ivy" books include *Zelda and Ivy, Zelda and Ivy and the Boy Next Door, Zelda and Ivy One Christmas,* and *Zelda and Ivy: The Runaways.* In the series opener, *Zelda and Ivy,* older sister Zelda tries to boss around younger sister Ivy in three humorous stories. In *Booklist,* Ilene Cooper noted that Kvasnosky "not only has a way with words; her illustrations are delightful, too." A reviewer for *Publishers Weekly* praised the author's "insightful look at sisterhood," noting that Kvasnosky's story "reach[es] out to readers regardless of their birth order." In *Horn Book* Martha V. Parravano wrote that, as an artist, Kvasnosky has a "gift for communicating a wealth of emotion through the dot of an eye or the angle of a tail," and *Bulletin of the Center for Children's Books* contributor Janice M. Del Negro predicted that the text will likely "elicit groans and chuckles of recognition" from young listeners. In *School Library Journal,* Luann Toth concluded of *Zelda and Ivy* that young readers "will recognize and relate to these three stories that take a gentle humorous look at sibling dynamics."

In *Zelda and Ivy and the Boy Next Door* the sisters are happy when Eugene moves in next door, thinking they will have a new playmate. However, the triangular nature of the new friendship presents difficulties when two gang up on one, and loyalties shift and change. Drama ensues when the trio attempt to set up a lemonade stand and play a game of pirates. Cooper described the fox sisters' second outing as "delightfully droll and at the same time awfully sweet," and Toth enthused of *Zelda and Ivy and the Boy Next Door:* "Encore Zelda and Ivy!" In the three easy-reading segments in *Zelda and Ivy, the Runaways* the fox sisters flee from home to avoid a hated lunch of cucumber sandwiches, create a very unusual time capsule, and invent a love potion. The "sibling dynamics" between Zelda and Ivy "are nicely enhanced" by Kvasnosky's artwork, noted Engberg, while in *School Library Journal* Laura Scott concluded that "bright, expressive cartoon illustrations complement the [author/illustrator's] fine writing."

A holiday-themed tale, *Zelda and Ivy One Christmas* finds the sisters with high hopes and a wealth of wishes for gifts, Zelda hopes for a fancy gown and Ivy desires a Princess Mimi doll. Hearing their gift wishes, elderly neighbor Mrs. Brownlie describes how she once went to a ball with her now-dead husband. Hoping to cheer up the widow on Christmas, Ivy suggests making a special bracelet. Zelda agrees, acting as if it were her idea in the first place. When the big day comes, Santa disappoints the sisters with matching bathrobes, but packages from a mysterious "Christmas Elf" reveal the doll and the desired gown. "As always, humor pervades the situations and the dialogue," noted Martha V. Parravano in a *Horn Book* review of *Zelda and Ivy One Christmas.* Ellen Mandel praised the tale in *Booklist,* calling it an "engaging return" for the sisters, and one that depicts the joy of giving: "companionship, affection, and memories, priceless rewards for any season."

In *One Lucky Summer* Steven Bennett is forced to move away from his Santa Cruz, California, home and its breezy beach weather, his best friend, and his Little League team when his family moves to hot Sacramento. His parents offer him little consolation: his photographer father is on assignment in Peru and his mother is busy authoring a cook book. Steven's bad luck continues when he discovers that his new next-door neighbor is a girl, and not just any regular girl, but one with dreams of becoming a ballerina. Even worse, Lucinda, the ballerina, does not take kindly to Steven's pet lizard, Godzilla, and is particularly upset when the boy accidentally ruins her favorite tutu. When Godzilla escapes from its cage during a trip to a woodland cabin, the two children band together to track it down, and discover a baby flying squirrel in the process. Their shared determination to keep the squirrel—dubbed Lucky—alive brings Steven and Lucinda closer together, and soon Steven is faced with a difficult decision: to let his pet lizard go or to give up the squirrel. Writing in *School Library Journal,* Alison Grant noted that Kvasnosky's debut "novel should prove to be a lucky choice for girls and boys alike." In *Booklist* Kay Weisman praised the author's "strong, believable characters and . . . good ear for dialogue," while a reviewer for *Publishers Weekly* called *One Lucky Summer* a "tightly written, affecting tale about adjustment and friendship."

"The seeds that grow into future books are often planted in young children," Kvasnosky once told *SATA.* "I know that because it is my experience. It is one reason I enjoy working with young writers and artists. Creating children's books is my dream job. The experiences I value most—nurturing a family, writing, graphic design, reading—all meet in this one enterprise."

## Biographical and Critical Sources

*PERIODICALS*

*Booklist,* September 15, 1995, April Judge, review of *See You Later, Alligator,* p. 175; July, 1996, Lauren Peterson, review of *Mr. Chips!,* p. 1830; October 1, 1996, Julie Corsaro, review of *A Red Wagon Year,* pp. 356-357; June 1, 1997, Carolyn Phelan, review of *If Somebody Lived Next Door,* p. 1719; April, 1998, Ilene Cooper, review of *Zelda and Ivy,* p. 1324; May 1, 1999, Ilene Cooper, review of *Zelda and Ivy and the Boy Next Door,* p. 1599; November 15, 2000, Ellen Mandel, review of *Zelda and Ivy One Christmas,* p. 648; March 1, 2002, Kay Weisman, review of *One Lucky Summer,* p. 1137; May 15, 2004, Ilene Cooper, review of *Frank and Izzy Set Sail,* p. 1625; June 1, 2006, Gillian Engberg, review of *Zelda and Ivy: The Runaways,* p. 87.

*Bulletin of the Center for Children's Books,* November, 1996, review of *Mr. Chips!,* p. 105; January, 1997, Amy E. Brandt, review of *What Shall I Dream?,* pp. 177-178; April, 1998, Janice M. Del Negro, review of *Zelda and Ivy,* p. 285; June, 1999, review of *Zelda and Ivy and the Boy Next Door,* p. 357; December, 2000, review of *Zelda and Ivy One Christmas,* p. 151; May, 2002, review of *One Lucky Summer,* p. 329; April, 2004, Hope Morrison, review of *Frank and Izzy Set Sail,* p. 333.

*Horn Book,* July-August, 1998, Martha V. Parravano, review of *Zelda and Ivy,* pp. 475-476; November-December, 2000, Martha V. Parravano, review of *Zelda and Ivy One Christmas,* p. 747; July-August, 2006, Betty Carter, review of *Zelda and Ivy: The Runaways,* p. 444.

*Kirkus Reviews,* July 1, 1996, review of *Mr. Chips!,* p. 970; March 15, 2004, review of *Frank and Izzy Set Sail,* p. 272; May 15, 2006, review of *Zelda and Ivy: The Runaways,* p. 519.

*Publishers Weekly,* May 2, 1994, review of *Pink, Red, Blue, What Are You?* and *One, Two, Three, Play with Me!,* p. 305; May 15, 1995, review of *There Once Was a Puffin,* p. 71; June 24, 1996, review of *Mr. Chips!,* p. 58; May 12, 1997, review of *If Somebody Lived Next Door,* p. 75; May 11, 1998, review of *Zelda and Ivy,* p. 67; April 8, 2002, review of *One Lucky Summer,* p. 228; May 10, 2004, review of *Frank and Izzy Set Sail,* p. 58.

*School Library Journal,* August, 1994, Linda Wicher, review of *Pink, Red, Blue, What Are You?* and *One, Two, Three, Play with Me!,* p. 139; November, 1995, Nancy Seiner, review of *See You Later, Alligator!,* p. 74; August, 1996, Marianne Saccardi, review of *Mr. Chips!,* p. 126; September, 1996, Judith Constantinides, review of *What Shall I Dream?,* p. 182; July, 1997, Christy Norris, review of *If Somebody Lived Next Door,* p. 69; June, 1998, Luann Toth, review of *Zelda and Ivy,* p. 113; May, 1999, Luann Toth, review of *Zelda and Ivy and the Boy Next Door,* p. 92; October, 2000, review of *Zelda and Ivy One Christmas,* p. 60; April, 2002, Alison Grant, review of *One Lucky Summer,* p. 114; June, 2004, Andrea Tarr, review of *Frank and Izzy Set Sail,* p. 112; June, 2006, Laura Scott, review of *Zelda and Ivy: The Runaways,* p. 81.

*ONLINE*

*Laura McGee Kvasnosky Home Page,* http://www.LMKBooks.com (August 27, 2007).

# L

## LEE, Chinlun

### Personal

Born in Taipei, Taiwan; father an art teacher; married; husband a veterinarian. *Education:* Royal College of Art (London, England), degree (illustration), 1999. *Hobbies and other interests:* Animals.

### Addresses

*Home*—Koashung, Taiwan.

### Career

Illustrator and author of children's books.

### Writings

*SELF-ILLUSTRATED*

*The Very Kind Rich Lady and Her One Hundred Dogs,* Candlewick Press (Cambridge, MA), 2001.

*Good Dog, Paw!,* Candlewick Press (Cambridge, MA), 2004.

*ILLUSTRATOR*

Michael Rosen, *Totally Wonderful Miss Plumberry,* Candlewick Press (Cambridge, MA), 2006.

### Sidelights

A native of Taiwan, Chinlun Lee grew up with a love of art. As a child she developed her skill, aided by an encouraging art-teacher father, and as an adult she has successfully made art her career. Leaving her country for several years to earn a degree in illustration from London's prestigious Royal College of Art, Lee now lives in southern Taiwan, where she both writes and illustrates books for children.

Dogs figure prominently in Lee's original self-illustrated picture books *The Very Kind Rich Lady and Her One Hundred Dogs* and *Good Dog, Paw.!* To illustrate her first published book, *The Very Kind Rich Lady and Her One Hundred Dogs,* Lee had to portray dogs of all sizes, shapes, and colors. Fortunately, she did not have to stray far to find animals to sketch; her husband is a veterinarian and her studio is upstairs from his office. In the book, which is based on a true story, Lee introduces readers to a wealthy lady who devotes much of her time and money to feeding, brushing, petting, and playing with one hundred dogs. In addition to its own food bowl, each of the one hundred pets also has its own special name, its own place in the woman's heart, and its own special sleeping spot on the woman's bed! Calling Lee's brightly colored art a "doggy delight," Ilene Cooper added in *Booklist* that the final picture of sleeping dogs "is pure whimsy." A *Publishers Weekly* critic noted the "understatement" in Lee's affectionate story, and was even more enthusiastic about her "appealingly naive" art. Citing the illustrator's use of "flat, Egyptian-style perspective," the *Publishers Weekly* contributor concluded that Lee's "subtle use of color and texture" signal her "sophisticated" talent.

*Good Dog, Paw!* was actually inspired by Lee's own dog. In the book, a black-and-white cocker spaniel named Paw lives with a veterinarian named April, who gives the pup a ten-point check-up every morning. Every day, Paw joins April in her pet clinic, where he is both a companion and a helper. When sick animals enter the clinic and are frightened and feeling bad, for example, Paw sings to them, passing along encouragement as well as the health tips he has learned from his veterinarian companion. Noting that Lee's "lively" and "detailed" drawings feature "impressionistic pastel tints [that] extend the text's sunny tone," *Horn Book* contributor Anita L. Burkam praised the "warm relationship" between Paw and April. In *Publishers Weekly* a reviewer found the two characters to be "a perfect match," noting in particular that dog and owner "tend not only to their patients' health, but to their hearts as

***Chinlun Lee captures the mercurial emotions of young children in her illustrations for Michael Rosen's picture book* Totally Wonderful Miss Plumberry.** (Illustration © 2006 by Chinlun Lee. All rights reserved. Reproduced by permission of the publisher, Candlewick Press, Inc., Cambridge, MA on behalf of Walker Books Ltd., London.)

well." "Lee's simple, present-tense text allows Paw's self-confident voice to ring out," wrote a *Kirkus Reviews* writer, the critic calling the pup a "cheerful" and "personable" character.

In addition to her own stories, Lee has also contributed her engaging pencil-and-watercolor illustrations to British author Michael Rosen's *Totally Wonderful Miss Plumberry.* In this gentle story, a young girl named Molly brings a special gem to class for show and tell. Although the gem is at first overlooked in the busy classroom, Molly ultimately gains an affirmation of her own feelings when her teacher also finds something magical in the colored stone. Describing Lee's pencil and watercolor art as "engaging" and "somewhat idyllic," *School Library Journal* contributor Piper L. Nyman wrote that the illustrator effectively captures both the "emotions" of the young girl and the "fickle attention" of her young classmates. In *Kirkus Reviews,* a reviewer praised Lee for her "light touch, nice colors and [the] expressive faces" on her young characters.

## Biographical and Critical Sources

*PERIODICALS*

*Booklist,* May 15, 2001, Ilene Cooper, review of *The Very Kind Rich Lady and Her One Hundred Dogs,* p. 1759; April 15, 2004, Gillian Engberg, review of *Good Dog, Paw!,* p. 1446; August 1, 2006, Ilene Cooper, review of *Totally Wonderful Miss Plumberry,* p. 96.

*Horn Book,* May-June, 2004, Anita L. Burkam, review of *Good Dog, Paw!,* p. 317.

*Kirkus Reviews,* March 15, 2004, review of *Good Dog, Paw!,* p. 272; August 15, 2006, review of *Totally Wonderful Miss Plumberry,* p. p. 850.

*New York Times Book Review,* July 15, 2001, review of *The Very Kind Rich Lady and Her One Hundred Dogs,* p. 24.

*Publishers Weekly,* May 28, 2001, review of *The Very Kind Rich Lady and Her One Hundred Dogs,* p. 86; April 26, 2004, review of *Good Dog, Paw!,* p. 64.

*School Library Journal,* July, 2001, Lisa Gangemi Kropp, review of *The Very Kind Rich Lady and Her One Hundred Dogs,* p. 84; August, 2004, Corrina Austin, review of *Good Dog, Paw!,* p. 89; September, 2006, Piper L. Nyman, review of *Totally Wonderful Miss Plumberry,* p. 183.

*ONLINE*

*Walker Books Web site,* http://www.walkerbooks.co.uk/ (August 27, 2007), "Chinlun Lee."*

* * *

## LeFRAK, Karen

### Personal

Married Richard LeFrak (a land developer); children: Harrison, James. *Education:* Mount Holyoke College, B.A. (magna cum laude); Hunter College, M.A. *Hobbies and other interests:* Playing classical piano, breeding show poodles.

### Addresses

*Home and office*—New York, NY.

### Career

Philanthropist. Member, New York State Council on the Arts; New York Philharmonic, director and member of executive, marketing, and education committees, assistant archivist of Volunteer Council. Previously worked in archival management and historical editing; former actress and nursery-school teacher. Member, Central Park Conservancy Women's Committee and Sloan-Kettering Memorial Cancer Center administrative board. Member of board, American Kennel Club and Canine Health Foundation.

### Member

Delta Society (honorary board member).

### Awards, Honors

James Hammerstein Award, and New York Women's Agenda Star Breakfast Awards, both 2004, both for work aiding victims and families of September 11th Twin Towers tragedy; Frederick Law Olmstead Award.

### Writings

*Jake the Philharmonic Dog,* illustrated by Marcin Baranski, Walker (New York, NY), 2006.

### Sidelights

Karen LeFrak and her husband, Richard LeFrak, are actively involved in several of New York City's major philanthropies. LeFrak's interest in the arts has led to her positions as a director of the New York Philharmonic, her membership in the New York State Council on the Arts, and her work chairing the New York Orchestra's 150th Anniversary Ball. LeFrak's civic involvement, along with her work for the American Kennel Club's DOGNY project and her volunteer work with therapy dogs, has also combined to inspire her picture book *Jake the Philharmonic Dog.*

Written to help children learn about the performing arts, *Jake the Philharmonic Dog* introduces readers to Richie, the orchestra's principle stage hand, and his dog, Jake. When Richie takes the music-loving Jake to work one day, the dog discovers the many different instruments used in the orchestra, and saves the day by finding the conductor's missing baton. "Children will enjoy Jake's charming personality," wrote a *Kirkus Reviews* contributor of LeFrak's canine hero, and Mary Elam wrote in *School Library Journal* that *Jake the Philharmonic Dog* will "appeal to dog lovers and may serve as a painless introduction to the orchestra as well."

Unlike his fictional counterpart in *Jake the Philharmonic Dog,* the real-life Jake, a mixed-breed terrier,

*Cover of Karen LeFrak's* **Jake the Philharmonic Dog,** *featuring artwork by Marcin Baranski.* (Walker & Company, 2006. Illustration © 2006 by Marcin Baranski. Reproduced by permission.)

comes to the Philharmonic every day. "I saw this little dog kind of stretching with all the musicians as they left for rehearsal break," LeFrak recalled to Robin D. Schatz of the Bergen County, New Jersey *Record.* in discussing the inspiration for her picture book. "I'd been a music teacher for children for many years and thought he'd be a perfect vehicle to teach children about music and the people who perform it." LeFrak's proceeds from *Jake the Philharmonic Dog* are donated to the New York Philharmonic.

## Biographical and Critical Sources

*PERIODICALS*

*Kirkus Reviews,* August 15, 2006, review of *Jake the Philharmonic Dog,* p. 846.

*New York Times,* October 28, 2001, Julie V. Ionvine, "The Healing Ways of Dr. Dog," p. ST8.

*Publishers Weekly,* September 11, 2006, review of *Jake the Philharmonic Dog,* p. 53.

*Record* (Bergen County, NJ), January 4, 2007, Robin D. Schatz, "New York Philharmonic's House Dog, a Literary Figure," p. F04.

*School Library Journal,* September, 2006, Mary Elam, review of *Jake the Philharmonic Dog,* p. 177.

*ONLINE*

*Jake the Philharmonic Dog Web site,* http://www.jakethephilharmonicdog.com/ (August 6, 2007).

*Walker Books Web site,* http://www.walkeryoungreaders.com/ (August 6, 2007), "Karen LeFrak."*

* * *

# LESSEM, Don 1951-
# ("Dino" Don Lessem)

***Don Lessem*** (Photo courtesy of Don Lessem.)

## Personal

Born December 2, 1951, in New York, NY; son of Lawrence (a dentist) and Gertrude (a psychologist) Lessem; married Paula Hartstein (a reading specialist), June 8, 1978 (divorced, July 1, 1999); children: Rebecca, Erica. *Education:* Brandeis University, B.A. (Oriental art history; cum laude), 1973; University of Massachusetts—Boston, M.S. (bio-behavioral studies), 1978. *Politics:* "Disgusted." *Religion:* Jewish. *Hobbies and other interests:* Travel, tennis, raising pygmy goats Paris and Nicole.

## Addresses

*Home and office*—Troodon Manor, P.O. Box 404, Media, PA 19063. *Agent*—Al Zuckerman, Writers House, 21 W. 26th St., New York, NY 10010. *E-mail*—DinoDonL@aol.com.

## Career

Writer, exhibit building and dinosaur skeleton reconstruction. Science journalist for *Boston Globe* and other periodicals; Dinosaur Productions, Waban, MA, president, beginning 1995; Dinosaur Exhibitions, Waban, president, beginning 1996; Dinodon, Inc., president, beginning 2002; Exhibits Rex, president, beginning 2004; DKV Sponsorship, president, 2005; Genghis Khan Exhibits, president, beginning 2006. Writer and host of episodes of television programs *Discovery* and *Nova* for Public Broadcast System (PBS). Technical advisor on films and for theme parks. Founder of charities Jurassic Foundation, Dinosaur Society, and Mongolian Cultural Preservation Fund.

## Member

International Association of Amusement Parks and Aquaria, American Association of Museums, Association of Science and Technology Centers, Society of Vertebrate Paleontology.

## Awards, Honors

Several National Science Teachers Association awards; Knight Science Journalism fellowship, Massachusetts Institute of Technology, 1988.

## Writings

*FOR CHILDREN*

*Life Is No Yuk for the Yak: A Book of Endangered Animals,* illustrated by Linda Bourke, Crane Russak (New York, NY), 1977.

(With John R. Horner) *Digging up Tyrannosaurus Rex,* Crown (New York, NY), 1992.

*The Iceman,* Crown (New York, NY), 1994.

*Jack Horner: Living with Dinosaurs,* illustrated by Janet Hamlin, Scientific American Books for Young Readers (New York, NY), 1994.

*Inside the Amazing Amazon: Incredible Fold-out Cross Sections of the World's Greatest Rainforest,* illustrated by Michael Rothman, Crown (New York, NY), 1995.

(With Donald Glut) *Dinosaur Encyclopedia,* Random House (New York, NY), 1996.

*Ornithomimids: The Fastest Dinosaur,* illustrated by Brian Franczak, Carolrhoda (Minneapolis, MN), 1996.

*Raptors!: The Nastiest Dinosaurs,* illustrated by David Peters, Little, Brown (Boston, MA), 1996.

*Seismosaurus: The Longest Dinosaur,* illustrated by Donna Braginetz, Carolrhoda (Minneapolis, MN), 1996.

*Troodon: The Smartest Dinosaur,* illustrated by Brian Franzack, Carolrhoda (Minneapolis, MN), 1996.

*Utahraptor: The Deadliest Dinosaur,* illustrated by Donna Braginetz, Carolrhoda (Minneapolis, MN), 1996.

(With Rodolfo Coria) *Supergiants! The Biggest Dinosaurs,* illustrated by David Peters, Little, Brown (Boston, MA), 1997.

*Bigger than T-Rex,* Random House (New York, NY), 1997.

*Skeleton Detective,* Random House (New York, NY), 1997.

*Dinosaur Worlds: New Dinosaurs, New Discoveries,* Boyds Mills Press (Honesdale, PA), 1997.

*Dinosaurs to Dodos: An Encyclopedia of Extinct Animals,* illustrated by Jan Sovak, Scholastic (New York, NY), 1999.

*The Ultimate Dinosaur Field Guide,* Klutz Press, 1999.

*Looking Lousy,* Morrow (New York, NY), 1999.

*All the Dirt on Dinosaurs,* illustrated by Kevin Wasden, Tor Kids (New York, NY), 2001.

*Tyrannosaurus Rex,* illustrated by Hall Train, Candlewick Press (Cambridge, MA), 2002.

*The Dinosaur Atlas: A Complete Look at the World of Dinosaurs,* illustrated by John Bindon, Firefly Books (New York, NY), 2003.

*Dinosaurs A to Z: The Ultimate Dinosaur Encyclopedia,* illustrated by Jan Sovak, Scholastic (New York, NY), 2004.

*Fun with Learning: Dinosaurs,* illustrated by Jan Sovak, Scholastic (New York, NY), 2005.

*Dinosaurs* (interactive book), illustrated by Phil Wilson, Publications International (Lincolnwood, IL), 2007.

Regular columnist for *Highlights for Children* magazine under name Dino Don; author and editor of *Dino Times* (newsletter). Contributor to periodicals, including *Boston Globe* and *New York Times.*

*"WHEN DINOSAURS LIVED" SERIES; AS "DINO" DON LESSEM*

*Baby Dinosaurs,* illustrated by John Bindon, Grosset & Dunlap (New York, NY), 2001.

*Biggest Dinosaurs,* illustrated by John Bindon, Grosset & Dunlap (New York, NY), 2001.

*Giants of the Sky,* illustrated by John Bindon, Grosset & Dunlap (New York, NY), 2002.

*Sea Monsters,* illustrated by John Bindon, Grosset & Dunlap (New York, NY), 2002.

*"MEET THE DINOSAURS" SERIES; AS "DINO" DON LESSEM*

*Duck-billed Dinosaurs,* illustrated by John Bindon, Lerner (Minneapolis, MN), 2005.

*The Fastest Dinosaurs,* illustrated by John Bindon, Lerner (Minneapolis, MN), 2005.

*Feathered Dinosaurs,* illustrated by John Bindon, Lerner (Minneapolis, MN), 2005.

*Giant Meat-eating Dinosaurs,* illustrated by John Bindon, Lerner (Minneapolis, MN), 2005.

*Horned Dinosaurs,* illustrated by John Bindon, Lerner (Minneapolis, MN), 2005.

*Sea Giants of Dinosaur Time,* illustrated by John Bindon, Lerner (Minneapolis, MN), 2005.

*The Smallest Dinosaurs,* illustrated by John Bindon, Lerner (Minneapolis, MN), 2005.

*The Smartest Dinosaurs,* illustrated by John Bindon, Lerner (Minneapolis, MN), 2005.

*Flying Giants of Dinosaur Time,* illustrated by John Bindon, Lerner (Minneapolis, MN), 2005.

*Giant Plant-eating Dinosaurs,* illustrated by John Bindon, Lerner (Minneapolis, MN), 2005.

*The Deadliest Dinosaurs,* illustrated by John Bindon, Lerner (Minneapolis, MN), 2005.

*Armored Dinosaurs,* illustrated by John Bindon, Lerner (Minneapolis, MN), 2005.

*OTHER*

*How to Flatten Your Nose,* Klutz Press, 1978.

*Aerphobics: The Scientific Way to Stop Exercising* (humor), Morrow (New York, NY), 1980.

*The Worst of Everything: The Experts' Listing of the Most Loathsome and Deficient in Every Realm of Our Lives,* McGraw-Hill (New York, NY), 1988.

*Kings of Creation: How a New Breed of Scientists Is Revolutionizing Our Understanding of Dinosaurs,* illustrated by John Sibbick, Simon & Schuster (New York, NY), 1992, published as *Dinosaurs Rediscovered: New Findings Which Are Revolutionizing Dinosaur Science,* Touchstone (New York, NY), 1993.

(With John R. Horner) *The Complete T. Rex: How Stunning New Discoveries Are Changing Our Understanding of the World's Most Famous Dinosaur,* Simon & Schuster (New York, NY), 1993.

(With Donald F. Glut) *The Dinosaur Society's Dinosaur Encyclopedia,* Random House (New York, NY), 1993.

(With Spencer Koelle) *Why French Women Smell Bad,* Merde Press (Media,PA), 2005.

## Sidelights

Science journalist and author Don Lessem specializes in writing nonfiction for children. His engaging style and contagious excitement about his topic, coupled with his dedication to providing accurate, accessible information, have made Lessem's books popular with readers and critics alike. Nicknamed "Dino" Don, Lessem is best known for his books on dinosaurs and the scientists who have dedicated their lives to uncovering the mysteries of these long-extinct creatures. Beginning his book-writing career with *Life Is No Yuk for the Yak: A Book of Endangered Animals,* which profiles endangered species alongside lighthearted limericks and Linda Bourke's cartoon illustrations, Lessem often combines science facts with humor. The majority of Lessem's books, which include *Digging up Tyrannosaurus Rex, Dinosaurs A to Z: The Ultimate Dinosaur Encyclopedia,* and *Sea Giants of Dinosaur Time,* outline the history of and current findings about a wide variety of dinosaurs: their discovery, habits, environments, and time periods.

Lessem's books on dinosaurs and paleontologists have garnered widespread praise for their ability to present detailed information in an attractive, uncluttered format. Critics have cited his prose style as both clear and inspirational, reflecting Lessem's own enthusiasm for his subject. "Dinosaurs are my writing life, at least much of it," the author once told *SATA.* "My job as I see it is to communicate the latest discoveries of dinosaurs to anyone who gives a hoot, especially kids. I do so via exhibits I build, such as Lost World; writing a column for *Highlights for Children* magazine; creating CD's for Microsoft; creating the largest dinosaur charity and its children's newspaper (the Dinosaur Society and *Dino Times*); creating Web sites; advising on theme parks and movies; writing and hosting *Nova* and *Discovery* documentaries; AND writing books." In his *Highlights* column, Lessem responds to over one thousand dino-related questions from young readers each year.

Born in 1951, Lessem first became interested in dinosaurs at age five. Years later, after studying biobehavioralism at the University of Massachusetts and establishing a career as a science writer for major newspapers, he traveled widely. When Lessem first began writing books in the late 1970s, he strayed from nonfiction to straight-out humor. Then, as he later recalled, in the late 1980s he began to focus almost exclusively on dino-related books. "I got onto dinosaurs visiting a Montana dig for a newspaper while an MIT science journalism fellow in 1988. I find the new discoveries, the remote locales, the characters who study dinosaurs, and the scavenger hunting that is much of the science to be continually fascinating. Many, at least those under the age of ten, share that interest, fortunately, or I'd be working nights at McDonald's."

Notable among Lessem's many books on dinosaurs are *Dinosaur Worlds: New Dinosaurs, New Discoveries* and *Dinosaurs A to Z.* In *Dinosaur Worlds* several of the most important excavations yielding dinosaur remains are introduced to young readers. Lessem also provides information on the environments, prey, and life cycles of a large number of the prehistoric creatures. *Dinosaur Worlds* "is a book that report writers and dinophiles won't want to miss," averred Stephanie Zvirin in *Booklist.*

***Cover of Lessem's* Supergiants!, *a picture book about supersized dinosaurs that features paintings by David Peters.*** (Little, Brown & Company, 1997. Reproduced by permission.)

*Dinosaurs A to Z* assembles 700 entries and 350 color illustrations by Jan Sovak into a single volume that even the most knowledgeable dino buff will find illuminating. From habitat and diet to taxonomic classification and pronunciation guide, the volume presents its many facts in an easily accessible alphabetical format. *Childhood Education* reviewer Joseph McSparran praised the work as a "fascinating reference book" that serves as an "exciting and complete resource," while in *Booklist* a contributor noted that Lessem's text is "thorough and interesting and not too difficult for elementary-school readers, who will be excited to have this book." "Only dinosaurs are covered, with no flying reptiles or ichthyosaurs to confuse things," added *School Library Journal* contributor Steven Engelfried, the critic summing up *Dinosaurs A to Z* as an "attractive and useful resource."

In *The Dinosaur Atlas* Lessem collects even more facts about the ancient Earth-roamers, this time framing his text with the rise and ultimate fall of the prehistoric creatures. Geology, paleontology, the evolution of fifty different species, and the Earth's evolving ecosystem all come under examination, in a text that is "lively and enlightening, focusing on especially interesting examples rather than vague generalizations," in the opinion of Engelfried. Lessem breaks his subject into three sections, each representing a different era in dino evolution: Triassic, Jurassic, and Cretaceous. He balances his focused text with informative sidebars, a well-researched bibliography, maps, and "excellent" illustrations by John Bindon that, according to a *Booklist* reviewer, add to the book's value. Praising both text and format in her *Resource Links* review, Judy Cottrell called *The Dinosaur Atlas* a "refreshing" and "wonderful book which takes a geographical approach to the study of dinosaurs."

Lessem profiles individual dinosaurs in such books as *Raptors!: The Nastiest Dinosaurs, Ornithomimids: The Fastest Dinosaur, Troodon: The Smartest Dinosaur, Seismosaurus: The Longest Dinosaur,* and *Utahraptor: The Deadliest Dinosaur,* all part of a series on special dinosaurs published by Carolrhoda. In each of these books, the author gathers information regarding the discovery of the fossil remains of each dinosaur type and the paleontologists who found them, as well as on how information about the creature's abilities and habits has been deduced from fossil evidence. Lessem then goes on to speculate about the possible evolutionary descendants of his subject. "Lessem treats a popular topic adeptly, humorously, and with a balance of information that is both relevant and stimulating to read," remarked Olga Kuharets in a review of both *Seismosaurus* and *Utahraptor* for *School Library Journal.* In her *Booklist* review of both *Ornithominids* and *Troodon,* Frances Bradburn commented that these "finely crafted" books offer "a fascinating look at how paleontologists discover the fossilized remains of these huge beasts." In addition, Lessem's texts have been praised by critics for their clarity and organization of a wealth of fascinating material.

Lessem's dedication to introducing children and adults to the lives of the scientists behind the scientific discoveries has yielded such works as *Kings of Creation: How a New Breed of Scientists Is Revolutionizing Our Understanding of Dinosaurs* and *Jack Horner: Living with Dinosaurs.* In *Kings of Creation* the author presents an overview of the wealth of new information that became available in the late twentieth century. Beginning in the 1970s, the popular image of dinosaurs was completely revised by a group of scientists who uncovered signs of intelligence, speed, and nurturing in species previously thought to be stupid, slow, and hostile even to their own offspring. Leading scientists, significant digs, and many new theories are all featured in a work in which Lessem, according to a reviewer for *Publishers Weekly,* "presents a lively sampling of current and significant work on dinosaurs worldwide. . . . This is the best book on the subject since Robert Bakker's *Dinosaur Heresies* and a treat for buffs."

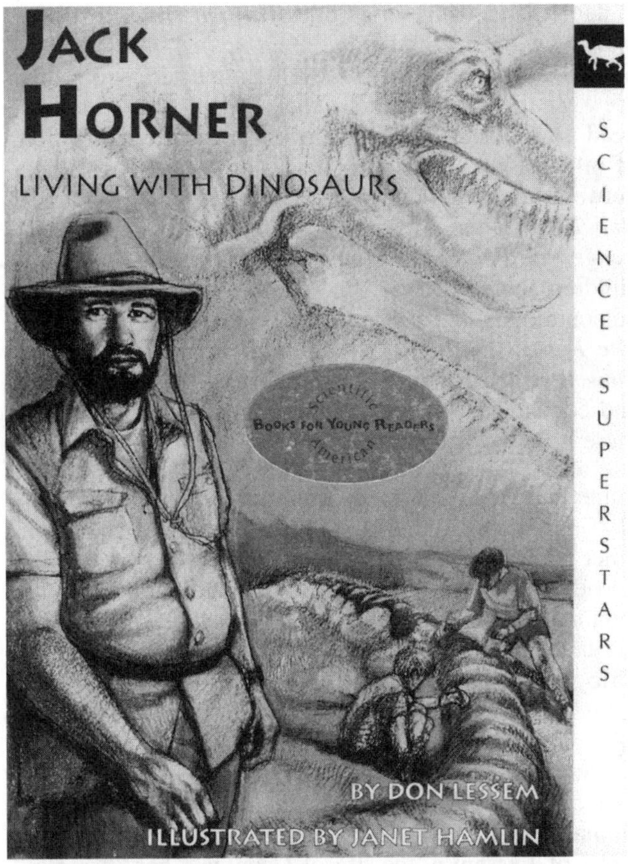


***Cover of* Jack Horner, *Don Lessem's biography of a noted American dinosaur hunter that features an illustration by Janet Hamlin.*** (W.H. Freeman & Company, 1994. Illustration © 1994 by Janet Hamlin. Reproduced by permission.)

*Jack Horner* is a biography about John R. Horner, chief curator of paleontology at the University of Montana and a scientific advisor on the popular motion picture *Jurassic Park.* In this work, Lessem presents both personal background on Horner and information about the scientist's most famous discoveries. The author "writes with zest, showing the determination and excitement that accompanied Horner's explorations," remarked Susan Dove Lempke in a review of *Jack Horner* for the *Bulletin of the Center for Children's Books.* Evelyn Tiffany-Castiglioni noted in *Appraisal* that "Lessem's portrayal of Horner feels authentic: a plainspoken, quiet, thoughtful man who is most at home walking on the badlands where dinosaurs walked before him." Writing in the same publication, Patricia Manning maintained that Lessem's writing style in *Jack Horner* is "perfectly tailored to fourth and fifth graders," and a *Kirkus Reviews* writer concluded that the "book works thanks to Lessem's own enthusiasm for dinosaurs and his impressive knack for writing in kid-speak."

In his "Meet the Dinosaurs" series, Lessem addresses young dino fans. The dozen picture books in this collection pair basic facts with colorful illustrations by

Bindon. Reviewing series titles *Horned Dinosaurs, Armored Dinosaurs,* and *Giant Meat-eating Dinosaurs* for *School Library Journal,* Steven Engelfried wrote that the "Meet the Dinosaurs" books "meet the perennial need for dinosaur books that offer the right combination of information and action." Focusing on the connection between dinosaurs and birds, Gillian Engberg wrote in *Booklist* that the "detailed drawings" and "simple language" in *Feathered Dinosaurs* will engage younger children and serve as a "fine place to start" for budding paleontologists. In a *School Library Journal* review of *The Fastest Dinosaurs* and *Flying Giants of Dinosaur Time,* Patricia Manning cited Lessem's "chatty style," and concluded: "Simple, eye-catching, and informative, these books will fly off the shelves."

Sometimes taking a break from dinosaurs, Lessem has also authored several nonfiction titles that focus on other topics of interest to him. In *The Iceman* he describes the discovery of a 5,000-year-old mummy in the mountains of Europe and explains what scientists have gleaned from the discovery regarding the life of prehistoric Europeans. Moving to South America, his book *Inside the Amazing Amazon: Incredible Fold-out Cross Sections of the World's Greatest Rainforest* combines Lessem's clearly written text with oversized, fold-out illustrations by Michael Rothman that detail plant and animal life in the world's largest rainforest. Another interest of Lessem's, the life of Genghis Khan, has also been the focus of research, and Lessem's international traveling exhibition *The Genius of Genghis Khan* was designed to coordinate with a planned biography. As the writer noted, Khan is "a much misunderstood figure."

Discussing his lifelong love affair with prehistoric creatures, Lessem more recently told *SATA:* "When I was five, my aunt Sylvie took me to see the T. Rex at the Natural History Museum in New York City. I still haven't recovered.

"When my own children were young, I was sent out to dinosaur digs in the American West by the *Boston Globe.* I fell in love with dinosaurs again, as did my children more briefly. For me it was, and remains, the mystery of lost worlds, the romance of exotic locales, and the detective work of the fossil scavenger hunt that excite me. My desire to communicate the wonders of nature—past and present—are what drives my work."

In addition to his career as a writer, Lessem is the founder of two dinosaur-related nonprofit organizations which have raised millions of dollars for dinosaur research: the Dinosaur Society and the Jurassic Foundation. In 1998 his Dinosaur Productions created the first full-size reproduction of the 45-foot-long Giganotosaurus, the largest of all land carnivores, for the Academy of Natural Sciences in Philadelphia. The following year he erected the first skeleton mount of the 100-foot-long Argentinosaurus, the largest animal ever to walk the earth, for the Fernbank Museum of Natural History in Atlanta. His natural-history touring exhibits featuring dinosaurs have appeared at the largest natural history museums in North America. "My aspiration," he once told *SATA,* "is to continue providing children with what for so long they have craved and lacked: current and accurate information on new scientific discoveries and the methods behind them.Their early fascination with dinosaurs, well-cultivated, can spread to a lifetime interest in all of science."

## Biographical and Critical Sources

*PERIODICALS*

*Appraisal,* winter, 1995, Patricia Manning and Evelyn Tiffany-Castiglioni, reviews of *Jack Horner: Living with Dinosaurs,* pp. 112-114; winter-spring, 1996, pp. 35-36.

*Booklist,* April 1, 1992, Jon Kartman, review of *Kings of Creation: How a New Breed of Scientists Is Revolutionizing Our Understanding of Dinosaurs,* p. 1419; February 15, 1996, Frances Bradburn, review of *Ornithomimids* and *Troodon,* p. 1014; September 1, 1996, p. 997; November 15, 1996, Stephanie Zvirin, review of *Dinosaur Worlds,* pp. 583-584; December 15, 2003, review of *Dinosaurs A to Z,* p. 766; March 1, 2004, review of *The Dinosaur Atlas,* p. 1228; June 1, 2005, Gillian Engberg, review of *Feathered Dinosaurs,* p. 1816.

*Bulletin of the Center for Children's Books,* September, 1994, review of *The Iceman,* p. 17; December, 1994, Susan Dove Lempke, review of *Jack Horner,* p. 135.

*Childhood Education,* summer, 2004, Joseph McSparran, review of *Dinosaurs A to Z,* p. 212.

*Kirkus Reviews,* May 15, 1994, p. 702; December 1, 1995, p. 1703; November 15, 1994, review of *Jack Horner,* p. 1534.

*Publishers Weekly,* March 2, 1992, review of *Kings of Creation,* p. 58; November 4, 1996, review of *Dinosaur World,* p. 78.

*Resource Links,* October, 2003, Judy Cottrell, review of *The Dinosaur Atlas,* p. 25.

*School Library Journal,* March, 1978, p. 138; July, 1994, Jeanette Larson, review of *The Iceman,* p. 111; January, 1996, Susan Oliver, review of *Inside the Amazing Amazon: Incredible Fold-out Cross Sections of the World's Greatest Rainforest,* p. 120; September, 1996, Olga Kuharets, review of *Seismosaurus* and *Utahraptor,* p. 218; October, 1996, Cathryn A. Camper, review of *Raptors!: The Nastiest Dinosaurs,* pp. 135-136; September, 1997, Cathryn A. Camper, review of *Supergiants!: The Biggest Dinosaurs,* p. 232; December, 1997, Cathryn A. Camper review of *Bigger than T. Rex,* p. 140; December, 2003, Steven Engelfried, review of *Dinosaurs A to Z* and *The Dinosaur Atlas,* p. 170; February, 2005, Steven Engelfried, review of *Armored Dinosaurs,* p. 123; July, 2005, Patricia Manning, review of *The Smartest Dinosaurs* and *The Fastest Dinosaurs,* both p. 90; September, 2005, Patricia Manning, review of *Sea Giants of Dinosaur Time,* p. 193.

*Voice of Youth Advocates,* August, 1997, review of *Dinosaur Worlds,* p. 165; April, 2004, Rollie Welch, review of *Scholastic Dinosaurs, A to Z,* p. 68.

*ONLINE*

*Boyds Mills Press Web site,* http://www.boydsmillspress.com/ (August 27, 2007), "Don Lessem."
*Dino Don's Dinosaur World,* http://www.dinodon.com (August 27, 2007).

* * *

## LILLY, Nate

### Personal
Male.

### Addresses
*Home and office*—Chicago, IL. *E-mail*—natelilly@gmail.com.

### Career
Illustrator.

### Illustrator
Elise Broach, *Cousin John Is Coming!,* Dial Books for Young Readers (New York, NY), 2006.

### Sidelights
Nate Lilly made his debut as a children's book illustrator with the publication of *Cousin John Is Coming!,* a picture book featuring a text by Elise Broach. In Broach's tale, young Ben is petrified when he learns from his mother that his cousin John will be paying the family a visit. Upon hearing the news, Ben goes through a series of flashbacks, recalling the many atrocities he and his pet cat previously suffered at John's hands—from terrifying moments being suspended over a pond full of alligators to being forced to walk the plank in a game of pirates. Ben's anguish is finally put to rest when he finds a way to prevent his cousin's impending visit. A *Kirkus Reviews* critic, reviewing *Cousin John Is Coming!,* noted that Lilly's illustrations, which feature "cartoon figures" with "large round heads and expressive faces," "tell the story here." Several reviewers cited Lilly's attention to detail, among them a *Publishers Weekly* reviewer who characterized the illustrations as "slightly sinister" but with a "humorous attention to detail."

### Biographical and Critical Sources

*PERIODICALS*

*Kirkus Reviews,* June 1, 2006, review of *Cousin John Is Coming!,* p. 568.
*Publishers Weekly,* July 31, 2006, review of *Cousin John Is Coming!,* p. 75.
*School Library Journal,* July, 2006, Catherine Threadgill, review of *Cousin John Is Coming!,* p. 68.

*ONLINE*

*Nate Lilly Home Page,* http://www.natelilly.com (August 9, 2007).

* * *

## LONG, Ethan 1968(?)-

### Personal
Born c. 1968, in PA; married (divorced); second wife's name Heather; children: (first marriage) Katie; (second marriage) two sons. *Education:* Ringling School of Art and Design, graduated, 1991.

### Addresses
*Home and office*—Tallahassee, FL. *E-mail*—inquiries@ethanlong.com.

***Ethan Long*** (Photograph by Spencer Freeman. Courtesy of Ethan Long.)

## Career

Illustrator, author, animator, and educator. Creator of animated films, including *Farm Force: Send in the Clones,* Nicktoons, 2005. Instructor at schools, including LeMoyne Art Foundation, Tallahassee, FL; has served as artist-in-residence. Commercial clients include Nickelodeon Studios, Scholastic, and Barnes & Noble. *Exhibitions:* Work included in shows staged by Society of Illustrators Los Angeles and Society of Illustrators New York.

## Awards, Honors

Nextoons Film Festival Viewer's Choice Award, 2005, for *Farm Force* (animated film).

## Writings

*SELF-ILLUSTRATED*

*Tickle the Duck!,* Little, Brown & Co. (New York, NY), 2006.

*Stop Kissing Me,* Little, Brown & Co. (New York, NY), 2007.

Author and illustrator of "Landfill" (weekly cartoon).

*ILLUSTRATOR*

Jason Eaton, *The Day My Runny Nose Ran Away,* Dutton Children's Books (New York, NY), 2002.

Esther Hershenhorn, *The Confessions and Secrets of Howard J. Fingerhut,* Holiday House (New York, NY), 2002.

Tom Birdseye, *Oh Yeah!,* Holiday House (New York, NY), 2003.

Mary Amato, *Snarf Attack, Underfoodle, and the Secret of Life: The Riot Brothers Tell All,* Holiday House (New York, NY), 2004.

Margie Palatini, *Stinky Smelly Feet: A Love Story,* Dutton Children's Books (New York, NY), 2004.

Ann Whitford Paul, *Mañana, Iguana,* Holiday House (New York, NY), 2004.

Elizabeth Spurr, *Halloween Skyride,* Holiday House (New York, NY), 2005.

Teddy Slater, *The Best Thanksgiving Ever!,* Scholastic (New York, NY), 2005.

Karen M. Stegman-Bourgeois, *Trollerella,* Holiday House (New York, NY), 2006.

Mary Amato, *Drooling and Dangerous: The Riot Brothers Return!,* Holiday House (New York, NY), 2006.

Teddy Slater, *The Spookiest Halloween Ever!,* Scholastic (New York, NY), 2006.

Ann Whitford Paul, *Fiesta Fiasco,* Holiday House (New York, NY), 2007.

Merrily Kutner, *The Zombie Nite Cafe,* Holiday House (New York, NY), 2007.

David Elliott, *One Little Chicken,* Holiday House (New York, NY), 2007.

Jan Carr, *Greedy Apostrophe: A Cautionary Tale,* Holiday House (New York, NY), 2007.

## Sidelights

In addition to his work as an animator, cartoonist, and educator, Ethan Long has gained a following among young readers. His quirky cartoon illustrations, which have graced the pages of such humorous books as Mary Amato's *Drooling and Dangerous: The Riot Brothers Return!,* Marge Palatini's *Stinky Smelly Feet: A Love Story,* Karen M. Stegman-Bourgeois's *Trollerella,* and Jan Carr's *Greedy Apostrophe: A Cautionary Tale,* also take center stage in several original picture books. In *Tickle the Duck!* and *Stop Kissing Me!* Long introduces a somewhat confrontational duck whose constant beligerant orders and determination echo those of a demanding child.

Born in Pennsylvania, Long was busy drawing by age three. He spent much of his childhood in Camp Hill, he and his family moved to Connecticut in his mid-teens. After high-school graduation Long enrolled at the Ringling School of Art and Design, a decision that took him south to Sarasota, Florida. Now married and the father

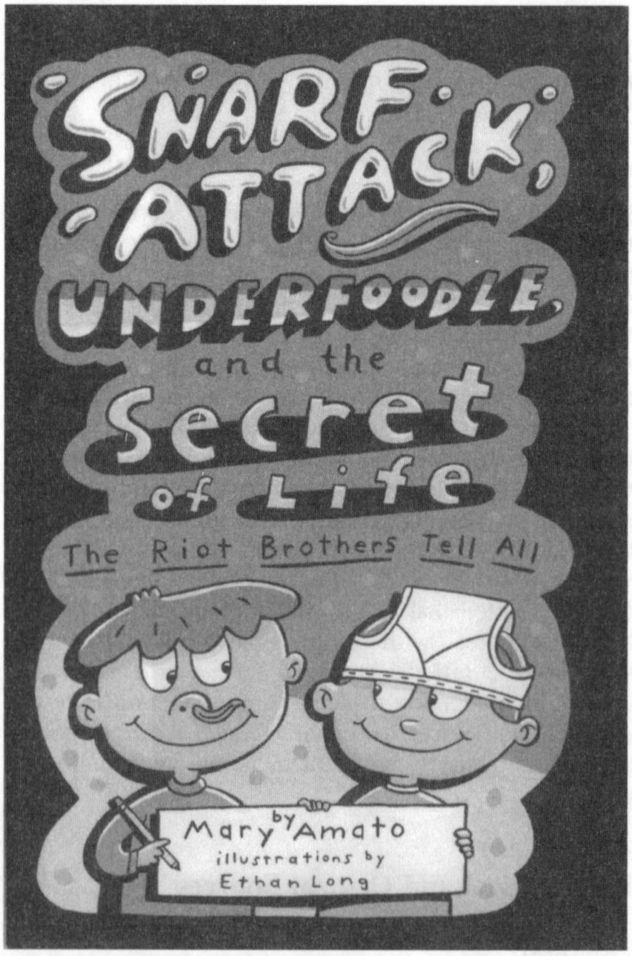


***Long's quirky art is a perfect match for Mary Amato's middle-grade saga* Snarf Attack, Underfoodle, and the Secret of Life, *a chapter book starring the mischievous Riot brothers.*** (Holiday House, 2004. Illustration © 2004 by Ethan Long. Reproduced by permission.)

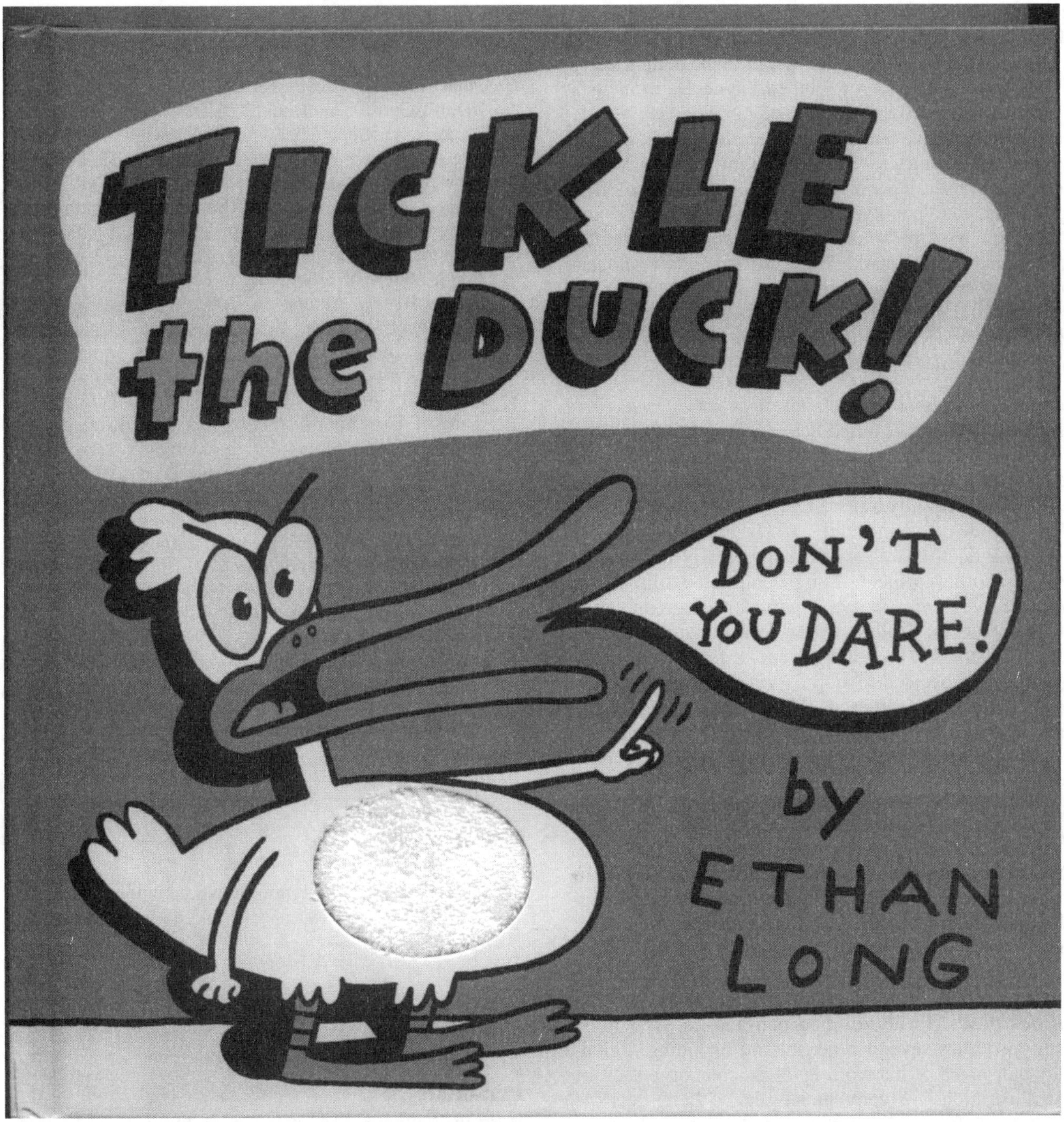


***Cover of Long's self-illustrated picture book* Tickle the Duck, *in which readers can test the patience of a testy but feathery fowl.*** (Little, Brown & Company, 2006. Illustration © 2006 by Ethan Long. Reproduced by permission. )

of three, he continues to make his home in the Sunshine state. Despite his training and talent, on his home page Long modestly credited many of his ideas to his children and his family's cats, Barnum and Bailey.

The art for Jason Eaton's 2002 picture book *The Day My Runny Nose Ran Away* was Long's first published work, marking a prolific career that has included illustrating texts by David Elliott, Teddy Slater, Tom Birdseye, Ann Whitford Paul, and Palatini. Amato's "Riot Brothers" series about rambunctious brothers Wilbur and Orville is a perfect outlet for Long's quirky art. His "playful cartoon illustrations extend the fun" of the brothers' debut in *Snarf Attack, Underfoodle, and the Secret of Life: The Riot Brothers Tell All,* according to *Booklist* reviewer Ed Sullivan, while Roger Leslie concluded in the same periodical that the artist's cartoon drawings "add significantly to the . . . humor" featured in the siblings' return in *Drooling and Dangerous.* In Birdseye's *Oh Yeah!,* which finds two young campers confronting their fears of the dark, Long's warm-toned "colored-pencil and acrylic" images "burst with energy . . . and feature jagged edges and the deliciously menacing imagined threats" of the story's young protagonists, according to *School Library Journal* contributor Marge Loch-Wouters. "The expressions on Long's bright and quirky punctuation people will delight early elementary listeners," concluded Jayne Damron in a *School Library Journal* review of *Greedy Apostrophe,* Carr's imaginative intro to punctuation. The "bright, stylized art" Long creates for Palatini's *Stinky Smelly Feet* was praised by a *Kirkus Reviews* writer, the critic noting that the "pop-eyed animals" populating the tale of a duck with personal problems contribute to the book's "hysterical detail." The illustrator's "vibrant cartoon illustrations in watercolors and gouache propel the text" of Paul's *Mañana, Iguana,* according to Mary Elam, reviewing the bilingual picture book for *School Library Journal.*

Long's first original picture book, *Tickle the Duck!,* was published in 2006. A board book designed for toddlers, it features an interactive element—Long incorporates actual fluffy spots on the body of his cranky character—and its equally interactive sequel, *Stop Kissing Me!,* includes a sound chip. *Tickly the Duck!* has its roots in a duck character that belligerently asserted itself in another project, Long's animated film *Farm Force: Send in the Clones,* a pilot for a cartoon series for Nickelodeon Studios. After seeing award-winning author/illustrator Mo Willems' books featuring a surly pigeon, Long decided to stop fighting the fowl's persistent efforts to take center stage in the film and gave the duck its own story. According to Lana Berkowitz in the *Houston Chronicle,* Long's daughter Katie "provided inspiration for the story. When she was a toddler, Long says, Katie would tell him to stop tickling her, but then she'd want more."

Creating full-color illustrations for a picture-book project requires about twelve months, accordingto Long, who added that he can complete the line drawings for a chapter book in less than half that time. Another twelve months is required for planning, which includes the months needed to create characters and draw them in various poses. In addition to pen-and-ink drawings, Long also uses several other media, including digital. Although much of his work involves creating poster art and illustrations for commercial clients, Long gets the greatest satisfaction illustrating for children, and he expands this through his work visiting schools.

## Biographical and Critical Sources

*PERIODICALS*

*Booklist,* October 15, 2002, John Peters, review of *The Day My Runny Nose Ran Away,* p. 411; July, 2004, Ed Sullivan, review of *Snarf Attack, Underfoodle, and the Secret of Life: The Riot Brothers Tell All,* p. 1841; November 1, 2004, Connie Fletcher, review of *Mañana, Iguana,* p. 493; May 15, 2006, Roger Leslie, review of *Drooling and Dangerous: The Riot Brothers Return,* p. 44; May 15, 2007, Shelle Rosenfeld, review of *Fiesta Fiasco,* p. 51.

*Bulletin of the Center for Children's Books,* February, 2006, Elizabeth Bush, review of *Tickle the Duck!,* p. 273.

*Houston Chronicle,* November 28, 2005, Lana Berkowitz, "Don't Goose This Duck!," "STAR" section, p. 1.

*Kirkus Reviews,* September 15, 2002, review of *The Day My Runny Nose Ran Away,* p. 1388; July 15, 2003, review of *Oh Yeah!,* p. 961; May 1, 2004, review of *Stinky Smelly Feet,* p. 446; September 15, 2004, review of *Mañana, Iguana,* p. 917; May 1, 2006, review of *Drooling and Dangerous,* p. 453; August 15, 2006, review of *Trollerella,* p. 852.

*Publishers Weekly,* August 26, 2002, review of *The Day My Runny Nose Ran Away,* p. 68; April 26, 2004, review of *Stinky Smelly Feet,* p. 65, and *Snarf Attack, Underfoodle, and the Secret of Life,* p. 66.

*School Library Journal,* September, 2002, Mary Elam, review of *The Day My Runny Nose Ran Away,* p. 189; August, 2003, Marge Loch-Wouters, review of *Oh Yeah!,* p. 122; June, 2004, Marge Louch-Wouters, review of *Stinky Smelly Feet,* p. 116; July, 2004, Jean Lowery, review of *Snarf Attack, Underfoodle, and the Secret of Life,* p. 66; September, 2004, Mary Elam, review of *Mañana, Iguana,* p. 176; August, 2005, Wendy Woodfill, review of *Halloween Sky Ride,* p. 106; September, 2006, Martha Topol, review of *Trollerella,* p. 185; October, 2006, Kristine M. Casper, review of *Drooling and Dangerous,* p. 102; May, 2007, Linda M. Kenton, review of *Fiesta Fiasco,* p. 106; July, 2007, Jayne Damron, review of *Greedy Apostrophe: A Cautionary Tale,* p. 73.

*Tallahassee Democrat,* July 20, 2006, Mark Hinson, "Driven to Draw."

*ONLINE*

*Ethan Long Home Page,* http://www.ethanlong.com (August 8, 2007).

* * *

# LORD, Cynthia

## Personal

Born in Waltham, MA; married; children: two children. *Education:* Attended college.

## Addresses

*Home*—Brunswick, ME. *Agent*—Adams Literary, 7845 Colony Rd., C4 No. 215, Charlotte, NC 28226. *E-mail*—cindy@cynthialord.com.

## Career

Educator and writer. Former teacher of first-and sixth-grade in New England public schools.

## Member

Society of Children's Book Writers and Illustrators, Maine Writers' and Publishers' Alliance.

***Cynthia Lord*** (Photograph by John Bald. Courtesy of Cynthia Lord.)

## Awards, Honors

Society of Children's Book Writers and Illustrators work-in-process grant, 2004; Smartwriters.com contest winner; Newbery Honor Book designation, Schneider Family Book Award in middle-school category, Michigan Library Association Mitten Award, New York Public Library 100 Titles for Reading and Sharing inclusion, National Council of Teachers of English Notable Children's Book in the Language Arts designation, American Library Association Notable Book designation, and nominations for numerous child-selected state awards, all 2007, all for *Rules.*

## Writings

*Rules* (middle-grade novel), Scholastic (New York, NY), 2006.

Also author of short fiction and of curriculums for educational publishers.

## Sidelights

With her first book, former middle-school teacher Cynthia Lord achieved what many writers only dream of: earning the Honor Book designation from the prestigious Newbery Award committee. Her middle-grade novel, *Rules,* was inspired by Lord's experience raising an autistic child. "David is based loosely upon my son when he was a young child," the author noted on her home page, referencing one of her novel's characters. Although "some incidents in the book came from real experience . . . , most of the events, details, and characters in *Rules* came from my imagination," Lord added. "The first line I ever wrote on the first blank page was: 'At our house, we have a rule,' and the story, the characters, the title, all sprang from that seed."

Dubbed "a heartwarming first novel" by *Booklist* contributor Cindy Dobrez, *Rules* draws readers into the story of twelve-year-old Catherine, who lives with her parents and autistic younger brother David in coastal Maine. Although Catherine is a caring girl and loves her little brother, she is embarrassed by some of the things the boy does, such as hugging strangers or dropping his toys into the fish tank. She also feels burdened by having to care for her brother much of the time. To help David understand his surroundings and learn to navigate daily life, Catherine develops a series of simple rules for him to follow. Over the summer, sadness over a departed best friend, feelings of guilt over her anger that David takes the bulk of her parents' attention, the approach of adolescence, and her growing affection for a wheelchair-bound boy named Jason combine to cause Catherine confusion. To deal with her feelings, the girl turns to art, and also sets down a series of ground rules that she hopes will define her world. Ultimately, the preteen "begins to understand that normal is difficult, and perhaps unnecessary, to define," as Connie Tyrell Burns noted in a *School Library Journal* review of Lord's award-winning novel debut. Referencing Catherine's conflicting feelings, a *Kirkus Reviews* writer wrote that "middle-grade readers will recognize her longing for acceptance," and in *School Library Journal* Connie Tyrrell Burns called the preteen "an endearing narrator who tells her story with both humor and heartbreak." In her novel Lord "candidly capture[s] . . . the delicate dynamics" within a family coping with disability, Burns added, and in *Publishers Weekly* a critic described *Rules* as "a rewarding story that may well inspire readers to think about others' points of view."

In an online interview with Debbi Michiko Florence, Lord discussed the experience of writing *Rules,* as well as her thoughts on the writing life. "One personal rule I tell children who ask me for writing advice is *Read, write, learn, and dream,*" she told Florence. Her advice for beginning writers: "Don't be afraid to try something, even if you think it won't work. Sometimes I am not the best judge of what my story needs and trying a suggestion can open a new possibility."

## Biographical and Critical Sources

*PERIODICALS*

*Booklist,* February 15, 2006, Cindy Dobrez, review of *Rules,* p. 98.

*Bulletin of the Center for Children's Books,* May, 2006, Deborah Stevenson, review of *Rules,* p. 411.

*Kirkus Reviews,* March 1, 2006, review of *Rules,* p. 234.

*Publishers Weekly,* April 15, 2006, review of *Rules,* p. 188.

*School Library Journal,* April, 2006, Connie Tyrrell Burns, review of *Rules,* p. 142.

*ONLINE*

*Cynthia Lord Home Page,* http://www.cynthialord.com (August 8, 2007).

*Debbi Michiko Florence Web site,* http://www.debbimichikoflorence.com/ (April, 2006), interview with Lord.

# M

## MACKALL, Dandi Daley 1949-
## (Dandi)

### Personal

Born Dorothy Ann Daley, March 24, 1949, in Kansas City, MO; daughter of F.R. (a physician) and Helen (a nurse) Daley; married Joseph S. Mackall (a professor and writer); children: Jennifer, Katy, Dan. *Education:* University of Missouri—Columbia, B.A., 1971; University of Central Oklahoma, M.A., 1989; also attended Institute of Biblical Studies (Arrowhead, CA) and Trinity Evangelical Divinity School. *Politics:* "Independent." *Religion:* Christian. *Hobbies and other interests:* Horseback riding, tennis, walking, painting.

### Addresses

*Home and office*—1254 Tupelo Lane, West Salem, OH 44287. *E-mail*—dandi@dandibooks.com.

### Career

Author, educator, and lecturer. Freelance manuscript reviewer and editor, 1978-86; University of Central Oklahoma, Edmond, lecturer in writing for children, 1986-89; freelance writer and public speaker, 1989—. Southwest Community College, Creston, IA, instructor, 1984-86; Southern Nazarene University, instructor, 1986-89; Ashland University, instructor, 1990-94; Institute of Children's Literature, instructor. Speaker at conferences; guest on television and radio programs.

### Member

Society of Children's Book Writers and Illustrators (religious coordinator, 1990-94), PEN International, Phi Beta Kappa.

### Awards, Honors

Silver Medallion Award, for *Degrees of Guilt* and *God Made Me; Romantic Times* Pick of the Month designation, for *Love Rules;* American Library Association Best Books for Young Readers nomination, 2006, and Ohioana Award finalist, 2007, both for *Eva Underground;* Distinguished Alumna Award, University of Missouri, 2006.

### Writings

*FOR CHILDREN*

*The Best Christmas Ever,* Standard Publishing (Cincinnati, OH), 1986.
*A Secret Birthday Gift,* Standard Publishing (Cincinnati, OH), 1987.
*A Super Friend,* Standard Publishing (Cincinnati, OH), 1987.
*Me First,* Standard Publishing (Cincinnati, OH), 1987.
*Allyson J. Cat,* Standard Publishing (Cincinnati, OH), 1989.
*Allyson J. Cat Coloring Book,* with cassette, Standard Publishing (Cincinnati, OH), 1989.
*The Christmas Gifts That Didn't Need Wrapping,* illustrated by Dawn Mathers, Augsburg-Fortress (Minneapolis, MN), 1990.
*It's Only Ali Cat,* Standard Publishing (Cincinnati, OH), 1990.
*An Ali Cat Christmas,* illustrated by Kathryn Hutton, Standard Publishing (Cincinnati, OH), 1991.
*Kay's Birthday Surprise,* illustrated by Dawn Mathers, Augsburg-Fortress (Minneapolis, MN), 1992.
*A Gaggle of Galloping Ghosts,* Hanna Barbera, 1995.
*No Biz like Show Biz,* Hanna Barbera, 1995.
*Millionaire Astro,* Hanna Barbera, 1995.
*Home Sweet Jellystone,* Hanna Barbera, 1995.
*Seasons,* Landoll's, 1995.
*Baby Animals,* Landoll's, 1995.
*Secret Night,* Landoll's, 1995.
*Who's a Goblin?,* Landoll's, 1995.
*The Halloween Secret,* Landoll's, 1995.
*Circus Counting,* Landoll's, 1995.
*ABC's of Lunch,* Landoll's, 1995.

**Dandi Daley Mackall** (Courtesy of Dandi Daley Mackall.)

*Things That Go,* Landoll's, 1995.
*Bugs and Butterflies,* Landoll's, 1995.
*Under the Water,* Landoll's, 1995.
*Santa's Toy Shop,* Landoll's, 1995.
*Scooby Doo and Scrappy in 1.2.3,* Hanna Barbera, 1996.
*Pebbles and Bamm Bamm in a Colorful Game,* Hanna Barbera, 1996.
*Jetsons in Shape,* Hanna Barbera, 1996.
*Yogi and Boo Boo ABC's,* Hanna Barbera, 1996.
*Picture Me at Walt Disney World's 25th Anniversary,* Disney (New York, NY), 1997.
*Christmas Buttons,* illustrated by Bryan Fyffe, Playhouse Publishing, 1997.
*Halloween Buttons,* illustrated by Bryan Fyffe, Playhouse Publishing, 1997.
*Chicken Soup for the Kid's Soul,* Batgirl, 1998.
*Joseph, King of Dreams* (movie adaptation), Dreamworks, 1998.
*Easter Adventure,* Concordia (St. Louis, MO), 1998.
(Compiler) *Why I Believe in God: And Other Reflections by Children,* Prima Publishing (Rocklin, CA), 1999.
*Portrait of Lies,* created by Terry Brown, Tommy Nelson (Nashville, TN), 2000.
*Off to Bethlehem!,* HarperCollins (New York, NY), 2000.
*No, No Noah!,* Tommy Nelson (Nashville, TN), 2000.
*The Don't Cry, Lion,* Tommy Nelson (Nashville, TN), 2000.
*Little Lost Donkey,* Tommy Nelson (Nashville, TN), 2000.
*Go, Go Fish!,* Tommy Nelson (Nashville, TN), 2000.
*Moses, Pharaoh, and the Snake,* Broadman (Nashville, TN), 2000.
*Silent Dreams,* illustrated by Karen A. Jerome, Eerdmans (Grand Rapids, MI), 2001.
(Compiler) *What Children Know about Angels,* Sourcebooks (Naperville, IL), 2001.
(Compiler) *101 Things Kids Wonder,* Sourcebooks (Naperville, IL), 2001.
(Compiler) *Kids' Rules for Life: A Guide to Life's Journey from Those Just Starting Out,* Sourcebooks (Naperville, IL), 2001.
*Until the Christ Child Came,* illustrated by Sally Wern Comport, Concordia (St. Louis, MO), 2002.
*Off to Bethlehem!,* illustrated by R.W. Alley, HarperFestival (New York, NY), 2002.
*Off to Plymouth Rock!,* illustrated by Gene Barretta, Tommy Nelson (Nashville, TN), 2002, issued with CD, 2005.
*It Must Be Halloween,* illustrated by Barry Gott, Little Simon (New York, NY), 2002.
*Love and Kisses, Bunny* (board book), illustrated by Hala Wittwer, Little Simon (New York, NY), 2003.
*First Day,* illustrated by Tiphanie Beeke, Harcourt (San Diego, CA), 2003.
*Who'll Light the Chanukah Candles?,* illustrated by Keiko Motoyama, Little Simon (New York, NY), 2003.
*Are We There Yet?,* illustrated by Shannon McNeill, Dutton (New York, NY), 2004.
*A Tree for Christmas,* illustrated by Dominic Catalano, Concordia (St. Louis, MO), 2004.
*Merry Creature Christmas!,* illustrated by Gene Barretta, Tommy Nelson (Nashville, TN), 2004, issued with CD, 2005.
*Journey, Journey, Jesus,* illustrated by Gene Barretta, Tommy Nelson (Nashville, TN), 2004.
*A Friend from Galilee,* illustrated by Jan Spivey Gilchrist, Augsburg Fortress (Minneapolis, MN), 2004.
*Made for a Purpose,* illustrated by Glin Dibley, Zonderkidz (Grand Rapids, MI), 2004.
*My Happy Easter Morning,* illustrated by Rachel O'Neill, Zonderkidz (Grand Rapids, MI), 2005.
*My Christmas Gift to Jesus* (board book), illustrated by Rachel O'Neill, Zonderkidz (Grand Rapids, MI), 2005.
*My Big Birthday* (board book), illustrated by Rachel O'Neill, Zonderkidz (Grand Rapids, MI), 2005.
*My Secret Valentine* (board book), illustrated by Rachel O'Neill, Zonderkidz (Grand Rapids, MI), 2005.
*Jesus in Me,* illustrated by Jenny B. Harris, Standard Publishing (Cincinnati, OH), 2005.
*In the Beginning,* illustrated by James Kandt, Tommy Nelson (Nashville, TN), 2005.
*I'm His Lamb,* illustrated by Jane Dippold, Standard Publishing (Cincinnati, OH), 2005.
*Jesus Said, "Go Tell the World," so I've Got a Job to Do,* illustrated by Jane Dippold, Standard Publishing (Cincinnati, OH), 2005.
*The Legend of Ohio,* illustrated by Greg LaFever, Sleeping Bear Press (Chelsea, MI), 2005.
*God Blesses Me,* illustrated by Jane Dippold, Standard Publishing (Cincinnati, OH), 2005.

*The Best Thing Is Love,* illustrated by Claudine Gèvry, Standard Publishing (Cincinnati, OH), 2005.

*Praying Jesus' Way,* illustrated by Claudine Gèvry, Standard Publishing (Cincinnati, OH), 2005.

*This Is the Lunch That Jesus Served,* illustrated by Benrei Huang, Augsburg Fortress (Minneapolis, MN), 2005.

*The Shepherd's Christmas Story,* illustrated by Dominic Catalano, Concordia (St. Louis, MO), 2005.

*The Golden Rule,* illustrated by Jane Dippold, Standard Publishing (Cincinnati, OH), 2005.

*Three Wise Women of Christmas,* illustrated by Diana Magnuson, Concordia (St. Louis, MO), 2006.

*God Shows the Way,* illustrated by Claudine Gèvry, Standard Publishing (Cincinnati, OH), 2006.

*The Armor of God,* illustrated by Jenny B. Harris, Standard Publishing (Cincinnati, OH), 2006.

*Seeing Stars,* illustrated by Claudine Gèvry, Simon & Schuster (New York, NY), 2006.

*I Love You, Mommy,* illustrated by Karen Lee Schmidt, Standard Publishing (Cincinnati, OH), 2006.

*I Love You, Daddy,* illustrated by Karen Lee Schmidt, Standard Publishing (Cincinnati, OH), 2006.

*God Made Me,* illustrated by Hiroe Nakata, Simon & Schuster (New York, NY), 2006.

*A Glorious Angel Show,* illustrated by Susan Mitchell, Integrity Publishers 2006.

*Treetops Are Whispering,* illustrated by Vincent Nguyen, Simon & Schuster (New York, NY), 2007.

*Rudy Rides the Rails: A Depression-Era Story,* illustrated by Chris Ellison, Sleeping Bear Press (Chelsea, MI), 2007.

*Easter Is for Me,* illustrated by Anton Petrov, Concordia (St. Louis, MO), 2007.

*For God So Loved the World: My First John 3:16 Book,* illustrated by Elena Selivanova, Thomas Nelson (Nashville, TN), 2007.

*Make Me a Blessing,* Simon & Schuster (New York, NY), 2007.

*The Blanket Show!,* illustrated by David Hohn, WaterBrook/Random House (New York, NY), 2007.

*A Gaggle of Geese and a Clutter of Cats,* WaterBrook/Random House (New York, NY), 2007.

*The Legend of Saint Nicholas: A Story of Christmas Giving,* illustrated by Guy Porfirio, Zonderkidz (Grand Rapids, MI), 2007.

*Christmas Light,* Concordia (St. Louis, MO), 2007.

*The Wonder of Christmas,* Concordia (St. Louis, MO), 2008.

*The Legend of the Christmas Cookie: An Inspirational Story of Sharing,* illustrated by Deborah Chabrian Zonderkidz (Grand Rapids, MI), 2008.

*The Legend of the Easter Robin,* Zonderkidz (Grand Rapids, MI), 2008.

*It Was Not Such a Silent Night,* Dutton (New York, NY), 2008.

*A Girl Named Dan,* Sleeping Bear Press (Chelsea, MI), 2008.

*The Legend of the Valentine: An Inspirational Story of Love,* illustrated by Edward Gazsi, Zonderkidz (Grand Rapids, MI), 2009.

*The Legend of Christmas Holly,* Zonderkidz (Grand Rapids, MI), 2009.

Also author of pop-up books *Daniel and the Lion's Den, Noah's Ark,* and *Jonah and the Whale,* all 1995; author of *The Princess and the Pea, Town and Country Mouse,* and "My First Book" series. Author of coloring books, under pseudonym Dandi. Contributor to books, including *Christmas Programs for Organizations,* Standard Publishing (Cincinnati, OH), 1986. Contributor to periodicals, including *Guidepost, Moody Monthly, Christianity Today, Power for Living, Christian Parenting,* and *Today's Christian Woman.* Author of humor column in an Iowa newspaper, 1984-86.

Author's works have been translated into over a dozen languages.

*"LITTLE BLESSINGS" PICTURE BOOKS*

*Blessings Everywhere,* illustrated by Elena Kucharik, Tyndale House (Wheaton, IL), 2000.

*God Makes Nighttime Too!,* illustrated by Elena Kucharik, Tyndale House (Wheaton, IL), 2000.

*Rain or Shine,* illustrated by Elena Kucharik, Tyndale House (Wheaton, IL), 2000.

*Birthday Blessings,* illustrated by Elena Kucharik, Tyndale House (Wheaton, IL), 2001.

*Count Your Blessings,* illustrated by Elena Kucharik, Tyndale House (Wheaton, IL), 2002.

*ABC's,* illustrated by Elena Kucharik, Tyndale House (Wheaton, IL), 2002.

*Many-Colored Blessings,* illustrated by Elena Kucharik, Tyndale House (Wheaton, IL), 2005.

*Blessings Come in Shapes,* illustrated by Elena Kucharik, Tyndale House (Wheaton, IL), 2005.

*"FIRST THINGS FIRST" BOARD-BOOK SERIES*

*Things I Do,* illustrated by Megan Halsey, Augsburg Fortress (Minneapolis, MN), 2002.

*Rainbow Party,* illustrated by Megan Halsey, Augsburg Fortress (Minneapolis, MN), 2002.

*The Lost Sheep,* illustrated by Megan Halsey, Augsburg Fortress (Minneapolis, MN), 2002.

*Made by God,* illustrated by Megan Halsey, Augsburg Fortress (Minneapolis, MN), 2002.

*"IMAGINATION" PICTURE-BOOK SERIES*

*The Shape of Things,* illustrated by Jill Newton, Augsburg Fortress (Minneapolis, MN), 2003.

*Color My World,* illustrated by Jill Newton, Augsburg Fortress (Minneapolis, MN), 2003.

*Cloud Counting,* illustrated by Jill Newton, Augsburg Fortress (Minneapolis, MN), 2003.

*Animal Babies,* illustrated by Jill Newton, Augsburg Fortress (Minneapolis, MN), 2003.

*"READY, SET, READ!" BEGINNING-READER SERIES*

*God Made Me,* illustrated by Michelle Neavill, Augsburg-Fortress (Minneapolis, MN), 1992.

*Jesus Loves Me,* illustrated by Kathy Rogers, Augsburg-Fortress (Minneapolis, MN), 1994.

*So I Can Read,* illustrated by Deborah A. Kirkeeide, Augsburg-Fortress (Minneapolis, MN), 1994.

*COMPILER; "KIDS SAY" SERIES*

*Kids Say the Cutest Things about Mom!,* Trade Life Books (Tulsa, OK), 1996.

*Kids Say the Cutest Things about Dad!,* Trade Life Books (Tulsa, OK), 1997.

*Kids Say the Cutest Things about Love,* Trade Life Books (Tulsa, OK), 1998.

*"PICTURE ME" SERIES; UNDER PSEUDONYM DANDI*

*Picture Me as Goldilocks,* illustrated by Wendy Rasmussen, Picture Me Books (Akron, OH), 1997.

*Picture Me as Jack and the Beanstalk,* illustrated by Wendy Rasmussen, Picture Me Books (Akron, OH), 1997.

*Picture Me as Little Red Riding Hood,* illustrated by Wendy Rasmussen, Picture Me Books (Akron, OH), 1997.

*Picture Me with Jonah,* Picture Me Books (Akron, OH), 1997.

*Picture Me with Noah,* Picture Me Books (Akron, OH), 1997.

*Picture Me with Moses,* Picture Me Books (Akron, OH), 1997.

*Picture Me with Jesus,* Picture Me Books (Akron, OH), 1997.

*"PUZZLE CLUB" MYSTERY SERIES*

*The Puzzle Club Christmas Mystery,* illustrated by Mike Young Productions, Concordia (St. Louis, MO), 1997.

*The Puzzle Club Activity Book,* Concordia (St. Louis, MO), 1997.

*The Puzzle Club Picture Book,* Concordia (St. Louis, MO), 1997.

*The Mystery of Great Price,* Concordia (St. Louis, MO), 1997.

*The Puzzle Club Case of the Kidnapped Kid,* Concordia (St. Louis, MO), 1998.

*The Puzzle Club Poison-Pen Mystery,* Concordia (St. Louis, MO), 1998.

*The Puzzle Club Musical Mystery,* Concordia (St. Louis, MO), 1998.

*The Puzzle Club Meets the Jigsaw Kids,* Concordia (St. Louis, MO), 1999.

Also author of *The Counterfeit Caper, The Case of the Missing Memory,* and *The Petnapping Mystery,* 1997-2000.

*MIDDLE-GRADE AND YOUNG-ADULT NOVELS*

*Kyra's Story: Degrees of Guilt,* Tyndale House (Wheaton, IL), 2003.

*Sierra's Story: Degrees of Betrayal,* Tyndale House (Wheaton, IL), 2004.

*Love Rules,* Tyndale House (Wheaton, IL), 2005.

*Eva Underground,* Harcourt (Orlando, FL), 2006.

*Maggie's Story,* Tyndale House (Carol Stream, IL), 2006.

*Larger-than-Life Lara,* Dutton (New York, NY), 2006.

*Crazy in Love,* Dutton (New York, NY), 2007.

*"CINNAMON LAKE" MYSTERY SERIES*

*The Secret Society of the Left Hand,* illustrated by Kay Salem, Concordia (St. Louis, MO), 1996.

*The Case of the Disappearing Dirt,* illustrated by Kay Salem, Concordia (St. Louis, MO), 1996.

*The Cinnamon Lake Meow Mystery,* illustrated by Kay Salem, Concordia (St. Louis, MO), 1997.

*Don't Bug Me Molly!,* illustrated by Kay Salem, Concordia (St. Louis, MO), 1997.

*Of Spies and Spider Webs,* illustrated by Kay Salem, Concordia (St. Louis, MO), 1997.

*The Cinnamon Lake-ness Monster,* illustrated by Kay Salem, Concordia (St. Louis, MO), 1997.

*Soup Kitchen Suspicion,* illustrated by Kay Salem, Concordia (St. Louis, MO), 1998.

*The Presidential Mystery,* illustrated by Kay Salem, Concordia (St. Louis, MO), 1999.

*"HORSEFEATHERS!" SERIES; YOUNG-ADULT NOVELS*

*Horsefeathers!,* Concordia (St. Louis, MO), 2000.

*Horse Cents,* Concordia (St. Louis, MO), 2000.

*A Horse of a Different Color,* Concordia (St. Louis, MO), 2000.

*Horse Whispers in the Air,* Concordia (St. Louis, MO), 2000.

*Horse Angels,* Concordia (St. Louis, MO), 2000.

*Home Is Where Your Horse Is,* Concordia (St. Louis, MO), 2000.

*"WINNIE THE HORSE GENTLER" NOVEL SERIES*

*Bold Beauty,* Tyndale House (Wheaton, IL), 2002.

*Midnight Mystery,* Tyndale House (Wheaton, IL), 2002.

*Unhappy Appy,* Tyndale House (Wheaton, IL), 2002.

*Wild Thing,* Tyndale House (Wheaton, IL), 2002.

*Eager Star,* Tyndale House (Wheaton, IL), 2002.

*Gift Horse,* Tyndale House (Wheaton, IL), 2003.

*Friendly Foal,* Tyndale House (Wheaton, IL), 2004.

*Buckshot Bandit,* Tyndale House (Wheaton, IL), 2004.

*"BLOG ON" YOUNG-ADULT NOVEL SERIES*

*Grace Notes,* Zonderkidz (Grand Rapids, MI), 2006.

*Love, Annie,* Zonderkidz (Grand Rapids, MI), 2006.

*Just Jazz,* Zonderkidz (Grand Rapids, MI), 2006.

*Storm Rising,* Zonderkidz (Grand Rapids, MI), 2006.

*Grace under Pressure,* Zonderkidz (Grand Rapids, MI), 2007.

*Jazz Off Key,* Zonderkidz (Grand Rapids, MI), 2007.

*Storm Warning,* Zonderkidz (Grand Rapids, MI), 2007.

*"STARLIGHT ANIMAL RESCUE" NOVEL SERIES*

*Runaway,* Tyndale House (Wheaton, IL), 2008.
*Mad Dog,* Tyndale House (Wheaton, IL), 2008.
*Kat Shrink,* Tyndale House (Wheaton, IL), 2008.
*Fur Ball,* Tyndale House (Wheaton, IL), 2008.

*FOR ADULTS*

*The Blessing Is in the Doing,* Broadman (Nashville, TN), 1983.
*A Spiritual Handbook for Women,* Prentice-Hall (Englewood Cliffs, NJ), 1984.
*Remembering . . . ,* Tyndale House (Wheaton, IL), 1985.
*When the Answer Is No,* Broadman (Nashville, TN), 1985.
*Splitting Up: When Your Friend Gets a Divorce,* Harold Shaw (Wheaton, IL), 1988.
*Just One of Me,* Harold Shaw (Wheaton, IL), 1989.
*Kindred Sisters: New Testament Women Speak to Us Today; A Book of Meditation and Reflection,* Augsburg Fortress (Minneapolis, MN), 1996.
*101 Ways to Talk to God,* Sourcebooks (Naperville, IL), 2000.

*OTHER*

(Compiler) *Kids Are Still Saying the Darndest Things,* Prima Publishing (Rocklin, CA), 1993.
(Compiler) *Kids Say the Greatest Things about God: A Kid's-Eye View of Life's Biggest Subject,* Tyndale House (Wheaton, IL), 1995.
*Problem Solving* (nonfiction), Ferguson (Chicago, IL), 1998, 2nd edition, 2004.
*Teamwork Skills* (nonfiction), Ferguson (New York, NY), 1998, 2nd edition, 2004.
*Self-Development* (nonfiction), Ferguson (Chicago, IL), 1998, 2nd edition published as *Professional Ethics and Etiquette,* 2004.
*Portrait of Lies,* Tommy Nelson (Nashville, TN), 2001.
*Please Reply!,* Tommy Nelson (Nashville, TN), 2002.
*Kids Say the Best Things about Life: Devotions and Conversations for Families on the Go,* Jossey-Bass (San Francisco, CA), 2004.
*Kids Say the Best Things about God: Devotions and Conversations for Families on the Go,* Jossey-Bass (San Francisco, CA), 2004.

## Adaptations

Three titles in the "Puzzle Club" mystery series were adapted as animated television programs. *Kindred Sisters* has been adapted as an audiobook.

## Sidelights

A prolific writer whose work has been published in over twenty countries, Dandi Daley Mackall has hundreds of books to her credit, the majority of which reflect her Christian faith. Mackall's works range from picture books and novels for children and young adults to historical fiction and nonfiction for a variety of ages. Mackall finds the seeds of stories everywhere, especially in her own life and her experiences raising her three children. For example, the writer's lifelong love of horses is reflected in her "Winnie the Horse Gentler" novel series, about a twelve year old who is able to communicate with horses. The time-honored mantra of the American family road trip inspired her picture book *Are We There Yet?,* while another picture book, *First Day,* reflects universally shared worries as the first day of school approaches. Mackall's young-adult novel *Eva Underground* is based on memories of her eighteen-month venture into Poland in the 1970s, where she experienced life behind the iron curtain prior to the end of the cold war. Readers of *Eva Underground* are treated to a "distinctive human portrayal of a troubling time and place," according to *School Library Journal* reviewer Suzanne Gordon, while a *Kirkus Reviews* contributor stated that "modern Communism is rarely depicted in children's literature, and never before this well." In *Booklist* Stephanie Zvirin dubbed *First Day* "cheerful" and "encouraging." *Are We There Yet?,* featuring what a *Publishers Weekly* contributor described as a "cleverly rhymed" text, also benefits from illustrations by Shannon McNeill that the reviewer praised as "chock full of detail."

Taking place in 1978, *Eva Underground* introduces Eva Lott, a Chicago high school senior. While still grieving her mother's death, Eva finds her secure suburban world further disrupted when her father, a college teacher, decides to put his energy into fighting as part of the Polish anti-communist underground. Making the dangerous border crossing, Eva begins to understand the plight of the Polish people. While her father helps organize an underground press, the American teen becomes involved with one of the underground's young radicals, and ultimately learns the cost of freedom. "Mackall effectively conveys the harsh realities of living under a Communist regime," noted *Booklist* reviewer Ed Sullivan, the critic adding that Eve's story also reflects the optimism of the Polish people following the election of Karol Wojtyla as Pope John Paul. Also reviewing *Eva Underground,* Claire Rosser wrote in *Kliatt* that "the romance and adventure" Mackall weaves into her fast-moving plot will sweep along most YA readers," while a *Kirkus Reviews* writer commented that Eva's narration "draws the reader inexorably into the story."

Geared for upper elementary-grade readers, *Larger-than-Life Lara* introduces Laney Grafton, a friendly fourth grader who sets down on paper the experiences of the new girl in school, carefully and consciously framing her tale in the multi-part structure her language arts teacher has taught her. Laney's subject, grossly overweight, ten-year-old Lara Phelps, has problems at her new school, where she quickly takes Laney's place as the subject of many schoolyard jokes. Through it all, Lara wins Laney's admiration due to her upbeat attitude, compassion, and ready smile, but ultimately something happens that breaks even Lara's buoyant spirit. "Thoroughly enjoyable and unexpectedly wry," *Larger-than-Life Lara* ". . . is as intelligent as it is succinct," noted *School Library Journal* contributor Elizabeth Bird, while in *Booklist* Carolyn Phelan commented that Mackall's story includes "touching moments and offers food for thought" for younger readers.

Mackall once told *SATA:* "I love to write! I even love to rewrite and revise. When I was a ten-year-old tomboy, I won my first contest with fifty words on 'why I want to be bat boy for the Kansas City A's.' But the team wouldn't let a girl be bat boy—my first taste of rejection! I've amassed drawerfuls of rejections since, but along the way I've hung in there and have seen hundreds of my books into print.

"Although I began writing books for grownups—humor, how-to's, inspirationals—when my children were born, I added children's books to the mix. Beginning with board books and baby books when my children were infants, I progressed through picture books and chapter books, middle-grade fiction and nonfiction, never dropping an age group, but simply adding another one. With our teens all in high school, I started a new series of young-adult fiction, 'Horsefeathers!' I grew up with horses, backyard horses: the kind you keep as friends in your own backyard. It's been great to draw on my earlier horse-loving days to build my main character in the series, a teenaged, female horse whisperer.

"I'm blessed with a husband who is also a writer and understands why the beds aren't made and there's nothing on the table at dinner time, and I'm blessed with children who offer encouragement and a never-ending supply of stories. I believe that God has stories already created for us if we're listening and looking and willing to work like crazy to make those stories the best they can be. I suppose that's really why I write."

## Biographical and Critical Sources

*PERIODICALS*

*Booklist,* November 1, 1993, Denise Perry Donavin, review of *Kids Are Still Saying the Darndest Things,* p. p. 500; August, 2003, Stephanie Zvirin, review of *First Day,* p. 1994; March 1, 2006, Ed Sullivan, review of *Eva Underground,* p. 81; May 1, 2006, Carolyn Phelan, review of *Seeing Stars,* p. 86; August 1, 2006, Carolyn Phelan, review of *Larger-than-Life Lara,* p. 78.

*Bulletin of the Center for Children's Books,* October, 2002, review of *Off to Bethlehem!,* p. 67; May, 2006, Loretta Gaffney, review of *Eva Underground,* p. 413; October, 2006, Deborah Stevenson, review of *Larger-than-Life Lara,* p. 82.

*Christian Parenting Today,* summer, 2002, review of "Winnie the Horse Gentler" series, p. 62.

*Kirkus Reviews,* November 1, 2002, review of *Off to Bethlehem!,* p. 1621; February 15, 2006, review of *Eva Underground,* p. 186.

*Kliatt,* March, 2006, Claire Rosser, review of *Eva Underground,* p. 15.

*Publishers Weekly,* September 23, 2002, review of *Until the Christ Child Came . . . ,* p. 36; May 5, 2003, review of *Are We There Yet?,* p. 209; August 25, 2003, review of *First Day,* p. 62; September 22, 2003, review of *Who'll Light the Chanukah Candles?,* p. 68; December 15, 2003, review of *Love and Kisses, Bunny,* p. 76; March 22, 2004, review of *Kids Say the Best Things about Life: Devotions and Conversations for Families on the Go,* p. 16.

*School Library Journal,* October, 1997, Jane Marino, review of *The Puzzle Club Christmas Mystery,* p. 44; October, 2002, Eva Mitnick, review of *Off to Bethlehem!,* p. 61; January, 2003, review of *Rainbow Party,* p. 106; April, 2003, Laurie von Mehren, review of *Silent Dreams,* p. 134; September, 2003, Lisa Gangemi Kropp, review of *First Day,* p. 184; January, 2004, Olga R. Kuharets, review of *Cloud Counting,* p. 102; January, 2005, Cass Kvenild, review of *Professional Ethics,* p. 144; June, 2006, Suzanne Gordon, review of *Eva Underground,* p. 161; September, 2006, Elizabeth Bird, review of *Larger-than-Life Lara,* p. 212.

*Voice of Youth Advocates,* August, 1998, pp. 223-224; December, 2000, review of "Horsefeathers!" series, p. 343; February, 2007, Vikki Terrile, review of *Crazy in Love,* p. 528.

*ONLINE*

*Cynsations Blog,* http://cynthialeitichsmith.blogspot.com/ (April 20, 2006), Cynthia Leitich-Smith, interview with Mackall.

*Dandi Daley Mackall Home Page,* http://www.dandibooks.com (July 27, 2007).

*Winnie the Horse Gentler Web site,* http://winniethehorsegentler.com/ (July 27, 2007).

*Autobiography Feature*

# Dandi Daley Mackall

Dandi Daley Mackall contributed the following autobiographical essay to *SATA:*

## *What's In a Name?*

With a name like "Dandi Daley," what else could I become? I had to be a children's writer. I used to think I'd own my own newspaper and call it *The Dandi Daily.* That goal changed, but I don't remember a time when I didn't want to write and tell stories. Most nights before I could read myself, my mom read fairy tales to me. Then my dad would come in, and he'd make up stories. The best part was that I got to help.

When I was very young, the stories went like this:

"Once upon a time, there were four horses on a high hill. Their colors were . . ." Here, I'd get to fill in the blank: "Black, white, brown, and green." Then Dad would take over again: "And their names were . . ." Back to me: "Blackie, Whitey, Brownie, and Greenie."

When I got a bit older, Dad began a story series with a larger-than-life character called "Big-Foot Dan." I couldn't wait for the next adventure of this amazing character, who could out-race Superman, out-fight Mighty Mouse, and outrun Speedy Gonzalez. And I got to determine the winner of each race, who, of course, was always Big-Foot Dan. I was in college before I made the wry connection between my childhood hero, Big-Foot Dan, and my own rather large feet.

## *Stories and their Tellers*

I was blessed with two great storytellers for parents. Mom's stories came from real life and held me as captivated as Big-Foot Dan had. My mother grew up in a family of eleven kids during the Great Depression. The first girl in her house to go to college, she became a nurse. When World War II broke out and her brothers all went off to war, so did she, as an army nurse. During her training, she met and fell in love with an army doctor, who would become my story-telling father. Only a couple of weeks after they met, they were married. A couple of weeks later, Mom was shipped out to France and Dad to Germany. Mom's stories of shivering in the French winds and Dad's AWOL escapades to meet his bride in foreign cities made me feel as if I'd lived through those days, too.

When I was in elementary school, my two favorite words were "'Member when . . .?" Twice a year, my parents drove my sister, Maureen, and me from our little town of Hamilton, Missouri, to the even-littler town of Cissna Park, Illinois. In that magical place, dozens and dozens of my cousins convened at my grandparents' house, the same house my mom grew up in. The grown-ups would shove all of us kids to long tables in the kitchen, while they settled in around an even longer table in the dining room. Between the two was a swinging door. I received one black eye and half a dozen nose punches from that door as I leaned against it, waiting to hear those mystical words: "'Member when . . .?"

"'Member when Helen"—my mother!—"played basketball for Cissna Park? She was a foot shorter than anyone on the court, but she could steal and dribble and sink that ball better than any of 'em"

My dinner growing colder, I'd stay at my station by the swinging door and wait until someone succeeded in getting my grandmother to tell the story about crossing the ocean from Germany to America in hopes of finding a new life here.

Some of my favorite stories starred my mom's cousin Norman, who broke every rule and led the troops into unimaginable mischief. What I loved most was the way each of the "Norman" stories ended. The teller of the tale would grow quiet, the smile fading like melted wax. Then the words would come: "I really miss Norman." Norman died long before I was born, but he had a profound influence on me. Later, when I'd get into my own mischief, I'd remember the ending to the Norman stories, proof that he was loved. There's a power in story, an enduring truth, a kind of magic that lives on.

## *The Beginnings of Writing*

By the time I entered first grade, I knew I wanted to be a writer of stories. The only problem was that I couldn't write. Miss Tomlin had us practice printing letters on graph paper. The plan was to make that letter fit in that box. Mine rarely fit. And the worst letter, the scurviest letter in the alphabet, was *S.* Not only did it have to fit in the box, but it had to be fat in the right place, skinny in the right place, and curve in the right direction. I remember one day, as I struggled to make that letter work for me, Miss Tomlin walked by, examined my pitiful *S*s, and commented, "Make them fit in the box, Dandi." I was already trying as hard as I could. Then she turned to the girl next to me (later to be known as "Perfect-S-Susie") and exclaimed, "Now *there's* a proper *S!* Dandi, make yours like Susie's."

How was I ever going to be a writer when I couldn't even make the letter *S* stay in the box? And then I made a wonderful discovery. My dad had a manual typewriter that he always left in the hallway outside his office, which was in the home of my other grandparents. My granddad had been the only medical doctor in our county, and when he had a heart attack, my dad had come back to Hamilton to help. Dad ended up practicing medicine there for over forty years.

For a few years, some of my cousins lived in the big Daley house, and we entertained ourselves by writing stories together. We kept a sheet of paper in the typewriter, and anyone was free to type a sentence or paragraph between fierce games of softball and capture the flag. Our stories had more turns and twists than Alfred Hitchcock's. But what I realized was this. Standing at the typewriter, I hit the round *S* key. And just like that, on the sheet of paper, there appeared a perfect *S*—fat in the right place, skinny in the right place, turning just like an *S* is supposed to turn. And today, as I sit at my computer, with one swift movement of my ring finger, *magic!* I produce a perfect *S!* There's always a way to make your dream happen.

### *Dreams*

I admit that I had another, very short-term, dream in the first grade. In the town where I grew up, population 1,701 before the shoe factory closed, there wasn't much to do. So when Miss Tomlin announced, "Class, you are going to put on the Christmas play!" it was a major event. I realize that today kids might even groan at that announcement, but not us. "Yea!" we screamed. "A Christmas play! . . . What's a Christmas play?" (We didn't get out much.)

Miss Tomlin went on to explain that there would be a lead role, the part of the little girl who would visit Wonderland and meet Mr. and Mrs. Santa Claus. And that's when I knew—I wanted that part more than anything in the whole world. Next day, as soon as I stepped into class, I shouted, "Miss Tomlin! Miss Tomlin! Who gets the part of the little girl who gets to skip to Wonderland and meet Mr. and Mrs. Claus and sing and dance on stage by herself?" Miss Tomlin smiled. "I haven't decided yet, Dandi."

Next day, I started, "Miss Tomlin! Miss Tomlin! Who gets the part of the little girl . . .?" My teacher interrupted: "Haven't decided yet, Dandi." By the end of the week, she was waiting at the window as I walked up to the school. "Haven't decided yet, Dandi!" she hollered down.

But the day came when she sat us all down and announced, "Everyone will get a part in our play. And the lead role," the moment I'd been waiting for, "the part of the little girl who gets to visit Wonderland," this was it . . . fingers crossed, "goes to . . . Susie!" I couldn't believe it. Perfect-S-Susie got the part. And as for me? I was a Christmas gift. My mom had to wrap a big box with Christmas wrapping paper for my costume, and I had to wear a stupid red bow on top of my head.

The night of the performance, Susie was singing in front of the curtain. Backstage, I sat with my friends, who were trees, snowflakes, stars. And I told them stories, something I'd started doing when we arrived early on school mornings. I landed onto one story about how the whole town of Hamilton was putting on a play for the whole world to see, and everybody wanted the part of the beautiful princess. At one point, I looked up and saw that every kid in my class had joined us. They were all listening to *me* and my story. *Not bad,* I thought. And when I came to the part in my story where the director said, "I'm sorry that only one person can have the lead role of the beautiful princess. But that part, of course, goes to . . . Dandi!," it was magic. In my story, I could make things turn out any way I wanted. The way they were supposed to. For Perfect-S-Susie, I bestowed the role of understudy for the Wicked Witch of the West End. Stories have such power.

I was remembering that night of my Hamilton Christmas play when I wrote the play production scenes in *Larger-than-Life Lara.*

When I was eight years old, our family took its first real vacation (that didn't end up at Grandma's in Illinois), and Dad drove us from Missouri to New York City. When we got there, we checked into our tiny hotel room, jumped on the beds, then headed out. Mom and my older sister, Maureen, wanted to shop. Not me. I went with Dad on an exploration. Nothing could have been farther removed from my farming community than this noisy, busy city, filled with skyscrapers and taxis.

I guess I must have wandered ahead of my dad because all of a sudden I found myself on a street corner, next to the most amazing sight I'd ever seen. There, leaning against a shopping cart filled with old sacks of who-knew-what, stood an old woman, her face shriveled like a rotten potato. She wore gloves with no fingers, a crumpled hat with a broken brim, and layers of dirty, holey clothes. *And* she was smoking a cigar.

I guess I must have been staring too hard to suit her because she leaned down, her face so close I could see specks in her eyes, and she blew smoke in my face.

Coughing, scared of this strange cigar-smoking woman, I heard my dad's footsteps coming up behind me. *Good!* I thought. *Dad's going to rescue me.*

Instead, my dad did the coolest thing. He didn't pick me up and rush me to safety. Instead, he said, "Dandi, don't stare. That's rude. Introduce yourself."

Feeling betrayed, I turned back to the bag lady. "I'm . . .," *cough, cough,* ". . . Dandi," I managed.

"Well," said the lady, "I'm Boxcar Betty, and I ride the rails." She stuck out her hand—dirtiest hand I'd ever seen. I shook it.

I asked her what she meant by "ride the rails." And she told me. She launched into stories about hopping freights and being a hobo, about living on the streets of New York City, in a box, or under the bridge with her buddies, like "Fast-Fingers Freddy." "Pickpockets can be kind as kind can be," she assured me. She told me about the "Jugman," who played the shell game on 42nd Street, and about "Toots," a "working girl" I could only catch on Tuesdays.

Dusk fell, and Dad said we had to get back to the hotel. I would have stayed the entire three days on that corner, listening to the stories and dreams of Boxcar Betty. As Dad and I walked back, I saw a different city. Instead of the taxis and fancy store windows, I noticed a man who had no feet, selling newspapers on the corner. I caught a glimpse of the Jugman, moving his walnut shells on a tiny table down the alley on 42nd Street. I grew a heart for the homeless.

Those "characters" lived for years in my head, until one day they popped out in a picture book set on the streets of New York City, where the Jugman, Fast-Fingers Freddy, a man who had no feet, and Boxcar Betty walked again in *Silent Dreams.* Several years later, Boxcar Betty forced her way into my story of a hobo during the Great Depression, a picture book called *Rudy Rides the Rails: A Depression Era Story.*

### *You Win Some, You Lose Some*

When I wasn't reading or writing, I had two outdoor passions, playing baseball and riding horses. Horses were like family. We always had at least a couple, and I rode every day, usually bareback. Knowing and loving horses gave me the background I needed to write three series of horse fiction. (And I'll come back to the horse books in a bit.)

But it was my passion for baseball that taught me my next lesson about writing. Every recess during elementary school, and most weekends, I played softball. By the fifth grade, I was the only girl still playing with the guys, but I could hit better than any of them, except a kid named Roger and maybe my buddy Ray on a good day.

Then one Saturday I showed up for a game of pick-up ball, and Roger met me at the third-base line. "You can't play, Dandi," he said.

"How come?" I asked. "Field wet?"

He shook his head. "Nope. This game is for boys only."

And that was that. They wouldn't let me play because I was a girl. It felt like the universe was collapsing on me.

About that time, the *Kansas City Star* ran a contest put on by Charlie O. Finley, owner of the Kansas City A's, the city's professional baseball team. It was a "Batboy Contest," and all you had to do was write in fifty words or less why you wanted to be batboy for the Kansas City A's. I couldn't imagine anything more exciting than handing those batters bats. I wanted to be batboy.

So the next Saturday, Ray came over so I could help him write his essay. We sat outside with our Big Chief tablets and wrote. I remember the smell of the wheat field across the road and fresh-cut grass, the neighbor's dog barking far away, how hot the sidewalk was where we sat to write our essays. I wrote then a lot like I write now, getting down a sentence, hating it, crossing it out, trying again. Good writing comes in the revising and rewriting.

After what seemed like minutes, Ray announced, "I'm done!"

"Read it," I demanded, hoping it wouldn't be good.

He read: "I really, really, really, really, really, really want to be batboy for the Kansas City A's because they are so very, very, very, very . . . good."

Relieved that his was so horrible, I let out a laugh.

"Oh yeah?" Ray snapped. "Well, you can't even be in the contest." He threw the entry from the newspaper at me and stormed off.

I read the contest form. There in small letters at the bottom were the words: "For boys only."

The next week I spent every spare minute working on my essay until I had the exact fifty words I wanted. Before I hiked to the mailbox, I thought about the way my dad always called me "Dan" when we played ball: "Here comes one high and on the outside corner, the way you like it, Dan." Or "Nice hit, Dan!" So I signed that contest entry "Dan Daley."

I won. But when the Kansas City officials discovered I was a girl, they wouldn't let me be batboy. They mailed me an A's hat and an A's jacket (which I kicked into my closet because I had suddenly become a St. Louis Cardinal fan). But I didn't get to hand players their bats.

What I did get was the hint that maybe I could actually write. Plus, I got my first taste of rejection, something every writer will have to learn to deal with. I've published over four hundred books, which means I've gotten over four hundred acceptances. But I've probably raked in at least twice that number of rejections. It's part of the process. And the entire story is now in a picture book called *A Girl Named Dan.*

***Dandi at age eight on her first horse, a pinto named Sugar she first rode at age three*** (Courtesy of Dandi Daley Mackall.)

My best friend growing up was named Sugar, and she weighed about a thousand pounds. Did I mention Sugar was my horse? Many mornings I'd take my pinto mare out on the country roads, then gallop back home to get ready for school. I talked to that horse, convinced she understood as nobody else did. Then one day I went down to the pasture, and my horse was lying on her side. Not breathing. Dead.

I didn't think I could handle it. How could I keep going without our early morning rides, our talks, her horse smell, the way her soft coat grew thick in the winter and her breath came out in white clouds? I came from a family filled with love, but we were tough, too tough to cry. So every time I felt I couldn't stand the longing for my horse, I'd run back to my bedroom and pull out my notebooks. And I'd write. At first, I wrote down all the great things Sugar and I had done together—how she ran away, with me clinging to her neck; how I tried, and failed, to get her to pull a cart; how she slipped on the ice once, and I fell off and slid underneath her, sprawled between her four hooves, but she refused to move.

When I ran out of *real* stories, I made them up. I had stories about "Sugar the Wonder Horse" and "Sugar the Super Horse." And somehow, when I wrote about Sugar, the pain of missing her faded. It was as if a piece of my horse was still there. I'm still writing about Sugar. You meet her, and many other horses I've known, in my "Winnie the Horse Gentler" series and "Horsefeathers!" series and "Starlight Animal Rescue" series. Stories have that power.

## *The Risk of Publishing*

My reading picked up. The town's tiny library was only open two afternoons a week, but I managed to read every horse book they had, then every Agatha Christie mystery and every detective story I could get my hands on. I bought my own copies of *To Kill a Mockingbird* and *Gone with the Wind.* I dreamed of writing books like that, making other kids feel the way those books made me feel.

In junior high, I taught myself to type, which earned me a shot at volunteering in the principal's office instead of sitting in study hall. My job was to type up the announcements for the day and run them off on this strange mimeograph machine that smelled like the color purple, if purple had a smell. Since we didn't have a PA system or intercoms, I'd deliver a copy of the announcements to each classroom, to be read by every teacher to the students.

My first day on the job, though, the temptation was too great. As I typed the soon-to-be-published page, I couldn't help taking ownership. First, I added a quote for the day. Nobody objected. A couple of teachers offered ideas for future quotes. But my sense of ownership grew as I typed each paper. This was, after all, my paper. So one morning as I typed the heading *The Daily Bulletin,* it struck me. This was the beginning of owning my own newspaper. It should be called *The Daley Bulletin,* spelled my way. And so I did.

I waited for the wrath I was sure would come. But nobody noticed. Nobody except Ray, who'd read *The Daley Bulletin* posted on the hall bulletin board. I might have continued all year like this if I'd been left it at that. But the next day, I typed *The Dandi Daley Bulletin.* And that ended my short career as a newspaper publisher.

Yet, my newspaper writing career was about to begin. I started writing letters to various publications, and my letters were almost always published in the Letters to the Editor section of newspapers and magazines. It's still a great way to break into print. In fact, it's how I published my first poem.

During high school summers, I worked at our brand-new swimming pool. But the days dragged on long and boring, and evenings were even worse. We whistle-twirling lifeguards wished for rain, resorting to primitive rain dances that would set us free from the torment of watching other people's kids. There were always a few of the same kids who never went home. Their parents left them at the pool until closing, huddled into towels on cold nights, turning us into glorified babysitters. We, on the other hand, were quick to close the pool if those kids took a dinner break. One week, the mother of one of our pool kids wrote a letter of complaint to the town's weekly paper, alleging that the lifeguards closed the pool before closing time and her little darlings didn't get to swim.

And so, on just such a night, while I sat in my lifeguard tower, I wrote:

### *Ode to a Lifeguard*

O woe is the life of a lifeguard, who sits on her stand all day.
Noble is she who sits and stares while all around her play.
On her throne of steel and wood, she sits to gaze away
At life below. Her sweating brow makes sure it stays that way.
And woe is the life of a basketgirl.* Orders, she gets plenty.
Two said "Thank-you." One said "Please."
That's out of a hundred and twenty.
It hurts my heart when'er I hear that someone is not pleased.
Unfair claims of "closing early" bring me to my knees.
I have sat wrapped in my towel on many a chilly night,
Pitying children mother left to get them out of sight.
I could complain of words I heard, words that make me bitter.
I'm a philosopher and noble guard, not a babysitter.

*With no lockers in the changing room, swimmers were given baskets that were turned in to a "basket girl," to be returned when they left the pool.

I was so proud when my hometown newspaper ran my poem on the front page . . . that is, until my mom started receiving calls from offended parents.

I kept writing letters and experiencing a thrill every time my words appeared in print. The Vietnam "Conflict" was just starting to get media attention, and it irritated me the way the *Kansas City Star,* among others, reported deaths as "casualties," as if there were anything "casual" about being killed in the jungles of Vietnam. The words were almost always the same: "The Viet Cong" suffered heavy losses. Our casualties were light." And so I wrote a "Ballad of Vietnam." I've lost the poem, but the first lines are still in my head:

*"The casualties were light,"* the paper read.
In jungles deep, a sniper added one.
*"And many of the enemy lay dead."*
For him, the end of life had just begun.

I remember that the rest of the ballad pictured a young bride receiving word that her husband had been killed, but not to worry because "the casualties were light."

Again, we got some angry calls after the article appeared. The country's opinion about that war hadn't turned yet. I was learning that writers take risks putting thoughts into words.

I wrote a letter to President Johnson and suggested we give money and build hospitals in Vietnam instead of sending more soldiers and guns there. I even said "please." In return, I received a letter from the FBI, saying that they were keeping my letter on file. I was fourteen. I framed the letter.

### *Language*

Sometimes I look back at the education I received from my small-town school, where I graduated valedictorian of my class of forty-nine students, most of whom had started kindergarten with me. I'm grateful for the good, old-fashioned English writing tools I picked up there. English teachers were big on diagramming sentences, knowing a dangling participle from a split infinitive, a direct object from a predicate nominative. Pretty boring stuff, but I left with an understanding of language that's helped in creative writing and gotten me editing jobs when I needed them.

We didn't write creatively in school—no stories, no flights of fancy. Our tests were fill-in-the-blank and don't-forget-the-dates. When a social studies teacher fresh out of college tried to give us an essay test, the whole school rebelled. I nailed two questions and loved the essay form, gladly giving up those fill-in-the-blank tests. I found I could take the little knowledge I had and make it sound like more. No way I could pull that off when all they wanted was the right word or date. The only problem was that there were ten questions to that social studies essay test, and I only made it through two of them before the bell rang. It was the one and only essay test I had in high school.

After high school, I got a scholarship to attend the University of Missouri, a terrific journalism school and just the place to expand the horizons of *The Dandi Daley.* The first day I strolled into my honors English class our instructor skipped introductions and said, "I'd like everyone to write a description of an unusual building for the rest of the hour." I couldn't decide on a building, so I made one up, haunted as I recall. I used proper sentences no one could fault, double-checked the use of my commas, making sure no sentence fragment or run-on sentences were in *my* paper. When I handed it in, I felt pretty good about my first college writing masterpiece. After all, I'd gotten A pluses in English in high school.

Imagine the pain, the humiliation, when our instructor passed back our papers at the beginning of the following class and mine had a D scrawled on it. Frantically, I turned the pages of my essay, looking for the errors I must have missed. But they weren't there—no red-pencil corrections of grammar or sentence structure, no inserted commas or deleted words. Just a big fat D. I stayed after class and gathered courage to ask the instructor, "Would you please help me understand why I got such a low grade when I didn't make any mistakes?"

She grinned as if she'd already read my mind. "You made up that old house, didn't you?"

"I thought that was okay," I said, defending myself.

"Nothing wrong with fiction," she responded. "But if you're going to make up a building, or a setting, it better sound so real that the reader won't be able to tell. Use your senses and paint the details until we feel what you feel about this place."

Before the semester was over, I'd "painted" my way to an A in her class. And more importantly, I'd learned another secret about the power of a good story. It can make the reader share emotion with the author.

At the University of Missouri, I made one false start toward journalism. It didn't take me long to figure out I wasn't a good fit in the land of "just the facts, Ma'am." Journalism profs wanted us to stick to the facts, even when we could have made those facts into something much more fun, or much more interesting. Every student in arts and sciences had to take a language, so I started my freshman year with French. I'd taken two years of German in high school and loved figuring out another language. Nothing teaches the intricacies of your own language like taking a different language.

French wasn't only intriguing, it sounded beautiful. I was hooked, and I piled on more and more French classes, using up all my electives. I wanted to sound like native speakers, so I talked the dean into letting me use my scholarship money to attend the Université d'Aix-Marseilles in Aix-en-Provence, France, during my junior year. I lived in a dorm, on the foreign-student floor, with dorm mates from Madagascar, Venezuela, Peru, and all over the world. I met people who would become minor characters in my books over the next twenty years.

When I got back to Missouri to finish my degree, my university advisor informed me that if I wanted to graduate on time, I'd better major in a foreign language. And besides, he continued, people just didn't make a living by writing. I could always write as a hobby. With no idea how I'd eventually make my living, I tackled Italian, Spanish, and more French and graduated in foreign languages.

Meanwhile, I began playing with article writing, mostly just to see if I could actually sell something. I wrote about all kinds of things and sold articles to *Reader's Digest, Western Horseman, Family Circle, Woman's Day, Worldwide Challenge,* and others. I can still remember the thrill of seeing "By Dandi Daley" on those articles.

### *A Change of Plans*

Steeped in foreign languages and convinced I could never make a living as a writer, I applied for grad school and won a full-ride scholarship to Stanford University. Only something had happened to me while I was still at Mizzou, and my plans changed dramatically. Although I'd gone to church with my parents when I'd lived in Hamilton, my university years were a time of questioning whether there was a God, and if so, so what? War raged in Vietnam, and we staged sit-ins and protests at home. I wanted peace inside, in spite of what was going on in the world. I began reading the stories of Jesus for myself, amazing stories. Eventually, I found that peace, not in religion, but in a personal relationship with Jesus, and this relationship has carried me through a lot of life since then, kept me relatively sane, and helped me realize my dreams.

And so my poor parents, still elated from the news of their daughter getting a full-ride scholarship for a Ph.D. at Stanford, had to hear my latest news: "Mom, Dad, about that scholarship, I'm passing on it. Instead, I'm going to become a missionary and go behind the Iron Curtain and live with twenty Polish university students so I can teach them the Bible and teach them how to write so they can defy their communist government, using an illegal printing press, of course, and report what's really going on behind the Berlin Wall. Love ya—Bye."

Now that I'm a parent, I appreciate the fact that Mom and Dad didn't lock me in my old room. They were very cool about it, mustering all of their resources to try to let me make my own decisions. The next time I went home, we didn't bring up the subject. But my dad had plastered my old bedroom with newspaper articles he'd cut out about Eastern Europe: *No Food in Poland. Riots Erupt. Communist Leaders Vow to Stamp out the Church! No Freedom of the Press in Warsaw—Three Students Shot.*

I spent a year and half on the border of Czechoslovakia and Poland, living in a house with twenty Poles and no hot water, my tiny room so cold the snow stayed on my boots all night. It was one of the best times of my life. I learned so much more than I taught, got much more than I gave. And I wrote my first book.

## *My First Book*

For the first three months in Poland, I was trying to survive the cold in a house that was heated only when the basement wood stove was fired up for meals. Since most of our meals consisted of bread with something cold and weird on it, the house was generally freezing. I never saw meat the whole time I lived in Poland. Even when soup or cabbage got cooked, the oven heat had to rise through a single stovepipe to the floors above. I lived on the top floor. But my Polish friends had plucked the feathers from consenting geese and made me a down comforter. After supper, I'd race for the warmth of that comforter and read in bed. I read every novel Charles Dickens wrote (smuggled in from the West), mysteries in French, *War and Peace.*

And then I decided it was time to write. With pen and a notebook, I began a humorous book for grown-ups, questioning what we're supposed to do when nothing goes right and things don't turn out our way. I can still remember closing that notebook, convinced I'd just written a blockbuster, my first book, penned "undercover" in Poland. The book, *When the Answer Is No,* had nothing to do with my experiences undercover in a communist country. The Poles I worked with asked me to wait ten years to write about them and their underground movement, Oasis, so they wouldn't be in danger from their government. In fact, even more years would go by before I wrote up those experiences in a young-adult novel titled *Eva Underground.* By that time, the story had become "historical fiction," but for me, the memories had deepened and the images intensified with time.

When I got back to the States, I thought the hard part of writing was done. All I had to do was type in my handwritten book and let those publishers fight for it. When I finished typing, I couldn't believe I only had ninety-nine typed pages. Even I knew that wasn't long enough for a humorous book for grown-ups. So I gave it a title page, then applied Wite-Out to the page numbers, inserted each page into my electric typewriter, and bumped up each page's number. I ended up with one hundred pages. Much better.

As it turned out, *When the Answer Is No* got "no" for an answer. I'd made a dozen photocopies of my masterpiece and mailed one to every publisher I could. My selection process consisted of looking in the back of books I owned and sending a copy to the publisher if they'd listed their full address and zip code.

Half a dozen publishers didn't bother to return the manuscript. A few sent cards informing me they didn't publish this kind of book. Two editors took the time to write personal notes. One editor's note was so critical that I wadded up the letter and stuffed it into my desk. The other editor suggested I attend a writer's conference and learn how to submit a manuscript. I took that advice. And in the course of one Saturday, I learned twenty-seven things I had done wrong in submitting my one hundred pages. I hadn't researched publishers to find out the kinds of books they needed or if they only wanted three chapters and an outline instead of the whole book. I hadn't included return postage and a self-addressed, stamped mailer for the manuscript's likely return. I hadn't written a cover letter, introducing myself and briefly giving the point of the book and indicating why I'd selected them.

Once I got over my humiliation, I rewrote and resubmitted to both editors who had taken the time to give me a personal rejection on the manuscript, even the highly critical editor whose letter I'd stuffed in my desk. I had to dig out that crumpled-up letter and respond to all the points in my rewrite. It was that publisher who finally sent me my first letter of acceptance for a book. I called everyone I knew and announced, "I'm a real live author!"

As I waited for the development and production of *When the Answer Is No,* I started the next book. A year later, the critical publisher backed out on the contract, and the company folded. But it was too late. I thought I was an author. And my second book had been accepted by a different publisher, my third by still another publisher. My first seven books were adult nonfiction, humor, and inspirationals: *How Not to Procrastinate, Remembering, Just One of Me,* and *A Spiritual Handbook for Women.*

## *Love, Mystery, and Children's Books*

I was writing part-time and teaching part-time, while picking up a master's degree in English and creative writing from the University of Central Oklahoma when I met, fell in love with, and married Joe Mackall. We introduced ourselves in late January, married in July. My parents wryly asked why we waited so long.

Joe had been working at the *Washington Post* and had even covered the police beat. But he'd decided he wanted to do more of his own writing. Joe tells this

***Daughters Jen (top) and Katy, at home in Norman, Oklahoma, 1988***
(Courtesy of Dandi Daley Mackall.)

story better than I do, but according to him, he spotted me in the hallway and turned into a detective. By the next day when I came out of my How to Write Murder Mysteries class, he had gathered a notebook full of information on me. He waited until I came out of class, handed me a coffee—no sugar, light cream—and asked, "So what's your favorite way to kill people?" He had me.

Our next move was to Ohio, where we both taught part-time at Ashland University and wrote part-time at opposite ends of our house. It wasn't until I had children that I discovered children's books. During days, I'd teach, then write my nonfiction books and articles. But I looked forward to daughter Jenny's bedtime, when I could read her children's books with her. I couldn't believe how fun and lyrical picture books were. It amazed me that so much story and character could be compressed into a book for young readers.

One night, after I'd been laboring over a book on worry, trying to make it funny, I collapsed onto Jenny's bed with Dr. Seuss's *The Foot Book.* When we finished the book, and caught our breaths from laughing so hard, I said, "Jenny, your books are so much more fun than mine." Jenny, age five, replied, "So write children's books."

I couldn't get to sleep that night. And the next day, I wrote a first draft of "Jenny's Christmas," which became my first children's book, *The Best Christmas Ever.* Since then, I've written books for every age, nonfiction, fiction, rhyming, series books, board books, early chapter books, chapter books, middle-grade and young-adult/adult novels.

When we adopted two-week-old Katy, I put together a unique baby book, the kind moms and dads start as soon as they know a baby is on the way. *Remembering* has places for parents to write their own stories, where they grew up, went to school, how they met, the stories that they'd want their children to know and remember.

Katy got a little older, and I wrote board books, including the "Little Blessings" series, illustrated by Elena Kucharik, who created the Care Bears. But I didn't just want to do older books as my kids grew older, leaving younger books behind. So I wrote another classic baby book, for that baby still in the womb. This one was called *God Made Me.* I've kept this practice of adding age groups and genres, without letting go of the former type of book. I want to write everything!

I love writing rhyme, and I got a good break when a publisher's child happened to have claimed some of my rhyming board books as his favorite. As a result, I was asked to write a dozen rhyming fairy tales, but to spin them in funny ways. I came through on the assignment and was given another, to write concept books: numbers, letters, shapes, colors. Then I wrote a number of nature books, including one called *Under the Sea,* which is my only coauthored book. My daughter Jen had been fascinated by weird creatures that lived underwater, and she had gathered books from the library on the subject. So Jen did the research, I wrote the text, and we shared the byline: "By Jen and Dandi Mackall."

Those early books got me noticed by a few bigger companies, like Hanna-Barbera, producers of the television programs *Yogi Bear, The Flintstones, The Jetsons,* and *Scooby-Doo.* They hired me to write some concept board books using their characters. "Sounds like fun!" I replied over the phone, still wondering if somebody might be playing a trick on me. "Would you like all of them to rhyme?" I asked. "We don't do rhyming books," said the bigwig on the other end of the line.

I hung up and got started on *Scooby-Doo and Scrappy in 1,2,3.* But I knew right away that the story should rhyme. Little kids love rhyme, and it helps them learn. It was the same problem when I began writing *Yogi and Boo Boo ABC's, Pebbles and Bamm Bamm in a Colorful Game,* and *Jetsons in Shape.* Not wanting to blow a big chance, I wrote all four books in prose. Then I wrote four more in rhyme. I sent all eight manuscripts to Hanna-Barbera and got a call at the end of the week. "Okay," said the bigwig, "so I guess we now do rhyme." They bought all four rhyming texts, then hired me to write a bunch of pictures books based on their characters, like *Scooby Doo in A Gaggle of Galloping Ghosts.*

***The author with her horses, Cheyenne and Moby, Cinnamon Lake, Ohio, 2000*** (Courtesy of Dandi Daley Mackall.)

I wrote for Warner Brothers for a while after that and was flown to their Los Angeles studios to brainstorm with their writers and animators to come up with one hundred titles for future books about Tweety Bird, Taz, Bugs Bunny, and the gang. I can still remember feeling like the country mouse in the big city as I sat in a boardroom, surrounded by men in suits with briefcases and writing credits longer than my hair. Jokes and ideas flew around that table faster than the speed of light. At the break, I was exhausted. All I wanted was to go outside and breathe in fresh air. Instead, they wheeled in a TV. We watched cartoons during the break, and those men laughed harder than my kids would have.

Later, I got to write books to accompany the DreamWorks movie *Joseph, King of Dreams.*

Son Dan was into mysteries and baseball books. A story had to keep moving to get Danny to sit still and finish the book. So I tackled writing mystery and adventure. The day we first drove to our home in Cinnamon Lake, Ohio, I took one look around at the twisted trees, pitch dark night, and bumpy roads and told my husband, "There are mysteries out here."

"Cinnamon Lake Mysteries" was my first series, combining quirky characters, twisty plots, and nature. In the end, mysteries were solved because the kids knew nature and picked up on clues connected with that knowledge. Quentin, Molly, Dirt (the toughest first grader in the world), and the Cinnamon Lakers became members of our household. My kids would hop off the school bus and race inside to find out what Molly had been up to that day, or if Quentin and Dirt were still mad at each other.

### *Illustration*

Although I'd painted in oils from time to time, just for fun, I'd given up on any thoughts of illustrating my own books. But I suppose the dream lingered. After I turned in the first "Cinnamon Lake Mysteries" title, called *The Secret Society of the Left Hand,* my editor called and asked if I could just sketch out the layout of Cinnamon Lake: the location of the lake, the Lakers' treehouse, a house with no tree, and the clubhouse of the Vultures. Then our illustrator could make a map to go in all the books.

I did my best, a ribbon-circle for the lake, triangle trees, rough shapes for clubhouses.

A few days later, I got a call from my editor. She was laughing so hard that I could barely understand her.

"Dandi, guess what? We're going to use *your* drawing as the map to go into each book."

I could barely believe it. They'd chosen my drawings to put in the front of every book? *I* was finally going to be an illustrator. "This is so great!" I managed.

"Yeah." More laughter from my editor on the other end of the line. "We were in our publishing meeting, and the head of the company studied your drawing. Then he said, 'Hey! Let's use this one. It looks like a little kid drew it.'"

That was the beginning, and the end, of my life as an illustrator. It was a great outcome, as it turns out. I've had so many wonderful, talented illustrators since then, like Elena Selivanova for *For God So Loved the World;* Susan Mitchell for *A Glorious Angel Show;* Vincent Nguyen for *The Treetops Are Whispering;* Gene Barretta for *Off to Plymouth Rock!, Merry Creature Christmas,* and *Journey Easter, Journey!;* Diana Magnuson for *The Three Wise Women of Christmas;* Karen Lee Schmidt for *I Love You, Daddy* and *I Love You, Mommy;* James Kandt for *In the Beginning;* Greg LaFever for *The Legend of Ohio;* Dominic Catalano for *The Shepherd's Christmas Story;* Claudine Gèvry for *Seeing Stars;* Glin Dibley for *Made for a Purpose;* Jan Spivey Gilchrist for *A Friend from Galilee;* Hala Wittwer for *Love and Kisses, Bunny;* Barry Gott for *It Must Be Halloween;* Keiko Motoyama for *Who'll Light the Chanukah Candles?;* Tiphanie Beeke for *First Day;* Shannon McNeill for *Are We There Yet?;* Karen A. Jerome for *Silent Dreams;* R.W. Alley for *Off to Bethlehem!;* Sally Wern Comport for *Until the Christ Child Came;* Chris Ellison for *Rudy Rides the Rails;* and Elena Kucharik, Jill Newton, Megan Halsey, Hiroe Nakata, Jenny Harris, Jane Dippold, Kay Salem, and others.

### *Family Reading and Characters*

It's been fun to watch our three kids develop such different tastes in reading. I've learned from all of them. As the kids got a little older, we looked forward to each summer's family vacation as a time when we could rein them back in and experience things together, as a family. My goal for vacation spots has always been to find a remote cabin or lodge or house to rent in a town nobody has ever heard of and no sane tourist would care to see.

One summer we vacationed on Beals Island, Maine, renting a resident's house, while she was on vacation. There were no hotels or motels, no theaters or fast-food joints on the island. Only three hundred lobster fishermen and the odd new family. We loved it. Everywhere we walked, people greeted us with, "Ah, you're the

***The Mackall family vacationing in Glacier Lake, Montana, 2005: (left to right) Katy, Jen, Dandi, Joe, and Dan*** (Courtesy of Dandi Daley Mackall.)

outsiders, aren't you?" We hiked by day and read by night. I carry with me the mental image from one particular night when I looked up from my Ann Tyler novel to see Jen reading a medieval fantasy in a rocking chair; Katy perched on a bunk bed, reading *Lottery Rose;* Dan lost in a crime story he'd picked up in a gas station the day before; and Joe sitting next to me, cracking open a new Scott Russell Sanders book.

Our three kids have supplied me with endless characters and plot lines, dialogue, and dilemmas. Sometimes I think our children must have come from different planets. Jen, no longer Jenny, would have fit best in the eighteenth or nineteenth century. She doesn't like TV, has no interest in computers, and would be content to spin wool and read in the drawing room of some Victorian estate. She's loved reading about ancient history her whole life. When I need help with historical facts for a novel, Jen is my go-to gal.

Dan, on the other hand, is thoroughly immersed in whatever is barely starting to sweep the nation. To write a contemporary teen novel, all I have to do is tune in to Dan and his friends, their language sprinkled with the latest cool expressions and rhythms. One vacation, in an obscure little town in Rhode Island, I began writing *Degrees of Guilt: Kyra's Story.* I knew I was onto something when Dan let me read my rough draft of chapter one to him. Then he got up each morning with me so I could read the new installment from the day before. The young adult novel is a murder mystery, and Dan nagged me all the way back home to tell him who did it.

Daughter Katy is our special gift from God to make us better people. She suffers from a chronic and rare disorder called Alport's Syndrome, as well as from hereditary nephritis, or kidney failure. Since age three, when Katy woke up and couldn't hear because she had overnight lost forty percent of her hearing, she has struggled with hearing, speech, comprehension, learning skills, and general health. She's been in special-needs classes and multihandicapped classes her whole school life. Yet she is the happiest person I know. Nobody meets Katy and walks away unchanged. When she's well enough, she competes in Special Olympics swimming, bowling, and even basketball. Everybody in the world should be forced to attend at least one Special Olympics game, where parents and players cheer for everybody, even opposing players.

Katy inhabits many of my books in various forms. I never realized this until a fan wrote and asked me, "Mrs. Mackall, why do you have so many special-needs kids show up in your books?" My first reaction was, "Do not!" Then I thought about some of my books. True, there had been a girl with a speech problem in my first children's book, *Jenny's Christmas,* but it was just a bit part. Then there was the little sister in *Portrait of Lies;* the autistic boy in *Winnie the Horse Gentler;* a pivotal, wonderful girl named Sandy, sister to the main character in *Crazy in Love;* not to mention the theme of bullying in *Larger-than-Life Lara.*

Stories bring out those things that are closest to our hearts, whether we realize this as we write, or not.

## *Write, Write, Write*

When Katy started having serious medical problems, and serious hospital bills, we knew our lifestyle had to change. We needed better medical insurance, and one of us needed to be home at all times. So my husband and I made a pact: the first one to make more money writing than teaching got to quit teaching, and the other one would go back to school and get a Ph.D. in order to teach full-time at the university and get medical benefits for the family.

A few months later, I won. So Joe went back to school, kept teaching part-time, and wrote, picking up that Ph.D. in record time. The teaching schedule works well for him, giving him the structure to schedule in writing time. He's published amazing essays, started an award-winning literary journal, *River Teeth: A Journal of Nonfiction Narrative,* and published chapters in anthologies, such as *Short Takes: Brief Encounters with Contemporary Nonfiction.* And Joe has managed to write two critically acclaimed books, *The Last Street before Cleveland: An Accidental Pilgrimage* and *Plain Secrets: An Outsider among the Amish.*

For me, having the whole day to write works perfectly. I get up early, between five and six, and write every minute that I'm not getting other family members to wherever they're going that day. I write all day, until someone makes me stop, usually Katy wondering if we have anything to eat for dinner. With two writers in the house, our children have grown up not asking "What's for dinner?" but "*Is* there dinner?"

Normally, I use the mornings for "fresh" writing, those feisty first drafts I like to spill from my head before Editor Dandi gets in the way and blocks the wild, but sometimes best, ideas. Around noon, I'll take my mini-tape player and walk five miles around our lake, talking scenes or ideas or dialogue into my tape player. Neighbors think I'm talking to myself and keep their distance.

Afternoons, I prefer to revise and rewrite, maybe working on a different manuscript. I love the rewrite stage, knowing that I can only make this story better. I love searching for the right image, the precise word that will sear the scene into the reader's brain forever. My rough drafts are usually twice as long as I want the finished manuscript, and I like to cut, cut, cut, making the prose tighter and tighter.

At any given time, I might have four stories brewing, four contracts I'm writing on, four deadlines. I can only work on one long fiction at a time because I want that voice to be stronger and stronger. But I can easily "change channels" in my head and write on several shorter pieces at the same time—a rhyming board book, a literary prose picture book, materials for the public relations people. I've been described as having "ADD" of writers. In a normal year, I may have from ten to twenty-two new books published, with four to six publishers. Each title will be completely different in style and content, many geared for different audiences.

### *The Sound of Story*

Books "come" in many different ways, although mine can usually be traced to something in my life, even if I hadn't realized it as I was writing. Sometimes, I *hear* a lyrical text in my head and know it's a picture book. As I write this, I have just finished a Christmas picture book called *Not Such a Silent Night,* for future release with Dutton/Penguin. Each verse relates the classic and traditional Christmas story, with onomatopoeia for sounds that must have been present on that first Christmas. I had the rhythm of that book before I'd typed a single word of text, and I can still "hear" the melody of the lines. I could sing the story to you, but I'm afraid my singing falls into the same category as my illustrating.

I've had many picture books that began with a word or phrase that stuck with me. "Splashing, crashing, flashing" played in my brain until I could see the Mayflower ship on that dangerous trip in *Off to Plymouth Rock!*

I love to play with words and rhythm and give each book its own melody, but I'm a stickler when it comes to rhyme and the regularity of rhythm. No off-rhyme for me. "Sack" and "backed" don't rhyme, and neither do "gain" and "again," or a host of other not-quite combinations we authors are tempted to use to make the line work for us. I scan all of my verse the way my ancient English teachers forced us to do in poetry classes, marking poetic feet into series of accented and unaccented syllables. It's the most rigid thing I do as a writer, and I think it's essential for verse. We can always read our own rhyming verses aloud and make them sound just right, pausing an extra beat or speeding up two syllables to make them sound like one. But my readers won't know when to do that. The only way to be sure any reader can pick up my rhyming picture book and read it right the first time is to scan.

*The Legend of Ohio* doesn't rhyme, but it has its own music. The story is based on an Iroquois oral tradition given to me by a "Keeper of Old Things" for the Algonquin tribe. It's a wonderful story about Chief Tarachiwagon, "The Man Who Held Up the Sky," leading his people into what is now America when "The Moving White Stone Mountain," or the glaciers, forced the people of the North to flee with the animals toward "The Grandfather Mountains," the Appalachians. The story had never been written down, and I wanted desperately to get it right. So I read scores of Native American legends and learned all I could about oral traditions. I knew the sound of the story was as important as the story itself.

### *Writing from Life*

I had published over a hundred books and given dozens of author visits, encouraging students to write what they know, to take advantage of the world they have around them and use those details as inroads to their best fiction, when it occurred to me that I wasn't taking my own advice. I'd never written a horse book, even though I know more about horses than I do about anything, with the possible exception of writing. So I dug into my memories of Sugar, Rocket, Misty, Towaco, Angel, Lancer, Cindy Loo, and the other horses of my past. I drew from our experiences with our own horses, Cheyenne and Moby. Out of this came my first horse series, "Horsefeathers!," eight novels for young adults. The setting was based on my old hometown in Missouri.

Later, I developed a horse series for middle-grade readers, "Winnie the Horse Gentler," and set the story in my neck of the woods in Ohio, using Ashland Middle School as part of the setting. Daughter Katy is my first reader on all animal books. Her specific job is to keep the animal genders straight, making sure I haven't slipped and written "his" mane when I'm referring to a mare, or "her" tail when writing about a male dog.

I added to my experience with horses by reading training manuals and how-to-gentle books, gathering facts and methods I tried out on our own horses. Whenever I felt the story sagging, I headed out to the pasture and went for a long ride. The perfect mix of life and art.

I can't seem to make myself extend my series fiction beyond eight books. I'll still be going strong at number eight, but it just feels that if I go past that, my characters can't keep growing. So I begin another project that's grabbed my attention. I stopped after eight books in "Cinnamon Lake Mysteries," "TodaysGirls.com," "Horsefeathers!," "Winnie the Horse Gentler," and "Blog On!," the last a middle-grade series about four extremely different characters who come together to build a Web site and do positive blogging. In the case of "Winnie," we got so much fan mail demanding more that I've written a spin-off series, "Starlight Animal Rescue." The only exception to my series rule was "Puzzle Club Mysteries," a fast-paced detective series that ended up being animated for television.

Some books take years to come to the surface. Though I lived in Poland behind the "Iron Curtain" from 1978 to 1979, ideas simmered until the setting, plot, voice, and tone came together as historical fiction in *Eva Underground,* published by Harcourt and nominated for ALA Best Book for Young Adults in 2007 and the Ohioana Award. I'd toyed with a novel about those years in Poland and even had a few false starts: an

*The author signing copies of* The Legend of Ohio Rock! *for students in Youngstown, Ohio, 2005* (Courtesy of Dandi Daley Mackall.)

adult novel, a memoir, a contemporary novel that flashed back to the communist era, and a novel written solely in Eva's point of view. But the book came together as soon as I realized I needed to tell Tomek's story, too, to show Poland's struggle through the eyes of a young Polish man, alternating viewpoints with Eva, the young American girl torn from her life in Chicago.

When you read *Eva Underground,* don't forget that most of the events that happen to Eva—from picking plums to moving the printing press after waiting for the bent man in a big black hat—happened to me first. Unlike Eva, I didn't go with my father or leave a boyfriend back home, but the details came from my own experiences. I dedicated the book to my Polish friend, now living in Russia, Gosia Muchowiecka.

Once in a great while, a book comes as if by magic, unraveling itself on the computer screen as my fingers move like frightened spiders across the keys, trying to keep up with the images in my head. Laney Grafton woke me up at 3:00 a.m. to tell me her story, or rather *not* to tell me her story. The words that ran through my head sounded like a tough, angry girl was spitting them at me: "This isn't about me. This story, I mean. So already you got a reason to hang it up."

I crawled out of bed, crossed the hall to my office, wrote down those words, and went back to sleep. Truth is, I've written down lots of things in the middle of dark nights. Usually, in the light of day, nothing makes sense. But this time it was different.

Next morning I sat at my computer, typed in the words, and then kept typing, without any idea where I was headed. Most of the time when I write, I have the whole story in my head before I begin. I'll have fleshed out character studies for main characters, built my setting, nailed the climax, and gotten down at least a rough outline.

Not this time. I was flying blind. But Laney didn't let me down. She kept narrating the story, denying it was about her.

This book surprised me during the whole writing process. At the end of day one, I stopped when Laney and her entire class turned to look at someone, or something, that had appeared in their classroom doorway. I could see every face, drop-jawed and wide-eyed, staring at whatever was in that doorway, but I had no idea who or what it was. I stopped writing, walked around the lake, tried to cook up possibilities. An odd substitute teacher? A stray dog? Something delivered to the classroom? A squirrelly kid like one in my fourth-grade class? The next day I sat down and started typing, and there she was, "Larger-than-Life Lara."

Laney talked me through that whole story. But she did more than that. She talked *about* story. As the action unfolds, the reader learns all about how to write fiction, how to build characters, what a climax is. The story picks up speed all the way to the end, with chapter titles, like "Details," "Dialogue," "Suspense," "Minor Characters," "Setting," "Climax," "Resolution." In many ways, I think this book, my four hundredth, is the best thing I've written.

*Crazy in Love,* a young adult novel, began the same way *Larger-than-Life Lara* had, with a strong voice calling me to her story. My main character, Mary Jane, is a senior in high school, who admits in her first sentence that she does hear voices. But she rushes on to assure us that the voices are all hers and she needs them desperately because she has fallen mad crazy in love with a girlfriend's boyfriend. I had a good idea where the story was taking me, but "MJ" kept me laughing out loud in the privacy of my office for months.

I write for many reasons, including laughter, mine and, hopefully, my readers' laughter. I write because, all advice to the contrary, I make a nice living writing. I write because sometimes life with a chronically ill daughter would consume every waking moment if I didn't disappear into the book I'm writing, the voices I'm hearing. I write because I believe I have things to say, and I trust they'll come out in words that never sound preachy or teachy but will connect one human to another. I write because what else would I do with all of these voices and stories swirling through my head? And I'm grateful for every one of them, for the power of a story that can reach inside.

***With husband, Joe, 2005*** (Courtesy of Dandi Daley Mackall.)

I write because I love the fans who write to me their honest thoughts, like this one from a young girl in the East:

> *Dear Mrs. Mackall, I love your books so much! I want to read every book you write because they are so real that I feel like I'm there. I feel like I'm one of the characters in your book. I read your books over and over. And besides, since my guinea pig died, I have nothing else to do.*

Each of us has a story of birth, first words, first friend, first day of school, first love. Life is a series of these moments, these stories we live and tell. We all share in the magic of story.

* * *

## MACNAUGHTON, Tina

### Personal

Born in Edinburgh, Scotland. *Education:* John Moore's University, B.A. (illustration; with honours). *Hobbies and other interests:* Traveling, sailing, films, reading, going to art galleries; nature and animals.

### Addresses

*Home and office*—56 Rookwood Court, Guilford, Surrey GU2 4EL, England. *E-mail*—tina@tinamacnaughton.com.

### Career

Illustrator and graphic designer. Worked as graphic designer for Hasbro and Grosvenor for London; freelance illustrator.

### Writings

*SELF-ILLUSTRATED*

*The Fairy Who Could Not Fly,* Kids Play (New York, NY), 2007.

*ILLUSTRATOR*

Christina M. Butler, *One Snowy Night,* Good Books (Intercourse, PA), 2004.

Christina M. Butler, *Snow Friends,* Good Books (Intercourse, PA), 2005.

Claire Freedman, *Snuggle Up, Sleepy Ones,* Good Books (Intercourse, PA), 2005.

Susie Jenkin-Pearce, *Pugwug and Little,* Gullane (London, England), 2005, published as *A Pal for Pugwug,* Gingham Dog Press (Columbus, OH), 2006.

Christina M. Butler, *One Winter's Day,* Good Books (Intercourse, PA), 2006.
Marni McGee, *While Angels Watch,* Good Books (Intercourse, PA), 2006.
Claire Freedman, *One Magical Day,* Good Books (Intercourse, PA), 2007.

Also illustrator of picture books *Little Fallow* and *Brown Bear's Wonderful Secret* for Gullane; *An Arkful of Animal Stories* for Lion Hudson; and *The Littlest Owl* and *The Little Lost Robin* for Little Tiger Press.

## Sidelights

While Tina Macnaughton has created the original board book *The Fairy Who Could Not Fly,* she is best known as the illustrator of stories for other writers, among them Claire Freedman's *Snuggle Up, Sleepy Ones* and *One Magical Day,* Susie Jenkin-Pearce's *A Pal for Pugwug,* Marni McGee's *While Angels Watched,* and Christina M. Butler's *One Winter's Day.* In a review of *Snuggle Up, Sleepy One,* a *Publishers Weekly* critic wrote that "Macnaughton's soft pastel animals portraits . . . are cute and snug," while a *Kirkus Reviews* contributor maintained that the illustrator's use of "lavish color" contributes to a picture book that "will lull young sleepyheads pleasantly into la-la land." *While Angels Watch* "achieve[s] a rather magical air, mainly due to the appealing illustrations," according to another *Kirkus Reviews* writer, and in *School Library Journal* Maryann H. Owen maintained that Macnaughton's "soft-focus pictures charmingly enhance the simple text" of *One Magical Day.*

Born in Edinburgh, Scotland, Macnaughton earned an honors degree in illustration, then worked as a graphic designer in London for several years before turning to children's book illustration. In her artwork, she strives for a soft, delicate look and she often uses oil pastels on tinted paper. Many of Macnaughton's illustration projects feature animal characters, and like many illustrators, she is constantly on the lookout for interesting images of creatures of all sorts, as well as of plants and other elements she can incorporate into her picture-book settings.

Asked about her job as a book illustrator, Macnaughton noted on the Little Tiger Press Web site: "The best thing is creating worlds and characters in your head and making them come alive on paper. Not only that, it's very very fulfilling to know that so many people gain pleasure from looking at my pictures." Her advice for aspiring illustrators? "You have to be very self-motivated and organised. A lot of people fail because they are not prepared to work hard. On a practical note you need financial back-up in the form of savings or a part-time job in the beginning for at least one or two years. Never enter into this with big debts because you need to give it plenty of time to grow and allow you to work at it full-time. Finally, don't let any rejection make you depressed or destroy your confidence—even the very best artists get turned down."

***Tina Macnaughton's soft-edged pastel art is a perfect match for Susie Jenkin-Pearce's picture book* A Pal for Pugwug.** (Illustration © 2005 by Tina Macnaughton. Reproduced by permission of School Specialty, Inc.)

## Biographical and Critical Sources

*PERIODICALS*

*Kirkus Reviews,* May 15, 2005, review of *Snuggle Up, Sleepy Ones,* p. 588; October 1, 2005, review of *Snow Friends,* p. 1077; May 1, 2006, review of *While Angels Watch,* p. 463; September 15, 2006, review of *One Winter's Day,* p. 948.
*Publishers Weekly,* June 27, 2005, review of *Snuggle Up, Sleepy Ones,* p. 61; March 27, 2006, review of *While Angels Watch,* p. 82.
*School Library Journal,* November, 2005, Amelia Jenkins, review of *Snow Friends,* p. 83; November, 2006, Rachel G. Payne, review of *One Winter's Day,* p. 86; August, 2007, Maryann H. Owen, review of *One Magical Day,* p. 80.

*ONLINE*

*Little Tiger Press Web site,* http://www.littletigerpress.com/ (August 27, 2007), interview with Macnaughton.
*Tina Macnaughton Home Page,* http://www.tinamacnaughton.com (August 27, 2007).

## MADISON, Alan

### Personal

Married; children: two.

### Addresses

*Home and office*—New York, NY. *E-mail*—alan@madisonia.com.

### Career

Scriptwriter and children's book author. Food Network, script writer for television programming; scriptwriter for soap operas and films; freelance writer. Coach for middle-school and high-school basketball.

### Writings

*FOR CHILDREN*

*Pecorino's First Concert,* illustrated by AnnaLaura Cantone, Atheneum (New York, NY), 2005.

*Pecorino Plays Ball,* illustrated by AnnaLaura Cantone, Atheneum (New York, NY), 2006.

*The Littlest Grape Stomper,* illustrated by Giselle Potter, Schwartz & Wade (New York, NY), 2007.

*Velma Gratch and the Way Cool Butterfly,* illustrated by Kevin Hawkes, Atheneum (New York, NY), 2007.

### Sidelights

Alan Madison has worked in many aspects of writing: everything from magazine articles and soap operas to

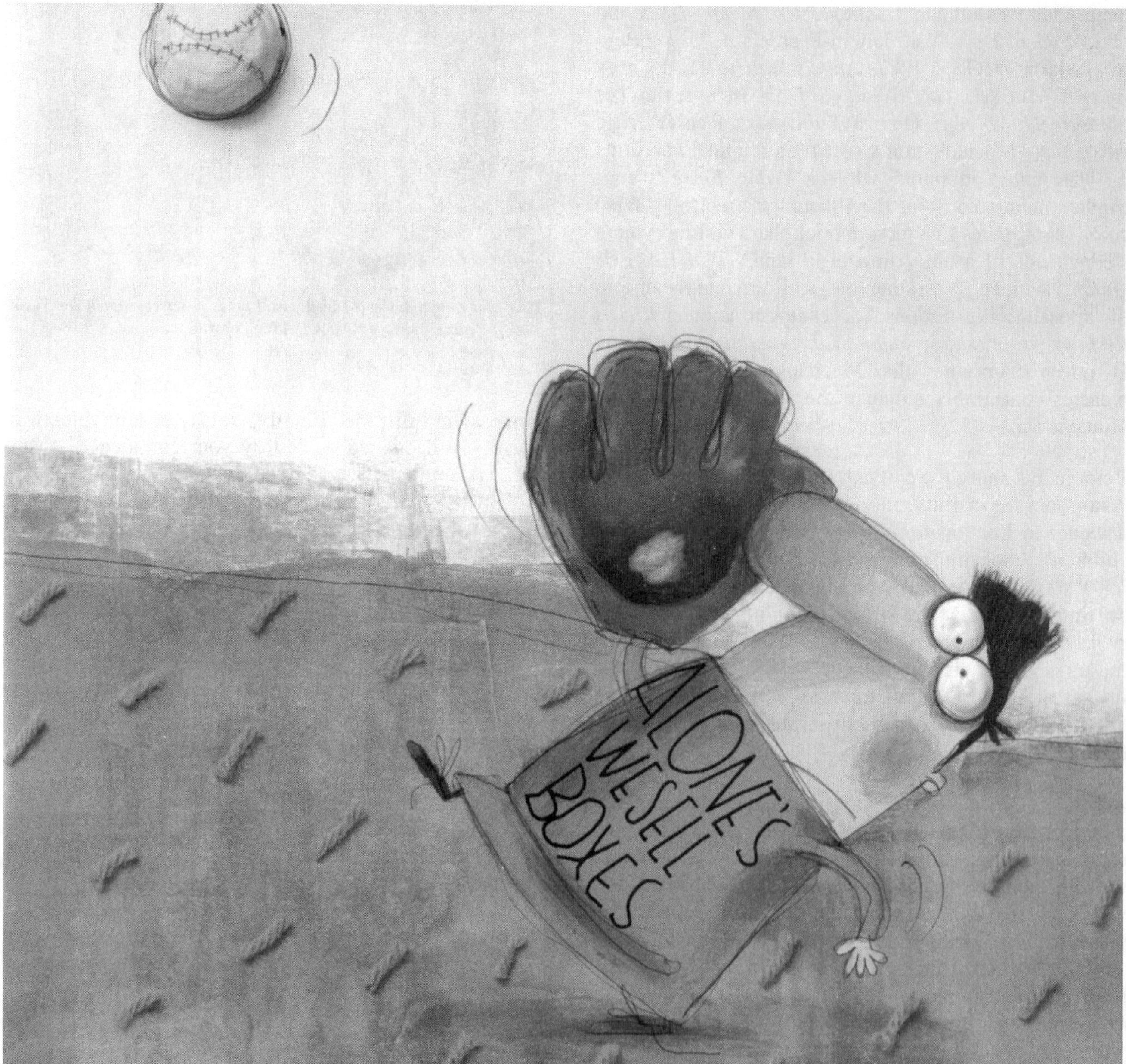


***In her artwork for* Pecorino Plays Ball, *AnnaLaura Cantone brings to life author Alan Madison's determined young hero.*** (Illustration © 2006 by AnnaLaura Cantone. Reprinted by permission of Atheneum Books for Young Readers, an imprint of Simon & Schuster Macmillan.)

fortune cookies. "The fortune cookie was the best thing I ever wrote," Madison explained on his home page. "It said, 'Write a children's book.'" Following the advice of his own fortune-cookie script, Madison embarked on a career as a children's book author with the picture book *Pecorino's First Concert.*

The hero of Madison's picture-book debut, Pecorino is a curious young boy who, on his first trip to an orchestral performance, explores the instruments on stage and gets stuck inside a tuba. Mary Elam, writing in *School Library Journal,* called *Pecorino's First Concert* an "entertainingly silly tale." Agreeing that the book's characters and story are silly, a *Kirkus Reviews* contributor added: "The language and character names are silly, too, and will delight readers who revel in wordplay."

Pecorino's adventures continue in *Pecorino Plays Ball,* in which the silly boy attempts to learn the basics of baseball but finds that he cannot even manage to chew his gum correctly. This failing turns out to be a blessing, however, when a sticky glove and a fly ball combine to make the lad a hero. A *Kirkus Reviews* contributor commented on "Madison's delight in jokes and silly words, with which he's liberally salted his tale." GraceAnne A. DeCandido, writing in *Booklist,* deemed *Pecorino Plays Ball* to be "silly, decidedly odd, and generally giggle inducing," and in her *School Library Journal* review Roxanne Burg calle the picture book "lighthearted nonsense."

In *The Littlest Grape Stomper* Madison introduces a new odd-ball hero. Sixto Poblano is a boy with six toes on each foot, and his physical difference is known to all because he often goes barefoot. Although having extra toes sometimes make Sixto clumsy, when he is recruited to stomp grapes the boy quickly becomes a hero. "In florid prose, Madison . . . elevates Sixto to legendary status," wrote a contributor to *Publishers Weekly* in a review of *The Littlest Grape Stomper.* A *Kirkus Reviews* contributor predicted that young readers "will enjoy both Sixto's triumph and the overall goofiness of this small tall tale."

Velma Gratch, the quirkily named heroine of Madison's picture book *Velma Gratch and the Way Cool Butterfly,* begins the first grade knowing that she can not live up to the stellar examples set by her two older sisters. However, when Velma visits a butterfly conservatory, a place where neither of her sisters has been, a butterfly flutters close to the girl and roosts on Velma's finger, refusing to move for days. Madison wraps butterfly facts into his unusual story, showing Velma going through her own metaphorical journey from cocoon to butterfly.

## Biographical and Critical Sources

*PERIODICALS*

*Booklist,* February 1, 2006, GraceAnne A. DeCandido, review of *Pecorino Plays Ball,* p. 56.

*Kirkus Reviews,* June 15, 2005, review of *Pecorino's First Concert,* p. 686; January 1, 2006, review of *Pecorino Plays Ball,* p. 43; January 15, 2007, review of *The Littlest Grape Stomper,* p. 77.

*Publishers Weekly,* August 8, 2005, review of *Pecorino's First Concert,* p. 234; January 8, 2007, review of *The Littlest Grape Stomper,* p. 50.

*School Library Journal,* August, 2005, Mary Elam, review of *Pecorino's First Concert,* p. 102; March, 2006, Roxanne Burg, review of *Pecorino Plays Ball,* p. 198.

*Tribune Books* (Chicago, IL), February 26, 2006, Mary Harris Russell, review of *Pecorino Plays Ball,* p. 7.

*ONLINE*

*Alan Madison Home Page,* http://www.madisonia.com (August 6, 2007).

*Simon and Schuster Web site,* http://www.simonsays.com/ (August 6, 2007), "Alan Madison."

* * *

# MAGOON, Scott 1972-

## Personal

Born Wayland Renrick Magoon, August 31, 1972; son of Wayland and Bonnie Magoon; married; children: two sons. *Education:* Northeastern University, B.A. (English literature), 1995. *Hobbies and other interests:* Reading, video games, sledding, jazz, movies.

## Addresses

*Home and office*—Boston, MA. *Agent*—c/o Writers House, Rebecca Sherman, 21 W. 26th St., New York, NY 10010. *E-mail*—scott@scottmagoon.com.

## Career

Graphic designer and illustrator. Candlewick Press, Boston, MA, book designer, 2003-06; Houghton Mifflin, Boston, MA, associate art director in Children's Trade Division, 2005—.

## Writings

Kara LaReau, *Ugly Fish,* Harcourt (Orlando, FL), 2006.

*Hugo and Miles In: I've Painted Everything!,* Houghton Mifflin (Boston, MA), 2007.

A.W. Flaherty, *The Luck of the Loch Ness Monster,* Houghton Mifflin (Boston, MA), 2007.

Kara LaReau, *Rabbit and Squirrel,* Harcourt (Orlando, FL), 2008.

*"BABY BERLITZ" SERIES*

*Count on Me, Baby!,* Berlitz Publishing (Singapore), 2004.

*Peek-a-boo Family,* Berlitz Publishing (Singapore), 2004.

*Babies Animal Friends,* Berlitz Publishing (Singapore), 2004.

## Sidelights

Scott Magoon, a book designer and self-taught illustrator, has contributed artwork to various children's titles, including the "Baby Berlitz" picture-book series. In addition to his work for other writer, Magoon combines his quirky art with an original story in *Hugo and Miles In: I've Painted Everything!* He also serves as an associate art director for Boston-based publisher Houghton Mifflin, where he designs children's titles. As Magoon noted on his home page, the "best stories for kids always seem to come with a message of hope." In his opinion, children's stories should reinforce the concept that, in the end, everything will be okay.

Magoon's philosophy of children's book applies to each of the works he has chosen to illustrate. With a text by Kara LaReau, *Ugly Fish* details the story of an unkind fish that bullies the smaller fish living in the same tank. Life for these smaller fish improves substantially when Ugly Fish receives a new tank that, even larger and uglier, makes the bullied fish the target of bullying. *School Library Journal* reviewer Julie Roach noted that Magoon's "edgy" pen-and-ink, digitally colored cartoon illustrations perfectly complement LaReau's "dry and wicked humor." As Roach added, the humor of Magoon's illustrations lightens the sometimes unpleasant effect of Ugly's predations.

In *Hugo and Miles In: I've Painted Everything!* Magoon tells a story that focuses on the concept of creativity and inspiration. Describing the author/illustrator's use of both pencil and digital color, Marianne Saccardi noted in *School Library Journal* that Magoon's images "provide [an] ample supply of visual jokes" and concluded that the book will inspire "new ways to see everyday objects."

## Biographical and Critical Sources

*PERIODICALS*

*Bulletin of the Center for Children's Books,* July-August, 2006, Deborah Stevenson, review of *Ugly Fish,* p. 505.

*Kirkus Reviews,* May 15, 2006, review of *Ugly Fish,* p. 519.

*Publishers Weekly,* June 26, 2006, review of *Ugly Fish,* p. 50; May 21, 2007, review of *Hugo and Miles In: I've Painted Everything!,* p. 54.

*School Library Journal,* July, 2006, Julie Roach, review of *Ugly Fish,* p. 82; March, 2007, Marianne Saccardi, review of *Hugo and Miles In: I've Painted Everything!,* p. 176.

*ONLINE*

*Houghton Mifflin Web site,* http://www.houghtonmifflin.com/ (August 9, 2007), "Scott Magoon."

*Scott Magoon Home Page,* http://www.scottmagoon.com (August 9, 2007).

* * *

# McALLISTER, Angela

## Personal

Born in England; married; children: two children.

## Addresses

*Home*—Dorset, England.

## Career

Children's book author and illustrator.

## Writings

*FOR CHILDREN*

*The King Who Sneezed,* illustrated by Simon Henwood, Morrow (New York, NY), 1988.

*Snail's Birthday Problem,* illustrated by Susie Jenkin-Pearce, Viking (New York, NY), 1989.

*Nothing to Do,* Bodley Head (London, England), 1989.

*Nothing to Cook,* Bodley Head (London, England), 1989.

*The Whales' Tale,* illustrated by Michaela Bloomfield, Aurum (London, England), 1990, published as *When the Ark Was Full,* Dutton (New York, NY), 1990.

*Nesta, the Little Witch,* illustrated by Susie Jenkin-Pearce, Viking (New York, NY), 1990.

*The Enchanted Flute,* illustrated by Margaret Chamberlain, Aurum (London, England), 1990.

*The Acorn Sailor,* illustrated by Alex Ayliffe, Aurum (London, England), 1990.

*The Christmas Wish,* illustrated by Susie Jenkin-Pearce, Aurum (London, England), 1990, Viking (New York, NY), 1991.

*Matepo,* illustrated by Jill Newton, Aurum (London, England), 1990, Dial (New York, NY), 1991.

(Self-illustrated) *The Battle of Sir Cob and Sir Filbert,* Clarkson N. Potter (New York, NY), 1991.

*Mungo Moonbats,* Dent (London, England), 1991.

*Paradise Park,* illustrated by Martin Pierce, Bodley Head (London, England), 1991.

*Magic from the Ground,* Dent (London, England), 1992.

*One Breeze-scented, Sun-sparkling Morning,* illustrated by Susie Jenkin-Pearce, Hutchinson (London, England), 1992.

*Dinny's Diplodocus,* Bodley Head (London, England), 1992.

*Jessie's Journey,* illustrated by Anne Magill, Macmillan (New York, NY), 1992.

*The Babies of Cockle Bay,* illustrated by Susie Jenkin-Pearce, Hutchinson (London, England), 1993, Barron's (Hauppauge, NY), 1994.

*The Snow Angel,* illustrated by Lothrop, Lee & Shepard (New York, NY), 1993.
*Sleepy Ella,* illustrated by Susan Winter, Dent (London, England), 1993, Doubleday (New York, NY), 1994.
*Felix and the Dragon,* illustrated by Jane Tattersfield, Dent (London, England), 1993, illustrated by Mary Claire Smith, Orion (London, England), 2005.
*Midnight at the Oasis,* illustrated by Frances Lloyd, Bodley Head (London, England), 1994.
*Daniel's Train,* illustrated by Alan Curless, Hutchinson (London, England), 1994.
*The Wind Garden,* illustrated by Claire Fletcher, Bodley Head (London, England), 1994, Lothrop, Lee & Shepard (New York, NY), 1995.
*The Ice Palace,* illustrated by Angela Barrett, Putnam (New York, NY), 1994.
*Scaredy Ghosts,* illustrated by Susie Jenkin-Pearce, Hippo (London, England), 1998.
*The Clever Cowboy,* illustrated by Katherine Lodge, D.K. Publishing (New York, NY), 1998.
*Jack and Lily,* illustrated by Phillida Gili, Orion (London, England), 2001.
(Reteller) *The Tortoise and the Hare: An Aesop's Fable,* illustrated by Jonathan Heale, Frances Lincoln (London, England), 2001.
*Be Good Gordon,* illustrated by Tim Archbold, Bloomsbury (London, England), 2001.
*The Baddies' Goodies,* illustrated by Sally Anne Lambert, Bloomsbury (London, England), 2002, published as *Barkus, Sly, and the Golden Egg,* Bloomsbury (New York, NY), 2002.
*Blue Rabbit,* illustrated by Jason Cockcroft, Bloomsbury (London, England), 2003, published as *The Little Blue Rabbit,* Bloomsbury (New York, NY), 2003.
*Harry's Box,* illustrated by Jenny Jones, Bloomsbury (New York, NY), 2003.
*Night-night, Little One,* illustrated by Maggie Kneen, Random House (New York, NY), 2003.
*Found You, Little Wombat!,* illustrated by Charles Fuge, Gullane (London, England), 2003.
*Little Jack Rabbit,* illustrated by Sue Porter, Gullane (London, England), 2003.
*Elephant in a Rowboat,* illustrated by Holly Swain, Gullane (London, England), 2004.
*Brave Bitsy and the Bear,* illustrated by Tiphanie Beeke, Macmillan (London, England), 2004, Clarion (New York, NY), 2006.
*Jasmine's Lion,* illustrated by Marie-Louise Fitzpatrick, Doubleday (London, England), 2005.
*Big Yang and Little Yin,* illustrated by Eleanor Taylor, Gullane (London, England), 2005.
*Monster Pet,* illustrated by Charlotte Middleton, Margaret K. McElderry Books (New York, NY), 2005.
*Trust Me, Mom!,* illustrated by Ross Collins, Bloomsbury (New York, NY), 2005.
*The Tide Turner,* Orion (London, England), 2006.
*Ruby and Little Joe,* illustrated by Terry Milne, Simon & Schuster (London, England), 2006, published as *Mama and Little Joe,* Margaret K. McElderry Books (New York, NY), 2007.
*Just like Sisters,* illustrated by Sophie Fatus, Atheneum (New York, NY), 2006.
*Digory the Dragon Slayer,* illustrated by Ian Beck, Bloomsbury (New York, NY), 2006.
*Take a Kiss to School,* illustrated by Sue Hellard, Bloomsbury (New York, NY), 2006.
*Digory and the Lost King,* illustrated by Ian Beck, Bloomsbury (New York, NY), 2007.

Author's works have been translated into Welsh.

## Adaptations

*Digory the Dragon Slayer* was adapted as an audiobook by BBC Audiobooks America, 2006.

## Sidelights

Angela McAllister is a prolific British author of picture books and chapter books. Since her first book was published in the late 1980s, McAllister has produced, on average, three books a year since, entertaining readers in the United States as well as her native England with titles such as *The Wind Garden, Harry's Box, The Whales' Tale,* and *Digory the Dragon Slayer.* Citing the author's "nimble prose" in *Harry's Box* for bringing to life a story about the power of imagination, a *Publishers Weekly* contributor added that in her repetitive text McAllister "echo[es] . . . the ambitions of imaginative kids everywhere." While usually collaborating with other illustrators, such as Katherine Lodge, Angela Barrett, Sue Hellard, and frequent collaborator Susie Jenkin-Pearce, McAllister also dons the illustrator cap for *The Battle of Sir Cob and Sir Filbert.* Reviewing this story, which finds two knights engaged in a fight during which they ultimately destroy the very things they are fighting for, a *Publishers Weekly* reviewer wrote that McAllister's pen-and-ink art "displays her humor in yet another medium and brings new dimension to her talent."

McAllister honed her storytelling talents while growing up in a large family, and she well knows the value of humorous nonsense and wordplay, as well as upbeat endings, among young readers. Her first published book, *The King Who Sneezed,* introduces aptly named King Parsimonious, a monarch who is so foolish that he does not realize that his own stinginess has caused his castle to become damp and uncomfortable. The Yippeeville Pancake Tossin' Contest brings together a host of quirky characters in *The Clever Cowboy,* as a group of spatula-wielding buckaroos attempt to out-toss each other and wind up blanketing the sun with a poorly aimed flapjack, while a young mole finds the second day of school easier to deal with when armed with a pocketful of kisses in *Take a Kiss to School.* Long-distance pen pals Nancy and Ally finally meet in *Just like Sisters,* and realize that their friendship is just as strong in real life—even though Nancy is a human child and Ally is an alligator. Reviewing *The Clever Cowboy* in *Publishers Weekly,* a critic cited the "spirited mood" carried by McAllister's "western vernacular," while a *Kirkus Reviews* contributor deemed *Take a Kiss to School* "heart-

***Cover of Angela McAllister's middle-grade fantasy* Digory the Dragon Slayer, *featuring artwork by Ian Beck*** (Illustrations © 2006 by Ian Beck. Reproduced by permission of Bloomsbury Children's Books.)

warming" and "a sweet take on an old theme." Calling *Just like Sisters* a "fresh, but odd spin on pen pals," a *Kirkus Reviews* writer added that artist Sophie Fatus's inclusion of "coy details" in her "colorful illustrations add understated humor" to McAllister's story. "A strong intertwining of text and illustration" make *Just like Sisters* "a charming celebration of friendship," concluded Elaine Lesh Morgan in *School Library Journal.*

In the chapter book *Digory the Dragon Slayer* McAllister introduces readers to a young boy who enjoys nothing better than spending time alone in the forest near his village playing his lute and making up songs. One day Digory finds a strange object in the woods. When the object is discovered to be a dragon's tooth, the boy is hailed as a dragon slayer. Forced to leave off writing songs, Digory soon finds himself mounted on an old, deaf horse named Barkley, wearing a suit of homemade armor. Reluctantly setting to slay dragons, rescue distressed damsels, and eventually marry a beautiful princess, the boy ultimately meets his destiny at the castle of King Widget, where both a fun-loving princess named Enid and a fearsome dragon live. Digory's adventures continue in *Digory and the Lost King,* as the young knight follows the trail of the missing King Weget and the monarch's long-missing twin brother. Digory finds even more expected of him, however, when he is mistaken for a powerful wizard. McAllister's "lighthearted plot and the strong underlying message about courage and individuality" in *Digory the Dragon Slayer* makes the book "a good choice for fantasy fans," according to *School Library Journal* contributor Elaine E. Knight. Discussing the sequel, Knight cited the "amusing" pen-and-ink art by Ian Beck for contributing to *Digory and the Lost King,* the critic adding that McAllister's "lighthearted fantasy spoof is filled with mock heroic dialogue and derring-do."

## Biographical and Critical Sources

*PERIODICALS*

*Booklist,* March 15, 1992, Julie Corsaro, review of *The Battle of Sir Cob and Sir Filbert,* p. 1389; September 1, 1992, Hazel Rochman, review of *Jessie's Journey,* p. 67; October 1, 1993, Janice Del Negro, review of *The Show Angel,* p. 353; October 15, 1994, Mary Harris Veeder, review of *The Ice Palace,* p. 437; March 15, 1995, Julie Corsaro, review of *The Wind Garden,* p. 1335; October 1, 1998, GraceAnne A. DeCandido, review of *The Clever Cowboy,* p. 336; June 1, 2003, Lauren Peterson, review of *The Little Blue Rabbit,* p. 1787; August, 2003, John Peters, review of *Harry's Box,* p. 1989; August 1, 2006, Hazel Rochman, review of *Take a Kiss to School,* p. 95.

*Bulletin of the Center for Children's Books,* January, 1989, review of *The King Who Sneezed,* p. 129; May, 1990, review of *When the Ark Was Full,* p. 221; January, 1992, review of *The Enchanted Flute,* p. 133; December, 1998, review of *The Clever Cowboy,* p. 137; April, 2004, Janice Del Negro, review of *The Tortoise and the Hare: An Aesop's Fable,* p. 339.

*Kirkus Reviews,* June 1, 2002, review of *Barkus, Sly, and the Golden Egg,* p. 807; October 15, 2002, review of *Be Good, Gordon,* p. 1534; February 15, 2003, review of *Night-night, Little One,* p. 312; June 15, 2003, review of *Harry's Box,* p. 861; October 15, 2005, review of *Trust Me, Mom!,* p. 1143; May 1, 2006, review of *Digory the Dragon Slayer,* p. 463; May 15, 2006, review of *Just like Sisters,* p. 521; June 15, 2006, review of *Take a Kiss to School,* p. 635; July 1, 2006, review of *Felix and the Blue Dragon,* p. 679; October 1, 2006, review of *Brave Bitsy and the Bear,* p. 1020; March 1, 2007, review of *Mama and Little Joe,* p. 227.

*Publishers Weekly,* December 14, 1990, review of *Matepo,* p. 66; January 13, 1992, review of *The Battle of Sir Cob and Sir Filbert;* October 24, 1994, review of *The Ice Palace,* p. 61; November 9, 1998, review of *The Clever Cowboy,* p. 75; December 9, 2002, review of *Night-night, Little One,* p. 81; May 26, 2003, review of *The Little Blue Rabbit,* p. 68; July 7, 2003, review of *Harry's Box,* p. 71; June 12, 2006, review of *Take a Kiss to School,* p. 51.

*School Library Journal,* February, 1989, Kathy Piehl, review of *The King Who Sneezed,* p. 72; April, 1990, Susan H. Patron, review of *Snail's Birthday Problem,* p. 93; September, 1990, Kathy Piehl, review of *When the Ark Was Full,* p. 206; March, 1991, Lisa S. Murphy, review of *Nesta, the Little Witch,* p. 175; June, 1991, Susan Scheps, review of *Matepo,* p. 85; December, 1991, Susan L. Rogers, review of *The Enchanted Flute,* p. 96; June, 1992, Lauralyn Persson, review of *The Battle of Sir Cob and Sir Filbert,* p. 98; January, 1993, Elizabeth Hanson, review of *Jessie's Journey,* p. 81; November, 1993, Shirley Wilton, review of *The Snow Angel,* p. 86; July, 1994, Alexandra Marris, review of *Sleepy Ella,* p. 85; October, 1994, Patricia Lothrop Green, review of *The Ice Palace,* p. 125; April, 1995, Patricia Pearl Dole, review of *The Wind Garden,* p. 104; October, 1998, Roxanne Burg, review of *The Clever Cowboy,* p. 107; September, 202, Marie Orlando, review of *Barkus, Sly, and the Golden Egg,* p. 200; January, 2003, Bina Williams, review of *Be Good, Gordon,* p. 105; March, 2003, Carolyn Janssen, review of *Night-night, Little One,* p. 198; July, 2003, Wendy Woodfill, review of *The Little Blue Rabbit,* p. 101; October, 2003, Kathleen Whalin, review of *Harry's Box,* p. 130; July, 2005, Shawn Brommer, review of *Monster Pet!,* p. 78; December, 2005, Robin L. Gibson, review of *Trust Me, Mom!,* p. 118; June, 2006, Elaine Lesh Morgan, review of *Just like Sisters,* p. 121; July, 2006, Lisa Gangemi Kropp, review of *Take a Kiss to School,* p. 82; August, 2006, Elaine E. Knight, review of *Digory the Dragon Slayer,* p. 92; October, 2006, Linda Staskus, review of *Brave Bitsy and the Bear,* p. 116; April, 2007, Amy Lilien-Harper, review of *Mama and Little Joe,* p. 112; July, 2007, Elaine E. Knight, review of *Digory and the Lost King,* p. 81.*

* * *

# McCALL, Wendell
# See PEARSON, Ridley

See PEARSON, Ridley

* * *

# McCARTY, Peter 1966-

## Personal

Born 1966, in Westport, CT; married 1995; children: Henry, Suki (daughter). *Education:* Attended University of Colorado; School of Visual Arts, graduated, 1992.

## Addresses

*E-mail*—petermccarty@optonline.net.

## Career

Illustrator. School of Visual Arts, New York, NY, instructor.

## Awards, Honors

Marion Vannett Ridgway Memorial Award, *New York Times* Best Books designation, Cooperative Children's Book Center Choice designation, Red Clover Award nomination, and Minnesota Book Award nomination, all 1997, and Bank Street College of Education Best Children's Book of the Year designarion, 1998, all for *Night Driving* by John Coy; *New York Times* Best Illustrated Book designation, 1999, for *Bunny on the Move;* Caldecott Honor designation, Society of Illustrators Gold Medal, and *New York Times* Best Illustrated Book designation, all 2002, all for *Hondo and Fabian;* Charlotte Zolotow Award, 2007, for *Moon Plane.*

## Writings

*SELF-ILLUSTRATED*

*Little Bunny on the Move,* Henry Holt (New York, NY), 1999.

*Baby Steps,* Henry Holt (New York, NY), 2000.

*Hondo and Fabian,* Henry Holt (New York, NY), 2002.

*T Is for Terrible,* Henry Holt (New York, NY), 2004.

*Moon Plane,* Henry Holt (New York, NY), 2006.

*Fabian Escapes,* Henry Holt (New York, NY), 2007.

*ILLUSTRATOR*

David Getz, *Frozen Man,* Henry Holt (New York, NY), 1994.

John Coy, *Night Driving,* Henry Holt (New York, NY), 1996.

David Getz, *Life on Mars,* Henry Holt (New York, NY), 1997.

David Getz, *Frozen Girl,* Henry Holt (New York, NY), 1998.

Rosemary Wells, *Mary on Horseback: Three Mountain Stories,* Dial Books for Young Readers (New York, NY), 1998.

David Getz, *Purple Death: The Mysterious Flu of 1918,* Henry Holt (New York, NY), 2000.

Tor Seidler, *Terpin,* Laura Geringer Books (New York, NY), 2002.

Tor Seidler, *Brothers below Zero,* Laura Geringer Books (New York, NY), 2002.

## Sidelights

Noted for his evocative pencil illustrations, award-winning artist and author Peter McCarty has gained critical acclaim for his original picture books *Moon Plane, T Is for Terrible,* and the Caldecott Honor book *Hondo and Fabian.* From rabbits to cats and dogs to dinosaurs, McCarty's original stories feature animal characters whose childlike personalities endear them to young readers. In *T Is for Terrible,* for instance, a Tyrannosaurus Rex bemoans its status as a much-feared carnivore with few friends, while *Hondo and Fabian* introduces a pair of mischievous household pets. Reviewing *T Is for Terrible,* a *Publishers Weekly* critic maintained that "McCarty's impressive, diaphanous art" engages toddlers with its "soothing" images while his text appeals to children's sense of whimsy. In his intricate pencil drawings for *Baby Steps,* McCarty also proves his ability to depict human characters, in this case, his own infant daughter. As Jane Marino wrote in *School Library Journal,* the author/illustrator's affectionate "illustrations are amazing in their simplicity, managing to capture small moments in meticulous detail."

Although born in New England, McCarty moved frequently while growing up due to his father's job. Although he enjoyed art, by the time he graduated from high school in Boulder, Colorado, he had decided to be a scientist. Enrolling at the University of Colorado, McCarty took science and math classes, but during his senior year he realized that he would not be happy working in a laboratory setting. Instead of graduating, McCarty moved to New York City and enrolled at the School of Visual Arts. After graduating in 1992, he was awarded his first illustration project by publisher Henry Holt, creating art David Getz's *Frozen Man,* on the strength of a recommendation by his illustration teacher, artist William Low.

McCarty's work for *Frozen Man* was praised by several critics, among them Chris Sherman who wrote in *Booklist* that the illustrator's "delicate, hazy drawings enhance the mysterious air of the text." Continuing his working relationship with editors at Henry Holt, he also achieved success with his second illustration project, John Coy's *Night Driving.* Reviewing this 1996 picture book, which won several awards, *Booklist* contributor Bill Ott wrote that the illustrator's "hazy, evocative" pencil illustrations "effectively capture the cocoon-like intimacy" of a father and son taking their first long road trip together. While McCarty has created artwork for several more books by other authors, beginning with his first original picture book, 1999's *Bunny on the Move,* he has found his greatest satisfaction illustrating his own stories.

In *Hondo and Fabian* McCarty introduces two of his most endearing characters: a yellow Labrador retriever and a gray tabby cat. The book brings to life a contented pet's day: from napping to exploring and causing a bit of mischief to eating in preparation for another round of napping. McCarty's "staccato text," while brief, "captures a lot of action in a few words," maintained *Booklist* contributor Ilene Cooper, the critic going on to laud the book's unique pencil illustrations done on textured watercolor paper. Citing the artist's "candlelit palette," a *Publishers Weekly* reviewer noted that *Hondo and Fabian* conveys a "warm, nostalgic mood" which creates "an effect at once ingenuous and sophisticated." In an appraisal of the picture book for the *New York Times Book Review,* Penelope Green admitted that McCarty's text relays "the sparest of plots." It is in the artwork, Green explained, that the story resonates with readers: "The faces—they will break your heart," she wrote, adding that "Hondo's nose evokes all the eager wet noses that have ever thrust themselves into your hand."

Hondo and Fabian return in *Fabian Escapes,* which finds the curious tabby escaping the confines of the family house to explore the flower garden and meet the dogs next door, before racing back to hide under the porch. Meanwhile, the portly pup neatly steals some butter from the kitchen table before being requisitioned for a game of "dress up" by his family's toddler. Praising McCarty's soft-edged colored-pencil art, a *Publishers Weekly* reviewer added that, despite the book's title, in *Fabian Escapes* the author/illustrator "maintains an even keel in this wry look at pets' everyday lives."

Capturing the same nostalgic mood as *Hondo and Fabian* and *Night Driving, Moon Plane* finds a small boy watching an twin-engine airplane fly overhead and letting his imagination follow its amazing trip spaceward. Describing the book's plot as "more an idea than a story," Cooper explained that the author deftly captures "both the way children's imaginations work and the connections they make." "McCarty's narrative unfolds in a whisper," wrote a *Publishers Weekly* writer, the critic adding that the book's "quiet words and . . . soothing gray" artwork effectively transport young listeners on "an evanescent airplane journey." In *School Library Journal* Carolyn Janssen praised McCarty's monochromatic illustrations for creating the subdued "atmosphere of a silent movie," and a *Kirkus Reviews* writer praised the "gentle adventure" depicted in *Moon Plane* for "captur[ing] . . . the weightless wonder and timeless silence of flight in outer space."

## Biographical and Critical Sources

*PERIODICALS*

*Booklist,* November 15, 1994, Chris Sherman, review of *Frozen Man,* p. 595; December 15, 1999, Ilene Cooper, review of *Little Bunny on the Move,* p. 790; October 1, 2000, Ilene Cooper, review of *Baby Steps,* p. 348; February 15, 2002, Ilene Cooper, review of *Hondo and Fabian,* p. 1021; August 1, 2006, Edie Ching, review of *Hondo and Fabian,* p. 99; September 1, 2006, Ilene Cooper, review of *Moon Plane,* p. 125; March 15, 2007, Ilene Cooper, review of *Fabian Escapes,* p. 54.

*Bulletin of the Center for Children's Books,* December, 1996, review of *Night Driving,* p. 131; November, 1999, review of *Little Bunny on the Move,* p. 100; October, 2000, review of *Baby Steps,* p. 74.

*Horn Book,* September-October, 1996, Roger Sutton, review of *Night Driving,* p. 574; November, 1998, Joanna Rudge Long, review of *Mary on Horseback: Three Mountain Stories,* p. 744; May-June, 2007, Christine M. Heppermann, review of *Fabian Escapes,* p. 269.

*Kirkus Reviews,* January 15, 2002, review of *Brothers below Zero,* p. 108; March 1, 2002, review of *Hondo and Fabian,* p. 339; July 1, 2004, review of *T Is for Terrible,* p. 633; August 15, 2006, review of *Moon Plane,* p. 848.

*New York Times Book Review,* November 21, 1999, J.D. Biersdorfer, review of *Little Bunny on the Move;* May 19, 2002, Penelope Green, review of *Hondo and Fabian.*

*Publishers Weekly,* August 26, 1996, review of *Night Driving,* p. 97; September 27, 1999, review of *Little Bunny on the Move,* p. 104; October 2, 2000, review of *Baby Steps,* p. 81; February 25, 2002, review of *Hondo and Fabian,* p. 65; July 19, 2004, review of *T Is for Terrible,* p. 159; July 24, 2006, review of *Moon Plane,* p. 56; February 19, 2007, review of *Fabian Escapes,* p. 166.

*School Library Journal,* October, 1996, Lauralyn Persson, review of *Night Driving,* p. 91; December, 1999, Liza Graybill, review of *Little Bunny on the Move,* p. 103; October, 2000, Jane Marino, review of *Baby Steps,* p. 130; February, 2001, Jean Gaffney, review of *Purple Death: The Mysterious Flu of 1918,* p. 133; June, 2002, Jody McCoy, review of *Hondo and Fabian,* p. 100; May, 2006, Veronica Schwartz, review of *T Is for Terrible,* p. 69; September, 2006, Carolyn Janssen, review of *Moon Plane,* p. 178; June, 2007, Catherine Threadgill, review of *Fabian Escapes,* p. 114.

*ONLINE*

*Peter McCarty Home Page,* http://www.petermccarty.net (August 27, 2007).

* * *

# McLIMANS, David 1948-

## Personal

Born 1948; married (divorced); children: Hannah. *Education:* University of Minnesota, B.A., Boston University, M.F.A.

## Addresses

*Home and office*—2803 Ridge Rd., Madison, WI 53705. *E-mail*—dmcl@chorus.net.

## Career

Graphic designer, author, and editorial illustrator.

## Awards, Honors

Award of Excellence, Society of Newspaper Designers; Certificate of Excellence, *Print* magazine; *New York Times Book Review* Ten Best Children's Books designation, 2006, and Caldecott Medal Honor Book designation, 2007, both for *Gone Wild: An Endangered Animal Alphabet.*

## Writings

*SELF-ILLUSTRATED*

*Gone Wild: An Endangered Animal Alphabet,* Walker (New York, NY), 2006.

Contributor of editorial illustrations to periodicals, including *Progressive, Time, New York Times, Washington Post, Atlantic Monthly,* and *Harpers.*

## Sidelights

David McLimans had plenty of success as an illustrator, graphic designer, and political cartoonist before creating his first children's book, *Gone Wild: An Endangered Animal Alphabet.* The title, which received a Caldecott Medal Honor in 2007, started McLimans' new career as a children's book illustrator with a bang. Talking about the switch from magazine work to children's literature with *Prairie Wind* interviewer Tina P. Schwartz, McLimans explained: "When I worked for *Harper's* [magazine] I'd have approximately a week to ten days to come up with articles. I got burned out from editorial work. I wanted a project that took longer to plan and conceptualize. Also, I wanted my work to last much longer."

*Gone Wild* pairs the twenty-six letters of the English alphabet with correlating images of twenty-six endangered animal species. The book took three years to conceptualize and create, and "started with my concern for the environment," as McLimans told Schwartz. Spending much of his free time out of doors as a child, the author/illustrator later worked as a teen camp counselor, living during this period in a "shed in the woods without lights, electricity or running water," as he recalled to Melanie Conklin for the *Wisconsin State Journal.* This experience, combined with McLimans' graduate thesis project designing a typeface, became the inspiration for *Gone Wild.*

Reviewing McLimans' picture-book debut, a *Kirkus Reviews* contributor described the black-and-white, mixed-media art in *Gone Wild* as "26 page-filling, dramatic letter forms in silhouette." Julie Leibach, reviewing the work for *Audubon,* noted that "a glossary at the back of the book provides greater detail on the animals featured," a fact that underscores the book's message that the earth needs to be protected, according to the critic. In *School Library Journal* Kathy Piehl called "the letters . . . far from ordinary," and predicted that *Gone Wild* will be an effective consciousness-raiser on environmental issues as well as a starting point for graphic-arts projects. Another *School Library Journal* critic described McLimans' typeface as "large, graceful, [and] stylized." Susan Perren, writing for the Toronto *Globe and Mail,* concluded that the book's appeal will extend beyond children to "people everywhere . . . who mourn the imminent demise of too much of this world's wildlife."

## Biographical and Critical Sources


*PERIODICALS*

*Audubon,* March-April, 2007, Julie Leibach, "Art of the Wild," p. 132.

*Capital Times* (Madison, WI), November 14, 2006, Kevin Lynch, "Illustrating a Point: McLimans Goes from Political Work to a Children's Book," p. B1.

*Globe and Mail* (Toronto, Ontario, Canada), December 2, 2006, Susan Perren, review of *Gone Wild: An Endangered Animal Alphabet,* p. D18.

*Kirkus Reviews,* August 1, 2006, review of *Gone Wild,* p. 792.

*School Library Journal,* November, 2006, Kathy Piehl, review of *Gone Wild,* p. 121.

*Wisconsin State Journal,* January 28, 2007, Melanie Conklin, "Phone Message Surprises Madison Author," p. A2.

*ONLINE*

*David McLimans Home Page,* http://davidmclimans.com (April 6, 2007).

*Graphic Classics Web site,* http://www.graphicclassics.com/ (August 6, 2007), "David McLimans."

*Portal Wisconsin Web site,* http://www.portalwisconsin.org/ (August 6, 2007), interview with McLimans.

*Prairie Wind Online,* http://www.intelligentlight.com/PrairieWind/ (August 6, 2007), Tina P. Schwartz, interview with McLimans.

*Walker Books Web site,* http://www.walkeryoungreaders.com/ (April 6, 2007), "David McLimans."


* * *

# MESTA, Gabriel
# See MOESTA, Rebecca

* * *

# MOESTA, Rebecca 1956-
# (K.J. Anderson, a joint pseudonym, Gabriel Mesta, a joint pseudonym)

## Personal

Born November 17, 1956, in Heidelberg, Germany; surname pronounced "MESS-tuh"; daughter of an English/theology teacher and a nurse; married (divorced, 1991); married Kevin J. Anderson (a writer), 1991; children: Jonathan. *Education:* California State University—Los Angeles, B.A., 1980; Boston University, M.S.B.A., 1985.

## Addresses

*Home*—c/o Anderzone, P.O. Box 767, Monument, CO 80132. *E-mail*—anderzone@aol.com.

## Career

Writer. WordFire, Inc. (editorial, publishing, and publicity company), chief executive officer.

## Writings

*Little Things* (based on the *Buffy the Vampire Slayer* television series), Simon Pulse (New York, NY), 2002.

Contributor to periodicals, including *Analog.*

*"JUNIOR JEDI KNIGHTS" SERIES*

*Anakin's Quest,* Berkley (New York, NY), 1997.
*Vader's Fortress,* Berkley (New York, NY), 1997.
*Kenobi's Blade,* Berkley (New York, NY), 1997.

*WITH HUSBAND, KEVIN J. ANDERSON*

*Star Wars: The Mos Eisley Cantina Pop-up Book,* illustrated by Ralph McQuarrie, Little, Brown (Boston, MA), 1995.
*Star Wars: The Jabba's Palace Pop-up Book,* illustrated by Ralph McQuarrie, Little, Brown (Boston, MA), 1995.
*Titan A.E.: Akima's Story,* Ace (New York, NY), 2000.
*Titan A.E.: Cale's Story,* Ace (New York, NY), 2000.
*Supernova* (movie novelization), 2000.
(Under joint pseudonym Gabriel Mesta) *Starcraft: Shadow of the Xel'Naga* (video game tie-in), 2001.
*Star Trek: The Next Generation: The Gorm Crisis* (graphic novel), illustrated by Igor Kordey, WildStorm/DC Comics (La Jolla, CA), 2001.
(Under joint pseudonym K.J. Anderson) *League of Extraordinary Gentlemen* (movie novelization), 2003.
*Crystal Doors: Island Realm,* Little, Brown (New York, NY), 2006.
*Crystal Doors: Ocean Realm,* Little, Brown (New York, NY), 2006.

*"YOUNG JEDI KNIGHTS" SERIES; WITH KEVIN J. ANDERSON*

*Heirs of the Force,* Berkley (New York, NY), 1995.
*Shadow Academy,* Berkley (New York, NY), 1995.
*The Lost Ones,* Berkley (New York, NY), 1995.
*Lightsabers,* Berkley (New York, NY), 1996.
*Darkest Knight,* Berkley (New York, NY), 1996.
*Jedi under Siege,* Berkley (New York, NY), 1996.
*Shards of Alderaan,* Berkley (New York, NY), 1996.
*Diversity Alliance,* Berkley (New York, NY), 1997.
*Delusions of Grandeur,* Berkley (New York, NY), 1997.
*Jedi Bounty,* Berkley (New York, NY), 1997.
*The Emperor's Plague,* Berkley (New York, NY), 1997.
*Return to Ord Mandel,* Berkley (New York, NY), 1998.
*Trouble on Cloud City,* Berkley (New York, NY), 1998.
*Crisis at Crystal Reef,* Berkley (New York, NY), 1998.

## Sidelights

Rebecca Moesta knew early on that she wanted to be a writer and she loved reading and watching fantasy and science-fiction television programs as early as the sec-

***Cover of Rebecca Moesta and Kevin J. Anderson's futuristic fantasy novel* Crystal Doors: Island Realm.** (Little, Brown & Company, 2006. Reproduced by permission.)

ond grade. Moesta was an early fan of the movie *Star Wars,* and among her many collaborations with her husband, writer Kevin J. Anderson, are several novels that take place within the "Star Wars" universe. Collaborating with Anderson on several novelizations and movie tie-ins, Moesta has also penned a novel in the ongoing "Buffy the Vampire Slayer" series, and has written several "Star Wars" novels for middle-grade readers.

*Crystal Doors: Island Realm,* a novel co-authored with Anderson, is Moesta's first fantasy novel set in an independent universe. The first in a trilogy, *Crystal Doors: Island Realm* focuses on teen cousins Gwen and Vic as they become involved in a battle between sea-people and their land-dwelling enemies. When Gwen's parents are mysteriously killed and Vic's mother vanishes shortly thereafter, Gwen goes to live with Vic and Uncle Cap. When she and Vic wander through one of her uncle's experiments with crystals, the two teens find themselves transported to the alternate world of Elantya. The Elantyans are land-dwelling magic users that are being threatened by sea folk called merlons, who are stopping travel between worlds. The novel "combines science, myth and magic, engaging characters, and a touch of mystery," according to Michele Winship in *Kliatt.* A *Kirkus Reviews* contributor noted the "likable teen characters and exciting plot," and Saleena L. Davidson wrote in *School Library Journal* that the coauthors' "protagonists are realistically drawn and the adventures exciting."

When asked by an online interviewer for *TheForce.net* how she keeps her perspective when writing for a younger readership, Moesta explained: "I have a son, nieces and nephews, friends who have teenagers, friends who are teenagers, etc. I talk to them and try to find out what they think about." Along with continuing her writing, Moesta works as the CEO of WordFire, an editorial and P.R. company she owns with Anderson, and has served as a judge for the Writers of the Future contest.

## Biographical and Critical Sources

*PERIODICALS*

*Booklist,* July 1, 2006, Diana Tixier Herald, review of *Crystal Doors,* p. 51.

*Kirkus Reviews,* June 1, 2006, review of *Crystal Doors: Island Realm,* p. 577.

*Kliatt,* May, 2006, Michele Winship, review of *Crystal Doors: Island Realm,* p. 11.

*Publishers Weekly,* June 5, 2000, Karen Raugust, "Life after Earth," p. 25; July 15, 2002, Melissa Mia Hall, "WordFire and False Summits," p 50.

*School Library Journal,* September, 2006, Saleena L. Davidson, review of *Crystal Doors: Island Realm,* p. 212.

*Voice of Youth Advocates,* May, 2006, Arlene Garcia, review of *Crystal Doors: Island Realm,* p. 500.

*ONLINE*

*DragonCon Web site,* http://www.dragoncon.org/ (August 6, 2007), "Rebecca Moesta."

*TheForce.net,* http://www.theforce.net/ (August 6, 2007), "Rebecca Moesta."

*Rebecca Moesta Home Page,* http://www.wordfire.com (August 6, 2007).

* * *

## MORGAN, Stevie

See DAVIES, Nicola

* * *

## MUNTEAN, Michaela

### Personal

Born in Omaha, NB; married Nik Cohn (a writer). *Education:* University of Wisconsin, degree (comparative literature).

## Addresses

*Home*—Shelter Island, NY. *Agent*—Pippin Properties, 115 E. 38th St., Ste. 2H, New York, NY 10016.

## Career

Children's book author. Western Publishing, Racine, WI, editor of children's books for two years; *Humpty Dumpty* magazine, New York, NY, editor; Workman Publishing, New York, NY, editor, 1994-99; freelance writer. Formerly worked as a teacher.

## Writings

*FOR CHILDREN*

*The Detective's Word Puzzle Book,* illustrated by Peter Bramley, Doubleday (Garden City, NY), 1981.

*The Very Bumpy Bus Ride,* illustrated by Bernard Wiseman, Parents Magazine Press (New York, NY), 1981.

*A Garden for Miss Mouse,* illustrated by Christopher Santoro, Parents Magazine Press (New York, NY), 1982.

*The Old Man and the Afternoon Cat,* illustrated by Bari Weisman, Parents Magazine Press (New York, NY), 1982.

*Panda Bear's Secret,* illustrated by Christopher Santoro, Golden Press (New York, NY), 1982.

*All about Me!,* illustrated by Ellen Appleby, Parents Magazine Press (New York, NY), 1983.

*Bicycle Bear,* illustrated by Doug Cushman, Parents Magazine Press (New York, NY), 1983.

*Theodore Mouse Goes to Sea,* illustrated by Lucinda McQueen, Golden Press (New York, NY), 1983.

*Alligator's Garden,* illustrated by Nicole Rubel, Dial (New York, NY), 1984.

*The House That Bear Built,* illustrated by Nicole Rubel, Dial (New York, NY), 1984.

*Little Lamb Bakes a Cake,* illustrated by Nicole Rubel, Dial (New York, NY), 1984.

*Monkey's Marching Band,* illustrated by Nicole Rubel, Dial (New York, NY), 1984.

*Theodore Mouse up in the Air,* illustrated by Lucinda McQueen, Golden Press (New York, NY), 1986.

*The Little Engine That Could and the Big Chase,* illustrated by Florence Graham, Platt & Munk (New York, NY), 1988.

*Bicycle Bear Rides Again,* illustrated by Doug Cushman, Parents Magazine Press (New York, NY), 1989.

*Just Joking,* Golden Books (New York, NY), 1995.

*Dinomaze: Collosal Fossil Maze Book,* mazes by Elizabeth Carpenter, Workman Publishing (New York, NY), 2001.

*Brain Quest Bedtime: 175 Stories, Poem, Questions, and Answers—Even Jokes and Riddles to Read Together with a Little Bear Named Tillie,* illustrated by Kimble Mead, Workman Publishing (New York, NY), 2002.

*Do Not Open This Book!,* illustrated by Pascal Lemaître, Scholastic (New York, NY), 2006.

*"SESAME STREET MUPPETS" SERIES*

*I Like School,* illustrated by Tom Herbert, Western Publishing (New York, NY), 1980.

*If I Lived Alone,* illustrated by Carol Nicklaus, Western Publishing (New York, NY), 1980.

*I Have a Friend,* illustrated by Marsha Winborn, Western Publishing (New York, NY), 1981.

*Look What I Found!,* illustrated by Jim Costanza, Western Publishing (New York, NY), 1981.

*Big and Little Stories,* illustrated by Maggie Swanson, Western Publishing (New York, NY), 1982.

*Every Morning at Play Group,* illustrated by Tom Cooke, Western Publishing (New York, NY), 1984.

*Muppet Babies through the Year,* illustrated by Bruce McNally, Western Publishing (New York, NY), 1984.

*Grover's Book of Cute Little Words,* illustrated by Carol Nicklaus, Western Publishing (New York, NY), 1985.

*A, My Name Is Annabel: A Sesame Street Alphabet,* illustrated by Tom Brandon, Western Publishing (New York, NY), 1986.

*Monsters, Monsters!,* illustrated by Richard Walz, Western Publishing (Racine, WI), 1987.

*Oscar's Silly ABC's, and Other Stories,* illustrated by Tom Brannon, Western Publishing (Racine, WI), 1987.

*The Runaway Soup, and Other Stories,* illustrated by Tom Cooke, Western Publishing (Racine, WI), 1987.

*In the Country,* illustrated by Tom Cooke, Western Publishing (Racine, WI), 1989.

*Getting Ready for School,* illustrated by Tom Cooke, Western Publishing (Racine, WI), 1989.

*Bert and the Magic Lamp, and Other Good-night Stories,* illustrated by Tom Cooke, Western Publishing (Racine, WI), 1989.

*Henry's New Shoes, and Other Good-night Stories,* illustrated by Carol Nicklaus, Western Publishing (Racine, WI), 1989.

*Cookie Soup, and Other Good-night Stories,* illustrated by Joe Ewers, Western Publishing (Racine, WI), 1990.

*Ernie's Window: A Neighborhood Story,* illustrated by Tom Cooke, Western Publishing (Racine, WI), 1990.

*A Grouch's Christmas,* illustrated by Tom Leigh, Western Publishing (Racine, WI), 1990.

*Wet Paint: A Color Story,* illustrated by Tom Cooke, Western Publishing (Racine, WI), 1990.

*I Want to Be a Teacher,* illustrated by David Prebenna, Western Publishing (Racine, WI), 1991.

*I Want to Be an Astronaut,* illustrated by Joe Ewers, Western Publishing (Racine, WI), 1991.

*We're Counting on You, Grover!,* illustrated by Joe Ewers, Western Publishing (Racine, WI), 1991.

*What's in Oscar's Trash Can?, and Other Good-night Stories,* illustrated by Tom Cooke, Western Publishing (Racine, WI), 1991.

*Ernie and His Merry Monsters and Other Good-night Stories,* illustrated by Tom Leigh, Western Publishing (Racine, WI), 1992.

*I Want to Be a Veterinarian,* illustrated by Tom Cooke, Western Publishing (Racine, WI), 1992.

*Kermit and the New Bicycle: A Book about Honesty,* illustrated by Tom Brannon, Grolier (Danbury, CT), 1992.

*Kermit's Cleanup: A Book about Imagination,* illustrated by Tom Brannon, Grolier (Danbury, CT), 1992.

*Something Special: A Book about Love,* illustrated by Joel Schick, Grolier (Danbury, CT), 1992.

*Nursery Rhymes ABC,* illustrated by Tom Cooke, Grolier (Danbury, CT), 1992.

*The Runaway Soup, and Other Stories,* illustrated by Tom Cooke, Western Publishing (Racine, WI), 1992.

*Elmo's Alphabet,* illustrated by Richard Walz, Western Publishing (New York, NY), 1993.

*I Want to Be President,* illustrated by Tom Brannon, Western Publishing (Racine, WI), 1993.

*Imagine—Ernie Is King,* illustrated by David Prebenna, Western Publishing (Racine, WI), 1993.

*Imagine—Grover's Magic Carpet Ride,* illustrated by Tom Brannon, Western Publishing (Racine, WI), 1993.

*The Disaster on Wheels: A Book about Helping Others,* illustrated by Tom Leigh, Grolier (Danbury, CT), 1993.

*Elmo and the Baby Animals,* illustrated by David Prebenna, Western Publishing (Racine, WI), 1994.

*Grover and the Package,* illustrated by Carol Nicklaus, Western Publishing (Racine, WI), 1994.

*Kermit and Robin's Scary Story,* illustrated by Tom Leigh, Viking (New York, NY), 1995.

*Elmo Can—Taste! Touch! Smell! See! Hear!,* illustrated by Maggie Swanson, Western Publishing (Racine, WI), 1996.

*Which Witch Is Which?,* illustrated by Tom Brannon, Western Publishing (Racine, WI), 1996.

*Zip! Pop! Hop!, and Other Fun Words to Say,* illustrated by David Prebenna, Western Publishing (Racine, WI), 1996.

*Big Bird Meets Santa Claus,* Golden Books (New York, NY), 1997.

*Elmo Can—Quack like a Duck,* illustrated by Maggie Swanson, Golden Books (New York, NY), 1997.

*Growing up Grouchy,* illustrated by David Prebenna, Golden Books (New York, NY), 1997.

*Big Bird's Baby Book,* illustrated by Tom Brannon, Golden Books (New York, NY), 1998.

*Growing up Grouch: The Story of Oscar the Grouch,* illustrated by David Prebenna, Random House (New York, NY), 2000.

*"FRAGGLE ROCK" SERIES*

*They Call Me Boober Fraggle,* illustrated by Lisa McCue, Holt (New York, NY), 1983.

*The Doozer Disaster,* illustrated by Diane Dawson Hearn, Holt (New York, NY), 1984.

*The Tale of Traveling Matt,* illustrated by Lisa McCue, Holt (New York, NY), 1984.

*What Do Doozers Do?,* illustrated by Sue Venning, Holt (New York, NY), 1984.

*Fraggle Countdown,* illustrated by Diane Dawson Hearn, Holt (New York, NY), 1985.

*Meet the Fraggles,* illustrated by Barbara Lanza, Holt (New York, NY, 1985.

*Mokey and the Festival of the Bells,* illustrated by Michael Adams, Muppet Press (New York, NY), 1985.

## Sidelights

As the oldest of seven children, Michaela Muntean had ample opportunity to hone her skill as a storyteller, and she continues to use this skill as the prolific author of numerous children's books. In addition to her many books based on late puppeteer Jim Henson's popular "Sesame Street" and "Fraggle Rock" characters, Muntean has created a number of original picture-book titles, among them *Bicycle Bear, A Garden for Miss Mouse,* and *Do Not Open This Book!*

Muntean began her career in children's literature as an editor at Western Publishing Company, based in Racine, Wisconsin, where she wrote titles for both Western and the Golden Books imprint for two years. At Western she began contributing to the publisher's "Sesame Street" series, and she continued with the long-running series after leaving for New York City and a job as editor of *Humpty Dumpty* magazine. *Kermit's Cleanup: A Book about Imagination, Elmo's Alphabet,* and *Growing up Grouch: The Story of Oscar the Grouch,* are a few of the dozens of titles Muntean has created during her years contributing to the series.

In addition to her "Sesame Street" books, Muntean has also created *Theodore Mouse Goes to Sea* and *Just Joking* for Western Publishing, while also working with illustrators such as Nicole Rubel and Doug Cushman on picture books for other publishing houses. *Bicycle Bear* and *Bicycle Bear Rides Again,* which feature Cushman's art, introduce two bears who run a bicycle delivery service. In *Bicycle Bear Rides Again* when the older bear takes a vacation, he leave his young and less-experienced nephew, Trike Bear, to handle deliveries, with humorous results.

In *Do Not Open This Book!* Pascal Lemaître's whimsical cartoon art brings to life Muntean's interactive story about a rude pig with a penchant for prose. Admonishing readers to go away while he unleashes his verbal creativity, the persnickety porker becomes frustrated when the large words he nails to a cartoon wall are blown about and reorganized with each turn of the book's actual pages. Ultimately, the crabby pig writes a story about a giant pest, leaving blanks and instructing young readers to cast themselves in the story. Lemaître's "loose-lined, messy-looking cartoons in glossy, bold colors suit the truculent tone" of Muntean's tale, noted *School Library Journal* contributor Joy Fleishhacker, and in *Booklist* critic Jennifer Mattson praised *Do Not Open This Book!* as a "playful send-up of the writing process." With its "irreverent, interactive premise," Mattson added, Muntean's story will inspire young readers "with a fresh understanding of the powerful qualities of words."

## Biographical and Critical Sources

*PERIODICALS*

*Booklist,* March 15, 2006, Jennifer Mattson, review of *Do Not Open This Book!,* p. 53.

*Bulletin of the Center for Children's Books,* March, 2006, review of *Do Not Open This Book!,* p. 321.

*Kirkus Reviews,* February 15, 2006, review of *Do Not Open This Book!,* p. 188.

*New York Times Book Review,* November 12, 2006, review of *Do Not Open This Book!,* p. 22.

*Publishers Weekly,* January 27, 1984, review of *Alligator's Garden,* p. 75; January 9, 2006, review of *Do Not Open This Book!,* p. 52.

*School Library Journal,* January, 1983, review of *A Garden for Miss Mouse,* p. 63; March, 1983, Terri M. Roth, review of *The Old Man and the Afternoon Cat,* p. 165; March, 1984, Craighton Hippenhammer, review of *Bicycle Bear,* p. 148; September, 1984, Candy Colborn, review of *Muppet Babies through the Year,* p. 107; November, 1984, Sue Venning, review of *What Do Doozers Do?,* p. 114; March, 1985, Jean Gaffney, review of *The Doozer Disaster,* p. 156; November, 1985, Susan Powers, review of *Meet the Fraggles,* p. 74; February, 1986, Carolyn Noah, review of *Mokey and the Festival of the Bells,* p. 70; March, 1996, Mary Ann Bursk, review of *Kermit and Robin's Scary Story,* p. 176; April, 2006, Joy Fleishhacker, review of *Do Not Open This Book!,* p. 114.

*Tribune Books* (Chicago, IL), Mary Harris Russell, review of *Do Not Open This Book!,* p. 7.

*ONLINE*

*Pippin Properties Web site,* http://www.pippinproperties.com/ (August 17, 2007), Michaela Muntean.

# P

## PATRON, Susan 1948-

### Personal

Born March 18, 1948, in San Gabriel, CA; daughter of George Thomas (a business owner) and Rubye (a homemaker) Hall; married Rene Albert Patron (a rare book restorer), July 27, 1969. *Education:* Pitzer College, B.A., 1969; Immaculate Heart College, M.L.S., 1972.

### Addresses

*Home*—CA.

### Career

Librarian and author. Los Angeles Public Library, Los Angeles, CA, children's librarian, 1972-79, senior children's librarian, 1979-2007. Served on several awards committees; taught courses in children's literature. Member of board of advisors, KCET public television's *Storytime* program.

### Member

Society of Children's Book Writers and Illustrators (member of board), Author's Guild, American Library Association, California Library Association, International Guild of Knot Tyers.

### Awards, Honors

American Library Notable Book designation, 1993, and *Parenting* magazine Certificate of Excellence, both for *Maybe Yes, Maybe No, Maybe Maybe;* Children's Literature Council of Southern California Dorothy McKenzie Award, Friends of Children oand Literature Award, PEN USA Literary Award finalist in children's literature category, and Newbery Medal for Children's Literature, all 2007, all for *The Higher Power of Lucky.*

### Writings

(With Christopher Weimann) *Marbled Papers: Being a Collection of Twenty-two Contemporary Hand-Marbled Papers,* Dawson's Book Shop, 1978.

*Burgoo Stew,* illustrated by Mike Shenon, Orchard Books (New York, NY), 1991.

*Five Bad Boys, Billy Que, and the Dustdobbin,* illustrated by Mike Shenon, Orchard Books (New York, NY), 1992.

*Bobbin Dustdobbin,* illustrated by Mike Shenon, Orchard Books (New York, NY), 1993.

*Maybe Yes, Maybe No, Maybe Maybe,* illustrated by Dorothy Donahue, Orchard Books (New York, NY), 1993.

*Dark Cloud Strong Breeze,* illustrated by Peter Catalanotto, Orchard Books (New York, NY), 1994.

*The Higher Power of Lucky,* illustrated by Matt Phelan, Atheneum (New York, NY), 2006.

Work included in anthology *Expectations,* published in Braille, 1992. Contributor of reviews to periodicals, including *School Library Journal* and *Five Owls.*

### Adaptations

*The Higher Power of Lucky* was adapted as an audiobook by Listening Library, 2007.

### Sidelights

Susan Patron grew up in Los Angeles, California, the middle of three sisters and, as she once told *SATA,* "a reader, dreamer, eavesdropper, washer of cars, shiner of shoes, mower of lawns, director of elaborate neighborhood plays, and teller of stories." Although she eventually pursued a career in library science, Patron also channeled her natural curiosity, her admitted expertise as an eavesdropper, and her skills as an observer into writing. Writing for the elementary grades, she has produced the books *Five Bad Boys, Billy Que, and the Dustdobbin, Dark Cloud Strong Breeze,* and *Maybe Yes, Maybe No, Maybe Maybe,* as well as her Newbery Medal-winning novel *The Higher Power of Lucky.* "I hope that by sharing vividly remembered feelings from childhood in my stories, I will be giving readers or listeners a way of recognizing and articulating their own," Patron noted of her work writing for children.

*Cover of Susan Patron's award-winning novel* **The Higher Power of Lucky,** *featuring artwork by Matt Phelan.* (Illustration © 2006 by Matt Phelan. Reprinted by permission of Atheneum Books for Young Readers, an imprint of Simon & Schuster Macmillan.)

Patron knew by age eight that she wanted to be a writer. "Confiding this ambition to my father, I received both encouragement (go ahead: if you want to be a writer, write) and excellent advice (learn how to type)," she recalled. "He also told me I wouldn't have to go far to find story ideas; all I had to do was keep my ears open. He was right. I began eavesdropping and hearing stories everywhere." After graduating with a B.A. from Pitzer College, she earned a library-science degree and in 1972 joined the staff of the Los Angeles Public Library, where she worked until her retirement in 2007. As a children's librarian, Patron read numerous children's books to groups of preschoolers and elementary school children. In addition to creating STORY: Seniors Taking the Opportunity to Reach Youth, an innovative program in which older adults were recruited and taught storytelling techniques, Patron also gained a familiarity with the stories young readers most enjoyed. Her first book, *Burgoo Stew,* was published in 1991, beginning her career as a children's book author. Describing the book as a "jaunty variation" on the classic story "Stone Soup," a *Publishers Weekly* reviewer praised Patron's debut picture book as "superbly narrated" and "an ideal read-aloud."

In Patron's novels *Five Bad Boys, Billy Que, and the Dustdobbin* and *Bobbin Dustdobbin,* the protagonist from *Burgoo Stew* returns to entertain readers. In these picture books Billy Que is joined by several of his ne'erdowell friends, as well as by Hob and Bobbin, a pair of "dustdobbins" that live amid the dust beneath Billy Que's bed. In *Five Bad Boys, Billy Que, and the Dustdobbin* Billy Que almost steps on the tiny Hob, prompting the angry creature to shrink the man to pencil height and assign him a series of tasks in the hopes that he become more tolerant of tiny creatures. Brought to life in watercolor art by Mike Shenon, *Bobbin Dustdobbin* finds a dustdobbin family threatened when the five bad boys arrive to celebrate Billy Que's birthday and offer to do gus chores—including sweeping the dust out from under the bed. Noting the "sly humor" in *Five Bad Boys, Billy Que, and the Dustdobbin,* as well as Shenon's "large, comical illustrations," *Horn Book* contributor Hanna B. Zieger deemed the work "an original and satisfying story to share." "Patron's ambitious text has plenty of verve," noted a *Publishers Weekly* contributor in reviewing *Bobbin Dustdobbin,* and Maeve Visser Knoth deemed the story "clever and very funny" in her *Horn Book* review. "I hear in my mind the voices of my Mississippi grandparents, Baby R. Della and Homer, as these stories spin out," Patron explained of her "Billy Que" books, adding that "they are meant to be told or read aloud like stories from the folk tradition."

*Dark Cloud Strong Breeze* takes a folkloric approach to a modern predicament as a girl and her father find themselves locked outside their automobile as an ominous rainstorm approaches. While Dad fumbles with the lock, the daughter takes a more active approach to the problem, and goes in search of a locksmith. As each step toward an ultimate solution brings its own problem, the girl soon enlists the help of a succession of other people and animals to solve the problem. "Patron's distinctive language makes this an obvious choice" for storytelling, according to *Booklist* reviewer Kay Weisman, and in *Publishers Weekly* a critic cited the story's "insistently rhythmic rhyme" as well as praising illustrator Peter Catalanotto's "splendid paintings." Describing *Dark Cloud Strong Breeze* as "a rhythmic, circular tale for very young children [that] moves back and forth between the fanciful and the mundane, the wish-world and the everyday one," Patron herself was especially pleased with the book's illustrations. "I had long admired the way that the artist Peter Catalanotto paints both [fanciful and mundane] qualities into his beautiful illustrations, so I asked my editor, Richard Jackson—a man of great vision—whether he thought Mr. Catalanotto might be interested in working on my story. To my great happiness, he was."

Moving to slightly older readers, Patron's elementary-grade novel *Maybe Yes, Maybe No, Maybe Maybe* focuses on middle sister PK, who is sandwiched between the drama of beautiful, pre-adolescent older sister Megan and the incessant questions posed by tenacious little sister Rabbit. With a working mom, the sisters look to each other much of the time, and imaginative PK provides the spark to inspire creativity and fun; as a *Publishers Weekly* critic noted, "PK's dreamy and determined character is endearing; her small revelations are the very stuff that growing up is made of." When the family must move to a new apartment, their feelings of dislocation are soothed by PK's characteristically entertaining stories. "It is the author's distinctive voice and characters rather than the plot that drive this engaging novel," wrote *Horn Book* contributor Nancy Vasilakis in a review of *Maybe Yes, Maybe No, Maybe Maybe.* As Vasilakis added, Patron's book will appeal to "gifted readers" through its insightful story and beginning chapter-book readers due to its simple vocabulary.

A dozen years would pass between *Maybe Yes, Maybe No, Maybe Maybe* and Patron's next book, the Newbery Medal-winning novel *The Higher Power of Lucky.* The reasons for the lengthy span were several: a form of writer's block that prevented Patron from finding the emotional core of the story; the death of her mother enabled Patron to unlock the feelings of sadness and loss that motivate the actions of her young protagonist and ground them in the complex backstory. On the heels of her Newbery win, Patron was hard at work on a sequel to the novel, scheduled for publication in 2009.

In *The Higher Power of Lucky,* readers meet ten-year-old Lucky Trimble, a girl whose love of both stories and science inspires her to want more than what her small California desert mining town can offer. Lucky is fascinated with the emotional lives of others in town, particularly Short Sammy, a local hippie/recovering alcoholic who often speaks at the many twelve-step group meetings she overhears. Like the twelve-steppers, the girl hopes to discover her own "higher power," and she estimates that the tragic death of her mom, the disinterest of her widowed father, and the ennui she senses in her legal guardian combine intensity to qualify as hitting rock bottom. Fearing abandonment, Lucky ultimately runs away from home during a dust storm, and ultimately comes to term with her grief while learning to appreciate her unique situation and its many blessings. "Lucky is a true heroine, especially because she's not perfect," maintained Francisca Goldsmith in *Booklist,* and *School Library Journal* reviewer Adrienne Furness cited the novel's austere setting as well as its "quirky cast and local color." Dubbing *The Higher Power of Lucky* "a small gem," a *Kirkus Reviews* writer praised Patron as a "master of light but sure characterization and closely observed detail." In its short chapters, told in the third person, the book "reflect[s] the cyclical, episodic nature of life" in small-town California, noted *Horn Book* contributor Elissa R. Gershowitz, the critic praising Patron's "meandering yet meticulously crafted sentences" and "sensory descriptions" of her book's unique characters and stark desert setting.

## Biographical and Critical Sources

*PERIODICALS*

*Booklist,* September 15, 1991, review of *Burgoo Stew,* p. 153; November 1, 1992, Ilene Cooper, review of *Five Bad Boys, Billy Que, and the Dustdobbin,* p. 522; March 15, 1993, Deborah Abbott, review of *Maybe Yes, Maybe No, Maybe Maybe,* p. 1322; March 15, 1994, Kay Weisman, review of *Dark Cloud Strong Breeze,* p. 1374; December 1, 2006, Francisca Goldsmith, review of *The Higher Power of Lucky,* p. 178.

*Horn Book,* September-October, 1991, Ellen Fader, review of *Burgoo Stew,* p. 606; January-February, 1993, Hanna B. Zeiger, review of *Five Bad Boys, Billy Que, and the Dustdobbin,* p. 77; July-August, 1993, Nancy Vasilakis, review of *Maybe Yes, Maybe No, Maybe Maybe,* p. 459; March-April, 1994, Maeve Visser Knoth, review of *Bobbin Dustdobbin,* p. 225; May-June, 1994, Nancy Vasilakis, review of *Dark Cloud Strong Breeze,* p. 318; January-February, 2007, Elissa R. Gershowitz, review of *The Higher Power of Lucky,* p. 71; July-August, 2007, Richard Jackson, review of *The Higher Power of Lucky,* p. 339, and Susan Patron, transcript of Newbery Acceptance Speech.

*Kirkus Reviews,* July 15, 1991, review of *Burgoo Stew,* p. 939; September 1, 1992, review of *Five Bad Boys, Billy Que, and the Dustdobbin,* p. 1133; March 3, 1993; October 15, 2006, review of *The Higher Power of Lucky,* p. 1077.

*Publishers Weekly,* August 23, 1991, review of *Burgoo Stew,* p. 61; August 31, 1992, review of *Five Bad Boys, Billy Que, and the Dustdobbin,* p. 77; April 5, 1993, review of *Maybe Yes, Maybe No, Maybe Maybe,* p. 78; September 6, 1993, review of *Bobbin Dustdobbin,* p.95; January 31, 1994, review of *Dark Cloud Strong Breeze,* p. 88; March 6, 1995.

*School Library Journal,* October, 1991, review of *Burgoo Stew,* pp. 111-112; December, 1992, review of *Five Bad Boys, Billy Que, and the Dustdobbin*; March, 1993; October, 1993, p. 107, review of *Maybe Yes, Maybe No, Maybe Maybe;* December, 2006, Adrienne Furness, review of *The Higher Power of Lucky,* p. 152.

* * *

# PEARSON, Ridley 1953-
# (Wendell McCall, Steven Rimbauer)

## Personal

Born March 13, 1953, in Glencove, NY; son of Robert G. (a writer) and Betsy (an artist) Pearson; married second wife, Marcelle Marsh; children: Paige, Storey (daughters). *Education:* Attended University of Kansas, 1972, and Brown University, 1974.

## Addresses

*Home*—Sun Valley, ID. *Office*—P.O. Box 715, Boise, ID 83701. *Agent*—Albert Zuckerman, Writer's House, Inc., 21 W. 26th St., New York, NY 10010.

## Career

Novelist and screenwriter. Worked variously as a songwriter for a touring bar band, a dishwasher, and a housekeeper in a hospital surgery suite; composer of orchestral score for documentary film *Cattle Drive.* Bass guitarist for Rock Bottom Remainders (literary garage band), with Dave Barry, Amy Tan, and Stephen King.

## Member

Writers Guild of America.

## Awards, Honors

Raymond Chandler Fulbright fellowship in detective fiction, Oxford University, 1990.

## Writings

*NOVELS*

*Never Look Back: A Novel of Espionage and Revenge,* St. Martin's Press (New York, NY), 1985.
*Blood of the Albatross,* St. Martin's Press (New York, NY), 1986.
*The Seizing of the Yankee Green Mall,* St. Martin's Press (New York, NY), 1987.
*Undercurrents,* St. Martin's Press (New York, NY), 1988.
*Probable Cause,* St. Martin's Press (New York, NY), 1990.
*Hard Fall,* Delacorte (New York, NY), 1992.
*The Angel Maker,* Delacorte (New York, NY), 1993.
*No Witnesses,* Hyperion (New York, NY), 1994.
*Chain of Evidence,* Hyperion (New York, NY), 1995.
*Beyond Recognition,* Hyperion (New York, NY), 1997.
*The Pied Piper,* Hyperion (New York, NY), 1998.
*The First Victim,* Hyperion (New York, NY), 1999.
*Middle of Nowhere,* Hyperion (New York, NY), 2000.
*Parallel Lies,* Hyperion (New York, NY), 2001.
(As Steven Rimbauer) *The Diary of Ellen Rimbauer: My Life at Rose Red* (also see below), foreword by Stephen King, Hyperion (New York, NY), 2001.
*The Art of Deception,* Hyperion (New York, NY), 2002.
*The Body of David Hayes,* Hyperion (New York, NY), 2004.
*Cut and Run,* Hyperion (New York, NY), 2005.
*Killer Weekend,* Putnam's (New York, NY), 2007.

*"NEVERLAND ISLAND" SERIES; FOR CHILDREN*

(With Dave Barry) *Peter and the Starcatchers* (inspired by *Peter Pan* by J.M. Barrie), illustrated by Greg Call, Hyperion/Disney Editions (New York, NY), 2004.
(With Dave Barry) *The Missing Mermaid,* Hyperion/Disney Editions (New York, NY), 2005.
(With Dave Barry) *Escape from the Carnivale,* illustrated by Greg Call, Hyperion/Disney Editions (New York, NY), 2006.
(With Dave Barry) *Peter and the Shadow Thieves,* illustrated by Greg Call, Hyperion/Disney Editions (New York, NY), 2006.
(With Dave Barry) *Cave of the Dark Wind,* Hyperion/Disney Editions (New York, NY), 2007.
(With Dave Barry) *Peter and the Secret of Rundoon,* Hyperion/Disney Editions (New York, NY), 2007.

*OTHER*

*The Diary of Ellen Rimbauer* (television miniseries; based on the book of the same title), American Broadcasting Corp., 2003.
*The Kingdom Keepers* (middle-grade novel), Hyperion/Disney Editions (New York, NY), 2005.

Author of screenplay adaptations of his novels *Probable Cause* and *Undercurrents.* Also author, under pseudonym Wendell McCall, of novel *Aim for the Heart,* St. Martin's Press. Work included in anthology *Diagnosis: Terminal,* edited by E. Paul Wilson, Forge (New York, NY), 1996.

## Adaptations

*Angel Maker, No Witnesses,* and *Undercurrents,* were optioned for film by Home Box Office; *Hard Fall* was optioned for film by Amadeo Ursini; film rights to *Probable Cause* were acquired by Ted Hartley of RKO; *Peter and the Shadow Thieves,* was optioned for film by Disney, 2006. Several books by Pearson have been adapted as audiobooks by Brilliance Audio, including *Parallel Lies,* 2001; *Peter and the Shadow Thieves,* 2006; and *Escape from the Carnivale,* read by Jim Dale, 2006.

## Sidelights

Although Ridley Pearson is best known to adult readers for the police procedurals he has been writing since the mid-1980s, he has also gained a following among younger readers through the middle-grade adventure novel *The Kingdom Keepers,* as well as through the fantasy fiction he writes in collaboration with humorist Dave Barry for the "Never Land Adventure" series. Inspired by the world created in *Peter Pan*—the 1953 Disney film more than the play by well-known nineteenth-century English writer J.M. Barrie—the "Never Land Adventure" books focus on a group of children living on Mollusk Island, where adventures and fantasy collide. Featuring familiar characters such as Peter Pan, the orphaned Lost Boys, Captain Hook, and Tinker Bell as well as introducing Molly Astor, Black Stache the pirate, Lord Ombra, Little Scallop the mermaid, and the Starcatchers, the series includes *Peter and the Starcatchers, Peter and the Shadow Thieves,* and *Escape from the Carnivale.*

Pearson and Barry set the stage for their fantasy series in *Peter and the Starcatchers,* which finds Peter at the head of a band of orphans enslaved by pirate captain

Black Stache aboard the pirate ship *Never Land.* When the ship wrecks near a small island, the boys gain their freedom and find themselves allied with a secret society called the Starcatchers. Working with apprentice starcatcher Mary Astor, Peter and the boys hope to beat an evil band of Others in locating a lost trunk of starstuff, a magical material that gives those who possess it happiness, braininess, and the power of flight. Crocodiles, mermaids, jungle-dwelling natives, and other creatures all figure in the authors' series opener. Describing the novel as "compulsively readable," a *Kirkus Reviews* writer added that *Peter and the Starchasers* will draw even reluctant readers in with its "never-a-dull-moment plot." In *School Library Journal,* Margaret A. Chang deemed the novel a "smoothly written page-turner [that] just might send readers back to [Barrie's] . . . original." The "real lure is the richly drawn characters," wrote *Booklist* critic Ilene Cooper, noting that the book's villainous characters "exhibit just the right amount of swagger and smirk." In *Publishers Weekly* a critic concluded that "Peter Pan fans will find much to like in [Pearson and Barry's] . . . what-if scenario."

In *Peter and the Shadow Thieves* the Others come in search of the magic stardust. Led by the evil nonhuman, soul-stealing Lord Ombra, the Others intend to gain possession of this magic dust so that Lord Ombra can channel its power and rule the world. Tracking Molly and the Starcatchers to London, Ombra's ship quickly sails off in pursuit. Now Peter, Tinkerbell, and their friends must find the stardust first, and send it back into the heavens before Ombra achieves his evil goal. According to *School Library Journal* contributor Eva Mitnick, *Peter and the Shadow Thieves* is "filled with enough rollicking, death-defying adventure to satisfy anyone," and the novel's "breathless chases," set in a world of "Dickensian squalor," results in "scenes that are rich in color." Writing that Pearson and Barry "do not disappoint" in their second novel for young readers, *Booklist* reviewer GraceAnne A. DeCandido went on to note that *Peter and the Shadow Thieves* "sustain[s] the . . . lively pace" through "short chapters packed with action and well-chosen details."

As Pearson and Barry have expanded their collaboration, they have also expanded their audience to younger readers in books such as *Escape from the Carnivale.* Geared for preteen readers, this novel focuses on Little Scallop and her friends Aqua and Surf, as they venture beyond the safety of their island coral reef in search of pearls. When Surf is captured by the crew of the ship *Carnivale,* Lost Boy James must marshal his dolphin friends to free the mermaid from the ruthless pirate band. The characters in *Escape from the Carnivale* return in several other "Never Land Adventure" novels, among them *Cave of the Dark Wind.*

Pearson's first series of forensic thrillers for adults, which include *Chain of Evidence, The Angel Maker, Beyond Recognition,* and *The Body of David Hayes,* is set in the Pacific northwest. Based in Seattle, Washington, recurring series characters detective Lou Boldt and police psychologist Daphne Matthews follow the highly technical trails of evidence that Pearson's criminals leave behind, resulting in books that have won the author an enduring readership. In addition to catapulting readers into the detective's hunt for serial killers and other murderers, the novels focus on the on-again, off-again romance between Pearson's two sleuths. "Some procedurals stress forensic detail, while others emphasize the multidimensional humanity of the cops," wrote Bill Ott in his *Booklist* review of *Chain of Evidence.* "Pearson does both," Ott concluded, "and the combination continues to be unbeatable." Pearson "makes complicated, potentially disgusting facts almost entertaining," maintained a *Publishers Weekly* contributor in a review of *The Angel Maker,* the critic adding that the author's "engaging forensic detail . . . and brisk prose will have readers racing to the cliffhanger climax."

*Ridley Pearson and Dave Barry collaborate on the middle-grade fantast novel* **Escape from the Carnivale,** *part of their "Neverland Island" series featuring artwork by Greg Call.* (Illustration © 2006. Reproduced by permission of Hyperion Books for Children.)

Critics have consistently praised Pearson for his ability to create taut plots that incorporate the latest in forensic technology. In *No Witnesses* a serial killer bent on exacting revenge against a food company begins poisoning the company's products, faxing extortion notes, and using ATM's to retrieve ransom money, thereby leaving no physical trace for Detective Boldt to track. "Pearson's grasp of investigative technology is truly impressive," noted Marilyn Stasio in a *New York Times* review of the novel, while Ott found "the combination of meticulous investigative detail and excruciating, screw-tightening suspense . . . utterly riveting."

*Beyond Recognition* finds a serial killer disposing of victims' bodies with rocket fuel, which burns so hot it leaves almost no trace behind. Pearson brings the suspense home to Detective Boldt in *The Pied Piper,* as the detective's own daughter is kidnapped when Boldt gets too close to identifying a serial kidnapper, while *The Art of Deception* follows Boldt's investigation of a pair of suspicious deaths that ultimately point to a murderer who may not be finished yet. In *The Body of David Hayes* when a former beau of Liz Boldt seeks the detective's wife's help in resolving a fraud conviction the past romantic relationship threatens both Lou's current investigation and his marriage. "Moving from one punchy scene to the next, this fuse-burning suspense tale is wonderful reading for a wide audience," noted Molly Gorman in a *Library Journal* review of *Beyond Recognition,* and *Library Journal* contributor Jeff Ayers praised *The Art of Deception* for "atmospheric descriptions of Seattle . . . [that are] dead-on." Ott also commended Pearson's setting, noting that the novelist's "detail-rich treatment goes well beyond the typical clichés of dark passages and abandoned storefronts" and praising the "Boldt and Matthews" novels as among "the mystery genre's greatest pleasures." Noting Pearson's focus on "the sinews that hold together a long-term marriage" in *The Body of David Hayes,* Ott maintained that the novel "adds depth and resonance to the ongoing series."

*Cover of Pearson's 2006 middle-grade fantasy adventure* **The Kingdom Keepers,** *featuring artwork by David Frankland.* (Illustration © 2005 by David Frankland. Reproduced by permission of Hyperion Books for Children.)

In addition to his "Boldt-Matthews" series, Pearson has also written several standalone novels. He moves his setting to his adopted home town of Sun Valley, Idaho in the novel *Killer Weekend.* Here, in the proposed first novel in a new series, the author introduces Sheriff Walt Fleming as he battles the chaos that erupts in his resort community during an annual conference of celebrities and powerbrokers. Reviewing this novel in *Booklist,* Allison Block recalled Pearson's long and successful career, commending the author for his "cleverly interwoven plots and crisp, economical prose."

## Biographical and Critical Sources

*PERIODICALS*

*Booklist,* August, 1994, Bill Ott, review of *No Witnesses,* p. 1993; September 1, 1995, Bill Ott, review of *Chain of Evidence,* p. 6; December 15, 1996, Bill Ott, review of *Beyond Recognition,* p. 693; May 1, 2001, review of *Parallel Lies,* p. 1638; June 1, 2002, Bill Ott, review of *The Art of Deception,* p. 1646; February 1, 2004, Bill Ott, review of *The Body of David Hayes,* p. 933; September 1, 2004, Ilene Cooper, review of *Peter and the Starcatchers,* p. 121; June 1, 2006, GraceAnne A. DeCandido, review of *Peter and the Shadow Thieves,* p. 66; February 15, 2007, Allison Block, review of *Killer Weekend,* p. 4.

*Entertainment Weekly,* October 27, 1995, Tom De Haven, review of *Chain of Evidence,* p. 83; April 9, 2004, Adam B. Vary, review of *The Body of David Hayes,* p. 93.

*Kirkus Reviews,* July 1, 2002, review of *The Art of Deception,* p. 911; February 1, 2004, review of *The Body of David Hayes,* p. 105; August 1, 2004, review of *Peter and the Starcatchers,* p. 737; August 15, 2005, review of *The Kingdom Keepers,* p. 919; June 1, 2006, review of *Peter and the Shadow Thieves,* p. 568; August 1, 2006, review of *Escape from the Carnivale,* p. 789.

*Library Journal,* January, 1997, p. 149; May 1, 1998, p. 156; July, 2002, Jeff Ayers, review of *The Art of Deception,* p. 122.

*New York Times,* October 56, 1986, section 7, p. 28; August 1, 1993; November 20, 1994; October 22, 1995.

*Publishers Weekly,* February 8, 1993, review of *The Angel Makers,* p. 74; August 15, 1994, review of *No Witnesses,* p. 85; September 18, 1995, review of *Chain of Evidence,* p. 11; June 3, 1996, review of *Diagnosis: Terminal,* p. 62; December 16, 1996, review of *Beyond Recognition,* p. 42; July 13, 1998, review of *The Pied Piper,* p. 63; July 1, 2002, review of *The Art of Deception,* p. 53; July 8, 2002, Dena Croog, "'Rimbauer' Author Unmasked," p. 18; February 23, 2004, review of *The Body of David Hayes,* p. 46; August 23, 2004, review of *Peter and the Starcatchers,* p. 55; March 14, 2005, review of *Cut and Run,* p. 46; October 10, 2005, review of *The Kingdom Keepers,* p. 62; May 7, 2007, Bridget Kinsella, "Ridley Pearson Gets Real in Sun Valley," p. 37; May 14, 2007, review of *Killer Weekend,* p. 32.

*School Library Journal,* October, 2004, Margaret A. Chang, review of *Peter and the Starcatchers,* p. 154; January, 2006, Mara Alpert, review of *The Kingdom Keepers,* p. 142; August, 2006, Eva Mitnick, review of *Peter and the Shadow Thieves,* p. 64; January, 2007, B. Allison Gray, review of *Escape from the Carnivale,* p. 68.

*ONLINE*

*Book Haven,* http://www.thebookhaven.homestead.com/ (August 28, 2003), Amy Carother, review of *The Diary of Ellen Rimbauer: My Life at Rose Red.*

*Ridley Pearson Home Page,* www.ridleypearson.com (August 27, 2007).*

* * *

# PEREZ, Lucia Angela 1973-

## Personal

Born 1973, in TX; daughter of Gloria Osuna Perez (an artist); children. *Education:* University of Texas at Arlington, B.F.A.

## Addresses

*Home*—Southern CA. *E-mail*—the_angelperez@yahoo.com.

## Career

Illustrator, actress, and caterer. Art teacher and presenter at workshops. *Exhibitions:* Work exhibited in museums and galleries in Texas and Southern California.

## Illustrator

(With mother, Gloria Osuna Perez) Joe Hayes, reteller, *Little Gold Star/Estrellita de oro: A Cinderella Cuento,* Cinco Puntos Press (El Paso, TX), 2002.

Tish Hinojosa, *Cada niño/Every Child: A Bilingual Songbook for Kids,* Cinco Puntos Press (El Paso, TX), 2002.

Jorge Argueta, *Talking with Mother Earth/Hablando con Madre Tierra: Poems,* Groundwood Books (Toronto, Ontario, Canada), 2006.

Contributor of illustrations to educational materials, including *Treasures,* Macmillan McGraw-Hill. Work included in *Contemporary Chicano and Chicana Art,* Bilingual Press (AZ).

## Biographical and Critical Sources

*PERIODICALS*

*Booklist,* May 15, 2000, Ilene Cooper, review of *Little Gold Star/Estrellita de oro: A Cinderella Cuento,* p. 1756; June 1, 2002, Shelle Rosenfeld, review of *Cada niño/Every Child: A Bilingual Songbook for Kids,* p. 1714.

*School Library Journal,* June, 2000, Ann Welton, review of *Little Gold Star,* p. 132; June, 2002, Ann Welton, review of *Cado Niño,* p. 128; October, 2006, Maria Otero-Boisvert, review of *Talking with Mother Earth/Hablando con Madre Tierra: Poems,* p. 144.

*ONLINE*

*Lucia Angela Perez Home Page,* http://www.luciaperez.com (August 17, 2007).*

# R

## RIMBAUER, Steven
See PEARSON, Ridley

* * *

## ROBBERECHT, Thierry 1960-

### Personal
Born February 11, 1960, in Belgium.

### Addresses
*Home*—Brussels, Belgium.

### Career
Writer.

### Awards, Honors
Prix Bouquin-Malin, Communauté de Communes du Piémont Oloronais, 2004, for *Un cadavre derrière la porte.*

### Writings

*FOR CHILDREN*

*Ik kan weer lachen,* Clavis (Amsterdam, Netherlands), 2000.

*La belle nuit de Zaza la vache,* Nathan (Paris, France), 2000.

*Quand Papa était le roi,* Martinère Jeunesse (Paris, France), 2001.

*J'ai perdu mon sourire,* illustrated by Philippe Goossens, Martinière Jeunesse (Paris, France), 2001, translated as *Stolen Smile,* Random House (New York, NY), 2002.

*Eva in het land van de verloren zusjes,* Clavis (Amsterdam, Netherlands), 2003.

*Boze Draak,* illustrated by Philippe Goossens, Clavis (Amsterdam, Netherlands), 2003, translation published as *Angry Dragon,* Clarion (New York, NY), 2004.

*Het Meisje dat Terug in Mama's Buik Wilde,* illustrated by Philippe Goossens, Clavis (Amsterdam, Netherlands), 2004, translation published as *Back into Mommy's Tummy,* Clarion (New York, NY), 2005.

*Eva et Lisa,* Castor Flammarion (Paris, France), 2004.

*Benno is Nooit Bang,* illustrated by Philippe Goossens, Clavis (Amsterdam, Netherlands), 2005, translation published as *Sam Is Never Scared,* Clarion (New York, NY), 2006.

*Benno Buitengewoon,* illustrated by Philippe Goossens, Clavis (Amsterdam, Netherlands), 2005, translation published as *Sam Tells Stories,* Clarion (New York, NY), 2007.

*Benno Bloost,* illustrated by Philippe Goossens, Clavis (Amsterdam, Netherlands), 2006, translation published as *Sam's New Friend,* Clarion (New York, NY), 2007.

*Sarah en haar Spookjes,* illustrated by Philippe Goossens, Clavis (Amsterdam, Netherlands), 2006, translation published as *Sarah's Little Ghosts,* Clarion (New York, NY), 2007.

*FOR ADULTS*

*La disparition d'Hèléne Alistair* (novel), Casterman (Tournai, Belgium), 1996.

*Pagaille chez les samouraïs,* Casterman (Tournai, Belgium), 1997.

*Gaffe au Gourou,* Casterman (Tournai, Belgium), 1999.

*Corrida à Paris* (serial novel), Hachette (Paris, France), 2001.

*L'entuête à l'envers* (novel), Labor (Brussels, Belgium), 2005.

### Sidelights
Belgian author Thierry Robberecht began writing fiction for adults in the mid-1990s, and in 1996 publishing his first novel, *La disparition d'Hèléne Alistair.* Broadening his creative focus to include song lyrics and picture books for children while continuing his work as a

*Thierry Robberecht joins illustrator Philippe Goossens to bring to life an engaging story about a young pup coping with common childhood fears in* **Sam Is Never Scared.** (Illustration © 2005 by Clavis Uitgeverij Amsterdam-Hasselt. All right reserved. Reprinted by permission of Clarion Books, an imprint Houghton Mifflin Company.)

novelist, Robberecht writes in both French and Dutch. His picture books, which are popular with children in Europe, include collaborations with illustrator Philippe Goossens. Several have also been translated into English.

*Stolen Smile* was the first of Robberecht's children's books to reach an English-speaking audience. In the story a girl named Sophie discovers that her smile is missing. Many friends ask her what is wrong when the usually cheerful girl is unable to conjure even the most subtle grin. When she realizes that the teasing Willie has stolen her smile, Sophie confronts the boy in an effort to get it back. "Typical boy-girl playground angst fills this simple, short, and effective story," wrote Leslie Barban in a review of the book for *School Library*

*Journal.* In *Publishers Weekly* a critic dubbed *Stolen Smile* a "keenly observed drama."

In *Angry Dragon,* the narrator describes his anger as a dragon, and the angrier he gets, the more dragon-like the boy becomes. But when he finally lashes out, he feels bad for having done so, and his tears wash away the dragon. "The authenticity of the boy's emotions is clearly conveyed," wrote Maria B. Salvadore in *School Library Journal,* while a *Publishers Weekly* critic noted that "Robberecht's approach . . . reflects and legitimizes kids' feelings." The description of the narrator's tantrum is "simple, clear, nonjudgmental, and authentic," concluded *Horn Book* contributor Martha V. Parravano in a positive review of *Angry Dragon.*

A little girl copes with the loss of attention that results from due to her parents' preparations for the arrival of a baby brother in *Back into Mommy's Tummy.* When her birthday comes around, however, Robberecht's young heroine realizes that being bigger than a baby is not so bad after all. "Engagingly silly yet compassionate, this is a perfect tale to present to soon-to-be or fledging siblings," noted a *Kirkus Reviews* contributor. In *School Library Journal* Holly T. Sneeringer commented on the "easy conversational tone of the text," while Hazel Rochman wrote in *Booklist* that "the silliness and love make this story a great title for opening discussion."

Robberecht's recurring picture-book hero Sam the puppy—Benno in the original Dutch—is introduced in *Sam Is Never Scared.* As brought to life by Goossens's colorful art, Sam's friend Max is afraid of everything, and Sam sometimes teases him because of it. However, when Sam finds a spider crawling on his hand and becomes terrified, it is friend Max who helps him through. "Robberecht's text is the perfect springboard for conversations with young children," wrote a *Kirkus Reviews* critic, the reviewer noting that themes of peer pressure also appear in the story. Piper L. Nyman, reviewing *Sam Is Never Scared* for *School Library Journal,* noted that "both text and art deftly reflect the targeted age group." Sam returns in several other stories by Robberecht, including *Sam Tells Stories* and *Sam's New Friend.*

## Biographical and Critical Sources

*PERIODICALS*

*Booklist,* January 1, 2005, Jennifer Mattson, review of *Angry Dragon,* p. 874; December 1, 2005, Hazel Rochman, review of *Back into Mommy's Tummy,* p. 56; September 1, 2006, Julie Cummins, review of *Sam Is Never Scared,* p. 140.

*Horn Book,* January-February, 2005, Martha V. Parravano, review of *Angry Dragon,* p. 83.

*Kirkus Reviews,* September 1, 2004, review of *Angry Dragon,* p. 873; October 15, 2005, review of *Back into Mommy's Tummy,* p. 1145; August 15, 2006, review of *Sam Is Never Scared,* p. 850.

*Publishers Weekly,* November 4, 2002, review of *Stolen Smile,* p. 83.

*School Library Journal,* January, 2003, Leslie Barban, review of *Stolen Smile,* p. 110; December, 2004, Maria B. Salvadore, review of *Angry Dragon,* p. 118; February, 2006, Holly T. Sneeringer, review of *Back into Mommy's Tummy,* p. 108; October, 2006, Piper L. Nyman, review of *Sam Is Never Scared,* p. 124.

*ONLINE*

*Houghton Mifflin Web site,* http://www.houghtonmifflinbooks.com/ (August 6, 2007), "Thierry Robberecht."

*Livres à Gogo Web site,* http://www.livres-a-gogo.be/ (August 6, 2007), "Thierry Robberecht."

*Ricochet Jeunes Web site,* http://www.ricochet-jeunes.org/ (August 6, 2007), "Thierry Robberecht."*

* * *

# ROBERTSON, James I., Jr. 1930-
# (James Irvin Robertson, Jr.)

## Personal

Born July 18, 1930, in Danville, VA; son of J. Irvin (a banker) and Mae (Kympton) Robertson; married Elizabeth Green, June 1, 1952; children: Beth Robertson Brown, James I., III, Howard. *Education:* Randolph-Macon College, B.A., 1955; Emory University, M.A., 1956, Ph.D., 1959. *Religion:* Anglican.

## Addresses

*Home*—405 Stonegate Dr. NW, Blacksburg, VA 24060. *Office*—Department of History, Virginia Polytechnic Institute and State University, Blacksburg, VA 24061.

## Career

Historian and educator. University of Iowa, Iowa City, editor of *Civil War History,* 1959-61; George Washington University, Washington, DC, associate professorial lecturer, 1962-65; University of Montana, Missoula, associate professor of history, 1965-67; Virginia Polytechnic Institute and State University, Blacksburg, professor of history, 1967-76, C.P. Miles Professor of History, beginning 1976, chair of department, 1969-76, alumni distinguished professor, 1991—. Executive director, U.S. Civil War Centennial Commission, 1961-65; charter member of Virginia Civil War Sesquicentennial Commission. Certified football official, Atlantic Coast Conference.

*James I. Robertson, Jr.* (Photo courtesy of James I. Robertson, Jr.)

## Member

American Historical Association, Organization of American Historians, Jefferson Davis Association (member of board of directors), Ulysses S. Grant Association (member of board of directors), Southern Historical Association, Virginia Historical Society (member of board of directors).

## Awards, Honors

Harry S Truman Historical award; Mrs. Simon Baruch University award; Bennett Memorial Historical award of Randolph-Macon College; centennial medallion, U.S. Civil War Centennial Commission; honorary degrees from Randolph-Macon College and Shenandoah University.

## Writings

(Editor and author of foreword) Sarah Dawson, *A Confederate Girl's Diary*, Indiana University Press (Bloomington, IN), 1960.

(Editor and author of introduction and notes) *From Manassas to Appomattox: Memoirs of the Civil War in America*, Indiana University Press (Bloomington, IN), 1960.

*Virginia, 1861-1865: Iron Gate to the Confederacy* (booklet), Virginia Civil War Commission, 1961.

(Editor and author of introduction and notes) Walter Herron Taylor, *Four Years with General Lee*, Indiana University Press (Bloomington, IN), 1962, new edition, 1996.

(Editor) Dolly Sumner Burge, *Diary*, University of Georgia Press, 1962.

*The Stonewall Brigade*, Louisiana State University Press (Baton Rouge, LA), 1963.

*The Civil War: A Student Handbook*, U.S. Civil War Centennial Commission, 1963.

*The Sack of Lawrence: What Price Glory?*, World Co. (Lawrence, KS), 1963.

(Compiler) *Civil War History: Cumulative Index, 1955-1959*, Volumes I-V, State University of Iowa, 1963.

(Editor) John H. Worsham, *One of Jackson's Foot Cavalry*, McCowat-Mercer, 1965.

(Editor) *The Civil War Letters of General Robert McAllister*, Rutgers University Press (Rutgers, NJ), 1965.

(Editor with Allan Nevins and Bell I. Wiley) *Civil War Books: A Critical Bibliography*, two volumes, Louisiana State University Press (Baton Rouge, LA), 1967–69.

*The Concise Illustrated History of the Civil War*, Stackpole, 1971.

(Editor) *Four Years in the Stonewall Brigade*, Morningside Bookshop, 1972.

(Editor with Richard McMurry) *Rank and File: Civil War Essays in Honor of Bell Irvin Wiley*, Presidio Press, 1977.

(Compiler) *An Index Guide to the Southern Historical Society Papers, 1876-1959*, two volumes, Kraus International, 1980.

*Civil War Sites in Virginia*, University Press of Virginia (Charlottesville, VA), 1981.

*4th Virginia Infantry,* H.E. Howard (Lynchburg, VA), 1982, 2nd edition, 1991.

*18th Virginia Infantry,* H.E. Howard (Lynchburg, VA), 1984.

*Tenting Tonite: The Soldier's Life,* Time-Life Books (Alexandria, VA), 1984.

*General A.P. Hill: The Story of a Confederate Warrior,* Random House (New York, NY), 1987.

*Soldiers Blue and Gray,* University of South Carolina Press (Columbia, SC), 1988.

*Civil War Virginia: Battleground for a Nation,* University Press of Virginia (Charlottesville, VA), 1991.

*"Civil War!": America Becomes One Nation,* Knopf (New York, NY), 1992.

*The Civil War's Common Soldier,* Eastern National Park and Monument Association (Conshohocken, PA), 1994.

(Author of text) *Jackson and Lee: Legends in Gray: The Paintings of Mort Künstler,* Rutledge Hill Press (Nashville, TN), 1995.

*Stonewall Jackson: The Man, the Soldier, the Legend,* Macmillan (New York, NY), 1997.

(Author of text) *The Confederate Spirit: Valor, Sacrifice, and Honor: The Paintings of Mort Künstler,* Rutledge Hill Press (Nashville, TN), 2000.

(Editor with Hill Jordan and J.H. Segars) Bell Irvin Wiley, *The Bell Irvin Wiley Reader,* Louisiana State University Press (Baton Rouge, LA), 2001.

*Standing like a Stone Wall: The Life of General Thomas J. Jackson,* Atheneum Books for Young Readers (New York, NY), 2001.

(Author of text) *Gods and Generals: The Paintings of Mort Künstler* (companion to film *Gods and Generals*), Greenwich Workshop Press (Shelton, CT), 2002.

(Editor) *Stonewall Jackson's Book of Maxims,* Cumberland House (Nashville, TN), 2002.

(Editor) *Soldier of Southwestern Virginia: The Civil War Letters of Captain John Preston Sheffey,* Louisiana State University Press (Baton Rouge, LA), 2004.

(Editor, with William C. Davis) *Virginia at War, 1861,* University Press of Virginia (Lexington, VA), 2005.

*Robert E. Lee: Virginian Soldier, American Citizen,* Atheneum Books for Young Readers (New York, NY), 2005.

(Editor, with William C. Davis) *Virginia at War, 1862,* University Press of Virginia (Lexington, VA), 2007.

Editor of *Proceedings of the Advisory Council of the State of Virginia,* Virginia State Library, 1977. Contributor to anthology *Gods and Generals: The Illustrated Story of the Epic Civil War Film,* Newmarket Press (New York, NY), 2003. Contributor to periodicals. Member of board of editors, *Civil War History, Lincoln Herald,* and *American History Illustrated.*

## Sidelights

James I. Robertson, Jr. told *SATA:* "My interest in U.S. Civil War history is lifelong. I was born in the city known as the 'Last Capital of the Confederacy,' and had antecedents who fought in that war. I worked my way through college as a big-band drummer; and in the graduate-school years, I was also employed by an Atlanta funeral home. For twenty-eight years into my career, I devoted much of the autumns as a football official. For sixteen years, I served as a varsity official in the Atlantic Coast Conference.

"I regard myself as a social historian in a military period. My primary interest are not battles and leaders so much as they are the common soldiers, women behind the lines, and socio-military topics such as medicine, religion, prisons, and music.

"In recent years, I have tended to focus more on Virginia's role in the Civil War.

"The nature of my professorship involves my traveling across the country regularly for speaking engagements. I average 100 to 150 talks per year."

## Biographical and Critical Sources

*PERIODICALS*

*Booklist,* March 15, 1993, review of *"Civil War!": America Becomes One Nation,* p. 1341; November 15, 2005, Carolyn Phelan, review of *Robert E. Lee: Virginian Soldier, American Citizen,* p. 36.

*Bulletin of the Center for Children's Books,* July, 1992, review of *"Civil War!",* p. 303; September, 2001, review of *Standing like a Stone Wall: The Life of General Thomas J. Jackson,* p. 32; November, 2005, Deborah Stevenson, review of *Robert E. Lee,* p. 153.

*Choice,* February, 1998, M. Muir, Jr., review of *Stonewall Jackson: The Man, the Soldier, the Legend,* p. 1153; October, 2006, W.W. Rogers, Jr., review of *Virginia at War, 1861,* p. 361.

*Kirkus Reviews,* October 15, 2005, review of *Robert E. Lee,* p. 1145.

*Kliatt,* May, 2003, John E. Boyd, review of *Standing like a Stone Wall,* p. 54.

*Library Journal,* June 1, 1987, Joseph G. Dawson, III, review of *General A.P. Hill: The Story of a Confederate Warrior,* p. 107; February 15, 1997, Judy R. Reis, review of *Stonewall Jackson,* p. 142.

*New Yorker,* July 20, 1987, review of *General A.P. Hill,* p. 59.

*Publishers Weekly,* April 3, 1987, review of *General A.P. Hill,* p. 61; February 3, 1997, review of *Stonewall Jackson,* p. 86.

*School Library Journal,* June, 2001, Andrew Medlar, review of *Standing like a Stone Wall,* p. 180; January, 2005, Jane G. Connor, review of *Robert E. Lee,* p. 162.

*Voice of Youth Advocates,* October, 2005, review of *Robert E. Lee,* p. 340; December, 2001, review of *Standing like a Stone Wall,* p. 383.

* * *

# ROBERTSON, James Irvin, Jr.

See ROBERTSON, James I., Jr.

* * *

# ROOT, Barry

## Personal

Married Kimberly Bulcken (an illustrator); children: three children.

## Addresses

*Home and office*—1222 River Rd., Quarryville, PA 17566.

## Career

Illustrator.

## Awards, Honors

Best Illustrated Children's Book selection, *New York Times,* for *Someplace Else* by Carol P. Saul; Notable book designation, Carolyn W. Field Award, 2001, for *Brave Potatoes* by Toby Speed; Christopher Award, 2006, for *Game Day* by Tiki and Ronde Barber.

## Writings

*SELF-ILLUSTRATED*

*Gumbrella,* Putnam (New York, NY), 2002.

*ILLUSTRATOR*

Sam Swope, *The Araboolies of Liberty Street,* Potter (New York, NY), 1989, Farrar, Straus (New York, NY), 2001.

Roberto Piumini, *The Saint and the Circus* (translation of *Grazie di san Tonio* by Olivia Holmes), Tambourine (New York, NY), 1991.

JoAnne Stewart Wetzel, *The Christmas Box,* Knopf (New York, NY), 1992.

Marti Stone, *The Singing Fir Tree: A Swiss Folktale,* Putnam (New York, NY), 1992.

Mary Lyn Ray, *Pumpkins: A Story for a Field,* Harcourt (San Diego, CA), 1992.

Michael O. Tunnell, *Chinook!,* Tambourine (New York, NY), 1993.

Bill Martin, Jr., *Old Devil Wind,* Harcourt (San Diego, CA), 1993.

Mary Lyn Ray, *Alvah and Arvilla,* Harcourt (San Diego, CA), 1994.

Lee Bennett Hopkins, editor, *April, Bubbles, Chocolate: An ABC of Poetry,* Simon & Schuster (New York, NY), 1994.

M.L. Miller, *Those Bottles!,* Putnam (New York, NY), 1994.

Jennifer Armstrong, *Wan Hu Is in the Stars,* Tambourine (New York, NY), 1995.

Toby Speed, *Two Cool Cows,* Putnam (New York, NY), 1995.

Carol P. Saul, *Someplace Else,* Simon & Schuster (New York, NY), 1995.

Timothy R. Gaffney, *Grandpa Takes Me to the Moon,* Tambourine (New York, NY), 1996.

Tony Johnston, *Fishing Sunday,* Tambourine (New York, NY), 1996.

Toby Speed, *Whoosh! Went the Wish,* Putnam (New York, NY), 1997.

Jan Peck, *The Giant Carrot,* Dial (New York, NY), 1998.

Charlotte Towner Graeber, *Nobody's Dog,* Hyperion (New York, NY), 1998.

Kathi Appelt, *Cowboy Dreams,* HarperCollins (New York, NY), 1999.

Lee Wardlaw, *Saturday Night Jamboree,* Dial (New York, NY), 2000.

Toby Speed, *Brave Potatoes,* Putnam (New York, NY), 2000.

Robert Burleigh, *Messenger, Messenger,* Atheneum (New York, NY), 2000.

Susan Hill, *Backyard Bedtime,* HarperFestival (New York, NY), 2001.

Laura Godwin, *Central Park Serenade,* HarperCollins (New York, NY), 2002.

Terry Farish, *The Cat Who Liked Potato Soup,* Candlewick (Cambridge, MA), 2003.

Tiki and Ronde Barber, with Robert Burleigh, *By My Brother's Side,* Simon & Schuster (New York, NY), 2004.

Elizabeth Loredo, *Giant Steps,* Putnam (New York, NY), 2004.

Tiki and Ronde Barber, with Robert Burleigh, *Game Day,* Simon & Schuster (New York, NY), 2005.

Tiki and Ronde Barber, with Robert Burleigh, *Teammates,* Simon & Schuster (New York, NY), 2006.

Sarah Martin Busse and Jacqueline Briggs Martin, *Banjo Granny,* Houghton Mifflin (Boston, MA), 2006.

## Sidelights

Award-winning illustrator Barry Root has provided art for numerous picture books for young readers and he is both illustrator and writer for his original title *Gumbrella.* Root has worked with such well-known authors as Bill Martin, Jr. and Lee Bennett Hopkins, and has also illustrated picture books by famous football-star siblings Tiki and Ronde Barber. From circuses to football games to fables, Root's illustration projects range widely in subject, gaining him praise from critics. The illustrator's "zany depictions of the portly circus star and his startled menagerie are executed with a panache befitting the big top," wrote a *Publishers Weekly* critic of Root's contributions to Roberto Piumini's *The Saint and the Circus,* and in a review of his art for Michael O. Tunnel's *Chinook!* Nancy Vasilakis concluded in *Horn Book* that "children will relish the illustrations." Of Jennifer Armstrong's picture book *Wan Hu Is in the Stars,* a *Publishers Weekly* critic wrote that Root's "full-bleed gouaches perfectly complements the gentle buoyancy of the narrative," and Jan Peck's retelling of a Russian folk tale in *The Giant Carrot* benefits from Root's "depiction of the family's dirt farm and ramshackle log cabin [as] . . . full of sunshine and energy," according to a *Publishers Weekly* contributor. Writing of Elizabeth Laredo's picture book *Giant Steps, Booklist* critic Jennifer Mattson wrote that "the real stars" of the picture book "are Root's goofy, snaggle-tooth giants."

Beyond tall tales and fairy stories, Root has also illustrated collections of poetry as well as contemporary titles. In *April, Bubbles, Chocolate: An ABC of Poetry,* edited by Lee Bennett Hopkins, the collection's "random mix of moods and styles . . . is expressed in Root's bright, clear watercolor paintings," according to Hazel Rochman in *Booklist.* Reviewing the illustrator's work for *Central Park Serenade,* Laura Godwin's celebration of New York City, *Horn Book* contributor Roger Sutton noted that "Root's bird's-eye vision of Central Park" serves as an invitation "into a beautiful part of the world." A *Publishers Weekly* critic also complimented the artist's "vibrantly hued, intentionally hazy paintings." According to *School Library Journal* contributor Susan Marie Pitard, the volume's "verbal images and illustrations . . . work together seamlessly to present a joyful, busy portrait," while Karla Kushkin wrote in *Horn Book* that "Root paints . . . with a skilled

***Barry Root's warmhearted paintings appear in numerous picture books, among them* The Cat Who Liked Potato Soup, *by Terry Farish.*** (Illustration © 2003 by Barry Root. Reproduced by permission of the publisher Candlewick Press, Inc., Cambridge, MA.)

hand, using a palette so lush you can smell the warmth of summer in it."

Root also gained recognition for his artistic contribution to the football-related tales by the brothers Barber. "Root's sunny watercolors, often accented with lush, green trees, capture action on and off the field," wrote a *Publishers Weekly* contributor of *By My Brother's Side,* while in *Game Day,* the illustrator's "earth-toned watercolors capture the speed, action and colors" of the book's autumn setting, according to a *Publishers Weekly* writer. Carolyn Phelan, in her *Booklist* review of *Teammates,* maintained that "Root's vibrant watercolor-and-gouache paintings kick the story over the goalposts."

Root's first self-illustrated title, *Gumbrella,* is the story of an elephant who creates a hospital for small animals that are injured, but enjoys the company so much that it will not let the creatures go home when they have recovered. "Root cleverly depicts Gumbrella's single-minded altruism with visual winks . . . coupled with a sly voice," wrote a *Publishers Weekly* contributor. "The tone is light, the pictures are bright," noted a critic for *Kirkus Reviews,* while Anita L. Burkam maintained in *Horn Book* that "Root fully exploits the humor inherent in an elephant with a Florence Nightingale complex." Jody McCoy, reviewing *Gumbrella* for *School Library Journal,* predicted that "children will enjoy Root's first endeavor as both illustrator and author," and in *Booklist*

Ilene Cooper recommended the book as "a story hour choice that might spark discussion among little ones."

## Biographical and Critical Sources

*PERIODICALS*

*Booklist,* August, 1992, Hazel Rochman, review of *The Christmas Box,* p. 2020; October 15, 1992, Ellen Mandel, review of *Pumpkins: A Story for a Field,* p. 441; December 15, 1992, Janice Del Negro, review of *The Singing Fir Tree: A Swiss Folktale,* p. 742; April 15, 1993, Deborah Abbott, review of *Chinook!,* p. 1524; October 1, 1993, Carolyn Phelan, review of *Old Devil Wind,* p. 353; February 1, 1994, Ilene Cooper, review of *Those Bottles!,* p. 1010; May 1, 1994, Hazel Rochman, review of *April, Bubbles, Chocolate: An ABC of Poems,* p. 1603; June 1, 1995, Ilene Cooper, review of *Two Cool Cows,* p. 1789; June, 1995, Lauren Peterson, review of *Wan Hu Is in the Stars,* p. 1781; November 15, 1995, Lauren Peterson, review of *Someplace Else,* p. 565; May 15, 1996, Kay Weisman, review of *Fishing Sunday,* p. 1592; June 1, 1997, review of *The Araboolies of Liberty Street,* p. 1675; March 15, 1998, Hazel Rochman, review of *The Giant Carrot,* p. 1246; August, 1998, Ellen Mandel, review of *Nobody's Dog,* p. 2004; January 1, 1999, Ilene Cooper, review of *Cowboy Dreams,* p. 885; September 15, 2000, Shelle Rosenfeld, review of *Brave Potatoes,* p. 250; December 15, 2000, Amy Brandt, review of *Saturday Night Jamboree,* p. 829; January 1, 2001, review of *Messenger, Messenger,* p. 864; February 15, 2001, Hazel Rochman, review of *Messenger, Messenger,* p. 1152; June 1, 2002, Lauren Peterson, review of *Central Park Serenade,* p. 1737; November 15, 2002, Ilene Cooper, review of *Gumbrella,* p. 612; April 15, 2003, Carolyn Phelan, review of *The Cat Who Liked Potato Soup,* p. 1477; February 1, 2004, Jennifer Mattson, review of *Giant Steps,* p. 981; September 1, 2004, Todd Morning, review of *By My Brother's Side,* p. 114; September 1, 2005, Ilene Cooper, review of *Game Day,* p. 119; September 1, 2006, Carolyn Phelan, review of *Teammates,* p. 116; November 1, 2006, Hazel Rochman, review of *Banjo Granny,* p. 58.

*Bulletin of the Center for Children's Books,* July, 1994, review of *April, Bubbles, Chocolate,* p. 360; July, 1995, review of *Wan Hu Is in the Stars,* p. 376; October, 1995, review of *Someplace Else,* p. 68; October, 1996, review of *Grandpa Takes Me to the Moon,* p. 58; September, 1997, review of *Whoosh! Went the Wish,* p. 27; March, 1998, review of *The Giant Carrot,* p. 255; September, 1998, review of *Nobody's Dog,* p. 14; June, 2000, review of *Brave Potatoes,* p. 374; November, 2000, review of *Messenger, Messenger,* p. 98, review of *Saturday Night Jamboree,* p. 125; December, 2002, review of *Gumbrella,* p. 171; June, 2003, review of *The Cat Who Liked Potato Soup,* p. 387; February, 2004, Janice Del Negro, review of *Giant Steps,* p. 239; January, 2006, Elizabeth Bush, review of *Game Day,* p. 218; January, 2007, Deborah Stevenson, review of *Banjo Granny,* p. 205.

*Horn Book,* January-February, 1992, Nancy Vasilakis, review of *The Saint and the Circus,* p. 61; November-December, 1992, Nancy Vasilakis, review of *The Christmas Box,* p. 714, Ellen Fader, review of *Pumpkins,* p. 719; July-August, 1993, Nancy Vasilakis, review of *Chinook!,* p. 451; January-February, 1994, Mary M. Burns, review of *Old Devil Wind,* p. 65; July-August, 1994, Nancy Vasilakis, review of *April, Bubbles, Choclate,* p. 467; November-December, 1994, Ellen Fader, review of *Alvah and Arvilla,* p. 725; November-December, 1995, Nancy Vasilakis, review of *Someplace Else,* p. 737; May, 2000, review of *Brave Potatoes,* p. 300; September-October, 2002, Roger Sutton, "Not Just a Walk in the Park," p. 499, Karla Kuskin, review of *Central Park Serenade,* p. 552, Anita L. Burkham, review of *Gumbrella,* p. 559.

*Kirkus Reviews,* March 15, 2002, review of *Central Park Serenade,* p. 411; September 15, 2002, review of *Central Park Serenade,* p. 1399; May 1, 2003, review of *The Cat Who Liked Potato Soup,* p. 676; January 1, 2004, review of *Giant Steps,* p. 38; September 15, 2004, review of *By My Brother's Side,* p. 909; September 15, 2005, review of *Game Day,* p. 1020; September 15, 2006, review of *Teammates,* p. 946; November 1, 2006, review of *Banjo Granny,* p. 1121.

*New York Times Book Review,* November 12, 1989, Carol Muske, review of *The Araboolies of Liberty Street,* p. 38; October 25, 1992, review of *Pumpkins,* p. 28; May 22, 1994, Julie Zuckerman, review of *Those Bottles!,* p. 29; May 14, 2000, review of *Messenger, Messenger,* p. 26; September 21, 2003, review of *The Cat Who Liked Potato Soup,* p. 26.

*Publishers Weekly,* August 11, 1989, review of *The Araboolies of Liberty Street,* p. 457; November 1, 1991, review of *The Saint and the Circus,* p. 80; September 7, 1992, review of *The Christmas Box,* p. 66, review of *Pumpkins,* p. 92; October 12, 1992, review of *The Singing Fir Tree,* p. 78; March 15, 1993, review of *Chinook!,* p. 87; September 20, 1993, review of *Old Devil Wind,* p. 29; March 7, 1994, review of *Those Bottles!,* p. 69; September 5, 1994, review of *Alvah and Arvilla,* p. 109; May 8, 1995, review of *Two Cool Cows,* p. 294, review of *Wan Hu Is in the Stars,* p. 295; August 14, 1995, review of *Someplace Else,* p. 82; April 21, 1997, review of *Whoosh! Went the Wish,* p. 71; July 22, 1996, review of *Grandpa Takes Me to the Moon,* p. 241; December 8, 1997, review of *Two Cool Cows,* p. 74; December 22, 1997, review of *Someplace Else,* p. 61; February 16, 1998, review of *The Giant Carrot,* p. 210; June 15, 1998, review of *Nobody's Dog,* p. 59; January 18, 1999, review of *Cowboy Dreams,* p. 338; May 22, 2000, review of *Brave Potatoes,* p. 92; June 19, 2000, review of *Messenger, Messenger,* p. 79; April 30, 2001, review of *The Araboolies of Liberty Street,* p. 80; February 25, 2002, review of *Central Park Serenade,* p. 64; September 9, 2002, review of *Gumbrella,* p. 67; May 5, 2003, review of *The Cat Who Liked Potato Soup,* p. 221; February 23, 2004, review of *Giant Steps,* p. 76; August 30, 2004, review of *By My Brother's Side,* p. 55; October 3, 2005, review of *Game Day,* p. 70; October 30, 2006, review of *Banjo Granny,* p. 60.

*Quill and Quire,* December, 1994, review of *Alvah and Arvilla,* p. 35.

*School Library Journal,* December, 1989, Shirley Wilton, review of *The Araboolies of Liberty Street,* p. 90; November, 1991, Karen James, review of *The Saint and the Circus,* p. 106; October, 1992, review of *The Christmas Box,* p. 45; February, 1993, Cyrisse Jaffee, review of *The Singing Fir Tree,* p. 91; March, 1993, Susan Scheps, review of *Pumpkins,* p. 184; June, 1993, Lisa Dennis, review of *Chinook!,* p. 91; November, 1993, Joy Fleishhacker, review of *Old Devil Wind,* p. 86; April, 1994, Susan Scheps, review of *Those Bottles!,* p. 110; September, 1994, Sally R. Dow, review of *April, Bubbles, Chocolate,* p. 208; January, 1995, Martha Rosen, review of *Alvah and Arvilla,* p. 92; June, 1995, Kathy Piehl, review of *Two Cool Cows,* p. 95; July, 1995, Margaret A. Chang, review of *Wan Hu Is in the Stars,* p. 54; January, 1996, Betty Teague, review of *Someplace Else,* p. 95; April, 1996, review of *April, Bubbles, Chocolate,* p. 39; June, 1996, Virginia Golodetz, review of *Fishing Sunday,* p. 102; September, 1996, Kathy East, review of *Grandpa Takes Me to the Moon,* p. 178; September, 1997, Judith Constantinides, review of *Whoosh! Went the Wish,* p. 195; February, 1998, Beth Tegart, review of *The Giant Carrot,* p. 103; June, 1998, Lisa Dennis, review of *Nobody's Dog,* p. 106; February, 1999, Steven Engelfried, review of *Cowboy Dreams,* p. 77; June, 2000, Nina Lindsay, review of *Messenger, Messenger,* p. 102; July, 2000, Ruth Semrau, review of *Brave Potatoes,* p. 88; September, 2000, Jody McCoy, review of *Saturday Night Jamboree,* p. 211; May, 2002, Susan Marie Pitard, review of *Central Park Serenade,* p. 114; November, 2002, Jody McCoy, review of *Gumbrella,* p. 134; July, 2003, Steven Engelfried, review of *The Cat Who Liked Potato Soup,* p. 95; March, 2004, Eve Ortega, review of *Giant Steps,* p. 176; November, 2004, Ann M. Holcomb, review of *By My Brother's Side,* p. 122; January, 2006, Mary Hazelton, review of *Game Day,* p. 116; November, 2006, Rachel G. Payne, review of *Teammates,* p. 117; December, 2006, Tamara E. Richman, review of *Banjo Granny,* p. 95.

*Science Books & Films,* August, 1997, review of *Grandpa Takes Me to the Moon,* p. 163.

*Smithsonian,* November, 1992, review of *Pumpkins,* p. 201.

*Tribune Books* (Chicago, IL), June 23, 2002, review of *Central Park Serenade,* p. 5; May 18, 2003, review of *The Cat Who Liked Potato Soup,* p. 5.

*Wilson Library Bulletin,* April, 1992, Donnarae MacCann and Olga Richard, review of *The Saint and the Circus,* p. 94; December, 1993, Donnarae MacCann and Olga Richard, review of *Old Devil Wind,* p. 112.

*ONLINE*

*HarperCollins Web site,* http://www.harperacademic.com/ (August 6, 2007), "Barry Root."

*Simon & Schuster Web site,* http://www.simonsays.com/ (August 6, 2007), "Barry Root."

## RUBIN, Susan Goldman 1939-

### Personal

Born March 14, 1939, in New York, NY; daughter of Abraham (a manufacturing jeweler) and Julia (a homemaker) Moldof; married Hubert M. Goldman (a physician), June, 1959 (divorced, 1976); married Michael B. Rubin (a real estate broker), December 30, 1978; children: (first marriage) Katie Goldman Kolpas, John, Peter; (second marriage) Andrew. *Education:* Oberlin College, B.A. (English; with honors), 1959; graduate study at University of California—Los Angeles, 1961-62, attended extension program, 1980-91. *Politics:* Democrat *Religion:* Jewish. *Hobbies and other interests:* Cooking, going to movies and theater, reading.

### Addresses

*Home*—Malibu, CA. *Agent*—George M. Nicholson, Sterling Lord Literistic, Inc., 65 Bleecker St., New York, NY 10012. *E-mail*—susanrubin@yahoo.com.

### Career

Children's book writer and illustrator, 1975—; freelance writer of educational filmstrips, 1975-78. California State University Department of Continuing Education, Northridge, instructor, 1977-86; University of California Extension School Writer's Program, Los Angeles, instructor in creative writing, 1986—. Designers West, Los Angeles, editorial assistant, 1991-92.

### Member

Society for Children's Book Writers and Illustrators, PEN, Authors Guild, Authors League of America, Southern California Council on Literature for Children and Young People.

### Awards, Honors

National Endowment for the Humanities Travel to Collections grant, 1993; International Reading Association Young Adults' Choice designation, 1995, for *Emily Good as Gold;* Sydney Taylor Award Honor Book designation, 2000, and SCBWI Golden Kite Honor Book designation, 2001, both for *Fireflies in the Dark;* Children's Literature Council of Southern California Award for nonfiction, and American Library Association (ALA) Best Book for Young Adults, both 2000, both for *Margaret Bourke-White;* ALA Notable Book Designation, 2003, for *Degas and the Dance;* Association of Jewish Libraries Notable Children's Book of Jewish Content, 2006, for *The Flag with Fifty-six Stars;* Sydney Taylor Award Honor Book designation, 2006, and ALA Notable Book designation, 2007, both for *The Cat with the Yellow Star;* ALA Notable Book designation, and National Parenting Publications Gold Award, both 2006, and Southern California Independent Booksellers Association Book Award shortlist, 2007, all for *Andy Warhol: Pop Art Painter.*

## Writings

(And illustrator) *Grandma Is Somebody Special,* Albert Whitman (Morton Grove, IL), 1976.

(And illustrator) *Cousins Are Special,* Albert Whitman (Morton Grove, IL), 1978.

(And illustrator) *Grandpa and Me Together,* Albert Whitman (Morton Grove, IL), 1980.

*Walk with Danger* (young-adult mystery), Silhouette Books (New York, NY), 1986.

*The Black Orchid* (young-adult mystery), Crosswinds, 1988.

*Emily Good as Gold* (middle-grade novel), Browndeer/Harcourt (San Diego, CA), 1993.

*The Rainbow Fields,* illustrated by Heather Preston, Enchante Publishing, 1993.

*Frank Lloyd Wright* (biography; "First Impressions" series), Abrams (New York, NY), 1994.

*Emily in Love,* Browndeer/Harcourt (San Diego, CA), 1996.

*Margaret Bourke-White* (biography; "First Impressions" series), Abrams (New York, NY), 1996, published as *Margaret Bourke-White: Her Pictures Were Her Life,* 1999.

*The Whiz Kids Plugged In,* illustrated by Doug Cushman, Scholastic (New York, NY), 1997.

*The Whiz Kids Take Off!,* illustrated by Doug Cushman, Scholastic (New York, NY), 1997.

*Toilets, Toasters, and Telephones: The How and Why of Everyday Objects,* illustrated by Elsa Warnick, Harcourt (San Diego, CA), 1998.

*Fireflies in the Dark: The Story of Friedl Dicker-Brandeis and the Children of Terezin,* Holiday House (New York, NY), 2000.

*The Yellow House: Vincent van Gogh and Paul Gauguin Side by Side,* illustrated by Joseph A. Smith, Abrams (New York, NY), 2001.

*There Goes the Neighborhood: Ten Buildings People Loved to Hate,* Holiday House (New York, NY), 2001.

*Steven Spielberg: Crazy for Movies,* Abrams (New York, NY), 2001.

*Degas and the Dance: The Painter and the Petit Rats Perfecting Their Art,* Abrams (New York, NY), 2002.

*Searching for Anne Frank: Letters from Amsterdam to Iowa,* Abrams (New York, NY), 2003.

*L'Chaim!: To Jewish Life in America!: Celebrations from 1654 until Today,* Abrams (New York, NY), 2004.

*Art against the Odds: From Slave Quilts to Prison Paintings,* Crown (New York, NY), 2004.

*The Flag with Fifty-six Stars: A Gift from the Survivors of Mauthausen,* illustrated by Bill Farnsworth, Holiday House (New York, NY), 2005.

*Andy Warhol: Pop Art Painter,* Abrams (New York, NY), 2005.

(With Ela Weissberger) *The Cat with the Yellow Star: Coming of Age in Terezin,* Holiday House (New York, NY), 2006.

*Haym Salomon: American Patriot,* illustrated by David Slonim, Abrams (New York, NY), 2006.

*Edward Hopper: Painter of Light and Shadow,* Abrams (New York, NY), 2007.

*Delicious: The Life and Art of Wayne Thiebaud,* Chronicle Books (San Francisco, CA), 2007.

*Counting with Wayne Thiebaud,* Chronicle Books (San Francisco, CA), 2007.

*Andy Warhol's Colors,* Chronicle Books (San Francisco, CA), 2007.

Also author of educational filmstrips for McGraw-Hill, BFA, and Pied Piper Productions; contributor of short fiction to *Highlights for Children.*

Author's works have been translated into Italian, French, and Spanish.

## Sidelights

Susan Goldman Rubin is the author of a number of acclaimed nonfiction works for younger readers. In her biographies for children, Rubin focuses on individuals ranging from nineteenth-century Dutch painter Vincent van Gogh and documentary photographer Margaret Bourke-White to groundbreaking architect Frank Lloyd Wright and modern filmmmaker Steven Spielberg, while her other nonfiction works explore buildings, technology, and art history. In addition to nonfiction, Rubin is also the author of novels for middle graders, such as *Emily Good as Gold* and *Emily in Love,* and she has written the well-received young-adult mystery *The Black Orchid.* In several of her nonfiction titles, such as *The Flag with Fifty-six Stars: A Gift from the Survivors of Mauthausen, Fireflies in the Dark: The Story of Friedl Dicker-Brandeis and the Children of Terezin,* and *The Cat with the Yellow Star: Coming of Age in Terezin,* Rubin explores the dark period of world history known as the Holocaust.

While growing up in the Bronx, Rubin dreamed of becoming an artist and illustrating children's books. As a teen she took classes at New York City's Art Students League and also attended the High School of Music and Art. After graduation, Rubin enrolled at Oberlin College in Ohio, where she eventually received her B.A. with honors in English. "[When] I moved to California as a young wife and mother," she later recalled, "I couldn't easily go back to New York to show my portfolio and try to get illustrating assignments. So I began writing my own stories to give myself something to illustrate. When I sent my picture-book dummies to editors, I found, to my great surprise, that they were as interested in my writing as my artwork. With their rejection letters came suggestions for revisions." By now living in California, Rubin took writing classes at the University of California—Los Angeles Extension and earned her first publishing credit when one of her stories was published in *Highlights for Children* magazine.

Rubin's first published book, the self-illustrated *Grandma Is Somebody Special,* was inspired by events in her own family, as were the young-adult novels *Walk with Danger* and *The Black Orchid,* which "grew from incidents I read about in the newspaper," as Rubin

***Susan Goldman Rubin focuses on a poignant moment in Holocaust history in* The Flag with Fifty-six Stars, *a picture book featuring evocative paintings by Bill Farnsworth.*** (Illustration © by Bill Farnsworth. Reproduced by permission of Holiday House, Inc.)

recalled. Her middle-grade novels *Emily Good as Gold* and *Emily in Love* had their genesis in an educational filmstrip the author produced with her first husband. "We researched and photographed at a special school for handicapped children in Los Angeles," Rubin once explained, "and I was deeply moved by the students I met. I felt that our filmstrip would only scratch the surface in terms of changing people's negative attitudes toward those who are disabled. I thought a middle-grade novel featuring a heroine who is mentally retarded would be more effective." In *Emily in Love* Rubin follows her teen protagonist experiences at a regular high school. Determined to date a non-learning-disabled student, Emily unwisely takes advice from her friend and classmate Molly. The two host a party with the goal of wooing a boy named Hunt, but the party has a disastrous outcome, leaving Emily aware that she has deceived her family as well as her friends in her pursuit of romance. *Emily in Love* "succeeds in showing how alike Emily is to most fourteen-year-old girls," remarked *Voice of Youth Advocates* reviewer Melissa Thacker, while Stephanie Zvirin predicted in *Booklist* that the novel's theme will resonate with young readers. "There's a universal message here as Rubin clearly shows the effects of prejudice on self-esteem," Zvirin wrote.

Since the late 1990s Rubin has concentrated on nonfiction in her books for children. With its focus on home-based technology, *Toilets, Toasters, and Telephones: The How and Why of Everyday Objects* examines the industrial-design history of household items from vacuum cleaners and stoves to plumbing fixtures, and explains how these objects gained in popularity among consumers to the point at which they became commonplace. She also discusses several failed designs, such as revolving shelves for refrigerators. "The text is solid, serious, and backed by an impressive bibliography," wrote Randy Meyer in a *Booklist* review of the book.

In *Margaret Bourke-White: Her Pictures Were Her Life* Rubin focuses on one of the first female photojournalists, and includes fifty-six of the photographer's black-and-white images. One of *Life* magazine's "Founding Four" photographers and a women credited with capturing some of the most well-known images of the first half of the twentieth century, Bourke-White was dedicated and fearless, often taking great risks to secure her photographs. Bourke-White spent time on the battlefields of World War II, and her photographs of the skeletal survivors of Nazi Germany's recently liberated concentration camps were indelible. As Rubin notes in her biography, although Bourke-White's mother voiced anti-Semitic views, the photographer later learned that she herself was part Jewish on her father's side. In a review of *Margaret Bourke-White* Roger Leslie wrote in *Booklist* that "Rubin does a brilliant job of bringing in personal elements that resonate with real emotion." A *Publishers Weekly* reviewer predicted that the author's "understated, seemingly effortless narrative" aids readers in understanding "that many of the images they take for granted today had their roots in the work of this daring pioneer."

Rubin focuses on creative individuals—such as artists Edgar Degas and Andy Warhol, filmmaker Steven Spielberg, and architect Frank Lloyd Wright—in biographies designed to introduce young readers to innovations in the arts. Called "a lovely book" by *School Library Journal* contributor Robin L. Gibson, *Degas and the Dance: The Painter and the Petits Rats, Perfecting Their Art* profiles the French painter who captured the lives of the working-class ballerinas of the Paris Opera in hundreds of loosely rendered works. Praising the book as "gloriously illustrated," a *Kirkus Reviews* writer added that *Degas and the Dance* "paint[s] . . . a portrait of an extraordinarily dedicated artist." Also set in France, *The Yellow House: Vincent van Gogh and Paul Gauguin Side by Side* recounts the two-month period late in 1888 when French painter Paul Gauguin visited Vincent van Gogh's farmhouse in the south of France. In addition to the growing animosity that developed because of their explosive personalities, the two artists had vastly different temperaments and work habits: Gauguin was slow and deliberate, making preliminary drawings of his subject before committing paint to canvas, while the exuberant, emotional Van Gogh sometimes squeezed pigment directly from the tube onto his brush. The men quarreled frequently, hastening Gauguin's eventual departure and accelerating his host's declining mental health. A reviewer for *Publishers Weekly* concluded in a review of *The Yellow House* that Rubin's "incisive, accessible analysis of some of the paintings created during their time together accompanies crisp reproductions of their work."

*Andy Warhol: Pop Art Painter* focuses on work that is familiar to many young children. Drawing on the recollections of Warhol's friends, family, and colleagues, Rubin focuses on the painter's interest in shoes, Siamese cats, and the quirks of popular culture in which, he predicted, everyone would achieve fifteen minutes of fame. Noting that the author "treat[s] Warhol's idiosyncrasies as youthful rather than disturbing," a *Publishers Weekly* maintained that Rubin "offers safe, evasive commentary on a complicated person." Agreeing that Rubin appropriately skirts the more controversial aspects of the artist's life in her elementary-grade biography, *Booklist* reviewer Gillian Engberg praised *Andy Warhol* as "concise" and featuring "clear, straightforward language."

When Rubin decided to write a biography of Steven Spielberg, the director behind such films as *E.T.* and *Schindler's List,* she recognized that Spielberg traditionally avoided participating in such projects. Knowing that the director's mother, Leah Adler, operated a kosher restaurant called The Milky Way, Rubin decided to visit Adler at work, show her some of her books, and ask for advice in contacting the noted Hollywood director. Although Adler initially declined, she eventually reconsidered, telling Rubin, "'I like you. I like your books,'" as the author later recalled to an interviewer for *Publishers Weekly.* In *Steven Spielberg: Crazy for Movies* Rubin presents Spielberg's life through his own commentary as well as recollections from some of the most incisive critics of all: his family and friends. Many of these comments recall Spielberg's fascination with filmmaking at an early age, and his use of an 8-millimeter camera to create visual stories. The book pairs Rubin's text with also contains fascinating family photographs that add a personal depth to the biography. "Fans of film will revel in this behind-the-scenes look at Spielberg's childhood, movies and the choices that led to his stellar career," stated a *Publishers Weekly* reviewer.

As she did in *Margaret Bourke-White,* Rubin focuses her attention on the World War II era in several other works of nonfiction. In *Fireflies in the Dark* she profiles the life of a woman who collected and preserved a precious cache of 5,000 drawings and poems done by the children of the Terezin concentration camp, located in Czechoslovakia. The art, which was discovered following the war, was hidden by Friedl Dicker-Brandeis in suitcases hidden in the attic of one of the camp's barracks buildings, and Rubin learned of this discovery during a visit to the Simon Wiesenthal Center/Museum of Tolerance in Los Angeles, California. As she explains in her book, Dicker-Brandeis was an art therapist in Prague before she was deported to Terezin. She managed to take her art supplies with her and began giving secret art classes to some of the 15,000 children who passed through the camp. Only a hundred would survive to adulthood, and Dicker-Brandeis herself died at the Auschwitz camp in Poland. The drawings reproduced in Rubin's book reveal the tragic dreams of young people longing for parents and their lost worlds: some depict the landscapes of home villages, or families gathering for the Passover holiday, while still others document the horrors young artists experienced at the camp. In *Fireflies in the Dark* Rubin contains interviews with some of the camp's survivors and recounts their stories as well as that of Dicker-Brandeis. In *School Library Journal* Patricia Manning called the work a keen addition to the literature of the Holocaust as well as "elegant in appearance, devastating in content, almost overwhelming in its quiet intensity." Other reviewers offered similar praise. "There's no sensationalism here," declared *Booklist* critic Hazel Rochman. "Everything is distanced, but the sense of loss is overwhelming."

Rubin followed *Fireflies in the Dark* with *The Cat with the Yellow Star,* a middle-grade memoir that focuses on one of Dicker-Brandeis's young art students. Ela Stein Weissberger was a talented artist, and many of her drawings and paintings appear in *Fireflies in the Dark.* Praising *The Cat with the Yellow Star* as a "poignant biography" of Weissberger's experiences as a child during the Holocaust, Rochman noted in *Booklist* that the production of the opera *Brundibar* by Weissberger and her fellow inmates at Terezin add to the book's "hopeful message about the power of music, art, friends, and teachers." Rubin also focuses on the power of creativity during times of personal confinement in *Art against the Odds: From Slave Quilts to Prison Paintings,* which focuses on convicts, political refugees, concentration-and internment-camp inmates, and the mentally ill. In *Searching for Anne Frank: Letters from Amsterdam to Iowa* she details the pen-pal correspondence that existed between well-known teen diarist Anne Frank and her older sister Margot and two sisters the same age who lived in Iowa in the years leading up to World War II. The exchange of letters ended when the Frank sisters went into hiding to avoid the Nazi armies that occupied Holland.

In *There Goes the Neighborhood: Ten Buildings People Loved to Hate* Rubin recounts the harsh critical and public reception of some of the world's most famous structures, from the Washington Monument in America's capital city to Paris's Eiffel Tower. She also discusses Frank Lloyd Wright's daring design for New York City's Solomon R. Guggenheim Museum, as well as another controversial museum designed by two 1970s architects, the Centre Pompidou in Paris, France. These buildings share the distinction of being initially vilified by architecture critics, city officials, and the general

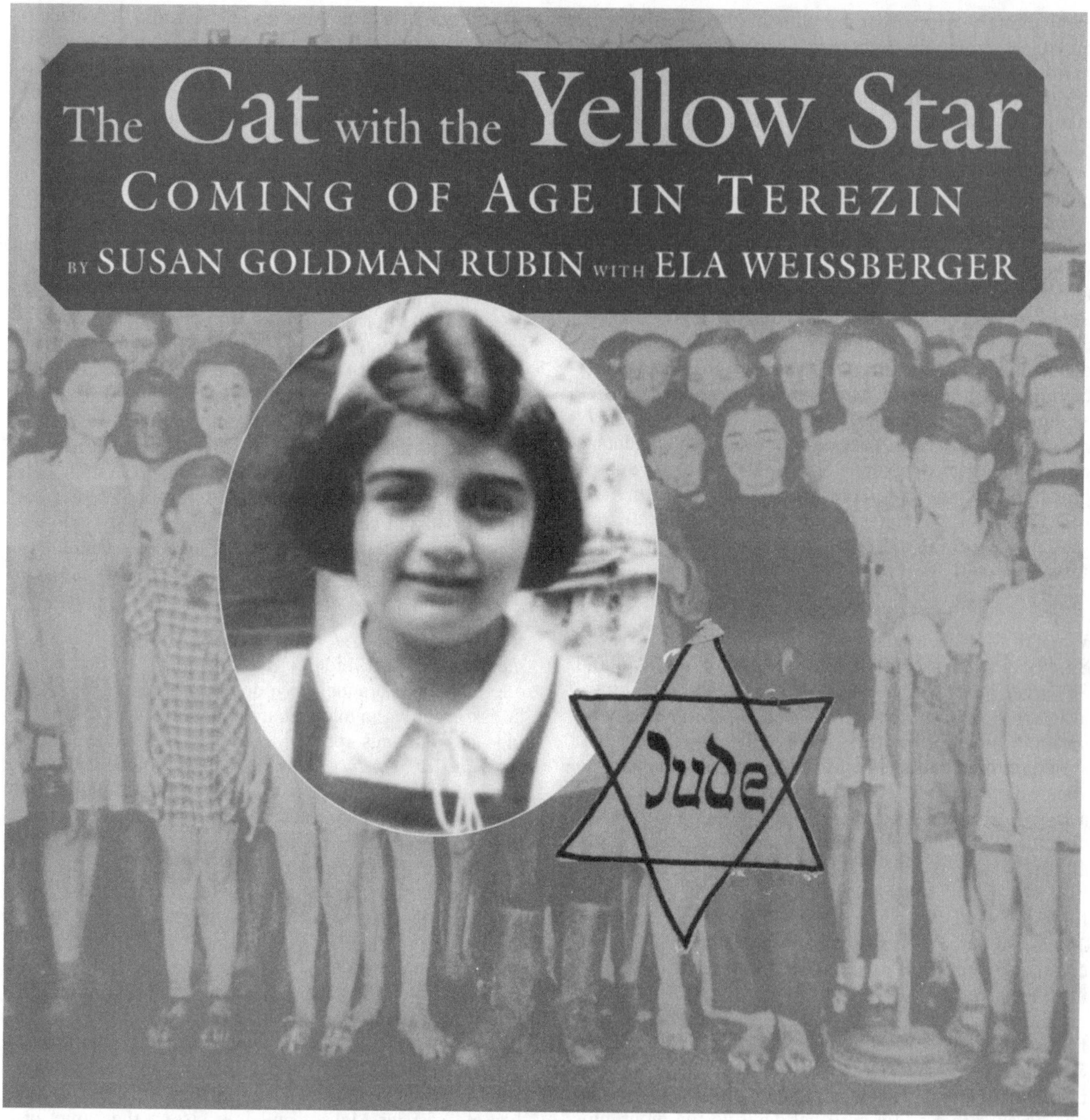


***Cover of Rubin's biography* The Cat with the Yellow Star, *the story of a girl's memories of her incarceration at the Terezin concentration camp.*** (Holiday House, Inc., 2006. Reproduced by permission of Holiday House, Inc.)

public alike until their uniqueness caused them to evolve into accepted landmarks. *There Goes the Neighborhood* "may well inspire readers to examine buildings . . . in new ways and bolster their courage to think differently," stated a *Publishers Weekly* reviewer. Noting that the volume is "written in simple, engaging language that never condescends," Engberg wrote that Rubin's "stories reveal how architects identified and solved aesthetic and engineering problems, and include fascinating" details about the history of each building, its neighborhood, and the visionary architects who designed them.

As a Jewish American, Rubin follows her interest in her cultural history in several books for young readers. In *L'Chaim!: To Jewish Life in America: Celebrations from 1654 until Today* she pairs her text with a wealth of photographs and other images that bring to life the long, colorful, and sometimes poignant history of Jews in North America. Beginning with the first Jewish settlement in 1654, Rubin follows the growth of Jewish Americans in business, labor, and society, documenting their significant role in shaping the United States. In *Haym Salomon: American Patriot* Rubin narrows her focus to one individual who played a significant role in the nation's early history. Salomon, a Polish immigrant to the American colonies at the time of the American Revolution, became a member of the patriotic Sons of Liberty in his adopted country. He also used his experience with European banking to establish the Bank of North America and help finance the young republic's push for independence. Although a *Publishers Weekly* contributor explained that little information exists about Salomon, in her biography Rubin "does a fine job of imbuing her hero's story with a sense of drama and urgency."

Rubin told *SATA:* "I feel so lucky to do the work I love. Researching and writing nonfiction these past few years has been tremendously exciting. One book leads to another. IN the course of research I use primary sources: interviews in person and by phone and e-mail, and travel to places I am writing about whenever possible. I look forward to sharing new books with young readers."

## Biographical and Critical Sources

*PERIODICALS*

*Booklist,* November 1, 1993, Stephanie Zvirin, review of *Emily Good as Gold,* p. 514; January 1, 1995, Hazel Rochman, review of *Frank Lloyd Wright,* p. 812; May 15, 1997, Stephanie Zvirin, review of *Emily in Love,* pp. 1573-1574; November 1, 1998, Randy Meyer, review of *Toilets, Toasters, and Telephones: The How and Why of Everyday Objects,* p. 488; November 1, 1999, Roger Leslie, review of *Margaret Bourke-White: Her Pictures Were Her Life,* p. 526; March 1, 2000, Stephanie Zvirin, review of *Margaret Bourke-White,* p. 1249; July, 2000, Hazel Rochman, review of *Fireflies in the Dark: The Story of Friedl Dicker-Brandeis and the Children of Terezin,* p. 2023; December 15, 2000, Gillian Engberg, review of *Fireflies in the Dark,* p. 811; August, 2001, Gillian Engberg, review of *There Goes the Neighborhood: Ten Buildings People Loved to Hate,* p. 2105; November 15, 2001, Gillian Engberg, review of *The Yellow House: Vincent van Gogh and Paul Gauguin Side by Side,* pp. 578-579; December 1, 2001, Randy Meyer, review of *Steven Spielberg: Crazy for Movies,* p. 641; December 1, 2002, Carolyn Phelan, review of *Degas and the Dance: The Painter and the Petit Rats Perfecting Their Art,* p. 662; November 1, 2003, Hazel Rochman, review of *Searching for Anne Frank: Letters from Amsterdam to Iowa,* p. 489; February 15, 2004, Gillian Engberg, review of *Art against the Odds: From Slave Quilts to Prison Paintings,* p. 1058; November 1, 2004, Stephanie Zvirin, review of *L'Chaim! To Jewish Life in America!: Celebrations from 1654 until Today,* p. 474; March 15, 2005, Hazel Rochman, review of *The Flag with Fifty-six Stars: A Gift from the Survivors of Mauthausen,* p. 1292; June 1, 2006, Hazel Rochman, review of *The Cat with the Yellow Star: Coming of Age in Terezin,* p. 100; November 1, 2006, Gillian Engberg, review of *Andy Warhol: Pop Art Painter,* p. 63.

*Bulletin of the Center for Children's Books,* November, 1993, review of *Emily Good as Gold,* p. 97; April, 1997, review of *Emily in Love,* p. 294; November, 2000, review of *Fireflies in the Dark,* p. 119; September, 2001, review of *There Goes the Neighborhood,* p. 33; December, 2001, review of *Steven Spielberg,* p. 151; January, 2003, review of *Degas and the Dance,* p. 210; January, 2004, Betsy Hearne, review of *Searching for Anne Frank,* p. 205; June, 2004, Deborah Stevenson, review of *Art against the Odds,* p. 436; January, 2005, Elizabeth Bush, review of *L'Chaim!,* p. 225.

*Horn Book,* March, 1999, Mary M. Burns, review of *Toilets, Toasters, and Telephones,* p. 229; January, 2000, review of *Margaret Bourke-White,* p. 102; September, 2000, review of *Fireflies in the Dark,* p. 599; November-December, 2003, Roger Sutton, review of *Searching for Anne Frank,* p. 76; July-August, 2006, Joanna Rudge Long, review of *The Cat with the Yellow Star,* p. 468.

*Kirkus Reviews,* November 1, 1999, review of *Margaret Bourke-White,* p. 1748; September 15, 2001, review of *The Yellow House,* p. 1366; October 15, 2001, review of *Steven Spielberg,* p. 1492; November 1, 2002, review of *Degas and the Dance,* p. 1613; October 15, 2003, review of *Searching for Anne Frank,* p. 1276; February 1, 2004, review of *Against the Odds,* p. 138; November 15, 2004, review of *L'Chaim!,* p. 1092; April 1, 2005, review of *The Flag with Fifty-six Stars,* p. 423; May 15, 2006, review of *The Cat with the Yellow Star,* p. 522; October 15, 2006, review of *Andy Warhol,* p. 1079.

*New York Times Book Review,* January 20, 2002, review of *Stephen Spielberg,* p. 14.

*Publishers Weekly,* October 25, 1993, review of *Emily Good as Gold,* p. 64; November 8, 1999, review of *Margaret Bourke-White,* p. 70; June 5, 2000, "A Lasting Legacy," p. 96; July 9, 2001, review of *There Goes the Neighborhood,* p. 69; September 3, 2001, review of *The Yellow House,* p. 87; November 12, 2001, review of *Steven Spielberg,* pp. 60-61; October 27, 2003, review of *Searching for Anne Frank,* p. 71; November 22, 2004, review of *L'Chaim!,* p. 61; March 21, 2005, review of *The Flag with Fifty-six Stars,* p. 51; March 20, 2006, review of *The Cat with the Yellow Star,* p. 57; November 27, 2006, review of *Andy Warhol,* p. 52; March 26, 2007, review of *Haym Salomon: American Patriot,* p. 93.

*School Library Journal,* October, 1993, Cindy Darling Codell, review of *Emily Good as Gold,* pp. 152-153; January, 1995, Jeanette Larson, review of *Frank Lloyd Wright,* p. 143; May, 1997, Renee Steinberg, review of *Emily in Love,* p. 139; November 1, 1998, Ann G. Brouse, review of *Toilets, Toasters, and Telephones,* p. 142; December, 1999, Carol Fazioli, review of *Margaret Bourke-White,* pp. 159-160; August, 2000, Patricia Manning, review of *Fireflies in the Dark,* p. 206; September, 2001, Mary Ann Carcich, review of *There Goes the Neighborhood,* p. 254; December, 2001, Shauna Yusko, review of *Steven Spielberg,* p. 171; January, 2002, Robin L. Gibson, review of *The Yellow House,* p. 124; December, 2002, Robin L. Gibson, review of *Degas and the Dance,* p. 129; November, 2003, Laura Reed, review of *Searching for Anne Frank,* p. 166; March, 2004, Sophie R. Brooker, review of *Art against the Odds,* p. 242; January, 2005, Sue Giffard, review of *L'Chaim!,* p. 154; May, 2005, Anne Chapman Callaghan, review of *The Flag with Fifty-six Stars,* p. 116; June, 2006, Teri Markson, review of *The Cat with the Yellow Star,* p. 184; November, 2006, Donna Cardon, review of *Andy Warhol,* p. 164; May, 2007, Heidi Estrin, review of *Haym Salomon,* p. 124.

*Voice of Youth Advocates,* June, 1997, Melissa Thacker, review of *Emily in Love,* p. 113; October, 2001, review of *There Goes the Neighborhood,* p. 307; June, 2002, review of *Steven Spielberg,* p. 141; October, 2003, review of *Searching for Anne Frank,* p. 336; February, 2005, Sophie Brookover, review of *L'Chaim!,* p. 508.

*ONLINE*

*Cynsations Web site,* http://cynthialeitichsmith.blogspot.com/ (May 30, 2005), Cynthia Leitich-Smith, interview with Rubin.

*Susan Goldman Rubin Home Page,* http://www.susangoldmanrubin.com (August 15, 2007).

# S

## SASAKI, Chris

### Personal

Male. *Hobbies and other interests:* Sports, photography, drawing, writing, music, camping.

### Addresses

*Home and office*—Toronto, Ontario, Canada.

### Career

Author. McLaughlin Planetarium, former senior producer and photographer; ICE Integrated Communications and Entertainment, Inc., former writer and creative director.

### Writings

*The Constellations: The Stars and Stories,* illustrated by Joe Boddy, Sterling Publishing (New York, NY) 2002.

*Detective Notebook: Secret Agent Codes,* illustrated by Jeff Sinclair, Sterling Publishing (New York, NY), 2004.

(Reteller) Arthur Conan Doyle, *The Adventures of Sherlock Holmes,* illustrated by Lucy Corvino, Sterling Publishing (New York, NY), 2005.

*Constellations: A Glow-in-the-Dark Guide to the Night Sky,* illustrated by Alan Flinn, Sterling Publishing (New York, NY), 2006.

(Reteller) H.G. Wells, *The War of the Worlds,* illustrated by Jamel Akib, Sterling Publishing (New York, NY), 2007.

(Reteller) H.G. Wells, *The Time Machine,* illustrated by Troy Howell, Sterling Publishing (New York, NY), 2008.

Contributor of science articles to various magazines.

### Sidelights

Chris Sasaki creates children's books that allow readers to explore the realms of astronomy. Sasaki's first publication, *The Constellations: The Stars and Stories,* includes eighty-eighty entries that describe and illustrate all of the constellations of the night sky. Descriptions detail the mythology behind each star pattern, instruct young readers on where and when to view each constellation, and include diagrams showing star locations. The book also includes additional resources, such as trivia, star charts, and a glossary. Gillian Engberg in her review of *The Constellations* for *Booklist,* remarked that Sasaki's book "demystifies stargazing." Sasaki's entries are "short and lively," Engberg added, noting that they are "written in relaxed, teen-friendly language." *School Library Journal* reviewer Linda Wadleigh commented that Sasaki's comprehensive volume will "serve the needs of those interested in astronomy."

*Constellations: A Glow-in-the-Dark Guide to the Night Sky* is Sasaki's companion title to *The Constellations.* Like its predecessor, Sasaki's second volume includes descriptions of constellations alongside images in which glow-in-the-dark stars are created with special ink. *Constellations* includes descriptions of eleven well-known constellations that contain elements of storytelling by including a discussion of the mythology connected to each constellation. A *Kirkus Reviews* critic noted that *Constellations* condenses the information found in Sasaki's first book. *School Library Journal* contributor Linda Wadleigh maintained that *Constellations* serves as a straightforward "introduction to the night sky."

### Biographical and Critical Sources

*PERIODICALS*

*Booklist,* February 15, 2003, Gillian Engberg, review of *The Constellations: The Stars and Stories,* p. 1062.

*Kirkus Reviews,* May 15, 2006, review of *Constellations: A Glow-in-the-Dark Guide to the Night Sky,* p. 523.

*School Library Journal,* July, 2003, Linda Wadleigh, review of *The Constellations,* p. 149; October, 2005, Rita Soltan, review of *The Adventures of Sherlock Holmes,* p. 156; August, 2006, Linda Wadleigh, review of *Constellations,* p. 111.

*Voice of Youth Advocates,* October, 2003, review of *The Constellations,* p. 336.

* * *

# SFAR, Joann 1971-

## Personal

Born August 28, 1971, in France. *Education:* Attended École des Beaux Arts. *Religion:* Jewish.

## Addresses

*Home*—France. *E-mail*—joannsfar@pastis.org.

## Career

Writer and illustrator, 1994—.

## Awards, Honors

René Goscinny Award, Angoulême International Comics Festival, 1998; Grand Prix de la ville d'Angoulême, 2004; Best International Series designation, Prix Saint-Michel (Belgium), 2004; Best International Writer designation, Max und Moritz prizes (Germany), 2004; Eisner Award for Best U.S. Edition of Foreign Material, 2006; Sproing award (Norway) for best foreign translated material, 2007, for *Le chat du Rabbin.*

## Writings

*COLLECTED COMIC BOOKS; SELF-ILLUSTRATED*

(With Emmanuel Guibert) *La fille du professeur* (graphic novel), Dupuis (Marcinelle, Belgium), 1997, translated by Alexis Siegel as *The Professor's Daughter,* First Second (New York, NY), 2007.

(With Lewis Trondheim) *Dungeon: Zenith, Volume 2: The Barbarian Princess* ("Donjon" series; includes *La princesse des barbares* and *Sortilege et avatar*), NBM (New York, NY), 2000.

*Vampire Loves* ("Grand Vampire" series, volumes 1-4; originally published 2001--03), translated by Alexis Siegel, First Second (New York, NY), 2006.

*Le chat du Rabbin* (includes volumes 1-3; originally published, 2002), Poisson Pilote, 2005, translated as *The Rabbi's Cat,* Pantheon (New York, NY), 2005.

*Little Vampire Does Kung Fu!* ("Petit vampire" series), translated by Mark and Alexis Siegel, Simon & Schuster Books for Young Readers (New York, NY), 2003.

*Little Vampire Goes to School* ("Petit vampire" series), translated by Mark and Alexis Siegel, Simon & Schuster Books for Young Readers (New York, NY), 2003.

(With Lewis Trondheim) *Dungeon: Zenith* ("Donjon" series), NBM (New York, NY), 2004.

*Les carnets,* L'Association, 2005.

*Grand Vampire 6,* Delcourt (Paris, France), 2005.

*Petit Vampire et le reve de Tokyo* ("Petit vampire" series), Delcourt (Paris, France), 2005.

(With Lewis Trondheim) *Donjon: Stanislas* ("Donjon" series), Delcourt (Paris, France), 2005.

(With Lewis Trondheim) *Donjon: Bercovici (monster 11)* ("Donjon" series), Delcourt (Paris, France), 2005.

*Pasquin,* L'Association, 2005.

*Petit Vampire et les enfants perdus* ("Petit vampire" series), Delcourt (Paris, France), 2005, translated as *Petit Vampire 8,* 2005.

(With Lewis Trondheim) *Dungeon: The Early Years* ("Donjon" series; contains *Donjon potron-minet, la chemise de la nuit* and *Donjon potron-minut, un justicier dans l'ennui*), illustrated by Christophe Blain, NBM (New York, NY), 2005.

*Klezmer* ("Tales of the Wild East" series; originally published, 2005), translated by Alexis Siegel, First Second (New York, NY), 2006.

(With Lewis Trondheim) *Dungeon: Twilight: Volume 1: Dragon Cemetery* ("Donjon" series), illustrated by Kerascoet, translated by Joe Johnson, NBM (New York, NY), 2006.

(With Lewis Trondheim) *Dungeon: Parade: Volume One: A Dungeon Too Many* ("Donjon" series), illustrated by Manu Larcenet, NBM (New York, NY), 2007.

(With Lewis Trondheim) *Dungeon: Twilight: Volume 2: Armageddon* ("Donjon" series), illustrated by Kerascoet, translated by Joe Johnson, NBM (New York, NY), 2007.

Also author, with Trondheim, of collected comic books *Dungeon: Zenith, Volume 1* and *Dungeon: Parade, Volume 1.* Author of other comic series, including (with José-Luis Munuera) "Les Potamoks," 1996-97; (with Pierre Dubois) "Pétrus Barbygère," 1997-97; "Le petit monde du Golem," 1998; (with Olivier Boiscommun) "Troll," 1999; (with Hervé Tanguerelle) "Le professeur Bell," 1999-2006; "La petite bibliothèque philosophique de Joann Sfar"; "Ukulélé"; "Harmonica"; "Socrate le demi-chien"; "Le minuscule mousquetaire"; "Le Borgne Gauchet"; "La ville des mauvais Reves"; "Merlin"; and "Paris-Londres."

Works have been translated into several languages, including German, French, Polish, and Dutch.

*"LES OLIVES NOIRES" SERIES; COMICS*

(With Emmanuel Guibert) *Pourquoi cette nuit est-elle différente des autres nuits?,* Dupuis (Marcinelle, Belgium), 2001.

(With Emmanuel Guibert) *Adam Harishon,* Dupuis (Marcinelle, Belgium), 2002.

(With Emmanuel Guibert) *Tu ne mangeras pas le chevreau dans le lait de sa mère,* Dupuis (Marcinelle, Belgium), 2003.

*ILLUSTRATOR; "SARDINE IN OUTER SPACE"/"SARDINE DE L'ESPACE" COMIC-BOOK COLLECTIONS*

(With Emmanuel Guibert) *Sardine de l'espace: le doigt dans l'oeil,* Broché (Paris, France), 2000, translated

by Sasha Watson as *Sardine in Outer Space: Volume One*, First Second (New York, NY), 2006.

(With Emmanuel Guibert) *Sardine de l'espace 2: le bar des ennemis,* Broché (Paris, France), 2000, translated by Sasha Watson as *Sardine in Outer Space: Volume Two*, First Second (New York, NY), 2006.

(With Emmanuel Guibert) *Sardine de l'espace 3: la machine à laver la cervelle,* Broché (Paris, France), 2001, translated by Sasha Watson as *Sardine in Outer Space: Volume Three*, First Second (New York, NY), 2007.

(With Emmanuel Guibert) *Sardine de l'espace 4: Les voleurs de Yaourt,* Broché (Paris, France), 2001, translated by Sasha Watson as *Sardine in Outer Space: Volume Four*, First Second (New York, NY), 2007.

(With Emmanuel Guibert) *Sardine de l'espace 5: le championnat de Boxe,* Broché (Paris, France), 2002.

(With Emmanuel Guibert) *Sardine de l'espace 6: le capitaine tout rouge,* Broché (Paris, France), 2002.

(With Emmanuel Guibert) *Sardine de l'espace 7: le grande sardine,* Broché (Paris, France), 2003.

(With Emmanuel Guibert) *Sardine de l'espace 8: les tatouages carnivores,* Broché (Paris, France), 2003.

(With Emmanuel Guibert) *Sardine de l'espace 9: les montagne électorale,* Cartonné (Paris, France), 2004.

(With Emmanuel Guibert) *Sardine de l'espace 10: le cyber disc-jockey,* Album, 2005.

## Sidelights

French writer and cartoonist Joann Sfar made his comic debut in 1994 with the comic-book series "Les adventures d' Ossour Hyrsidoux." Since then Sfar has gone on to win accolades as one of the most popular "new generation" of graphic novelists in Europe. His comic-book series, which have been collected into book-length volumes and translated into several languages, include "Les Potamoks," "Le professeur Bell," "Petit vampire," and "Le fille du professeur." Many of Sfar's series have special appeal for younger readers, and his award-winning "Sardine in Outer Space" and "Little Vampire" graphic novels have gained a loyal following among English-language readers.

Utilizing a comic-strip format, the compilation volumes *Little Vampire Does Kung Fu!* and *Little Vampire Goes to School* introduce readers to Little Vampire. In *Little Vampire Goes to School* Sfar's young bloodsucker is lonely because he must attend school at night all by himself. Against his teacher's advice, Little Vampire summons a crazy cast of friends, ranging from the Captain of the Dead to a handful of ghosts, to attend school with him. After discovering a human student's school book, Little Vampire begins to communicate with the boy, Michael, and the two are soon writing back and forth. When the captain of the Dead discovers what has been going on, he immediately wants to meet Michael to ensure that no ghostly secrets are revealed. A *Publishers Weekly* critic commented in a review of *Little Vampire Goes to School* that "readers of European series . . . will recognize Sfar's baroque illustration style and dense plotting, which recommends itself to an experienced audience."

*Cover of* **Dungeon: Zenith: The Barbarian Princess,** ***a collaborative comic-book anthology by Joann Sfar and Lewis Trondheim.*** (Nantier Beall Minoustchine Publishing, Inc., 2000. Reproduced by permission.)

Sfar continues the adventures of his nocturnal protagonist in *Little Vampire Does Kung Fu!* This time around Michael enlists the help of his new ghostly friends to help him get revenge on a school bully. When the apparitions accidentally eat the bully, Michael must sew his schoolmate back together in order to bring the boy back to life. Sfar's text is accompanied by his bright illustrations, which *School Library Journal* reviewer Steven Engelfried wrote "worked effectively with the intentionally wild plot." Engelfried noted that, while "the mildly gruesome illustration and off-the-wall storytelling will not appeal to all kids, . . . fans of comics, silliness, and dark humor will appreciate the unusual approach." *Booklist* critic Francisca Goldsmith also enjoyed Sfar's book, commenting that *Little Vampire Does Kung Fu!* "is a wonderful starting place for American kids to discover the fantastic possibilities of contemporary French comics."

Sfar joins with frequent collaborator Emmanuel Guibert to create the whimsical "Sardine in Outer Space" series. In the first volume, readers meet Sardine, Little Louie, and piratical Captain Yellow Shoulder, and follow the trio's adventures speeding through the galaxy in their oddly shaped space ship. During their interplanetary jaunts, they encounter a host of unusual creatures, such as the cha-cha flies of planet Ouchypoo and the trouble-making Supermuscleman. Noting the series' appeal to middle-grade readers, *Kliatt* reviewer George Galuschak cited the "potty humor" and "lively, imaginative stories" and in *School Library Journal* Dawn Rutherford wrote that the crew's adventures "are unrelentingly silly and will leave readers giggling." In *Booklist,* Francisca Goldsmith concluded that Sfar's "bouncy, bright art perfectly suits the Sardine troop's energy and sass," while *School Library Journal* contributor Benjamin Russell described it as "scratchy and primitive," adding that the author's drawings "also contain . . . the sort of raw, grotesque sensibility that so often clicks with young readers."

The collaborative series collected as *The Professor's Daughter* was actually written by Sfar to showcase Guibert's art. First published in France as *La fille du professeur,* the award-winning comic series follows the growing love between a mummy and the daughter of an academic. Another collaboration with Guibert, "Les olives noires" takes readers back to the days of Jesus as it follows a young Jew traveling through the land of Judea. A long-running collaboration with author Lewis Trondheim, the "Dungeon" series first appeared in 1998 and follows an unfolding saga in a fanciful fantasy world.

## Biographical and Critical Sources

*PERIODICALS*

*Booklist,* September 15, 2003, Francisca Goldsmith, review of *Little Vampire Does Kung Fu!,* p. 242; September 1, 2006, Jesse Karp, review of *Sardine in Outer Space 2,* p. 128; November 15, 2006, Tina Coleman, review of *Armageddon: Dungeon: Twilight,* p. 39; March 15, 2007, Tina Coleman, review of *The Professor's Daughter,* p. 56; Francisca Goldsmith, review of *Sardine in Outer Space 3,* p. 64.

*Horn Book,* July-August, 2007, Tanya D. Auger, review of *The Professor's Daughter,* p. 403.

*Kirkus Reviews,* August 1, 2003, review of *Little Vampire Does Kung Fu!,* p. 1023; August 15, 2006, review of *Sardine in Outer Space 2,* p. 841; January 15, 2007, review of *The Professor's Daughter,* p. 51; March 1, 2007, review of *Sardine in Outer Space 3,* p. 222.

*Kliatt,* July, 2006, George Galuschak, review of *Vampire Loves,* p. 29; May, 2007, Jennifer Feigelman, review of *The Professor's Daughter,* p. 32.

*Publishers Weekly,* April 3, 2006, review of *Vampire Loves,* p. 48; July 28, 2003, review of *Little Vampire Goes to School,* p. 95; June 12, 2006, review of *Sardine in Outer Space,* p. 52; February 5, 2007, review of *The Professor's Daughter,* p. 48.

*School Library Journal,* August, 2003, Joy Fleishhacker, review of *Little Vampire Goes to School,* p. 142; December, 2003, Steven Engelfried, review of *Little Vampire Does Kung Fu!,* p. 126; July, 2006, Benjamin Russell, review of *Sardine in Outer Space,* p. 125, and Dawn Rutherford, review of *Vampire Loves,* p. 131; January, 2007, John Leighton, review of *Armageddon,* p. 163; May, 2007, Heidi Dolamore, review of *The Professor's Daughter,* p. 172; July, 2007, Dawn Rutherford, review of *Sardine in Outer Space 3,* p. 124.

*ONLINE*

*BdParadisio Web site,* http://www.bdparadisio.com/ (March 19, 2005), "Joann Sfar."

*Joann Sfar Home Page,* http://www.pastis/org (April 27, 2007).

*Lambiek Web site,* http://www.lambiek.net/ (April 27, 2007), "Joann Sfar."*

* * *

# SHEBAN, Chris

## Personal

Married; children: two daughters. *Education:* Kent State University, B.A.

## Addresses

*Home and office*—2861 Shannon Court, Northbrook, IL 60062. *E-mail*—csheban@comcast.net.

## Career

Artist and illustrator.

## Awards, Honors

Silver Medals, Society of Illustrators; Gold Medal, Society of Illustrators, for *I Met a Dinosaur*; Gold Medal, Society of Illustrators, iParenting Media Award, and Children's BookSense 76 Selection, all for *The Story of a Seagull and the Cat Who Taught Her to Fly.*

## Illustrator

*FOR CHILDREN*

*Christmas Magic,* Kingfisher (New York, NY), 1994.

Jan Wahl, *I Met a Dinosaur,* Creative Editions (Mankato, MN), 1997.

J. Patrick Lewis, *The Shoe Tree of Chagrin,* Creative Editions (Mankato, MN), 2001.

Luis Sepúlveda, *The Story of a Seagull and the Cat Who Taught Her to Fly* (translation by Margaret Sayers Peden of *Historia de una gaviota y del gato que le enseñó a volar*), Arthur A. Levine (New York, NY), 2003.

Brian J. Heinz, *Red Fox at McCloskey's Farm,* Creative Editions (Mankato, MN), 2006.

Myla Goldberg, *Catching the Moon,* Arthur A. Levine (New York, NY), 2007.

Stephanie Greene, *Christmas at Stony Creek,* Greenwillow (New York, NY), 2007.

## Sidelights

Beginning his career in children's-book publishing as a jacket artists for novels by Kate DiCamillo, A. LaFaye, Jenny Nimmo, and others, Chris Sheban has gone on to illustrate a number of picture books for young readers. Including *Christmas Magic,* which features a pop-up Christmas tree, his work has earned gold and silver medals from the prestigious Society of Illustrators. Although he had worked as an artist prior to moving to book illustration, Sheban was initially intimidated by the idea of becoming a children's book illustrator. "When you walk into a bookstore, there are just tons of wonderful, wonderful picture books," he told Heather Vogel Frederick in *Publishers Weekly.* "Although it's inspiring to see all the different styles, it can be pretty overwhelming."

For Sheban's first picture-book project, Jan Wahl's *I Met a Dinosaur* he developed a soft-focused style. "This slightly dreamy visual style seamlessly unites fact and

***Chris Sheban has created cover art for a number children's books, among them* Dad, in Spirit, *a supernatural-themed novel by A. LaFaye.*** (Simon & Schuster Books for Young Readers, 2001. Illustration © 2001 by Chris Sheban. Reproduced by permission of the illustrator.)

***Paired with Luis Sepulveda's mystical text, Sheban's artwork for* The Story of a Seagull and the Cat Who Taught Her to Fly *enhances the story's dreamlike air.*** (Illustration © 2003 by Chris Sheban. Reproduced by permission of Scholastic Inc.)

fiction," wrote a *Publishers Weekly* contributor of the book. In *Booklist* Michael Cart called the illustrations "lavish—and occasionally witty." Sheban's second title, *The Shoe Tree of Chagrin Falls,* is an original tall tale by J. Patrick Lewis that is set in the Ohio Valley. "The luminous illustrations, done in a fine line and misty palette, allow tans and browns to dominate each landscape," wrote Jane Marino in her review of the book for *School Library Journal.* Discussing the story's main character, a *Kirkus Reviews* contributor noted that "brawny, gray-haired Susannah towers as convincingly in Sheban's dusky scenes." The illustrator's "comical visual characterizations carry the day" in *Red Fox at McCloskey's Farm,* according to a *Kirkus Reviews* contributor. Carolyn Janssen, writing in *School Library Journal,* predicted that Sheban's "illustrations will bring on belly laughs."

Along with picture books, Sheban's illustrations have also been featured in chapter books for older readers. In *The Story of a Seagull and the Cat Who Taught Her to Fly* his "delicate charcoal and pastel illustrations heighten the sense of magic," according to a *Publishers Weekly* critic. Shelle Rosenfeld, writing in *Booklist,* commented that Sheban's "black-and-white illustrations expressively portray the characters and settings," and Shawn Brommer concluded in *School Library Journal* that the illustrator's "soft-focus, black-and-white illustrations capture the action of the text." *The Story of a Seagull and the Cat Who Taught Her to Fly* won several awards, including a Society of Illustrators gold medal.

When asked about his career in children's books in an interview with Heather Vogel Frederick for *Publishers Weekly,* Sheban responded: "What I like about illustrating books is that the work is a little more enduring than your typical illustration job, which is printed once and you never see it again. I've really enjoyed the whole process, and I feel very, very fortunate."

## Biographical and Critical Sources

*PERIODICALS*

*Booklist,* November 1, 1997, Michael Cart, review of *I Met a Dinosaur,* p. 485; December 15, 2001, Linda Perkins, review of *The Shoe Tree of Chagrin Falls,* p. 731; September 1, 2003, Shelle Rosenfeld, review of *The Story of a Seagull and the Cat Who Taught Her to Fly,* p. 121.

*Kirkus Reviews,* September 1, 2001, review of *The Shoe Tree of Chagrin,* p. 1295; August 15, 2006, review of *Red Fox at McCloskey's Farm,* p. 842.

*Publishers Weekly,* September 22, 1997, review of *I Met a Dinosaur,* p. 80; December 22, 1997, Heather Vogel Frederick, "Flying Starts"; August 18, 2003, review of *The Story of a Seagull and the Cat Who Taught Her to Fly,* p. 79.

*School Library Journal,* November, 1997, Pamela K. Bomboy, review of *I Met a Dinosaur,* p. 102; February, 2002, Jane Marino, review of *The Shoe Tree of Chagrin,* p. 108; December, 2003, Shawn Brommer, review of *The Story of a Seagull and the Cat Who Taught Her to Fly,* p. 125.

*ONLINE*

*Arthur A. Levine Books Web site,* http://www.arthuralevinebooks.com/ (August 6, 2007), "Chris Sheban."

*Emily Inman Agency Web site,* http://emilyinman.com/contact.htm (August 6, 2007), "Chris Sheban."

*HarperCollins Web site,* http://www.harpercollins.com (August 6, 2007), "Chris Sheban."

*Scholastic Web site,* http://content.scholastic.com/ (August 6, 2007), "Chris Sheban."

*Workbook Web site,* http://www.workbook.com/ (August 6, 2007), "Chris Sheban.*

* * *

# SPEARS, Rick

## Personal

Born in CA. *Education:* University of Georgia, B.A.

## Addresses

*Home and office*—Atlanta, GA. *E-mail*—paleoartist@hotmail.com.

## Career

Paleoartist and author. Creator of sculptures of dinosaurs for various museums. Rock Eagle Natural History Museum, Eatonton, GA, exhibits coordinator; Fernbank Science Center, Atlanta, GA, exhibit designer/fabricator; Mackie's World T. Rex, Grand Rapids, MI, designer/fabricator.

## Awards, Honors

Quick Pick for Reluctant Readers nomination, Young Adult Library Services Association, New York Public Library Top 100 Titles for Reading and Sharing designation, and CYBILS Literary Award nomination in nonfiction category, all 2006, all for *Tales of the Cryptids.*

## Illustrator

Kelly Milner Halls, *Dino-Trekking: The Ultimate Dinosaur Lover's Travel Guide,* Wiley (New York, NY), 1996.

Kelly Milner Halls, *Dinosaur Mummies: Beyond Bare-Bones Fossils,* Darby Creek (Plain City, OH), 2003.

Kelly Milner Halls and Roxyanne Young, *Tales of the Cryptids: Mysterious Creatures That May or May Not Exist,* Darby Creek (Plain City, OH), 2006.

Contributor of illustrations to books, including *Guys Write for Guys Read,* by Jon Sciezska, and to magazines, including *Dinosaurus, Dig, Child Life, Family Fun,* and *AMNH Ology.*

## Sidelights

Rick Spears fell in love with dinosaurs when he was a child. Although he moved on and cycled through several other childhood interests, his love for dinosaurs returned while Spears was attending college, and it was then that he began doing what he calls "paleoart": the art of dinosaurs. As a paleoartist, Spears coordinates exhibits, creates sculptures depicting what dinosaurs may have actually looked like, and provides illustrations to magazines, books, and museum exhibits. His work in children's literature began in the early 1990s, when he was contacted by children's author Kelly Milner Halls. "I met Rick Spears . . . when I was researching *Dino-Trekking: The Ultimate Dinosaur Lover's Travel Guide* and needed a dinosaur expert for the state of Georgia," Halls recalled on her home page. The first person she contacted recommended her to Spears, saying: "When it comes to dinosaurs, Rick is the man." Halls and Spears hit it off, and together they have collaborated on several books, including two titles that focus exclusively on dinosaurs.

The first collaboration by Halls and Spears resulted in *Dino-Trekking.* Geared for dinosaur lovers, *Dino-Trekking* offers details of dinosaur related sites in all

***Rick Spears' art is featured in Kelly Milner Halls' nonfiction picture book* Dinosaur Mummies.** (Illustration © 2003. Reproduced by permission of Darby Creek Publishing.)

fifty United States and Canada. From museums to parks to exhibits, Hall and Spears' guide covers where the sites are and what things there are to do while you are there. It then rates the site's fun factor on a scale of from one to three bones. A *Publishers Weekly* critic called the listing of sites "exhaustive"

In *Dinosaur Mummies: Beyond Bare-Bones Fossils,* Halls and Spears to take paleontology beyond mere bones. They reveal what can be learned from looking at the remains of skin, organs, and even dinosaur dung. "Young dinosaur fans will latch onto this heavily illustrated report like starving velociraptors at a picnic," predicted a *Kirkus Reviews* contributor of the title. Carolyn Phelan, writing in *Booklist,* noted that Spears' watercolor-washed "drawings . . . show how the dinosaurs might have looked."

*Tales of the Cryptids: Mysterious Creatures That May or May Not Exist* departs from dinosaur fact to introduce creatures from myth and legend. Some of these, like the nightmarish giant squid, have been found to have their roots in real creatures. "Plenty of small watercolor and pencil sketches from Spears flesh out a scant assortment of blurry photos," wrote a contributor to *Kirkus Reviews.* Patricia Manning, reviewing *Tales of the Cryptids* for *School Library Journal,* noted that the "plethora of . . . photos and drawings in both color and black and white . . . will prove enticing." *Tales of the Cryptids* was selected as a Quick Pick for Reluctant Readers by the American Library Association's Young Adult Library Services Association.

In a discussion with Halls in *Child Life,* Spears explained how he designs his dinosaurs. "You must use your imagination to create something real," he explained. "They are a cross between fact and imagination." "If I had my way," Spears added, "I'd build a dinosaur park and museum where you would feel like you were actually in the prehistoric past."

## Biographical and Critical Sources

*PERIODICALS*

*Booklist,* November 1, 2003, Carolyn Phelan, review of *Dinosaur Mummies: Beyond Bare-Bones Fossils,* p. 492; November 15, 2006, GraceAnne A. DeCandido, review of *Tales of the Cryptids: Mysterious Creatures That May or May Not Exist,* p. 45.

*Bulletin of the Center for Children's Books,* October, 2003, Elizabeth Bush, review of *Dinosaur Mummies,* p. 61.

*Child Life,* April-May, 1996, Kelly Milner Halls, interview with Spears.

*Kirkus Reviews,* August 1, 1993, review of *Dinosaur Mummies,* p. 1017; August 15, 2006, review of *Tale of the Cryptids,* p. 72.

*Library Media Connection,* February, 2004, review of *Dinosaur Mummies,* p. 57.

*Publishers Weekly,* January 22, 1996, review of *Dino-Trekking: The Ultimate Dinosaur-Lover's Travel Guide,* p. 74.

*School Library Journal,* March, 1996, Cathryn A. Camper, review of *Dino-Trekking,* p. 209; December, 2003, Steven Engelfried, review of *Dinosaur Mummies,* p. 168; December, 2006, Patricia Manning, review of *Tales of the Cryptids,* p. 163.

*ONLINE*

*Dinosaur Mummy Web site,* http://www.dinosaurmummy.com/ (August 6, 2007).

*Kelly Milner Halls Home Page,* http://kellymilnerhalls.com/ (August 6, 2007).

*Tale of the Cryptids Web site,* http://www.talesofthecryptids.com/ (August 6, 2007).*

* * *

# STEGGALL, Susan 1967-

## Personal

Born March 8, 1967, in Poole, England; married Paul Rutherford (a teacher); children: Oscar, Ralph. *Education:* Middlesex Polytechnic, B.A. (graphic design; with honours); Oxford Brookes University, teaching certificate.

## Addresses

*Home and office*—Fordingbridge, Hampshire, England. *E-mail*—suesteggall@btopenworld.com.

***Sue Steggall*** (Photograph courtesy of Susan Steggall.)

## Career

Illustrator and educator. Graphic designer based in Glasgow, Scotland, 1989-90; primary school teacher, then infant coordinator in Cambridge, England, 1992-96; primary school teacher in Ringwood, Hampshire, England, 1996-97; school librarian in Fordingbridge, Hampshire, 1998-2006.

## Writings

*SELF-ILLUSTRATED*

*On the Road,* Kane/Miller (La Jolla, CA), 2005.

*Life of a Car,* Frances Lincoln (London, England), 2007, Henry Holt (New York, NY), 2008.

## Sidelights

Susan Steggall told *SATA:* "My first book, *On the Road,* was inspired by my two children, Oscar and Ralph, and their obsession with vehicles of all kinds. Oscar, especially, used to spend hours lining up parades of matchbox cars all around the house—along steps and radiators, across the back of the sofa, and around his sleeping brother's head. And they both used to love going on a car journey and spotting the different types of vehicles passing us by. Even at night, Oscar could tell a Peugeot from a Renault by the shape of the headlights!

"I soon started to get drawn into all of this. So I painted an A-Z of transport on their playroom wall—starting comfortably enough with ambulance, bus, and caravan but staggering to an awkward finished with yellow submarine and zeppelin! I developed this into a simple book format, but soon abandoned the alphabet idea and decided on following a simple journey instead.

"I have tried to create pages that are full of interest but retain a direct visual appeal. And I like to include the functional and the ordinary, things that probably aren't picturesque but may be interesting and familiar to young children.

"I build my collages up in stages. First, I sketch a rough layout in pencil. Then I tear out some crude shapes for the main elements, to get an idea of the balance of the page. From there, I gradually refine the picture, adding detail and shifting things around as I go. At the moment, my work is made almost entirely from very carefully torn paper, but I'm starting to wonder about this—after a while your hands can really ache, and it's a disaster if I break a nail! I like the gentleness of the torn edges though.

"I usually work whilst my children are at school, and sometimes whilst they're asleep. I have music, or the radio, on all the time and I tend to drink too much coffee and eat too many ginger biscuits—especially when I get to a tricky bit.

"Some of my favourite children's books are *Where The Wild Things Are* by Maurice Sendak, for the beautifully written text; *Do You Know Who Sunk the Boat?* by Pamela Allen, for the illustrations; and *The Grumpalump,* for both. I also love *The Giving Tree* by Shel Silverstein, for the idea, and *Owen and the Mountain,* by Malachy Doyle, for its simplicity. I don't like books that are obviously contrived, or adhere to a restrictive pattern, or those that seem to be imitating something else. I love poster art, well-designed labels and packaging, and hand-drawn typography."

## Biographical and Critical Sources

*PERIODICALS*

*Kirkus Reviews,* January 15, 2005, review of *On the Road,* p. 125.

*School Library Journal,* April, 2005, Wanda Meyer-Hines, review of *On the Road,* p. 113.

*Times Educational Supplement,* April 22, 2005, Jane Doonan, "First Journeys to Big Ideas," p. 12.

*ONLINE*

*Kane/Miller Publishers Web site,* http://www.kanemiller.com/ (August 15, 2007), "Sue Steggall."*

* * *

## STONE, Tanya Lee

### Personal

Married; children: two. *Education:* Oberlin College, B.A. (English); Southern Connecticut State University, M.A. (science education). *Hobbies and other interests:* Reading, writing, sushi, travel, singing, musical theater, playing piano, dancing.

*Tanya Lee Stone* (Courtesy of Tanya Lee Stone.)

### Addresses

*Home*—VT. *Agent*—Rosemary Stimola, Stimola Literary Studio, 308 Chase Ct., Edgewater, NJ 07020. *E-mail*—tanyastone@tanyastone.com.

### Career

Author. Worked for thirteen years as an editor for Holt, Rinehart & Winston, Macmillan, Grolier, and Blackbirch Press, New York, NY.

### Member

Society of Children's Book Writers and Illustrators, Authors Guild, National Council against Censorship, Assembly on Literature for Adolescents, PEN American Center, Authors Supporting Intellectual Freedom (AS IF!).

### Awards, Honors

Sydney Taylor Notable Book, 2003, for *Ilan Ramon, Israel's First Astronaut;* Quick Picks for Reluctant Readers selection, American Library Association, and Books for the Teen Age selection, New York Public Library, both for *A Bad Boy Can Be Good for a Girl.*

## Writings

*FICTION*

*A Bad Boy Can Be Good for a Girl* (young-adult novel), Wendy Lamb (New York, NY), 2006.

Also author of a play based on *A Bad Boy Can Be Good for a Girl.* Contributor to periodicals, including *Voice of Youth Advocates, School Library Journal,* and *New York Times.*

*PICTURE BOOKS*

*D Is for Dreidel: A Hanukkah Alphabet Book,* illustrated by Dawn Apperley, Price Stern Sloan (New York, NY), 2002.
*P Is for Passover: A Holiday Alphabet Book,* illustrated by Margeaux Lucas, Price Stern Sloan (New York, NY), 2003.
*M Is for Mistletoe: A Christmas Alphabet Book,* illustrated by Claudine Gevry, Price Stern Sloan (New York, NY), 2003.
*B Is for Bunny: A Springtime Alphabet Book,* illustrated by Sue Ramá, Price Stern Sloan (New York, NY), 2006.
*Elizabeth Leads the Way: Elizabeth Cady Stanton and the Right to Vote,* illustrated by Rebecca Gibbon, Henry Holt (New York, NY), 2008.
*Sandy's Circus,* illustrated by Boris Kulikov, Viking (New York, NY), 2008.

*NONFICTION*

*Medical Causes,* Twenty-first Century Books (New York, NY), 1997.
*Diana: Princess of the People,* Millbrook Press (Brookfield, CT), 1999.
*Rosie O'Donnell: America's Favorite Grown-up Kid,* Millbrook Press (Brookfield, CT), 2000.
(With Edward Ricciuti and Jenny Tesar) *America's Top 100,* Blackbirch Press (Woodbridge, CT), 2000.
*Laura Welch Bush: First Lady,* Millbrook Press (Brookfield, CT), 2001.
*Oprah Winfrey: Success with an Open Heart,* Millbrook Press (Brookfield, CT), 2001.
*Ilan Ramon: Israel's First Astronaut,* Millbrook Press (Brookfield, CT), 2003.
*Abraham Lincoln,* DK Publishing (New York, NY), 2005.
*Amelia Earhart,* DK Publishing (New York, NY), 2007.
*Up Close: Ella Fitzgerald,* Viking (New York, NY), 2008.
*Almost Astronauts: The Right Stuff at the Wrong Time,* Candlewick Press (Boston, MA), 2009.

*"AMERICA'S TOP TEN"SERIES*

*America's Top Ten National Monuments,* Blackbirch Press (Woodbridge, CT), 1998.
*America's Top Ten Construction Wonders,* Blackbirch Press (Woodbridge, CT), 1998.

*"MADE IN THE USA"SERIES*

*Teddy Bears: From Start to Finish,* photographs by Gale Zucker, Blackbirch Press (Woodbridge, CT), 2000.
*Snowboards: From Start to Finish,* photographs by Gale Zucker, Blackbirch Press (Woodbridge, CT), 2000.
*Toothpaste: From Start to Finish,* photographs by Jill Brady, Blackbirch Press (Woodbridge, CT), 2001.

*"LIVING IN A WORLD OF . . ." SERIES*

*Living in a World of Blue: Where Survival Means Blending In,* Blackbirch Press (Woodbridge, CT), 2001.
*Living in a World of Brown: Where Survival Means Blending In,* Blackbirch Press (Woodbridge, CT), 2001.
*Living in a World of Green: Where Survival Means Blending In,* Blackbirch Press (Woodbridge, CT), 2001.
*Living in a World of White: Where Survival Means Blending In,* Blackbirch Press (Woodbridge, CT), 2001.

*"MAKING OF AMERICA" SERIES*

*The Great Depression and World War II,* Raintree Steck-Vaughn (Austin, TX), 2001.
*The Progressive Era and World War I,* Raintree Steck-Vaughn (Austin, TX), 2001.

*"BLASTOFF!" SERIES*

*Mars,* Benchmark Books (New York, NY), 2002.
*Saturn,* Benchmark Books (New York, NY), 2003.
*Venus,* Benchmark Books (New York, NY), 2003.
*Mercury,* Benchmark Books (New York, NY), 2003.

*"WILD WILD WORLD" SERIES*

*Ants,* Blackbirch Press (Detroit, MI), 2003.
*Butterflies,* Blackbirch Press (Detroit, MI), 2003.
*Crocodilians,* Blackbirch Press (Detroit, MI), 2003.
*Dragonflies,* Blackbirch Press (Detroit, MI), 2003.
*Fireflies,* Blackbirch Press (Detroit, MI), 2003.
*Flamingoes,* Blackbirch Press (Detroit, MI), 2003.
*Grasshoppers,* Blackbirch Press (Detroit, MI), 2003.
*Hamsters,* Blackbirch Press (Detroit, MI), 2003.
*Kangaroos,* Blackbirch Press (Detroit, MI), 2003.
*Ladybugs,* Blackbirch Press (Detroit, MI), 2003.
*Lions,* Blackbirch Press (Detroit, MI), 2003.
*Lizards,* Blackbirch Press (Detroit, MI), 2003.
*Mantises,* Blackbirch Press (Detroit, MI), 2003.
*Mosquitoes,* Blackbirch Press (Detroit, MI), 2003.
*Sea Lions,* Blackbirch Press (Detroit, MI), 2003.
*Spiders,* Blackbirch Press (Detroit, MI), 2003.
*Turtles,* Blackbirch Press (Detroit, MI), 2003.

*"WILD AMERICA" SERIES*

*Earthworm,* Blackbirch Press (Detroit, MI), 2003.
*Mouse,* Blackbirch Press (Detroit, MI), 2003.

Also author of *Beaver, Crow, Rabbit, Deer, Raccoon, Turtle, Opossum, Skunk, Squirrel,* and *Toad.*

*"REGIONAL WILD AMERICA" SERIES*

*Unique Animals of the Pacific Coast,* Blackbirch Press (Detroit, MI), 2005.
*Unique Animals of the Northeast,* Blackbirch Press (Detroit, MI), 2005.
*Unique Animals of the Mountains and Prairies,* Blackbirch Press (Detroit, MI), 2005.
*Unique Animals of the Midwest,* Blackbirch Press (Detroit, MI), 2005.
*Unique Animals of the Islands,* Blackbirch Press (Detroit, MI), 2005.
*Unique Animals of the South,* Blackbirch Press (Detroit, MI), 2005.
*Unique Animals of Alaska,* Blackbirch Press (Detroit, MI), 2005.
*Unique Animals of the Southeast,* Blackbirch Press (Detroit, MI), 2005.
*Unique Animals of the Southwest,* Blackbirch Press (Detroit, MI), 2005.
*Unique Animals of Hawaii,* Blackbirch Press (Detroit, MI), 2005.

## Sidelights

Tanya Lee Stone is the author of dozens of nonfiction books for young readers, including titles in the "Regional Wild America," "Wild Wild World," and "Making of America" series. "I am passionate about nonfiction," Stone told *Suite 101* online interviewer Sue Reichard. "I just love coming across a little-known piece of history or an interesting topic in science and finding a way to get kids just as excited about it as I am." In 2006 Stone expanded into fiction with *A Bad Boy Can Be Good for a Girl,* a young-adult novel that was described as "one of the most honest treatments of teenage sexuality to be found in YA fiction" by *Kliatt* contributor Claire Rosser. "I absolutely love reading and writing within this genre," the author remarked to Teri S. Lesesne in *Teacher Librarian.* "The urgency, passion, drama, and importance, all wrapped up in transitioning from being a kid to an adult, is the stuff of life. I love immersing myself in it." In addition to her nonfiction titles, Stone has also published picture books that include *B Is for Bunny: A Springtime Alphabet Book.*

Stone, whose father was also an author, developed an early interest in telling tales. "I've been writing stories since I was seven years old," she noted on the *Random House* Web site. "Some of them were even published—in the school newspaper." After graduating from Oberlin College with a degree in English, Stone moved to New York City, where she spent thirteen years in the publishing industry. "My editorial background has definitely been an advantage in terms of craft," she explained to Cynthia Leitich Smith on the *Cynsations* Web site. "I edited hundreds and hundreds of books before I wrote my first one for publication."

***Cover of Stone's young-adult novel* A Bad Boy Can Be Good for a Girl, *featuring artwork by Gary Panter.*** (Illustration © 2006 by Gary Panter. Reproduced by permission of Wendy Lamb Books, an imprint of Random House Children's Books, a division of Random House, Inc.)

Since becoming an author, Stone has published dozens of titles about the natural world, and in her books for the "Living in a World of" series she examines animal camouflage. Ellen Heath, writing in *School Library Journal,* praised the "clever organization and . . . attractive, readable format" of the series titles. Stone's contributions to the "Regional Wild America" series, which focuses on animals from a variety of geographical regions, include *Unique Animals of the Mountains and Prairies* and *Unique Animals of Alaska.* Stone's "writing is clear," stated Kathy Piehl in a review for *School Library Journal,* "and the well-designed pages feature photographs that reinforce the written information." Stone has also written a number of well-received biographies, including *Oprah Winfrey: Success with an Open Heart*—dubbed "an upbeat title" by *Booklist* critic Gillian Engberg—and *Ilan Ramon: Israel's First Astronaut,* which *School Library Journal* contributor Jeffrey A. French deemed "an appealing and informative book."

*A Bad Boy Can Be Good for a Girl* concerns three high-school students—Josie, Nicolette, and Aviva—who each fall for and are betrayed by the same manipulative senior, a young man who wants them only for sex.

"Stone's novel in verse, more poetic prose than poetry, packs a steamy, emotional wallop," in the opinion of *Booklist* contributor Cindy Dobrez, and *School Library Journal* reviewer Susan Oliver similarly noted that "the free verse gives the stories a breathless, natural flow and changes tone with each narrator." In an interview with Brent Hartinger for the *AS IF!* Web site, Stone remarked that her focus in writing the novel was "in exploring the emotional ups and downs and realizations that go along with heading into that new and uncertain territory of intimate relationships." Her message to readers: "'Hey, this happens to all of us at one point or another—and pay attention, because this is how it happens, so if you can learn from these fictional girls' experiences, I hope it can help you avoid some pain and make you smarter about who you are and who you want to be.'"

*A Bad Boy Can Be Good for a Girl* marked the emergence of a new theme in Stone's body of work. Since writing that young-adult novel, she has focused on strong female characters and the empowerment of girls in books such as *Amelia Earhart, Up Close: Ella Fitzgerald,* and *Almost Astronauts: The Right Stuff at the Wrong Time. Almost Astronauts* is the story of thirteen women pilots who began astronaut training in 1961. Although NASA did not allow them to join the space program, their efforts paved the way for the first female astronauts—among them, Sally Ride—who were admitted in 1978. Women's history is a broad stroke that appeals to Stone and she uses it to highlight strong women as role models for girls.

Asked if she had any counsel for aspiring authors, Stone told Smith: "My advice is to make your nonfiction subject come to life for yourself as much as possible; make interesting connections, highlight unusual things kids may not know about a topic, and always keep in mind what is important to you, the writer, about your topic while you're writing. If you're passionate about the subject, I think that comes through in the writing." In thinking about what drives a writer's best work, whether it is nonfiction or fiction, Stone added: "It stems from an authentic desire to express both how we see the world as it is, and how we hope it can be."

## Biographical and Critical Sources

*PERIODICALS*

*Booklist,* December 15, 2000, Ilene Cooper, review of *Rosie O'Donnell: America's Favorite Grown-up Kid,* p. 818; June 1, 2001, Gillian Engberg, review of *Oprah Winfrey: Success with an Open Heart,* p. 1876; September 15, 2001, Ilene Cooper, review of *Laura Welch Bush: First Lady,* p. 218; April 1, 2003, Carolyn Phelan, review of *Mercury,* p. 1395; December 1, 2003, Kay Weisman, review of *Ilan Ramon: Israel's First Astronaut,* p. 680; January 1, 2006, Cindy Dobrez, review of *A Bad Boy Can Be Good for a Girl,* p. 86.

*Bulletin of the Center for Children's Books,* April, 2006, Karen Coats, review of *A Bad Boy Can Be Good for a Girl,* p. 375.

*Horn Book,* January-February, 2006, Christine M. Hepperman, review of *A Bad Boy Can Be Good for a Girl,* p. 90.

*Kirkus Reviews,* January 1, 2006, review of *A Bad Boy Can Be Good for a Girl,* p. 45.

*Kliatt,* January, 2006, Claire Rosser, review of *A Bad Boy Can Be Good for a Girl,* p. 12.

*Publishers Weekly,* February 24, 2003, review of *P Is for Passover,* p. 29.

*School Library Journal,* January, 1998, Kathleen Isaacs, review of *Medical Causes,* p. 120, and Stephani Hutchinson, review of *America's Top Ten National Monuments,* p. 132; February, 1998, Elden Younce, review of *America's Top Ten Construction Wonders,* p. 122; August, 1999, Lisa Gangemi Krapp, review of *Diana: Princess of the People,* p. 180; December, 2000, Steve Clancy, review of *Snowboards: From Start to Finish,* p. 166; June, 2001, Lana Miles, review of *The Progressive Era and World War I,* p. 160; September, 2001, Debbie Feulner, review of *Laura Welch Bush,* p. 222; January, 2002, Ellen Heath, reviews of *Living in a World of Green: Where Survival Means Blending In* and *Living in a World of White: Where Survival Means Blending In,* p. 126; October, 2002, Mara Alpert, review of *D Is for Dreidel: A Hanukkah Alphabet Book,* p. 64; October, 2003, Susan Patron, review of *M Is for Mistletoe: A Christmas Alphabet Book,* p. 68; January, 2004, Jeffrey A. French, review of *Ilan Roman,* p. 160; March, 2005, Kathy Piehl, review of "Regional Wild America" series, p. 203; January, 2006, Susan Oliver, review of *A Bad Boy Can Be Good for a Girl,* p. 144.

*Science Books & Films,* May, 2003, reviews of *Mars,* p. 23, and *Venus,* p. 116; November-December, 2005, Robert Goode Patterson, review of "Regional Wild America" series, p. 271.

*Teacher Librarian,* February, 2006, Teri S. Lesesne, "Opening Floodgates: An Interview with Tanya Lee Stone," p. 56.

*Voice of Youth Advocates,* April, 2006, Michele Winship, review of *A Bad Boy Can Be Good for a Girl,* p. 52.

*ONLINE*

*Assembly on Literature for Adolescents Web site,* http://ala-ya.org/ (August 27, 2007), *New Voices* interview with Stone.

*AS IF! Web site,* http://asifnews.blogspot.com/ (June 7, 2007), Brent Hartinger, interview with Stone.

*Cynsations Web site,* http://cynthialeitichsmith.blogspot.com/ (February 14, 2006), Cynthia Leitich Smith, interview with Stone.

*Random House Web site,* http://www.randomhouse.com/ (July 20, 2007), "Tanya Lee Stone."

*Suite101.com,* http://www.suite101.com/ (May 1, 2004), Sue Reichard, "Tanya Lee Stone: Superb Children's Author."

*Tanya Lee Stone Home Page,* http://www.tanyastone.com (July 20, 2007).

*Tanya Lee Stone Web log,* http://tanyaleestone.livejournal.com.

* * *

## SUMMERS, Barbara 1944-

### Personal

Born September 6, 1944, in Springfield, MA. *Education:* University of Pennsylvania, B.A.; attended Yale University and University of Paris, Sorbonne.

### Addresses

*Home and office*—Barbara Summers, Open the Unusual Door, Park West Station, P.O. Box 21044, New York, NY 10025.

### Career

Author and editor. City University of New York, New York, NY instructor in English composition. Formerly worked as a high-fashion model for Ford Models.

### Writings

(Editor) Brian Lanker, *I Dream a World: Portraits of Black Women Who Changed America,* Stewart, Tabori & Chang (New York, NY), 1989.
*Nouvelle Soul: Short Stories,* Amistad (New York, NY), 1992.
*The Price You Pay* (novel), Amistad (New York, NY), 1993.
*Skin Deep: Inside the World of Black Fashion Models,* Amistad (New York, NY), 1999.
*Black and Beautiful: How Women of Color Changed the Fashion Industry,* Amistad (New York, NY), 2001.
(Editor and author of introduction) *Open the Unusual Door: True-Life Stories of Challenge, Adventure, and Success by Black Americans,* Graphia (Boston, MA), 2005.

### Sidelights

Barbara Summers is a writer and educator with a background in the beauty industry. Along with her fiction, she has also written, edited, and collected several works about social activism and the hidden history of African-American women. Prior to writing, Summers worked as a fashion model for over fifteen years. Her knowledge of the significant part women of color played in changing the modern concept of beauty inspired her to move from fiction to nonfiction with the books *Skin Deep: Inside the World of Black Fashion Models* and *Black and Beautiful.*

*Skin Deep* is part biography and part an overview of the world inhabited by African-American fashion models from the 1940s through the late twentieth century. In

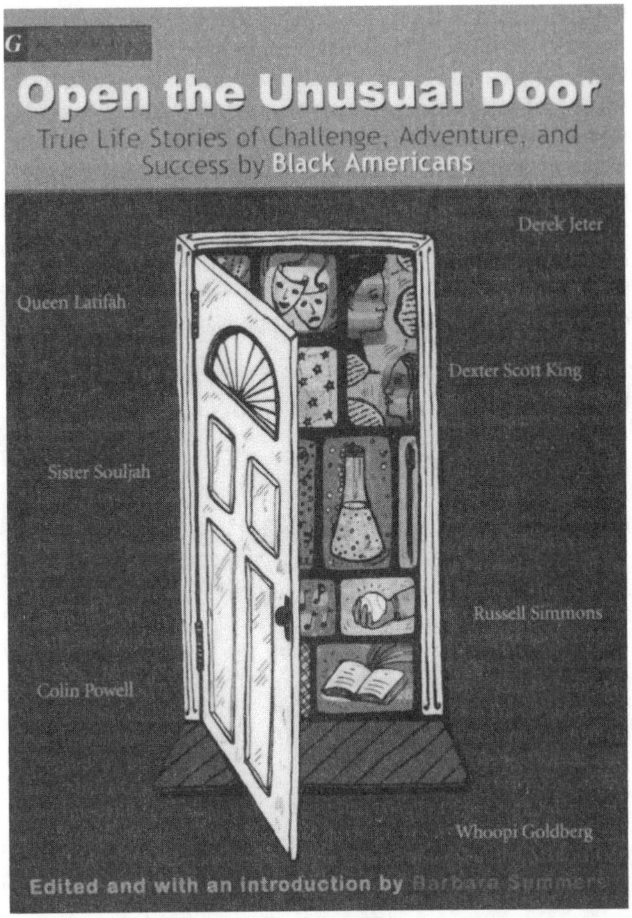


*Cover of Barbara Summers' inspirational collection* **Open the Unusual Door,** *featuring artwork by Gina Triplett.* (Illustration © 2005 by Gina Triplett. Reprinted by permission of Houghton Mifflin Company. All rights reserved.)

addition to exploring the role of models within the fashion industry, Summers describes the emergence of black designers and modeling agencies that promote models of color. Calling the book a "massive tome," Ann Burns added in her *Library Journal* review that in *Skin Deep* Summers "presents a fascinating portrait of black supermodels."

Edited by Summers, *Open the Unusual Door: True-Life Stories of Challenge, Adventure, and Success by Black Americans* is geared toward a younger audience. In addition to excerpts from the autobiographies of sixteen well-known African Americans, Summers gathers tales of challenges overcome that provide readers with insights into how life choices play out in one's life. The book includes the writings of athletes, entertainers, activists, writers, a scientist, and a statesman. "This little gem of a book should be a first purchase for public and school libraries," Carol Jones Collins asserted in *School Library Journal,* while Kay Weisman wrote in *Booklist* that the "thoughtful essays" in *Open the Unusual Door* "will make excellent discussion starters." Patricia Moore, writing for *Kliatt,* found the book to be "easily read but not easily forgotten."

As she noted on her home page, *Open the Unusual Door* was written because Summers "got tired of seeing the headlines: 'Black Kids Don't Read; or, Reading Scores for Black Students Are below Grade.' I'm a writer. If black kids who don't read grow up to be black adults who don't read, I'm going to be out of a job!" Her idea was to assemble a selection of essays relevant for a crucial target audience: young black students struggling with reading. "Challenges can be doors to opportunity—unusual, unexpected chances to change your life," she wrote, explaining the book's focus. "And there's nothing like using the real experiences of real people to show how this can happen."

## Biographical and Critical Sources

*PERIODICALS*

*American Visions,* April-May, 1994, Gary A. Puckrein, review of *The Price You Pay,* p. 33.

*Black Issues Book Review,* January, 1999, review of *Skin Deep: Inside the World of Black Fashion Models,* p. 51.

*Booklist,* January 1, 2006, Kay Weisman, review of *Open the Unusual Door: True-Life Stories of Challenge, Adventure, and Success by Black Americans,* p. 79.

*Kliatt,* March, 2006, Patricia Moore, review of *Open the Unusual Door,* p. 36.

*Library Journal,* December, 1993, review of *The Price You Pay,* p. 177; November 1, 1994, review of *Skin Deep,* p. 86; November 1, 1998, Ann Burns, review of *Skin Deep,* p. 117.

*Obsidian II,* fall-winter, 1993, Joyce Pettis, review of *Nouvelle Soul,* p. 136.

*Publishers Weekly,* October 26, 1992, review of *Nouvelle Soul,* p. 56; January 17, 1994, review of *The Price You Pay,* p. 408; August 31, 1998, review of *Skin Deep,* p. 65.

*School Library Journal,* December, 2005, Carol Jones Collins, review of *Open the Unusual Door,* p. 175.

*ONLINE*

*Open the Unusual Door Web site,* http://www.opentheunusualdoor.com/ (August 7, 2007), "Barbara Summers."

*Houghton Mifflin Books Web site,* http://www.houghtonmifflinbooks.com/ (August 6, 2007), "Barbara Summers."*

# U-W

## UBELL, Earl 1926-2007

*OBITUARY NOTICE*— See index for *SATA* sketch: Born June 21, 1926, in New York, NY; died of Parkinson's disease, May 30, 2007, in Englewood, NJ. Journalist and author. Ubell was an award-winning science journalist and editor who also wrote books that made complicated subjects more understandable to the general reader. Raised in a Yiddish-speaking home, he did not become fluent in English until he attended public school. Becoming editor of his high school newspaper, he embarked on a journalism career at the *New York Herald Tribune*. He worked there as a secretary, and, after serving in the U.S. Navy in the later days of World War II, returned to the paper as a reporter. Ubell studied physics at what is now the City College of the City University of New York, completing a B.S. in 1948. He was named science editor at the *Herald Tribune* in 1953. In this post, he famously reported on the Soviet Union's launching of the *Sputnik* satellite in 1957; he happened to be attending a conference at the Soviet embassy at the time, which gave him easy access to many good interviews. He also conducted interviews with such scientists as Albert Einstein and wrote feature pieces about the polio vaccine and the discovery of the structure of DNA. Ubell also won the 1957 Albert and Mary Lasker Medical Journalism Award for a series he wrote about heart attacks. In 1960, he earned the American Association for the Advancement of Science-Westinghouse Science Writing Award for an article he wrote explaining steady-state theory, which concerns the origin and evolution of the universe. Moving into broadcasting, from 1966 to 1972 he was health and science editor at WCBS-TV in New York City and, from 1972 to 1976, was a director at WNBC-TV. Ubell was not merely a reporter of science, he was actively involved in its practice. Over the years, he conducted laboratory work at the California Institute of Technology, Israel's Weizmann Institute of Science, and the Jackson Laboratory in Maine. A former president of the Council for the Advancement of Science Writing, he was considered an authority on the complex subject of X-ray crystallography. During the 1970s, Ubell spent time producing television programs on a variety of subjects, winning a local Emmy Award in 1970 for his work. Returning to WCBS in 1978 to resume work as science editor, Ubell remained there until he retired in 1995. He was also health editor for *Parade* magazine from 1983 to 1997. Ubell's decision to retire was prompted by his diagnosis of Parkinson's disease. He wrote about his fight with Parkinson's as one of his last stories. Acclaimed for his skill in making scientific topics interesting and comprehensible for the lay reader, Ubell brought this ability to his books for children, such as *The World of Living* (1965) and *The World of Candle and Color* (1969). His books for older readers include *How to Save Your Life* (1973) and *Parade Family Health Companion: A Reassuring Guide to Dealing with Life's Day-to-Day Health Issues* (1997), the latter coauthored with Randi Londer. The cofounder, with his wife, and chair of the Center for Modern Dance Education in Hackensack, New Jersey, Ubell won many more awards in appreciation for his contributions. Among these are the Samuelson Award from the New York League for Hard of Hearing, an award from the Milton Helpern Library of Legal Medicine, the 1982 Special Achievement award from the Deadline Club, the 1985 National Media award from the American Diabetes Association, the 1987 New York State Mental Health Council award, and the 1990 Annual Service award from the Dance Notation Bureau.

*OBITUARIES AND OTHER SOURCES:*

*PERIODICALS*

*Los Angeles Times,* May 31, 2007, p. B8.
*New York Times,* May 31, 2007, p. A17.
*Washington Post,* May 31, 2007, p. B5.

## WALROD, Amy 1973(?)-

### Personal

Born c. 1973. *Education:* Rhode Island School of Design, graduated, 1995.

### Addresses

*Home*—Cambridge, MA.

### Career

Illustrator. Formerly worked at a shoe store and as a pet sitter. Art instructor at summer camp, beginning 1991.

### Illustrator

James Howe, *Horace and Morris but Mostly Dolores,* Atheneum (New York, NY), 1999.

Philemon Sturges, reteller, *The Little Red Hen (Makes a Pizza),* Dutton (New York, NY), 1999.

Donna Jo Napoli and Richard Tchen, *How Hungry Are You?,* Atheneum (New York, NY), 2001.

James Howe, *Horace and Morris Join the Chorus (but What about Dolores?),* Atheneum (New York, NY), 2002.

Philemon Sturgis, *This Little Pirate,* Dutton (New York, NY), 2005.

Gennifer Choldenko, *How to Make Friends with a Giant,* Putnam's (New York, NY), 2006.

James Howe, *Horace and Morris Say Cheese (Which Makes Dolores Sneeze!),* Atheneum (New York, NY), 2009.

## Biographical and Critical Sources

*PERIODICALS*

*Booklist,* February 15, 1999, Ilene Cooper, review of *Horace and Morris but Mostly Dolores,* p. 1063; November 15, 1999, Marta Segal, review of *The Little Red Hen (Makes a Pizza),* p. 639; September 15, 2001, Michael Cart, review of *How Hungry Are You?,* p. 233; June 1, 2005, Hazel Rochman, review of *This Little Pirate,* p. 1824.

*Horn Book,* January-February, 2003, Susan P. Bloom, review of *Horace and Morris Join the Chorus (but What about Dolores?,* p. 58.

*Kirkus Reviews,* October 1, 2002, review of *Horace and Morris Join the Chorus (but What about Dolores?),* p. 147; June 1, 2006, review of *How to Make Friends with a Giant,* p. 570.

*Publishers Weekly,* February 15, 1999, review of *Horace and Morris but Mostly Dolores,* p. 1063; June 29, 1999, Nathalie op de Beeck, "Amy Walrod," p. 29; August 16, 1999, review of *The Little Red Hen (Makes a Pizza),* p. 83; August 20, 2001, review of *How Hungry Are You?,* p. 80; October 14, 2002, review of *Horace and Morris Join the Chorus (but What about Dolores?),* p. 83; May 9, 2005, review of *This Little Pirate,* p. 69; August 7, 2006, review of *How to Make Friends with a Giant,* p. 58.

*School Library Journal,* November, 2002, Shelley B. Sutherland, review of *Horace and Morris Join the Chorus (but What about Dolores?),* p. 126.*

* * *

## WALSH, Joanna 1970-

### Personal

Born May 24, 1970, in England; daughter of Ken (a teacher) and Lyn (a teacher) Walsh; married Robert Stevens (a lecturer); children: Florence, Elliot. *Education:* Hertford College, Oxford, M.A. (English), 1991; Central Saint Martin's College of Art, diploma (illustration), 1998.

### Addresses

*Home and office*—Oxford, England. *Agent*—Philippa Milnes Smith, 14 Vernor St., London W14 ORJ, England. *E-mail*—walshworks@aol.com.

### Career

Illustrator and writer, beginning 1995. Instructor at Swindon Art College, Roald Dahl Museum, and Story Centre; host of art workshops for children and adults; various artist residencies. *Exhibitions:* Work exhibited by British Design Council and at St. Anne's College Oxford.

## Writings

*SELF-ILLUSTRATED*

*Lion!,* Transworld, 1996.

*What If?,* Jonathan Cape (London, England), 1999.

*Amos Jellybean Gets It Right,* Hodder Headline (London, England), 2005.

*All Asleep,* Hodder Headline (London, England), 2007.

*ILLUSTRATOR*

Lynda Britnell, *Nettie's New Shoes,* Orion Children's Books (London, England), 1996.

Lynda Britnell, *Nettie's New House,* Orion Children's Books (London, England), 1996.

Lynda Britnell, *How Nettie Got Her Wings,* Orion Children's Books (London, England), 1996.

Lynda Britnell, *A Name for Nettie,* Orion Children's Books (London, England), 1996.

Adèle Geras, *The Magical Story House,* Macdonald Young (Hemel Hempstead, England), 1996.

Marjorie-Ann Watts, *Crocodile Tears: Three Stories,* new edition, Hodder Children's (London, England), 1996.

Caroline Plaisted, *My Day as a Bridesmaid,* Bloomsbury (London, England), 1996, published as *I'm in the Wedding, Too: A Complete Guide for Flower and Junior Bridesmaids,* Dutton Children's Books (New York, NY), 1997.

Ernest Henry, *Rub-a-dub-dub: New and Best-loved Poems for Babies,* Bloomsbury Children's Books (London, England), 1997.

Contributor of illustrations to periodicals, including London *Guardian, New York Times, World of Interiors, Die Woche, Economist,* and *Canadian National Post.*

## Sidelights

Joanna Walsh is an artist whose animated illustrations have been paired with texts by writers such as Adèle Geras, Lynda Britness, and Marjorie-Ann Watts, in addition to bringing to life her own original stories. Walsh's picture book *All Asleep,* which features babies sleeping everywhere from cribs to cars to outside under the starlit night sky, is a bedtime story for the very young, while *Amos Jelly Bean Gets It Right* is a humorous tale for the toddler set. Popular with children in her native England, Walsh also works as a teacher and hosts writing workshops for budding young artists as well as adults.

"I have an eclectic approach to writing and illustrating for children and adults," Walsh explained to *SATA.* "In all my work, the illustrations tell the story as much as the text and my work is concerned with the intertwined and sometimes conflicting relationship between the two. I also design for animation and illustrate for newspapers and magazines around the world."

## Biographical and Critical Sources

*PERIODICALS*

*Publishers Weekly,* January 13, 1997, review of *I'm in the Wedding, Too: A Complete Guide for Flower and Junior Bridesmaids,* p. 77.

*School Librarian,* spring, 1999, review of *Lion!,* p. 20.

*ONLINE*

*Joanna Walsh Home page,* http://www.walshworks.org.uk (August 8, 2007).

*Joanna Walsh Web log,* http://www.badaude.com/ (August 8, 2007).*

* * *

# WILSON, John 1951- (John Alexander Wilson)

## Personal

Born August 2, 1951, in Edinburgh, Scotland; son of James Annan (an engineer) and Evelyn Victoria Marguerite Wilson; married July 26, 1975; wife's name Jenifer Mary (a family therapist); children: Sarah, Fiona, Iain. *Education:* University of St. Andrews, B.Sc. (geology; with honours), 1975.

## Addresses

*Home*—British Columbia, Canada. *Office*—Box 316, Lantzville, British Columbia V0R 2H0, Canada. *E-mail*—johnwilson-author@shaw.ca.

## Career

Alberta Geological Survey, Alberta, Canada, research geologist, 1979-89; freelance writer, beginning 1989; Malaspina University College, Nanaimo, British Columbia, Canada, instructor in writing, 1991—.

## Member

Writer's Union of Canada, Children's Book Centre, Canadian Society of Children's Authors, Illustrators, and Performers, Children's Writers and Illustrators of British Columbia.

## Awards, Honors

British Columbia Arts Council grants, 1996, 1997, 2002, 2003; British Columbia Book Prize Honour Book designation, 1997, 2004, 2006; Geoffrey Bilson Prize shortlist, 1998, 2006; Canada Council for the Arts grant, 2001, 2005; New York Public Library Books for the Teen Age designation, 2001, 2004; Norma Fleck Award shortlist, 2002, 2004; Manitoba Young Readers Choice Award shortlist, 2004, 2006; White Pine Award shortlist, 2004; Hackamatack Award shortlist, 2004; Chocolate Lily Award shortlist, 2005; Stellar Award shortlist, 2005; numerous poetry, photography, and short fiction awards.

## Writings

*YOUNG-ADULT FICTION*

*Weet Trilogy* (includes "Weet," "Weet's Quest," and "Weet Alone"), illustrated by Janice Armstrong, Napoleon Publishing (Toronto, Ontario, Canada), 1995.

*Across Frozen Seas,* Beach Holme (Vancouver, British Columbia, Canada), 1997.

*Lost in Spain,* Fitzhenry & Whiteside (Markham, Ontario, Canada), 2000.

*Ghosts of James Bay,* Beach Holme (Vancouver, British Columbia, Canada), 2001.

*Adrift in Time,* Ronsdale Press (Vancouver, British Columbia, Canada), 2003.

*And in the Morning,* Kids Can Press (Toronto, Ontario, Canada), 2003.

*Flames of the Tiger,* Kids Can Press (Toronto, Ontario, Canada), 2003.

*The Flags of War,* Kids Can Press (Tonawanda, NY), 2004.

*Battle Scars,* Kids Can Press (Toronto, Ontario, Canada), 2005.

*Four Steps to Death,* Kids Can Press (Toronto, Ontario, Canada), 2005.

*Red Goodwin,* Ronsdale Press (Vancouver, British Columbia, Canada), 2006.

*Where Soldiers Lie,* Key Porter Books (Toronto, Ontario, Canada), 2006.

*The Alchemist's Dream,* Key Porter Books (Toronto, Ontario, Canada), 2007.

*YOUNG-ADULT NONFICTION*

*Norman Bethune: A Life of Passionate Conviction,* XYZ Publishing (Montreal, Quebec, Canada), 1999.

*Righting Wrongs: The Story of Norman Bethune,* illustrated by Liz Milkau, Napoleon Publishing (Toronto, Ontario, Canada), 2001.

*John Franklin: Traveller on Undiscovered Seas,* XYZ Publishing (Montreal, Quebec, Canada), 2001.

*Dancing Elephants and Floating Continents: The Story of Canada beneath Your Feet,* Key Porter (Toronto, Ontario, Canada), 2003.

*Discovering the Arctic: The Story of John Rae,* illustrated by Liz Milkau, Napoleon Publishing (Toronto, Ontario, Canada), 2003.

*OTHER*

*North with Franklin: The Lost Journals of James Fitzjames* (fiction), Fitzhenry & Whiteside (Allston, MA), 1999.

Contributor of stories, poetry, essays, articles and reviews to periodicals, including *Chicadee, Western Living, Today's Parent, Dugout, Pacific Way, Sky, Silver Kris, Island Parent, Alberta Report, Prospectors and Developers, Scanorama, Discovery, Punch Digest,* Toronto *Globe and Mail, Naniamo, Essence, Meridian, Quarter Moon Quarterly, Canadian Author, Branch Line, Calgary Cosmopolitan, Quill & Quire, Victoria Times-Colonist,* and *Canadian.* Contributor of columns to *Nanaimo* and *Meridian,* all 1993-94. Also author of technical papers and books.

Author's work has been translated into French.

## Sidelights

John Wilson told *SATA:* "When I was a nine-year-old boy, busily growing up in post-Second-World War Scotland, my heroes were fighter pilots sending Messerschmitts to a flaming doom, commandoes silently knifing Nazi guards, and spies being brutally tortured by the Gestapo. . . .

"Many major publishing houses . . . worked hard to replace the adventure/war books I used to crave with kinder, gentler, character-driven stories. True, some dealt with difficult problems—growing up gay, living on the street, family breakup—but they were real-life dilemmas facing real children in our modern world. They didn't encourage violence in boys. . . .

"[Eventually I found myself in the local library, looking for books at the appropriate reading level for my own son.] Try it sometime; it's a sobering exercise. Assume that a seven-or eight-year-old boy is reading at his age level or a little above and that he needs an exciting story to hold his interest. . . . There are some, but you will be able to take them home in a good-sized book bag. You will need a pickup truck for the books that will appeal to a girl of the same age and reading level. . . .

"Raising two girls does nothing to prepare one for raising a boy. Boys are not the failed girls that our school system would sometimes like to view them as. They are different. Their bodies are different and their brains are different. They act, react, and learn differently from girls. And they need to read different books.

"So, what makes a good book for boys? At the simplest level, a whole bunch of dead guys. . . .

"A dead guy in the first sentence is good because it captures the reader's attention and that is the second thing a book for boys must do, draw them in quickly. Boys live in an immediate world that requires instant gratification. They won't read fifty pages of background—the thrills have to be there, or at least promised, up front.

"And the thrills have to keep coming. . . .

"What doesn't get in the way of a boys' story is a detailed description of a neat weapon. Boys like to know how things work. They will happily read a description of a World War II Tiger tank that comes directly from Herr Krupp's owner's manual. How thick was its armour plating? What size of shell could it stop? How fast could it go? Where did the crew sit? What calibre was the machine gun in the turret? What happened to the crew if a shell got through the armour plating?. . .

"Several of my novels—including *And in the Morning, Flames of the Tiger, Battle Scars,* and *Four Steps to Death*—are war stories. They are set in different wars, but all involve boys who get caught up in the violence and horror. There are a lot of dead guys in them and a lot of descriptions of weapons, but they are not there for salacious entertainment and so that I can get a bigger royalty cheque. Okay, partly they are, but the main reason stems from something I learned talking to boys on book tours. War is cool. It was cool when Agamemnon attacked Troy, when the crusaders besieged Jerusalem, and when Germany invaded Belgium, and it is cool now. Why else do young men flock to fight?

"When the Americans were invading Iraq, it was a tough time to be a boy. An Abrams M1 battle tank with a 120-mm cannon featuring a DRS Technologies

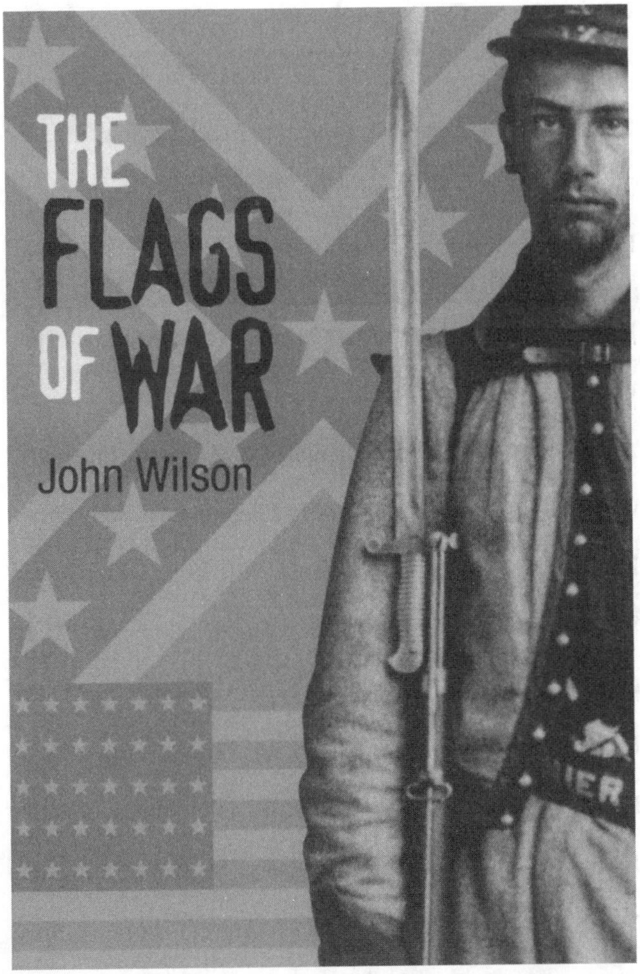


*Cover of John Wilson's young-adult novel* **The Flags of War,** *which takes readers back to the battlefields of the U.S. Civil War.* (Kids Can Press, 2004. Reproduced by permission of Kids Can Press Ltd., Toronto.)

second-generation GEN II TIS thermal-imaging gunner's sight, steel-encased depleted uranium armour, 12. 7-mm Browning M2 machine gun, and an L8A1 six-bareled smoke grenade discharger fitted on each side of the turret is unutterably cool to a twelve-year-old boy. He could see them on television and yet he was being told that the war was wrong. Perhaps his parents were going on peace marches. There was a conflict there. He could handle it by only talking tanks to his buddies and peace marches to his parents, but it couldn't be resolved—unless there was a safe place to talk about both aspects of war.

"That place is the past. The past is safe and a modern reader can get caught up in the thrill and learn that other boys have felt as he does without adult censure. In *And in the Morning,* for example, a boy in 1914 is swept up in the enthusiasm for war and can't wait to join up and fight. He sees war as a huge, exciting adventure.

"Of course, there's a danger here. If a book relates to a boy's attraction to war, it must also portray the other side—the rats, the rotting corpses, the terror of life in the trenches—in at least an equally convincing way. It must be graphic and many people are not comfortable with that.

"I once had a manuscript rejected as 'too grim.' Given that 'too grim' is an oxymoron to a twelve-year-old boy, let us assume the publisher was right. Let's take out all the graphic bits in *And in the Morning.* What's left? A book that says war is an exciting adventure but fails to point out that soldiers die horribly. Is this a perspective we want to encourage?

"George Santayana's observation that we will relive the past that we do not remember is particularly applicable to boys and violence. Pretending that boys do not feel an attraction to violence is only sweeping the problem under the rug. Ignoring the attraction doesn't make it go away, despite the warm, comfortable feeling we adults get every time a 'problem' book that deals with difficult issues we feel kids should know about wins a major literary award. We have to acknowledge the things that boys are interested in, even if we would rather they weren't. Only by doing that will we get their attention. Only by getting their attention can we get them to read. Only then can we make a larger point about the kind of world we would like them to create when they grow up."

## Biographical and Critical Sources

*PERIODICALS*

*Booklist,* March 15, 2003, Connie Fletcher, review of *And in the Morning,* p. 1319.

*Bulletin of the Center for Children's Books,* April, 2003, review of *And in the Morning,* p. 337.

*Canadian Review of Materials,* May 12, 2000, review of *Norman Bethune: A Life of Passionate Conviction;* June 8, 2001, review of *Lost in Spain;* November 2, 2001, review of *John Franklin: Traveller on Undiscovered Seas;* March 28, 2003, review of *And in the Morning;* September 5, 2003, review of *Flames of the Tiger;*

*Kirkus Reviews,* February 15, 2005, review of *Battle Scars,* p. 237.

*Resources Links,* June, 2005, Susan Miller, review of *Battle Scars,* p. 35; December, 2005, Philip Mills, review of *Four Steps to Death,* p. 39; June, 2006, Victoria Pennell, review of *Red Goodwin,* p. 30.

*School Library Journal,* December, 2000, Leah J. Sparks, review of *Lost in Spain,* p. 151; June, 2003, review of *And in the Morning,* p. 152; February, 2005, Christina Stenson-Carey, review of *The Flags of War,* p. 142; February, 2006, Christina Stenson-Carey, review of *Four Steps to Death,* p. 139.

*Voice of Youth Advocates,* April, 2001, review of *Lost in Spain,* p. 47; April, 2005, Julie Watkins, review of *The Flags of War,* p. 52; February, 2006, Delia Culberson, review of *Four Steps to Death,* p. 494.

*ONLINE*

*John Wilson Blog site,* http://johnwilson-author.blogspot.com (August 27, 2007).

* * *

## WILSON, John Alexander
## See WILSON, John

* * *

## WINTER, Susan

### Personal

Born in South Africa married; children: one son, one daughter. *Education:* Natal University, degree (social work); studied illustration at Chelsea School of Art.

### Addresses

*Home*—West London, England.

### Career

Illustrator and author of children's books. Formerly worked as a social worker in South Africa, then London, England.

### Writings

*SELF-ILLUSTRATED*

*Me Too,* Dorling Kindersley (New York, NY), 1993.
*I Can,* Dorling Kindersley (New York, NY), 1993.
*My Shadow,* Doubleday (New York, NY), 1994.
*A Baby Just like Me,* Dorling Kindersley (New York, NY), 1994.

*ILLUSTRATOR*

Mary Hoffman, *Henry's Baby,* Dorling Kindersley (New York, NY), 1993.
Angela McAllister, *Sleepy Ella,* Dent (London, England), 1993, Delaocorte (New York, NY), 1994.
Jean Richardson, *The Bear Who Went to the Ballet,* Dorling Kindersley (New York, NY), 1995.
Helen Cresswell, *A Gift from Winklesea* (originally published, 1969), Hodder (London, England), 1995.
Helen Cresswell, *Mystery at Winkelsea,* Hodder (London, England), 1995.
Helen Cresswell, *Whatever Happened in Winkelsea?,* Hodder (London, England), 1995.
Debbie Driscoll, adaptor, *Jenny Came Along,* Doubleday (New York, NY), 1995.
Eileen Moore, *The Ghost Watchers,* Hodder (London, England), 1997.
Tony Bradman, *Nicky and the Twins: The Lost Rabbit,* Collins (New York, NY), 1997.
Lee Davis, *The Bear Who Wanted to Read,* Dorling Kindersley (London, England), 1998.
Tony Bradman, *Nicky and the Twins: The Great Nappy Disaster,* Collins (London, England), 1998.
Francesca Simon, *Calling All Toddlers,* Orion (London, England), 1998, Orchard Books (New York, NY), 1999.
Richard Edwards, *Copy Me, Copycub,* HarperCollins (New York, NY), 1999.
Francesca Simon, *Toddler Times,* Orchard Books (New York, NY), 2000.
Anne Fine, *Bad Dreams,* Doubleday (London, England), 2000.
Opal Dunn, *Acker Backa Boo!: Playground Games from around the World,* Henry Holt (New York, NY), 2000.
Marion Dane Bauer, *If You Had a Nose like an Elephant's Trunk,* Holiday House (New York, NY), 2001.
Richard Edwards, *Where Are You Hiding, Copycub?,* HarperCollins (New York, NY), 2001.
Linda Ashman, *Sailing off to Sleep,* Simon & Schuster (New York, NY), 2001.
Richard Edwards, *Always Copycub,* HarperCollins (New York, NY), 2002.
Kathy Henderson, *Tabby Cat's Secret,* Frances Lincoln (London, England), 2002.
Joanne Ryder, *Come Along, Kitten,* Simon & Schuster (New York, NY), 2003.
Margaret Anastas, *Mommy's Best Kisses,* HarperCollins (New York, NY), 2003.
Richard Edwards, *Good Night, Copycub,* Frances Lincoln (London, England), 2003, HarperCollins (New York, NY), 2004.
Margaret Anastas, *A Hug for You,* HarperCollins (New York, NY), 2005.
David Bedford, *Little Otter's Big Journey,* Good Books (Intercourse, PA), 2006.
Diana Reynolds Roome, *Tulliver's Tunnel,* Frances Lincoln (London, England), 2006.
Richard Edwards, *Little Monkey's One Safe Place,* Frances Lincoln (London, England), 2006.
April Pulley Sayre, *Hush Little Puppy,* Henry Holt (New York, NY), 2007.

### Sidelights

Children's book author and illustrator Susan Winter began her working life as a social worker in her native South Africa. Moving to England, she continued to work as a counselor. Eventually Winter made her career switch to art, enrolling at the Chelsea School of Art to study book illustration after the birth of her second child. Her self-illustrated books include *A Baby Just like Me,* which a young black girl anticipates the close friendship she will have with her soon-to-be-born baby sister. In *Publishers Weekly,* a contributor praised *A Baby Just like Me,* writing that "Winter's straightforward text and realistic, full-page watercolors are a winning combination."

*As she does in Diana Reynolds Roome's* **Tulliver's Tunnel,** *Susan Winter often illustrates stories featuring animal characters.* (Illustration © 2006 by Susan Winter. Reproduced by permission of Frances Lincoln Children's Books.)

While Winter created original picture books early in her career, she now works primarily as an illustrator, and her art has been paired with text by authors such as Richard Edwards, David Bedford, Diana Reynolds Roome, Margaret Anastas, Marion Dane Bauer, Tony Bradman, Helen Cresswell, and Francisca Simon. In a review of Simon's *Calling All Toddlers,* a *Publishers Weekly* reviewer predicted that "toddlers will easily spot themselves in Winter's gentle, realistic depictions of [children] . . . acting silly, busy, naughty and nice."

Winter is best known for her collaborations with Edwards in the "Copycub" books, which include *Copy Me, Copycub, Always Copycub,* and *Good Night, Copycub.* In the series, a young bear cub imitates everything Mother Bear does. In *Copy Me, Copycub,* for example, the cub follows his mother home to their cozy den in time to snuggle in for a long winter's nap, while *Good Night, Copycub* finds the restless cub soothed by a bedtime story about the many ways other creatures drift off to sleep. Reviewing Winter's illustrations for *Always Copycub,* which finds the young cub playing tricks on his ever-patient mother, a *Kirkus Reviews* contributor wrote that the artist's "finely detailed watercolors vividly express the shifting emotions of the tale," and *School Library Journal* reviewer Janet M. Bair concluded that the book's "soft-toned watercolor pictures portray the cozy [family] relationship." Praising the series' "charming" bear character, Bina Williams wrote of *Good Night, Copycub* that Edwards' "simple tale is made all the more wonderful by Winter's soft watercolors."

## Biographical and Critical Sources

*PERIODICALS*

*Booklist,* November 15, 1993, Hazel Rochman, review of *Henry's Baby,* p. 63; October 15, 1994, Ilene Cooper, review of *My Shadow,* p. 440; February 15, 1996,

Carolyn Phelan, review of *The Bear Who Went to the Ballet,* p. 1027; April 15, 1999, Shelley Townsend-Hudson, review of *Calling All Toddlers,* p. 1537; September 1, 1999, Kathy Broderick, review of *Copy Me, Copycub,* p. 139; May 1, 2000, Kathy Broderick, review of *Toddler Time,* p. 1675; September 15, 2001, Helen Rosenberg, review of *If You Had a Nose like an Elephant's Trunk,* p. 230; January 1, 2002, Connie Fletcher, review of *Sailing off to Sleep,* p. 862; September 1, 2003, Lauren Peterson, review of *Come Along, Kitten,* p. 130; January 1, 2007, Diana Tixier Herald, review of *A Kiss in Winter,* p. 67; June 1, 2007, Hazel Rochman, review of *Hush, Little Puppy,* p. 76.

*Bulletin of the Center for Children's Books,* February, 1999, review of *Calling All Toddlers,* p. 217; March, 2004, Karen Coats, review of *Good Night, Copycub,* p. 270.

*Kirkus Reviews,* August 1, 2001, review of *If You Had a Nose like an Elephant's Trunk,* p. 1117; November 1, 2001, review of *Sailing off to Sleep,* p. 1546; January 1, 2002, review of *Always Copycub,* p. 44; March 1, 2003, review of *Mommy's Best Kisses,* p. 378; March 15, 2006, review of *Little Monkey's One Safe Place,* p. 288; September 15, 2006, review of *Little Otter's Big Journey,* p. 947.

*Publishers Weekly,* May 17, 1993, review of *Me Too* and *I Can,* p. 76; August 23, 1993, review of *Henry's Baby,* p, 71; September 12, 1994, review of *A Baby Just like Me,* p. 90; November 20, 1995, review of *The Bear Who Went to the Ballet,* p. 77; January 11, 1999, review of *Calling All Toddlers,* p. 70; July 26, 1999, review of *Copy Me, Copycub,* p. 90; July 9, 2001, review of *If You Had a Nose like an Elephant's Trunk,* p. 66; July 7, 2003, review of *Come Along, Little Kitten,* p. 70.

*School Library Journal,* February, 1994, Denise Furgione, review of *Me Too* and *I Can,* p. 92; September, 2001, Shara Alpern, review of *If You Had a Nose like an Elephant's Trunk,* p. 183; January, 2002, Maryann H. Owen, review of *Sailing off to Sleep,* p. 89; February, 2002, Janet M. Bair, review of *Always Copycub,* p. 100; April, 2003, Judith Constantinides, review of *Mommy's Best Kisses,* p. 114; July, 2003, Sandra Kitain, review of *Come Along, Kitten,* p. 104; February, 2004, Bina Williams, review of *Good Night, Copycub,* p. 111; March, 2005, Rebecca Sheridan, review of *A Hug for You,* p. 164; December, 2006, Linda L. Walkins, review of *Little Otter's Big Journey,* p. 95.

*ONLINE*

*HarperCollins Web site,* http://www.harpercollins.com/ (August 27, 2007), "Susan Winter."*

* * *

## WITHERS, Pam 1956-

### Personal

Born July 31, 1956, in Milwaukee, WI; daughter of Richard S. (an Episcopal minister) and Anita E. (a nurse) Miller; married Stephen G. Withers (a professor of chemistry), June, 1985; children: Jeremy. *Education:* Beloit College, B.A. *Hobbies and other interests:* Sports.

### Addresses

*Home*—Vancouver, British Columbia, Canada. *Agent*—Leona Trainer, Transatlantic Literary Agency, 72 Glengowan Rd., Toronto, Ontario M4N 1G4, Canada.

### Career

Runners World Magazine Co., Mountain View, CA, associate editor, 1978-79; *Adventure Travel,* New York, NY, associate editor, 1980-82; reporter and copy editor for newspapers in Seattle, WA, 1982-84; freelance writer.

### Member

Canadian Writers and Illustrators (president, 2005—), Canadian Association of Professional Speakers, Society of Children's Book Writers and Illustrators, Writers Union, Toastmasters of Today (president, 2003).

### Awards, Honors

Public speaking awards, Toastmasters of Today.

### Writings

*YOUNG-ADULT NOVELS*

*Raging River*, Whitecap Books (Vancouver, British Columbia, Canada), 2003.

*Peak Survival*, Whitecap Books (Vancouver, British Columbia, Canada), 2004.

*Adrenaline Ride*, Whitecap Books (Vancouver, British Columbia, Canada), 2004.

*Skater Stuntboys*, Whitecap Books (Vancouver, British Columbia, Canada), 2005.

*Camp Wild*, Orca Books (Custer, WA), 2005.

*Breathless*, Orca Books (Custer, WA), 2005.

*Surf Zone*, Whitecap Books (Vancouver, British Columbia, Canada), 2005.

*Vertical Limits*, Whitecap Books (Vancouver, British Columbia, Canada), 2006.

*Daredevil Club*, Whitecap Books (Vancouver, British Columbia, Canada), 2006.

*Wake's Edge*, Whitecap Books (Vancouver, British Columbia, Canada), 2007.

*OTHER*

(With John B. Izzo) *Values Shift: The New Work Ethic and What It Means for Business,* Prentice-Hall Canada (Don Mills, Ontario, Canada), 2000.

### Sidelights

Pam Withers told *SATA:* "My father and grandmother both encouraged me to write, and a high school journalism teacher was key in pushing me in that direction.

But basically, I wanted to be an author from the age of eight. I used to write stories in a little notebook and read them to my younger sisters, who seemed to like them!

"A British author by the name of Willard Price wrote a series of adventure books for boys. I used to read them to my son when he was ten, and they ended up being the largest influence on my desire to write a series of adventure books involving extreme sports. I'm also a fan of Farley Mowat, Will Hobbs and Gary Paulsen. Also, my misspent youth as a whitewater kayaker made it a given I'd write about sports, I think!

"I start a project by immersing myself in the sport I'm going to write about, either taking it up personally, or hooking up with people in the sport. I read magazines, Web sites and books devoted to the sport, watch tons of videos, and attend events. All these give me a sense of the action and jargon, and of the personalities drawn to the sport. They also give me ideas for plot twists. Then I select an athlete I want as my primary consultant.

*Cover of* Camp Wild, *by Canadian author and journalist Pam Withers.* (Orca Books Publishers, 2005. Reproduced by permission.)

*Cover of Withers' young-adult novel* Daredevil Club, *published in 2006.* (Orca Book Publishers, 2006. Reproduced by permission.)

"Next, I research the location I've chosen as the setting for my book, and research all aspects of my chosen subplot, and begin plotting in my head (playing it like a movie). When I have an outline started (or, more rarely, finished!), I begin writing. My athlete/consultant reads several chapters at a time, as I finish them, offering feedback and corrections and sometimes filling in blanks. Once I've done the research and interviews I need, it generally takes less than two months to write the book itself. I write about six hours a day, while my son is at school, taking lots of breaks for exercise. I am a very disciplined writer, and as a former journalist, am comfortable with deadlines.

"The most surprising thing I have learned as a writer is that I love the public-speaking circuit that goes with being an author. I speak to thousands of school children and aspiring adult writers per year, traveling extensively to do so. I never get tired of it! It energizes me.

"Of my books, *Skater Stuntboys* has always been my favorite, perhaps because it has the most complex plot (and because of Jake's surprise at the end), and also because it just came together the fastest and easiest of all of them. But now it's tied with *Vertical Limits.*"

## Biographical and Critical Sources

*PERIODICALS*

*Kliatt,* May, 2004, Barbara McKee, review of *Raging River,* p. 24; July, 2005, Heidi Hauser Green, review of *Camp Wild,* p. 27.

*Resource Links,* February, 2004, review of *Raging River,* p. 41; April, 2004, Brenda Dillon, review of *Peak Survival,* p. 42; February, 2005, Heather Empey, review of *Adrenaline Ride,* p. 43.

*School Library Journal,* November, 2004, Betsy Fraser, review of *Peak Survival,* p. 156.

*ONLINE*

*Canadian Review of Materials Online,* http://www.umanitoba.ca/outreach/cm/ (December 13, 2005), Dave Jenkinson, profile of Withers.

*Take It to the Extreme Web site,* http://www.takeittotheextreme.com/ (December 13, 2005).

* * *

# WOODRUFF, Liza 1971(?)-

## Personal

Born c. 1971, in RI; married; husband's name Tom; children: Thomas, Eden. *Education:* Muhlenberg College, degree (art and French); Art Institute of Boston, degree (illustration). *Hobbies and other interests:* Skiing, hiking, swimming, gardening.

## Addresses

*Home*—Charlotte, VT. *Agent*—Bernadette Szost, Portfolio Solutions, 136 Jameson Hill Rd., Clinton Corners, NY 12514. *E-mail*—liza@lizawoodruff.com.

## Career

Children's book illustrator. *Horn Book* magazine, Boston, MA, former member of circulation and marketing department.

## Illustrator

Cindy Neuschwander, *Amanda Bean's Amazing Dream: A Mathematical Story,* Scholastic (New York, NY), 1998.

Willy Welch, *Dancing with Daddy,* Whispering Coyote Press (Dallas, TX), 1999.

Marielle Alison, *How to Be a Bride and a Flower Girl, Too!,* Little Simon (New York, NY), 1999.

Martha F. Brenner, *Stacks of Trouble,* Kane Press (New York, NY), 2000.

Annie Cobb, *The Long Wait,* Kane Press (New York, NY), 2000.

Jan Wahl, *Mabel Ran away with the Toys,* Whispering Coyote (Watertown, MA), 2000.

Ron Roy, *Who Cloned the President?,* Golden Books (New York, NY), 2001.

Ron Roy, *Kidnapped at the Capital,* Golden Books (New York, NY), 2002.

*Deck the Halls,* HarperFestival (New York, NY), 2003.

DeMar Regier, *What Time Is It?,* Children's Press (New York, NY), 2005.

Donna Marie Pitino, *Too-Tall Tina,* Kane Press (New York, NY), 2005.

Dorian Cirrone, *Lindy Blues: The Missing Silver Dollar,* Marshall Cavendish (New York, NY), 2006.

Dorian Cirrone, *Lindy Blues: The Big Scoop,* Marshall Cavendish (New York, NY), 2006.

## Sidelights

Illustrator Liza Woodruff had an interesting start to her career in children's literature: before she became an illustrator she worked as a book reviewer for Boston's well-respected *Horn Book* magazine. Woodruff, who grew up in Rhode Island, began at *Horn Book* follow-

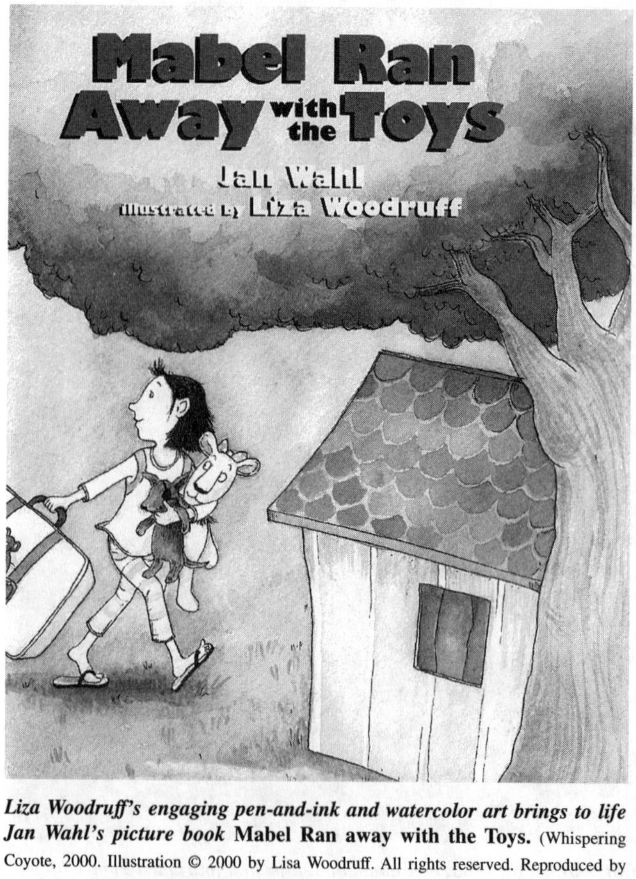


***Liza Woodruff's engaging pen-and-ink and watercolor art brings to life Jan Wahl's picture book* Mabel Ran away with the Toys.** (Whispering Coyote, 2000. Illustration © 2000 by Lisa Woodruff. All rights reserved. Reproduced by permission of Charlesbridge Publishing, Inc.)

ing her graduation from the Art Institute of Boston with a degree in illustration. She credits the five years she worked at the magazine with building her familiarity with the best authors and illustrators of children's books, as well as with gaining the mentors who encouraged her efforts to become a published illustrator.

Woodruff's first illustration project, creating artwork for Cindy Neuschwander's *Amanda Bean's Amazing Dream: A Mathematical Story,* was released in 1998. Reviewing the book for *Booklist,* Carolyn Phelan cited the "deft drawing, bright hues, and buoyant good humor of Woodruff's ink-and-watercolor illustrations" as contributing to the story's interest. The illustration projects that have followed included beginning readers by Martha F. Brenner, Ron Roy, and Dorian Cirrone, as well as picture books such as Jan Wahl's *Mabel Ran away with the Toys,* which features what *School Library Journal* reviewer Elizabeth Maggio described as "large and richly colored illustrations . . . [that] humorously follow the text." One of Woodruff's more recent projects, creating art for Cirrone's "Lindy Blues" chapter-book series earned the illustrator similar praise. Rachael Vilmar noted in *School Library Journal* that Woodruff's pen-and-ink "full-page drawings and spot art enliven" Cirrone's story in *Lindy Blues: The Missing Silver Dollar.*

## Biographical and Critical Sources

*PERIODICALS*

*Booklist,* September 15, 2998, Carolyn Phelan, review of *Amanda Bean's Amazing Dream: A Mathematical Story,* p. 239.

*Kirkus Reviews,* March 1, 2006, review of *Lindy Blues: The Missing Silver Dollar,* p. 227; September 15, 2006, review of *Lindy Blues: The Big Scoop,* p. 949.

*School Library Journal,* June, 2000, Anne Knickerbocker, review of *The Long Wait,* p. 104; September, 2000, Elizabeth Maggio, review of *Mabel Ran away with the Toys,* p. 210; February, 2001, Holly T. Sneeringer, review of *Stacks of Trouble,* p. 92; September, 2006, Rachael Vilmar, review of *Lindy Blues: The Missing Silver Dollar,* p. 164; October, 2006, Adrienne Furness, review of *Lindy Blues: The Big Scoop,* p. 103.

*ONLINE*

*Liza's Art Blog,* http://www.lizawoodruffart.blogspot.com (August 8, 2007).

*Liza Woodruff Home Page,* http://www.lizawoodruff.com (August 8, 2007).

# The Irish Bridget

Irish Studies
James MacKillop, *Series Editor*

Annie Walsh, an Irish immigrant, worked as a domestic in Providence until her marriage in 1883. *Courtesy of Daureen Aulenbach, Annie's great-granddaughter.*